Left
BRAIN

Right
BRAIN

A Series of Books in Psychology

Editors:
Richard C. Atkinson
Gardner Lindzey
Richard F. Thompson

Sally P. Springer
University of California at Davis

Georg Deutsch
University of Alabama at Birmingham

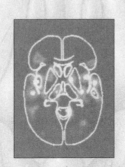

Left | Right
BRAIN | BRAIN

Perspectives from Cognitive Neuroscience

fifth edition

W. H. Freeman and C

To the memory of
Peter Deutsch
and
Fanny Margulies, Lilyan Margulies,
and Nathaniel Margulies

Library of Congress Cataloging-in-Publication Data

Springer, Sally P., 1947–
   Left brain, right brain: perspectives from cognitive neuroscience / Sally P. Springer, Georg Deutsch. — 5th ed.
     p.   cm. — (A Series of books in psychology)
   Includes bibliographical references and index.
   ISBN 0-7167-3110-X (hardcover: alk. paper). — ISBN 0-7167-3111-8
(pbk.: alk. paper)
    1. Cerebral dominance. 2. Brain—Localization of functions. 3. Left and right (Psychology)
4. Cognitive neuroscience.
I. Deutsch, Georg. II. Title. III. Series.
   [DNLM: 1. Laterality. 2. Brain—physiology. 3. Dominance, Cerebral.   WL 335 S753L 1998]
QP385.5.S67   1997
612.8′25—dc21
DNLM/DLC
for Library of Congress   97-27803
                                                     CIP

Text and Cover Designer: Blake Logan

Printed in the United States of America

First printing, 1997

Contents

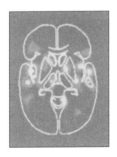

Preface / xi

Introduction / 1

PART I

The Discovery of Asymmetry: Clues from the Clinic / 7

Chapter 1
Evidence from Brain Damage and the Rise
of Neuropsychology / 9

The Doctrine of Cerebral Localization / 10
A Turning Point: The Findings of Paul Broca / 11
The Concept of Cerebral Dominance / 14
The Right Brain: The Neglected Hemisphere / 15
Further Insights from the Clinic / 19
Inferring Brain Function from Brain Damage:
The Rise of Contemporary Neuropsychology / 23
Cognitive Neuropsychology: Approaches and Assumptions / 25
The Cognitive Neuroscience Approach / 29

Chapter 2

Splitting the Brain: Insights from the Surgical Separation of the Hemispheres / 31

Cutting 200 Million Nerve Fibers: A Search for Consequences / 33
Everyday Behavior After Split-Brain Surgery / 39
Language and the Hemispheres / 42
Visuospatial Functions in the Hemispheres / 45
Information Processing in the Two Hemispheres / 48
Separated Awareness and Unifying Mechanisms / 52
What Do the Cerebral Commissures Really Do? / 56
Special Insights from the Study of Commissurotomy Patients / 57

PART II

Exploring Asymmetry in the Normal Brain / 59

Chapter 3

Psychology and Physiology: Building the Link Through Neuroimaging / 61

Functional Neuroimaging: Metabolic Techniques / 63
Functional Neuroimaging: Electrophysiological Techniques / 74
Issues Raised by Techniques Measuring Brain Activity / 83
Anatomical Asymmetries in the Two Hemispheres / 86
Anatomical Neuroimaging of the Living Brain / 89
Physiology and Psychology: Building the Link / 93

Chapter 4

Behavioral Approaches to Asymmetry / 97

Techniques Used in Behavioral Studies / 98
Why Does Lateralized Presentation Result in Asymmetric Performance? / 100
In What Ways Do the Hemispheres Differ? / 102

What Are Behavioral Tests Actually Measuring? / **107**
What Do the Tests Tell Us About the Nature of Asymmetries? / **111**

PART III

Handedness, Sex, and the Brain / **117**

. . . .

Chapter 5

The Puzzle of the Left-Hander / **119**

Historical Notions of Left-Handedness / **120**
The Difficulty of Determining Handedness / **123**
What Determines Handedness? / **124**
How is Handedness Related to Language Lateralization? / **130**
Handedness and Cognitive Abilities / **134**
The Controversy Over Longevity / **136**

Chapter 6

Sex Differences in Cognition and Asymmetry / **139**

The Case for Sex Differences in Asymmetry / **140**
Anatomical Evidence for Sex Differences / **143**
Sex Differences in Cognition: Linkages to Asymmetry / **145**
Are Sex Differences in Laterality Real? / **147**
The Origin of Sex Differences / **148**
Hormones and Cognitive Function / **149**
The Significance of Sex Differences / **155**

PART IV

From the Clinic to the Laboratory: Integrating Neuropsychology and Neuroimaging / **157**

. . . .

Chapter 7

Language, Voluntary Movement, and Perception / 159

Contemporary Neuropsychology / 159
Disorders of Speech and Language / 162
The Role of the Right Hemisphere in Language / 178
Disorders of Purposeful Movement / 182
Perceptual Disorders / 188
Visual Imagery / 195

Chapter 8

Attention, Memory, Music, and Emotion / 199

The Neglect Syndrome / 199
Amnesia and Localization of Memory / 204
Music and the Hemispheres / 220
Emotion / 225

PART V

The Evolution and Development of Asymmetry / 235

Chapter 9

Animal Asymmetries: The Search for the Biological Origins / 237

Avian Asymmetries: What the Bird's Brain Can Tell Us / 238
Paw Preference: Precursor to Handedness? / 240
Split-Brain Research with Animals / 242
Anatomical Asymmetries in Primates / 244
Pharmacological Asymmetries / 245
Behavioral Tests / 246
Theoretical Implications of Animal Asymmetries / 247

Chapter 10

Asymmetry Over the Life Span / 251

Brain Injury in Childhood: Laterality and Plasticity / 252
Hemispherectomy in Childhood: Removing Half a Brain / 253
The Search for the Beginnings of Lateralization / 256
The Role of the Corpus Callosum in Development / 259
Nature and Nurture in the Establishment of Asymmetries / 263
Some Theoretical Issues / 267

PART VI

Pathology and Asymmetry / 269

. . . .

Chapter 11

Links to Developmental Disabilities and Psychiatric Illness / 271

Learning Disability: Is There a Link to Asymmetry? / 272
Stuttering: The Case for Competition for Control of Speech / 278
Autism / 280
Hemispheric Asymmetry and Psychiatric Illness / 284
Implications for Treatment / 287

PART VII

Hypotheses and Speculation: Beyond the Data / 289

. . . .

Chapter 12

Attempts at Applying Asymmetry: "Hemisphericity," Education, and Culture / 291

Two Brains, Two Cognitive Styles? / 292
Hemisphericity / 294

Education and the Hemispheres / **298**
From Theory to Practice: Learning to Draw / **300**
Science, Culture, and the Corpus Callosum / **301**

Chapter 13

The Nature of Hemispheric Specialization / **303**

Is Dominance Based on Motoric Skills? / **304**
Hemispheric Specialization:
The Role of Novelty and Ambiguity / **308**
A Model of Callosal Function / **312**
Global Versus Local Processing and the Hemispheres / **315**
Emerging Principles of Visuospatial Lateralization / **317**
Computer Simulation and PDP Models of Neural Networks / **319**
A Little About Models, Reductionism, and Explanation / **324**
Left and Right in Biology and Physics / **326**

Chapter 14

Mind–Body, Consciousness, and the Hemispheres / **331**

Two Brains, Two Minds? / **332**
Language, Consciousness, and the Left Hemisphere / **337**
The Right Hemisphere and the Unconscious / **342**
Can Hemispheres Be Independent Selves? / **344**
Conscious Versus Unconscious Processes in the Clinic / **348**
The Binding Problem / **351**
Is the Mind–Body Problem a Dead Issue? / **354**

Postscript / **357**

Notes / **361**

Index / **397**

Postscript / **357**
Notes / **361**
Index / **397**

Preface

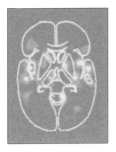

The fifth edition of *Left Brain, Right Brain* is appearing simultaneously at the end of the "Decade of the Brain" and at the beginning of the new millennium. It has been our privilege to chronicle the exciting developments in brain function in general, and in hemispheric asymmetry in particular, over the last 20 years. Our self-appointed task was a challenging one from the beginning and has been made ever more challenging over time as new developments, techniques, and approaches permitted investigators to ask, and answer, ever more sophisticated questions.

Throughout, we have striven to make the fascinating findings of contemporary brain research accessible to any serious reader, regardless of background, while at the same time ensuring that our presentation would be uncompromisingly accurate from a scientific perspective so that our academic colleagues would be comfortable using it as a text in their courses. We are heartened that the book continues to enjoy a significant lay audience, as well as adoptions in a wide range of courses at colleges and universities throughout the world. We also feel honored by the many foreign language translations of *Left Brain, Right Brain*.

While incorporating the growth and increasing sophistication of its topic, the fifth edition remains true to our original goals, taking the reader on an exciting intellectual adventure into the field now formally known as cognitive neuroscience. Although the term *cognitive neuroscience* has been in use for only a decade or so, the seeds of this interdisciplinary approach to brain function were sown many years before as investigators well beyond the traditional boundaries defined by neurology began to study and model the organization of higher cognitive processes such as language, memory, and perception. Today, neuropsychologists, cognitive psychologists, neuroimaging scientists, linguists, and computer scientists, among others, are working together in different ways to contribute to the understanding of the cerebral mechanisms underlying human mental function.

Left Brain, Right Brain, fifth edition, bears a subtitle: *Perspectives from Cognitive Neuroscience.* The title reflects a greater emphasis on our integration of evidence from multiple disciplines, especially the combination of new functional neuroimaging research and more traditional clinical brain-damage studies. Previous editions of the book have done this to an extent, but now it is more explicit and comprehensive. For a while, we considered another subtitle, *A Perspective on Cognitive Neuroscience,* reflecting our view that the study of hemispheric asymmetry contributes in significant ways to our understanding of brain function more broadly.

We are grateful to many people, only a few of whom we have space to acknowledge here, who have contributed in significant ways to our effort in this and previous editions. Investigators around the world responded to our e-mail requests for preprints of their latest work. Editors with books in progress arranged to send us copies of the chapters that were to appear in their forthcoming books. And several people, including Morris Moscovitch, Eran Zaidel, Sheri Berenbaum, and Michael Gazzaniga, took time to share their insights with us in person or through written comments provided to the publisher. We apologize for not being able to include all the excellent work sent or shown to us over the last few years, for it has truly been a struggle to keep the size of this book under control.

We would like to give particular recognition to the contributions to the fifth edition made by the late M. P. (Phil) Bryden, who passed away unexpectedly in August 1996. Phil had provided us with his detailed thoughts on what was new and worthy of consideration for inclusion, just as he had for each previous edition. We always looked forward to Phil's comments—they were so reasonable, balanced, helpful, supportive, and insightful. There are more references to Phil Bryden's work throughout *Left Brain, Right Brain* than to that of any other single author, reflecting both the breadth of his interests as well as his productivity. He was a true friend and colleague, and we mourn his passing.

A special word of thanks goes to Susan Brennan, Executive Editor at W. H. Freeman and Company, for believing that the fifth edition of *Left Brain, Right Brain* should be written and for providing the support we needed to produce it. The new eight-page color section, which we believe adds greatly to our presentation of neuroimaging findings, is a first for us and the direct result of her efforts. Preparation of the fifth edition was also greatly facilitated by a professional development leave from UC Davis for one of us (SPS).

And finally, our spouses, Håkon Hope and Martha Pezrow, deserve our gratitude, as before, for their continuing understanding and support of our efforts. They, as well as Mollie and Erik Hope, now 9 and 12, respectively, have made significant sacrifices so that the fifth edition could become reality. We thank them for their love and support throughout.

Introduction

A young male subject lies in a quiet, darkened room and is asked to imagine making his way through a series of complex passageways. Earlier, he had been given a tour of the passageways and told to remember as much about them as possible. As he continues to imagine walking through the hallways and visualizing what is there, a harmless amount of a special radioactive compound, or "tracer," is injected into his bloodstream. The tracer is picked up by the brain over the next 60 seconds, depending on the rate of cerebral blood flow. Shortly after, he is moved to a room where his head is placed inside a device called a SPECT scanner (for single photon emission computed tomography) that is used to determine the distribution of the tracer within his brain. Because the particular tracer used in this experiment remains "locked" in place throughout the brain, its distribution, even an hour after injection, captures the levels of regional blood flow and by inference, the level of brain activity in those regions associated with the visual imagery task.

Later, four collaborating scientists intently examine the computer-generated images of the activity in different cross sections of the subject's brain. "Ah," says one, "I told you that activity in primary visual cortex will occur even when one is only imagining a visual scene!" "Frankly, I'm surprised," says another, "Who would have thought that imagining a scene would involve almost the same cerebral regions that are involved when a subject actually looks at it." "Well, I'm not surprised by that," says the third, "but why is the activity so much greater in the visual regions of the right half of the brain?" "Well," says the first, "that fits with the evidence from the effects of brain injury that shows that the right hemisphere of the brain plays a more prominent role in complex spatial tasks, such as solving mazes." The fourth scientist, who is not really familiar with brain scanning or neuroanatomy, but nevertheless is extremely interested in the relationships between vision and visual imagery, stands quietly by and says to himself, "I really must alter my model of visual image storage and recall; my current model would not have predicted these results at all."

As they leave the laboratory, two of the investigators comment on how marvelous it is to "see the mind at work," using this new brain scanning technique and the experiments they devised. The other two voice objections to this statement. One says, "You mean the brain at work! Remember, we're only looking at external correlates of mental processes—and pretty crude ones at that! But don't get me wrong. I think we're getting closer to the brain processes responsible for mind. Perhaps in a few years . . ." The other investigator has a more profound objection. He states, "Well, I'm very impressed by these techniques and by today's experiment, and I feel that these findings shed some light on the organization of the brain and even on how we should model certain cognitive operations. But with respect to the mind—I just don't understand how external measurements reveal anything about the real experience of the subject. I'm not saying that the mind comes from something other than the brain, but I just don't see how these experiments shed much insight into the connection."

This scenario represents a glimpse of some of the questions being asked about human brain function in laboratories throughout the world from a new interdisciplinary perspective—cognitive neuroscience. Scientific studies of the human brain have taken on a new challenge in the last decade—to delve into the biological basis of memory, learning, imagery, emotion, and other higher mental functions and, perhaps, to discover how consciousness itself arises from the workings of the brain. Cognitive neuroscience arose from the need to transcend the limits of traditional academic disciplines in the quest to understand the mind and to better formulate the questions we can ask about the mind and its relationship to brain activity. Investigators from academic disciplines that until recently had little to do with one another—cognitive psychology, neurology, computer science, philosophy—are collaborating in an atmosphere of excited anticipation, hoping to unravel the secrets of the mind–brain connection.

Although cognitive neuroscience has only recently been recognized as a formal discipline, there is a long history behind the attempt to relate mental function to the operation of the brain, a history that is also filled with conceptual and philosophical conundrums that are yet to be resolved. The study of the effects of brain injury on mental status—a field known as neuropsychology—has provided the background and identified over the last 100 years many of the questions and apparent dilemmas that cognitive neuroscience now seeks to answer. An important part of this background of established brain–behavior relationships concerns asymmetries in the functioning of the left and right cerebral hemispheres.

The two hemispheres of the brain, tightly packed together inside the skull and linked by several distinct bundles of nerve fibers that serve as channels of communication between them, appear to be approximately mirror images of each other, very much in keeping with the general left–right symmetry of the human body. Functionally, control of the body's basic movements and sensations is evenly divided between the two cerebral hemispheres in a crossed fashion: The left hemisphere controls the right side of the body (right hand, right leg, and so on), and the right hemisphere controls the left side. Figure I.1 shows this arrangement.*

The left–right physical symmetry of the brain and body does not imply, however, that the right and left sides are equivalent in all respects. We have only to examine the abilities of our two hands to note asymmetry of function. Few people are truly ambidextrous; most have a dominant hand. And differences in the abilities of the two hands are but one manifestation of basic asymmetries in the functions of the two cerebral hemispheres.

A great deal of accumulated evidence shows that the left brain and the right brain are not identical in their capabilities or organizations and that the differences between the hemispheres extend to precisely the kinds of higher level mental functions that form the basis of inquiry in cognitive neuroscience. Research has demonstrated that asymmetries in the function of the two hemispheres include differences in the ability to produce and understand language and differences in the ability to process complex spatial relationships, among many others.

Such differences are of interest in and of themselves, but of even greater interest, perhaps, are the questions that follow from them. To what extent are hemispheric differences unique to human beings, and to what extent can they be found in other animals? Are hemispheric differences present at birth, or do they develop throughout childhood and adolescence? What differences exist in patterns of asymmetry

---

The Brain: A Neuroscience Primer by Richard F. Thompson (W. H. Freeman, 1998) is an excellent reference for readers seeking an overview of neuroanatomy.

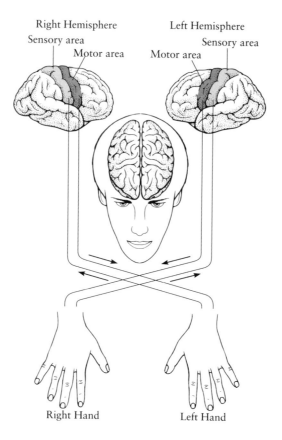

FIGURE I.1 Motor control and sensory pathways between the brain and the rest of the body are almost completely crossed. Each hand is served primarily by the cerebral hemisphere on the opposite side.

across people? What are the implications of those differences? Does the existence of two hemispheres imply the possibility of duality of consciousness, and, if not, how is unity of mind achieved? These are but a few of the questions that come to mind.

The chapters that follow emphasize the study of hemispheric asymmetries in the brain, in the greater context of the study of brain function in general. The division of the brain into two parts for study and analysis was a simple, anatomically driven distinction that has resulted in a wealth of surprising findings of great interest to investigators attempting to relate mental function to the brain and its activity. Much of cognitive neuroscience has been implicitly guided by the findings of investigations into cerebral asymmetry. At the same time, the approaches of cognitive neuroscience, which bring to bear evidence from a wide range of disciplines, are reshaping and honing our understanding of cerebral asymmetries and their relationship to human behavior and mental function. This interdisciplinary approach is a powerful one, and it is our hope that in the course of reading this book the reader will gain an understanding, not only of what is known about the differences in function between the hemispheres of the brain, but also of how investigators are studying the relationship between mind and brain more broadly.

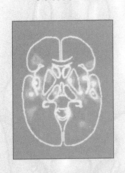

PART I

The Discovery
of Asymmetry

Clues from the Clinic

Chapter 1

Evidence from Brain Damage and the Rise of Neuropsychology

Anyone walking through a stroke ward in a hospital can see that patients are fairly evenly distributed between two groups: those with paralyzed left sides and those with paralyzed right sides. A stroke generally involves a stoppage of the blood supply to part of the brain and results in damage to the affected region. Because blood is supplied to each hemisphere separately, a stroke usually affects only one-half of the brain. Because each half controls the opposite side of the body, paralysis of the right side indicates a stroke in the left hemisphere, and left-sided paralysis indicates a stroke in the right hemisphere.

Throughout the long history of medicine, the clinical combination of speech disturbances with weakness or paralysis of the right half of the body has been reported again and again. These observations should have suggested a link between loss of speech and damage to the left hemisphere of the brain. The significance of the relationship, however, was not appreciated by the medical community as a whole until the second half of the nineteenth century.[1]

It is perhaps not surprising that this evidence of hemispheric asymmetry was overlooked for so long. Early anatomical studies showed that the halves of the brain were mirror images of each other, roughly equal in size and weight. Also, most scientists firmly believed that the brain functioned as a whole unit; thus, the scientists were not predisposed to "see" evidence that suggested otherwise.

By the first decades of the nineteenth century, however, serious attention was being given to the idea that particular functions could be assigned to specific regions of the brain. The notion that one could study the role of specific regions became known as the doctrine of cerebral localization.

The Doctrine of Cerebral Localization

Franz Gall, a late eighteenth century German anatomist, was the first to propose that the brain is not a uniform mass and that various mental faculties can be localized to different parts of the brain. The faculty of speech, he believed, is located in the frontal lobes, the part of each hemisphere closest to the front of the head. Unfortunately, Gall also claimed that the shape of the skull reflects the underlying brain tissue and that an individual's mental and emotional characteristics can be determined through a careful study of bumps on the head.

In many scientific circles, Gall was dismissed as a quack on the grounds that no good evidence existed to show that skull shape can be used reliably to predict anything about the person whose head is being measured. The basic idea that different functions are controlled by different regions within the brain, however, did attract many followers. Among them was Jean Baptiste Bouillaud, a French professor of medicine. Bouillaud was so certain Gall was correct in localizing speech to the frontal lobes that he offered 500 francs (a considerable sum at the time) to anyone who could produce a patient with damage to the frontal lobes that was unaccompanied by loss of speech.[2]

For many years, most scientists quietly aligned themselves with one of the two sides of this issue. One group firmly believed that speech is controlled by the frontal lobes; the other side argued that particular functions cannot be localized to specific regions of the brain. At the time, there was little in the way of new data to change anyone's mind, and each group held firmly to its position in the absence of compelling evidence to the contrary.

A Turning Point: The Findings of Paul Broca

The stalemate ended in 1861. At a meeting of the Society of Anthropology in Paris, Bouillaud's son-in-law, Ernest Auburtin, repeated Bouillaud's claim that the center controlling speech is in the frontal lobes. His remarks impressed Paul Broca, a young surgeon who was present.

A few days before the meeting, an old man suffering from a serious leg infection had been admitted to Broca's service at a local hospital. The infection was recent, but the patient had for many years suffered from loss of speech as well as from paralysis of one side of his body, known as hemiplegia. After the meeting, Broca approached Auburtin and suggested it might be useful for them to examine this patient together.

A day or so after their examination, the man died. Broca performed a postmortem examination of his brain and found a region of damaged tissue, or lesion, in part of the left frontal lobe. At the next meeting of the Society, Broca brought the brain and pointed out his findings. But no one seemed to pay much attention to his comments.

A few months later, Broca again reported to the Society that he had observed a similar lesion at autopsy in a second patient suffering from loss of speech. What changed the minds of the Society of Anthropology members is not clear, but this time Broca's report was received with great excitement and touched off heated debate and controversy. Broca soon found himself viewed as the chief proponent of cerebral localization of function. His new evidence did not convince everyone, however. Die-hard critics of the concept of localization directed their attacks at him. If speech is localized in the frontal lobes, he was challenged, why is it that monkeys with large frontal brain areas do not possess the ability to speak? Similarly, how can one account for the occasional case of extensive frontal lobe damage that does not produce loss of speech?

Broca was an unwilling participant in the controversy generated by his work. He later stated that his two reports to the Society of Anthropology were simply an attempt to bring to the attention of others a curious fact that he had observed by chance and that he did not desire to be involved in debates about the localization of speech centers. Despite his protests, however, Broca continued to figure centrally in the controversy. He went on to collect data from additional cases

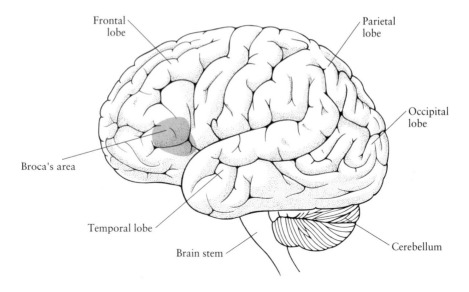

FIGURE 1.1 The location of Broca's area in the left cerebral hemisphere.

and was able to pinpoint more precisely the area of the brain involved in instances of speech loss. Figure 1.1 shows the location of this region, which has since become known as Broca's area. This figure also illustrates the division of a hemisphere into four lobes: frontal, parietal, occipital, and temporal.

Recognizing the Role of the Left Hemisphere

Although his two earliest cases had involved lesions of the frontal lobe of the left hemisphere, Broca did not immediately see the link between speech loss and the side of the lesion. For two years, he made no attempt to explain this coincidence. In commenting on other cases showing the same relationship, he noted: "Here are eight cases where the lesion is situated in the posterior portion of the third frontal convolution and a thing most remarkable in all of these patients [is that] the lesion is on the left side. I do not attempt to draw a conclusion and I await new findings."[3]

By 1864, however, Broca had become convinced of the importance of the left hemisphere in speech. In the following quote, he refers to loss of speech, which we now call aphasia, as aphemia:

I have been struck with the fact that in my first aphemics the lesion always lay not only in the same part of the brain but always the same side—the left. Since then, from many postmortems, the lesion was always left sided. One has also seen many aphemics alive, most of them hemiplegic, and always hemiplegic on the right side. Furthermore, one has seen at autopsy lesions on the right side in patients who had shown no aphemia. It seems from all this that the faculty of articulate language is localized in the left hemisphere, or at least that it depends chiefly upon that hemisphere.[4]

Although Broca is often credited with being the first to see the relationship between damage to the left hemisphere and loss of speech, the association had in fact first been noted almost 30 years earlier by Marc Dax, a French country doctor. Dax's observations, although sound in principle, were not well documented and were ignored by the scientific community. Historians have disagreed about whether or not Broca had been aware of Dax's earlier findings, but in any event Broca subsequently presented a considerably stronger case for the relationship between speech and the left hemisphere than had Dax.

Broca's Rule

Broca also went on to consider the relationship between handedness and speech. He suggested that both speech and manual dexterity are attributable to the inborn superiority of the left hemisphere in right-handers. "One can conceive," he speculated, "that there may be a certain number of individuals in whom the natural pre-eminence of the convolutions of the right hemisphere reverses the order of the phenomenon which I have just described."[5] These individuals, of course, are left-handers.

Broca's "rule" that the hemisphere controlling speech is on the side opposite the preferred hand was influential well into the twentieth century. The rule accounted nicely for the relationship between damage to the left hemisphere and aphasia in right-handers. But as more cases were studied, left-handers appeared to come in two varieties: those with speech in the hemisphere opposite their preferred hand (as predicted by Broca) and those with speech in the left hemisphere. The existence of the latter group was discovered through observations of left-handed patients who become aphasic following damage to the left hemisphere. These patients, often referred to as having crossed aphasia, show rather dramatically that left-handedness is not necessarily the simple converse of right-handedness.[6]

The precise nature of the relationship of handedness to hemispheric asymmetry is a question that remains to be resolved. We will return to it several times throughout this book.

The Concept of Cerebral Dominance

Within ten years of the publication of Broca's initial observations, the concept now known as cerebral dominance began to emerge as the major view of the relationship between the two hemispheres of the brain. In 1864 the great British neurologist John Hughlings Jackson wrote, "Not long ago, few doubted the brain to be double in function as well as physically bilateral; but now that it is certain from the researches of Dax, Broca, and others, that damage to one lateral half can make a man entirely speechless, the former view is disrupted."[7]

In 1868 Jackson proposed his idea of the "leading" hemisphere—a notion that may be viewed as the precursor of the idea of cerebral dominance. "The two brains cannot be mere duplicates," he wrote, "if damage to one alone can make a man speechless. For these processes [of speech], of which there are none higher, there must surely be one side which is leading." Jackson further concluded "that in most people the left side of the brain is the leading side—the side of the so-called will, and that the right is the automatic side."[8]

By 1870, other investigators began to realize that many types of language disorders could result from damage to the left hemisphere. Early work concentrating on speech production problems that resulted from injury to the left hemisphere had overlooked the fact that these same patients frequently had difficulty understanding the speech of others. Karl Wernicke, a German neurologist, is credited with showing that damage to the back part of the temporal lobe of the left hemisphere could produce difficulties in understanding speech.

Similarly, problems in reading and writing were identified in some patients and were shown to result from damage to the left hemisphere, not from damage to the right. Clearly, the picture emerging by the end of the nineteenth century was one in which the left hemisphere played a role of great importance in language functions in general and not just in speech per se. It had also become apparent that different kinds of language problems resulted from damage to different areas within the left hemisphere.

Further evidence supporting the notion that the left hemisphere possesses functions not shared by the right came from Hugo Liepmann's studies of apraxia. This disorder is generally defined as the inability to perform purposeful movements on command.* An apraxic patient might have no difficulty brushing his or her teeth in the context of a normal bedtime routine, but he or she would be unable to reproduce the same movements when instructed to pretend to brush in an unrelated context.

Liepmann had shown that, although such deficits are not due to a general inability to understand speech, they are associated with injury to the left hemisphere. He concluded that the left hemisphere controls "purposeful" movements as well as language but that the specific areas of the left hemisphere involved are different in the two cases.

Taken together, these findings formed the basis of a widely held view of the relationship between the two hemispheres. One hemisphere, usually the left in right-handers, was seen as the director of speech and other higher functions; the right, or "minor," hemisphere, was without special functions and subordinate to control by the "dominant" left. The origin of the term *cerebral dominance* is obscure, but it captures nicely the idea of one-half of the brain directing behavior. Although the concept originally associated with this term underestimates the role of the right hemisphere, the term is still widely used today.

The Right Brain: The Neglected Hemisphere

Almost as soon as the concept of cerebral dominance became popular, evidence suggesting that the right, or minor, hemisphere also possesses specialized abilities began to appear. John Hughlings Jackson's notion of the left hemisphere as "leading" was the intellectual grandparent of the idea of dominance. Interestingly, Jackson was also one of the first to consider that an extreme, one-sided view of the way mental functions are localized in the brain was wrong. "If then," he wrote in 1865, "it should be proven by wider experience that the faculty of expression

---

*Apraxia and other clinical disorders considered in this chapter are discussed in more detail in Chapter 7.

resides in one hemisphere, there is no absurdity in raising the question as to whether perception—its corresponding opposite—may be seated in the other."[9]

This speculation took more concrete form 11 years later when Jackson argued that the lobes at the rear of the brain are the seat of visual ideation or thought and that "the right posterior lobe is the leading side, the left the more automatic."[10] Jackson based this proposal on his observation of a patient who had a tumor in the right hemisphere and experienced difficulty recognizing objects, persons, and places.

Jackson's idea was way ahead of its time. Although other reports of a similar nature occasionally appeared, little attention was paid to Jackson's evidence. Investigators concerned themselves with localizing various functions within the left hemisphere and essentially ignored the right. By the 1930s, however, more data showing specialized roles for the right hemisphere had been collected, and scientists began to reconsider their ideas about the functions of the minor half of the brain.

Visuospatial Abilities in the Right Hemisphere

One important development was the discovery of significant and fairly consistent differences in the way subjects with left-hemisphere damage and those with right-hemisphere damage performed on standard psychological tests. The tests were originally developed to study and compare normal subjects along dimensions such as verbal ability, appreciation of spatial relationships, and ability to manipulate forms.

The first large-scale effort using these measures to study the effects of brain damage involved over 200 patients and more than 40 different tests, an average of 19 hours of testing per patient.[11] The results of this and subsequent studies were impressive. It was found, as a general rule, that damage to the left, or dominant, hemisphere results in poor performance on the tests that emphasize verbal ability. Although this finding was not too surprising, it was also found that patients with damage to the right hemisphere consistently do more poorly on nonverbal tests involving the manipulation of geometrical figures, puzzle assembly, completion of missing parts of patterns and figures, and other tasks involving form, distance, and space relationships. (Two visuospatial tasks are shown in Figure 1.2.)

The most striking evidence for specialized right-hemisphere function comes from direct observations of the patients themselves, who often display profound disturbances in orientation and awareness.

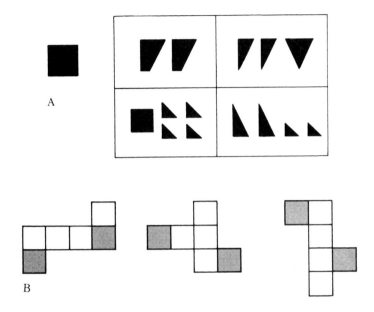

FIGURE 1.2 Visuospatial tasks. A. Which boxed set(s) can form the square on the outside? B. If you fold these patterns into cubes, in which cube(s) will the dark sides meet at one edge?

Such patients can be so disoriented in space that they are unable to find their way around a house in which they have lived for many years. Some show neglect, or hemispatial inattention: They consistently miss objects or events on their left. Certain agnosias—disturbances in the recognition or perception of familiar information—are also associated with damage to the right hemisphere. Spatial agnosia is a disorientation with respect to locations and spatial relationships. Some right-hemisphere patients have deficits in their ability to comprehend depth and distance relationships or to deal with mental images of maps and forms.

One of the most interesting forms of agnosia is facial agnosia. A patient with this condition is unable to recognize familiar faces and sometimes cannot discriminate between people in general. The deficit is quite specific. Recognition of scenes and objects, for example, may not be impaired. This problem has been found in cases where there was damage to both halves of the brain, although several investigators have argued for the importance of right-hemisphere lesions in this disorder.[12] We discuss this at greater length in Chapter 7.

The Role of the Right Hemisphere in Music

Additional evidence pointing to the specialization of the right hemisphere came from the observation that the ability to sing is frequently unaffected in patients suffering from severe speech disturbances. One of the earliest recorded cases of this type was described in 1745:

> He had an attack of a violent illness which resulted in a paralysis of the entire right side of the body and complete loss of speech. He can sing certain hymns, which he had learned before he became ill, as clearly and distinctly as any healthy person. . . Yet this man is dumb, cannot say a single word except "yes" and has to communicate by making signs with his hand.[13]

Similar cases were reported in the early 1900s and suggest that the right hemisphere controls singing.

Other evidence consistent with this idea comes from clinical reports that damage to the right half of the brain may result in the loss of musical ability, leaving speech unimpaired. This disorder, known as amusia, was most frequently reported in professional musicians who suffered from stroke or other brain damage. By the 1930s, the medical literature contained many case histories of people who suffered impairments in various aspects of musical ability after damage to the right hemisphere. Similar reports following damage to the left hemisphere were rarer, again suggesting that the right hemisphere is in some way critically involved in music.[14]

Why "Discovery" of the Right Brain Took So Long

All this evidence shows that the view of the right hemisphere as the minor or passive hemisphere is inappropriate. Why did it take most scientists 70 years after Broca's findings concerning the left hemisphere to recognize that the right hemisphere controls important functions? There may be several reasons for this time lag.

First, it seemed that the right hemisphere was able to withstand greater damage without producing any obvious impairments. Small lesions in particular areas of the left hemisphere drastically affected speech abilities, but comparable damage in the right hemisphere did not appear to cause any serious dysfunction. This disparity was originally interpreted as a sign of the less important role played by the right hemisphere in human behavior. Another possibility, however, is that this difference simply reflects the way processes are organized in the right hemisphere: Specific processes may be distributed over larger regions of brain tissue in the right half of the brain than in the left half.[15]

The most likely reason for the slow recognition of the importance of the right hemisphere, however, is that disabilities caused by lesions in the right hemisphere were not so easy to analyze and fit into the traditional ideas about brain function. Most damage to the right hemisphere did not abolish any obvious human abilities in an all-or-none fashion; instead, it disturbed behavior in fairly subtle ways.

It is important to keep in mind that the most debilitating effect of a stroke is the paralysis it often causes. The paralysis tends to be the patient's chief complaint or problem. Brain damage that arises from traumas such as accidents or gunshot wounds is also accompanied by complications that make it difficult to separate out subtle intellectual impairments from a host of other problems.

Despite its initially camouflaged role, the right hemisphere does play a vital part in human behavior. It is now clear that both hemispheres contribute to complex mental activity while differing to an extent in their function and organization. The idea that each hemisphere is specialized for different functions is known as complementary specialization.

Further Insights from the Clinic

To complete our brief introduction of the contributions of clinical data to the understanding of hemispheric asymmetry of function, we should mention two highly specialized neurosurgical procedures developed in the 1930s and 1940s. Designed to help the neurosurgeon determine which hemisphere was controlling speech and language function in an individual about to undergo brain surgery for epilepsy, these procedures have also contributed significantly to our knowledge of hemispheric asymmetry of function in general.

Direct Electrical Stimulation of the Hemispheres

Epilepsy is a disorder involving abnormal electrical activity that originates in a specific part of the brain and spreads to other regions. The abnormal activity produces reactions that may range from short blackouts lasting a second or two to full-blown grand mal seizures.

In the early 1930s, Wilder Penfield and his associates at the Montreal Neurological Institute pioneered the use of surgery, removing the area of the brain where the abnormal activity begins as a treatment for epilepsy in patients who did not respond well to drug therapy.[16] Although the procedure proved to be successful in many instances, surgeons were reluctant to undertake cases requiring the removal of tissue that was close to the parts of the brain controlling speech and language. They wished to avoid these regions to reduce the likelihood that the surgery would merely substitute one debilitating disorder (aphasia) for another (epilepsy).

Clearly, what was required was a method for determining with precision the location of the centers controlling speech and language in a given patient. To meet this need, Penfield and his colleagues developed a procedure that involved mapping these areas by using direct electrical stimulation of the brain at the time of surgery.

Preliminary work in the early 1900s had shown that, because the brain itself does not contain pain receptors, it is possible for a patient to remain fully conscious while a neurosurgeon removes a flap of skull under local anesthesia and applies small electrical currents directly to different regions of the brain surface. Such studies had shown that electrical stimulation of specific parts of the brain caused patients to see, hear, smell, or feel in an elementary way. Stimulation of other regions caused involuntary motor responses, such as the movement of an arm or a leg. The Montreal group was the first to use direct electrical stimulation as a tool for determining the location of the centers controlling speech and language in a given individual.

During a typical procedure using direct electrical stimulation to map speech areas, the patient is asked to identify a series of pictures as the neurosurgeon moves the stimulating electrode over the surface of the brain to locate areas that produce interference with naming. The interference is known as aphasic arrest.[17] Figure 1.3 maps the points on the left hemisphere where stimulation has resulted in speech disturbance.

Aphasic arrest is a sure sign that the region being stimulated is part of the speech area in the hemisphere specialized for language. Penfield noted that aphasic arrest never follows from the stimulation of sites within the non–language-specialized half of the brain. Over the last 20 years, work by neurologist George Ojemann has confirmed and extended these earlier findings.[18]

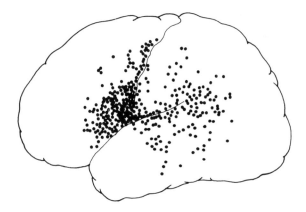

FIGURE 1.3 Points along the surface of the left hemisphere where electrical stimulation resulted in interference with speech. The interference included total speech arrest, hesitation, slurring, repetition of words, and inability to name. [From Penfield and Roberts, *Speech and Brain Mechanisms,* Fig. VII-3, p. 122. (Princeton, NJ: Princeton University Press, 1959). Reprinted by permission of Princeton University Press.]

The Wada Test: Anesthetizing a Hemisphere

Another test known as the Wada test after its inventor, Juhn Wada, has been very valuable in localizing functions across hemispheres. In the Wada test, the neurosurgeon temporarily anesthetizes one hemisphere at a time on separate days before surgery so that it can be determined which side of the brain normally controls the ability to speak.[19] The first step is the insertion of a small tube, or catheter, into the carotid artery on one side of the patient's neck. The carotid artery on each side brings blood to the hemisphere on the same side as the artery. Thus, when sodium amobarbital (a barbiturate chemically similar to the ingredients used in sleeping pills) is injected into the right artery, it is carried to the right hemisphere, putting just that half of the brain to sleep.

Moments before the drug is injected, the fully conscious patient lies flat on his or her back and is asked to count repeatedly from 1 to 20 while keeping both arms raised. Within seconds of the injection, dramatic results occur. First, the arm opposite the side of the injection falls limp. Because each half of the brain controls the opposite side of the body, the falling arm tells the neurosurgeon that the drug has reached the proper hemisphere and has taken effect. Second, the patient generally stops counting, either for a few seconds or for the duration of the drug's effect, depending on which hemisphere is affected. If the drug is injected on the same side as the hemisphere controlling speech, the patient remains speechless for 2 to 5 minutes, depending on the dose administered. If it is injected on the other side, the patient generally resumes counting within a few seconds and can answer questions with little difficulty while the drug is still inactivating the other half of the brain.

Sodium amobarbital work has been the basis for the most commonly cited data about the relationship between handedness and brain organization. In the largest study of this type, reported in 1977, over 95 percent of all right-handers without any history of early brain damage had speech and language controlled by the left hemisphere; the remainder had speech controlled by the right hemisphere. Contrary to Broca's rule, a majority of left-handers also showed left-hemisphere speech; however, the percentage (about 70 percent) was smaller in left-handers than in right-handers. Roughly 15 percent of left-handers had speech in the right hemisphere, and 15 percent or so showed evidence of speech control in both hemispheres (bilateral speech control).[20] More recent evidence from studies using the amobarbital technique, however, suggests that the incidence of pure right-hemisphere speech may actually be much lower than previously reported in patients with no history of early damage.[21] What was believed to be right-hemisphere speech was, in reality, bilateral speech representation in many cases.

The same 1977 study reported use of the Wada technique in patients who were known to have had some damage to the left hemisphere early in life. These patients showed a much higher incidence of right-hemisphere or bilateral speech: 70 percent of the left-handers and 19 percent of the right-handers fell into one or the other of these categories. This evidence points to the adaptability of the brain and to the limited value of handedness per se as an index of brain organization, particularly in left-handers.

The Wada test has proved to be invaluable as a powerful neuropsychological procedure in both clinical and research contexts. It is not, however, an absolute measure of hemispheric control of speech. It has been noted that methodological differences in the administration of the procedure as well as different criteria for determining mixed speech dominance can result in widely varying estimates of mixed speech dominance in patient populations.[22]

Inferring Brain Function from Brain Damage:
The Rise of Contemporary Neuropsychology

The clinical observations and neurological procedures we have just discussed formed the foundation of modern interest in hemispheric asymmetries. In the chapters that follow, we will explore how investigators have built upon and extended these observations and techniques in many different and fascinating ways to give us our current understanding of the two hemispheres and their functions. Along with new findings and developments have also come new ways of thinking about the relationships between the brain and behavior from the perspective of clinical studies. In this section we will discuss the changes in approach and conceptualization that have taken place over time.

Over 100 years' worth of observations of neurological patients have firmly established the field of neuropsychology—the investigation of disorders of perception, memory, language, thought, emotion, and action in patients suffering from neurological disease or injury. Broca's assertion that the seat of language is located in the posterior region of the left frontal lobe has been seen by many as a critical point in the establishment of neuropsychology. Broca's claim had two key parts: that language could be disrupted independently of other cognitive processes and that language could be localized to a specific region of the brain. Both were revolutionary in their implications and generated decades of research relating damage and disease in various parts of the brain to their consequences.

A model of the recognition and production of spoken and written words proposed in 1885 by neurologist L. Lichtheim illustrates the early neuropsychological approach.[23] Based on observations of a number of patients with brain injury, Lichtheim's model has five different "centers" that are interlinked. The model purports to explain several kinds of language disorders in terms of damage to one or more centers and/or the connections between them.

This approach to neuropsychology was sometimes referred to as diagram-making because it literally involved the generation of diagrams showing lines linking related centers. Although it enjoyed popularity into the early part of the twentieth century, as additional data were collected, diagram-making fell into disfavor because the actual observations of individual patients offered as support for the diagram models were often disappointingly weak and unconvincing. The approach was also criticized because anatomical data did not support the precise localization of centers controlling different functions that were postulated.

Even though some investigators continued to work within Lichtheim's diagram-maker tradition, by the 1930s a different approach to neuropsychology gained prominence. This new approach questioned the value of analyzing and reporting on single cases, as the diagram-makers had done, and substituted a group approach to data analysis. Patients were assigned to a group on the basis of general information about the site of brain injury (e.g., left or right temporal lobe), and the performance of the groups was then compared in a series of standardized, quantifiable tests to see whether the groups showed different patterns of deficits. The use of control groups of normal subjects matched for important variables (age, sex, and education, for example) also became an important part of neuropsychological investigations.

Although sound in principle, the group study also has problems that limit its usefulness. Because the members of each group can be expected to show variation in severity of impairment, preinjury levels of performance, and so on, large numbers of subjects are required to obtain differences between groups that are statistically significant. Thus, it could (and often did) take ten years or more of data collection to complete some studies. Furthermore, interesting and potentially very important differences between subjects get "washed out" or lost in the analysis. The group study is based on averaging results across subjects selected on the basis of certain criteria (e.g., lesion side); differences between individuals and even between slightly different groupings of individuals are obscured.

The mid-1960s saw the development of yet another approach to neuropsychology that would dramatically transform the field. Neurologist Norman Geschwind, whose work plays a prominent role in many of the chapters that follow, is often credited with being instrumental in starting that transformation.[24] Geschwind's own research led him to reconsider and appreciate the value of the diagram-makers and the single case study approach, and he called on his fellow investigators to reconsider as well.[25] At the same time, the discipline of cognitive psychology, which focuses on theories and models of normal cognitive function, began to firmly establish itself. The approaches of cognitive psychology were warmly embraced by Geschwind and other neurologists and neuropsychologists seeking to understand higher mental function both in the normal brain and in the diseased or injured brain.

The union of cognitive psychology and the renewed interest in the single case study approach to neuropsychology established contemporary neuropsychology, often referred to as cognitive neuropsychology. Cognitive neuroscience includes cognitive neuropsychology as one of several approaches to understanding the relationship between brain and behavior. The two terms sound similar, and thus it is important for the reader to keep the distinction between them clear as we turn our attention now to some of the approaches and assumptions of cognitive neuropsychology.

Cognitive Neuropsychology:
Approaches and Assumptions

Cognitive neuropsychology studies the underlying mechanisms of the psychological processes that are the basis of our mental life—thinking, reading, speaking, recognizing, remembering—through the effects of brain injury. Its first aim is to relate the patterns of cognitive performance in brain-injured patients to psychological operations that are necessary for normal cognitive function; the second is to actually draw conclusions about normal cognitive processes from observations of the effects of brain injury. Thus, cognitive neuropsychologists not only attempt to explain how brain injury disrupts normal function, but they also seek to increase our understanding of the way the normal brain and mind are organized by studying deficits that occur following brain injury.

The distinction between a traditional neuropsychological approach and that of cognitive neuropsychology is nicely made when considering a patient who, following brain injury, could no longer remember, or "find," many words that had long been part of his vocabulary. This condition is known as anomia. Is it better to say "He is anomic because of damage to his left hemisphere," asks neuropsychologist Andrew Ellis, or "He is anomic because of damage to the psychological processes which mediate spoken word finding?"[26] We will present both approaches in this book. Our interest in the left and right hemisphere implies attention to "where," whereas our overall concern with function and process will lead us to deeper issues of "how" and "why."

The Logic of Associations and Dissociations

Central to the logic of relating normal functioning to the effects of brain injury is the concept of dissociations. A dissociation occurs when a patient performs very poorly on a task (e.g., reading) and normally or at a much higher level on another task (e.g., recognizing faces). We could argue that different cognitive processes are involved in each case. However, another explanation could be equally plausible. Perhaps the same cognitive processes are involved in both tasks, but reading is more difficult than face recognition. If this were the case, we would be observing differences in performance due to level of difficulty and not differences in the cognitive processes involved.

This logical problem can be addressed if we can identify patients who show the reverse patterns of symptoms, for example, greater impairment in face recognition and normal performance in reading. Having examples of both patterns of impairment, known as a double dissociation, makes a much stronger case for the existence of separate processes involved in the tasks in question. In yet another situation, impairment in one task may be associated with impairment in other tasks. One plausible interpretation of this kind of observation is that all the tasks share a common process that is disrupted by brain damage. However, it is also possible that different sets of processes are involved, one for each task, and that these processes are mediated by areas in the brain close enough to be affected by one lesion. Such an association would be of neurological importance but of less interest from the perspective of a cognitive neuropsychologist.

The Concept of Modularity

The caveats about drawing conclusions from associations and dissociations follow from a view of mind–brain organization in which there are large numbers of semi-independent cognitive processes (or modules) that can be impaired independently. Mental life, according to the modularity hypothesis, is the result of the coordinated activity of many different modules, each of which engages its own form of processing independently of the activity in others.

The work of David Marr, who used computers to simulate complex human abilities, led him to propose that complex systems, be they brain or machines, evolve toward modular organization because of the potential for improvement and ease of detecting and correcting errors.* In support of this idea he stated:

> Any large computation should be split up and implemented as a collection of small sub-parts that are as nearly independent of one another as the overall task allows. If a process is not designed in this way, a small change in one place will have consequences in many other places. This means that the process as a whole becomes extremely difficult to debug or to improve, whether by a human designer or in the course of natural evolution, because a small change to improve one part has to be accompanied by many simultaneous compensating changes elsewhere.[27]

Modularity is one of the key assumptions underlying cognitive neuropsychology, although it cannot be directly proved or disproved. Several other assumptions are also implicit in the approach taken by cognitive neuropsychologists, and we will discuss these in greater detail in Chapter 7. For the moment, it is sufficient to understand that these assumptions form the basis for the belief that a careful analysis of the patterns of intact and impaired performance and the pattern of errors shown by a patient after brain injury should lead to valid conclusions about the nature and normal function of the processing components. In other words, the patient's pattern of performance will provide a guide to the nature of the underlying disruption. This in turn will refine our understanding of normal cerebral organization.

There are, however, obstacles to the interpretation of the pattern of symptoms shown by a patient. These include individual variation in performance, the effects of a brain that is compensating for the injury, and the fact that most injuries cause fairly widespread damage and probably affect multiple processes, or modules. These confounding factors have been acknowledged for many years as problems for neuropsychology and for all attempts at inferring brain function from brain damage.

The basic problem is that there is no simple way to relate the function of a piece of destroyed brain tissue to the disabilities a patient

---

*The use of computer simulation or "modeling" of human mental functions is an important part of the multidisciplinary approach of cognitive neuroscience to brain research. We will return to Marr's work briefly in Chapter 7 and to other approaches in Chapter 13.

seems to incur as a result of the damage. The oldest idea was to say simply that whatever a patient could not do was normally controlled by the area of the brain that was damaged. If a person had a lesion and could not see, for example, then the damaged area was said to control vision. If someone had a lesion in a different region and could not understand spoken language, then the area involved was said to be responsible for speech comprehension.

That approach has turned out to be much too simplistic. For one thing, most of the processes neatly labeled as visual perception, speech production, voluntary movement, or memory are really the result of many complex cerebral interactions. Whether they are diffusely spread over large areas of the brain or are limited to particular regions appears to be determined by which function we are studying, how precisely we are defining it, and how successfully we are able to limit our tests to what we assume they are testing. Just about any fairly limited damage to the brain is likely to interfere with a step or phase of some larger process (although not the entire process). It is also likely to interfere with a step or phase of more than one process. It is not unusual to see damage to a small area of the brain result in deficits in a number of different functions.

Another major problem in deducing brain function from clinical data is the fact that the brain tends to adjust its operations as best it can in the presence of damage. We cannot assume that the remaining intact areas of a damaged brain are operating as they would in a normal brain. It is not as though a piece is missing but everything else is working as it was before. In most cases of brain damage, there is some recovery of function over time, sometimes fairly dramatic recovery. The recovery can involve changes in the undamaged areas and is a tribute to the adaptability of the brain. This plasticity is a fascinating and obviously very useful feature, but it complicates the efforts of those who are trying to deduce brain function from clinical data.

These problems have not been eliminated by the assumptions of cognitive neuropsychology but have been placed in a slightly different perspective. Adjustments or compensation by the brain to injury is acknowledged as an important factor but is viewed as occurring strictly as a result of changes in the operations of undamaged modules, not to the creation of new modules. This notion allows investigators to assume that what appears to be missing at first, postinjury, is in fact attributable to the functions of impaired modules and that changes postinjury are due to reorganization of other modules.

The Cognitive Neuroscience Approach

The knowledge we gain about the role of particular brain regions from the effects of brain damage is extremely valuable but tentative and most useful in combination with knowledge of brain function obtained in other ways. In the next chapter we will consider the findings from studies with a limited number of so-called split-brain patients who have had the fibers connecting the two hemispheres surgically sectioned. These cases confirm and, indeed, dramatically illustrate the differences in hemispheric function identified through the study of the effects of brain damage. However, still other approaches that do not depend on great intrusions into normal functioning are necessary to demonstrate the nature and extent of asymmetries in the normal brain. Cognitive neuroscience brings together these approaches in an integrated attempt to understand the relationship between mind and brain.

We will examine some of these approaches, including the use of neuroimaging—techniques to visualize both the structure and certain aspects of the function of the brain—in later chapters. We will return to what has been discovered by neuropsychological studies of brain damage in Chapters 7 and 8, using the tools of cognitive neuroscience. Together, these approaches produce converging lines of evidence about the workings of the left brain, the right brain, and the two together.

Chapter 2

Splitting the Brain

Insights from the Surgical Separation of the Hemispheres

In 1940 a scientific report described the spread of epileptic discharge from one hemisphere to the other in the brains of monkeys.[1] The author concluded that the spread occurred largely or entirely by way of the corpus callosum, the largest of several commissures—bands of nerve fiber connecting regions of the left brain with similar areas of the right brain. Other investigators had already observed that damage to the corpus callosum from a tumor or other problem sometimes reduced the incidence of seizures in human epileptics.[2] Together, these findings paved the way for a new treatment for patients with epilepsy that could not be controlled in other ways: the split-brain operation, or commissurotomy, in which some of the fibers that connect the two cerebral hemispheres are cut.

The role of the corpus callosum was a mystery to early researchers, who expected to find functions associated with it commensurate with its large size and strategic location within the brain. Animal research, however, showed that the consequences of split-brain surgery on a healthy organism are minimal. The behavior of a split-brain monkey, for example, appeared indistinguishable from that monkey's behavior before the operation. The apparent absence of any noticeable changes following commissurotomy led some scientists to suggest facetiously that the corpus callosum's only function was to hold the halves of the brain together and keep them from sagging.

Speculation about the consequences of split-brain surgery goes back to the nineteenth century and the writings of Gustav Fechner, considered by many to be the father of experimental psychology. Fechner believed that consciousness was an attribute of the cerebral hemispheres and that continuity of the brain was an essential condition for unity of consciousness. If it were possible to divide the brain through the middle, he speculated, something like the duplication of a human being would result.

> Were it possible for the two halves of a man divided lengthwise to carry on living at all, that is, for the psychophysical activity in both halves to remain above the threshold, then we would undoubtedly see something equivalent to the doubling of a man. . . . Undoubtedly the two halves would begin with the same states of mind, the same dispositions, knowledge, memories, the same consciousness in general; by degrees, however, as they passed through different circumstances, they would develop differently.[3]

Fechner, however, considered this "thought experiment" involving separation of the hemispheres impossible to achieve in reality.

Fechner's views concerning the nature of consciousness did not go unchallenged. William McDougall, a founder of the British Psychological Society, argued strongly against the position that unity of consciousness depends on the continuity of the nervous system. To make his point, McDougall volunteered to have his corpus callosum cut if he ever got an incurable disease. He apparently wanted to show that his personality would not be split and that his consciousness would remain unitary.

McDougall never got the opportunity to put his ideas to the test, but the surgery Fechner thought an impossibility took place for the first time almost a century later. The issues these men raised have been among those explored by scientists seeking a fuller understanding of the corpus callosum and the two cerebral hemispheres through the study of split-brain patients.

Cutting 200 Million Nerve Fibers:
A Search for Consequences

· · · · · · · · · · ·

The First Split-Brain Operations on Humans

William Van Wagenen, a neurosurgeon from Rochester, New York, performed the first split-brain operations on patients with epilepsy in the early 1940s. Postsurgical testing showed surprisingly little evidence of deficits in perceptual and motor abilities or effects on everyday behavior. Also, unfortunately, some patients showed little or no improvement in their conditions after commissurotomy.[4]

Disappointed with the outcome, Van Wagenen soon stopped performing the commissurotomy procedure. Others, however, continued to study the functions of the corpus callosum in animals. A decade later, in the early 1950s, Roger Sperry at the California Institute of Technology and his graduate student Ronald Myers made some remarkable discoveries in cats that marked a turning point in efforts to study this enigmatic structure.[5]

In most higher animals, the visual system is arranged so that each eye normally projects to both hemispheres. By cutting into the optic nerve crossing the optic chiasm, however, experimenters can limit the sites where each eye sends its information. The remaining fibers in the optic nerve transmit information to the hemisphere on the same side: Visual input to the left eye is sent only to the left hemisphere, and input to the right eye projects only to the right hemisphere.

Myers and Sperry performed this operation on cats and subsequently taught each animal a visual discrimination task, for example, pressing a lever when the animal sees a circle but not pressing the lever when it sees a square. When this training is done with one eye covered, a normal cat or a cat with a sectioned optic chiasm can later perform the task using either eye. When both the corpus callosum and the optic chiasm were cut, however, they found that the results were dramatically different. The cat trained with one eye patched would learn to do a task well, but when the patch was switched to the other eye, the cat was totally unable to do the task. In fact, it had to be taught over again, taking just as long to learn the task as it had the first time. Myers and Sperry

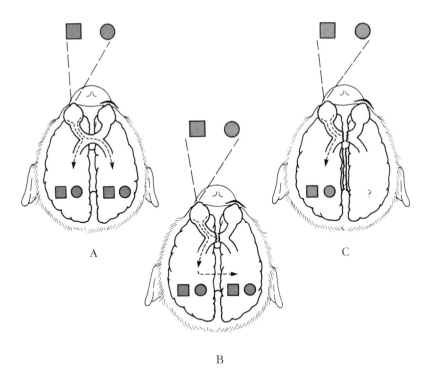

FIGURE 2.1 Split-brain experiment with cats. In a control situation, both eyes and both hemispheres see the stimuli. Experimental conditions alter this in the following ways: A. When one eye is patched, the other eye continues to send information to both hemispheres. B. When one eye is patched and the optic chiasm is cut, the visual information is transmitted to both hemispheres by way of the corpus callosum. C. When one eye is patched and both the optic chiasm and corpus callosum are cut, only one hemisphere receives visual information.

concluded that cutting the corpus callosum prevented the information going into one hemisphere from reaching the other hemisphere. They had, in effect, trained only one-half of a brain. Figure 2.1 schematically illustrates their experiment.

These and later findings led two neurosurgeons working near the California Institute of Technology to reconsider the use of split-brain surgery as a treatment for intractable epilepsy in human beings. Philip Vogel and Joseph Bogen reasoned that some of the earlier work with human patients had failed because the surgical disconnection between the cerebral hemispheres was not complete. Based on this logic, Bogen and Vogel performed a complete commissurotomy on the first of what was to be a new series (the California series) of patients suffering from intractable epilepsy. Figure 2.2 shows the corpus callosum and adjacent smaller commissures.

Bogen and Vogel's reasoning proved to be correct. In some of the cases, the medical benefits of the surgery even appeared to exceed expectations. In striking contrast to the reduction in seizure activity it produced, the operation appeared to leave patients unchanged in personality, intelligence, and behavior in general, just as had been the

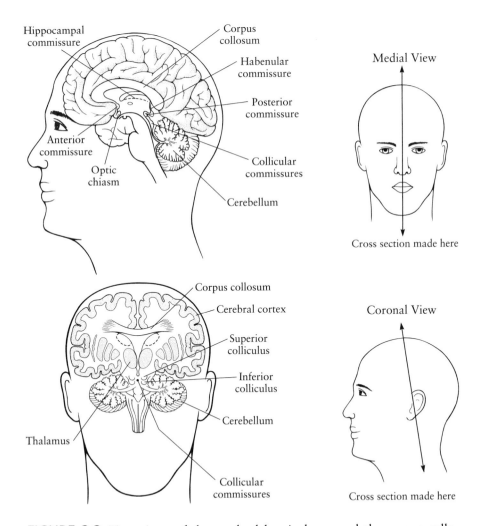

FIGURE 2.2 Two views of the cerebral hemispheres and the corpus callosum, the major nerve fiber tract connecting them. Other commissures are also shown.

case with Van Wagenen's patients. More extensive and ingenious testing conducted in Roger Sperry's laboratory, however, soon revealed a more complex story, for which Sperry was awarded the 1981 Nobel prize in physiology or medicine.

Testing for the Effects of Disconnecting Left from Right

Split-brain patient N.G., a California housewife, sits in front of a screen with a small black dot in the center. She is asked to look directly at the dot. When the experimenter is sure she is doing so, a picture of a cup is flashed briefly to the right of the dot. N.G. reports that she has seen a cup. Again, she is asked to fix her gaze on the dot. This time, a picture of a spoon is flashed to the left of the dot. She is asked what she saw. She replies, "No, nothing." She is then asked to reach under the screen with her left hand and to select, by touch only, from among several items the one that is the same as the one she has just seen. Her left hand palpates each object and then holds up the spoon. When asked what she is holding, she says, "Pencil."

Once again the patient is asked to fixate on the dot on the screen. A picture of a nude woman is flashed to the left of the dot. N.G.'s face blushes a little, and she begins to giggle. She is asked what she saw. She says, "Nothing, just a flash of light," and giggles again, covering her mouth with her hand. "Why are you laughing, then?" the investigator inquires. "Oh, doctor, you have some machine!" she replies.

The testing procedure just described has been widely used in studies with split-brain patients, and the testing arrangement is illustrated in Figure 2.3. The patient sits in front of a visual display that permits the investigator to control precisely the duration for which a picture or pattern is presented on a screen. The presentations are kept brief, about one- or two-tenths of a second (100 to 200 milliseconds), so that the patient does not have time to move his or her eyes away from the fixation point while the picture is still on the screen.* This procedure is necessary to ensure that visual information is presented initially to only one hemisphere. Stimuli presented to only one hemisphere are said to be lateralized.

---

*The rapid eye movements that occur when gaze is shifted from one point to another are known as saccadic eye movements or saccades. Although, once started, saccades are extremely rapid, they take about 200 milliseconds to initiate with the eye at rest. If a stimulus is presented for less than 200 milliseconds, then the stimulus is no longer present by the time an eye movement can occur.

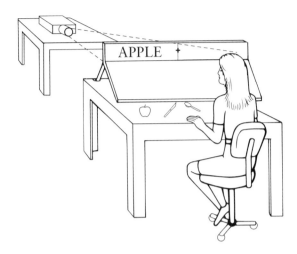

APPLE

FIGURE 2.3 Basic testing arrangement used to lateralize visual and tactile information and allow tactile responses.

The design of the human nervous system is such that each cerebral hemisphere receives information primarily from the opposite half of the body. This contralateral rule applies to vision and hearing as well as to body movement and touch (somatosensory) sensation, although the situation in vision and hearing is more complex.

In vision, the contralateral rule applies to the right and left sides of one's field of view (visual field) rather than to the right and left eyes per se. When both eyes are fixating on a single point, stimuli to the right of the point of fixation are registered in the left half of the brain, and the right half of the brain processes everything occurring to the left of the fixation point. This split and crossover of visual information results from the manner in which the nerve fibers from corresponding regions of both eyes are divided between the cerebral hemispheres. Figure 2.4 shows both the optics and the neural wiring involved.

In animal studies, as we have seen, visual information can be directed to one hemisphere by cutting the optic chiasm. The procedure is used only with animals, however, because it plays no part in the rationale for the split-brain operation on humans. Investigators wishing to transmit visual information to one hemisphere at a time in a human split-brain patient must do so through a combination of controlling the patient's fixation and presenting information to one side of space.

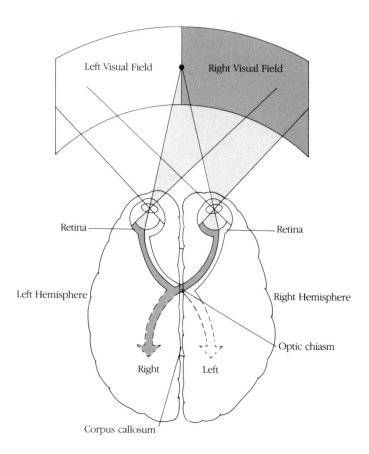

FIGURE 2.4 Visual pathways to the hemispheres. When fixating on a point, each eye sees both visual fields but sends information about the right visual field only to the left hemisphere and information about the left visual field only to the right hemisphere. This crossover and split is a result of the manner in which the nerve fibers leading from the retina divide at the back of each eye. The visual areas of the left and right hemisphere normally communicate through the corpus callosum. If the callosum is cut and the eyes and head are kept from moving, each hemisphere can see only half of the visual world.

With this background, let us return to the tests administered to patient N.G. In those tests, the patient saw everything to the left of the fixation point with the right side of her brain and everything to the right with her left hemisphere. The split in her brain prevented the normal interchange of information between the two sides that would have occurred before her surgery. In effect, each side of her brain was blind to what the other side was seeing, a state of affairs dramatically brought out by the knowledge that only one hemisphere controls speech.

As a consequence, the patient reported perfectly well any stimuli falling in the right visual field (projecting to the verbal left hemisphere), although she was unable to tell anything about what was flashed in her left visual field (sent to the mute right hemisphere). The fact that she "saw" stimuli in the left visual field is amply demonstrated by the ability of her left hand (basically controlled by the right brain) to select the spoon from among several objects that were hidden from her view. It is also demonstrated by her emotional reaction to the nude picture, despite her claim not to have seen anything.[6]

The patient's response to the nude picture is particularly interesting. She seemed puzzled by her own reactions to what had appeared. Her right hemisphere saw the picture and processed it sufficiently to evoke a general, nonverbal reaction—the giggling and the blushing. The left hemisphere, meanwhile, did not "know" what the right had seen, although its comment about "some machine" seems to be a sign that it was aware of the bodily reactions induced by the right hemisphere. It is very common for the verbal left hemisphere to try to make sense of what has occurred in testing situations where information is presented to the right hemisphere. As a result, the left brain sometimes comes out with erroneous and often elaborate rationalizations based on partial cues.

Everyday Behavior After Split-Brain Surgery

It is natural to wonder what disconnection effects can be observed in the everyday behavior of split-brain patients. Commissurotomy patients are often mute for a time after surgery, and sometimes they have difficulty controlling the left side of the body, which may even be paralyzed at first. As the patient recovers use of the left hand, competitive movements between the left and the right hands sometimes occur. This syndrome, known as the acute disconnection syndrome, usually passes quickly. It is probably due to the surgical division of the commissures and to general trauma resulting from the compression of the right hemisphere required to provide access to the nerve tracts between the hemispheres during the operation.

After recovering from the initial shock of major brain surgery, most patients report a feeling of improved well-being. Less than two days after surgery, one young patient was well enough to quip that he had a "splitting headache." Within a few weeks, the symptoms of the acute disconnection syndrome subside, thus making it necessary to use carefully contrived laboratory tests to reveal the effects of the operation.

In some cases, however, the effects of disconnection persist and manifest themselves in bizarre ways. One of the earliest patients, for example, described the time he found his left hand struggling against his right when he tried to put his pants on in the morning: One hand was pulling them up while the other hand was pulling them down. In another incident, the same patient was angry and forcibly reached for his wife with his left hand while his right hand grabbed the left in an attempt to stop it.[7]

The frequency with which such stories are mentioned in popular articles on split-brain research would lead one to believe that they are commonplace events. In fact, the frequency of such events is low in most patients. One exception is P.O.V., a female patient operated on by neurosurgeon Mark Rayport of the Medical College of Ohio. This patient reported frequent dramatic signs of interhemispheric competition for at least three years after surgery. "I open the closet door. I know what I want to wear. As I reach for something with my right hand, my left comes up and takes something different. I can't put it down if it's in my left hand. I have to call my daughter."[8]

Cases such as these support the concept that the cerebral commissures transmit information that is inhibitory in nature. In other words, activity in one hemisphere leads to callosal transmissions that serve to moderate, decrease, or stop certain activities in the other.

It seems likely that corpus callosum-mediated inhibition is an important process that is quickly masked by compensatory mechanisms in most split-brain patients. In fact, in a large majority of cases, the two sides of the body appear to continue to work in a coordinated fashion. Perhaps the rarity of patients with persistent disconnection effects indicates that more than callosal damage is necessary to prevent adjustment to the commissurotomy.

There is ample evidence, however, both from reports from the patients themselves and from sophisticated batteries of tests, that there are subtle changes in behavior and ability after surgery. Several patients, for example, have reported great difficulty in learning to associate names with faces after surgery. Verification of this problem came from a study in which subjects had to learn first names for each of three pictures of young men.[9] The investigators reported that subjects eventually learned the name–face associations by isolating some unique feature in each picture (for example, "Dick has glasses") rather than by associating the name with the face as a whole. This finding suggests that the deficit in the ability to associate names and faces may be due to a disconnection of the verbal naming functions of the left side of the brain from the facial-recognition abilities of the right side.

Deficits in the ability to solve geometry problems have been anecdotally linked to the sectioning of the corpus callosum. Patient L.B., a high school student with an IQ considerably above average, was transferred out of geometry into a class in general math after he experienced inordinate difficulty with the course. Another report told of a college student who had exceptional difficulty with geometry despite average grades in other courses. Studies with split-brain patients to determine the ability of each hemisphere to match two- and three-dimensional forms on the basis of common geometrical features showed that the right hemisphere was markedly superior, especially on the most difficult matches.[10] Thus, as in the preceding example, the patient's deficits may be the result of the disconnection of the speaking left hemisphere from the right-hemisphere regions specialized for such tasks.

Another complaint of some split-brain patients is that they no longer dream. Because dreaming is a process involving visual imagery, some investigators speculated that it might be the responsibility of the right half of the brain and thus disconnected from the left hemisphere in split-brain patients. This idea, however, has not been confirmed by research in which split-brain patients were monitored for brain-wave activity while sleeping and were awakened whenever the recordings indicated that they were dreaming. When asked to describe the dreams they had just been having, the patients provided the experimenters with descriptions of their dreams, a result contradicting the prediction that they would be unable to do so.[11]

Other anecdotal evidence documents poorer memory after surgery. Recent work suggests a physiological basis for these reports. Some patients, specifically those with damage to the hippocampal commissures* or other extracallosal structures, display memory deficits, whereas others do not.[12] In a study involving pre- and postsurgical memory tests, patients with commissurotomies that included the posterior region of the callosum showed memory impairments, with recall more affected

---

*The hippocampus is a subcortical structure that is divided into two parts, which are connected by a band of fibers. It is believed to play an important role in memory and is discussed in Chapter 8.

than recognition. Patients with partial callosal sections that excluded the posterior region did not show these deficits.[13] The investigators concluded that these results were consistent with the earlier work, because the hippocampal commissure is usually damaged during posterior sectioning, but not during anterior sectioning, of the corpus callosum.

Overall, it is not clear why a few patients seem to show persistent patterns of deficit after commissurotomy, whereas the majority of patients do not. Important differences among patients in their preoperative condition and surgical treatment probably exist, although we do not yet know what they are.

Language and the Hemispheres

Split-brain research has dramatically confirmed that, in most persons, control of speech is localized to the left hemisphere. But what about other language abilities? How well can the right hemisphere understand language, either written or spoken? What are its capabilities with respect to the various components of language—phonological or sound-based, syntactic or grammatical, and semantic or meaning? The split-brain patient provides investigators with a unique opportunity to answer these questions, because tests of such patients permit an assessment of the right hemisphere's abilities in isolation, decoupled from those of the language-rich left hemisphere. In contrast to studying the remaining language in aphasics with left-hemisphere damage as a measure of right-hemisphere language, split-brain research permits assessment of the positive language competence of the right hemisphere free from any inhibitory effects of the damaged left hemisphere.[14]

A major concern in interpreting work with split-brain patients, however, is how their unique neurological and surgical histories may affect the outcome of the research. In particular, some have argued that research with split-brain subjects may overestimate the degree of right-hemisphere language function as a result of reorganization of language following early left-hemisphere damage. Those who believe the approach is a valuable one, however, look for commonalities across patients who vary in their neurological history or who show little evidence of brain damage before their surgery. Subjects are also studied on a case-by-case basis to understand the factors that may be responsible for individual differences.

Eran Zaidel was the first investigator to undertake systematic investigations of right-hemisphere language in split-brain patients.[15] Working primarily with two patients, L.B. and N.G., from the original Bogen and Vogel series, Zaidel developed a contact lens device that permits the patient to move his or her eyes freely without a time limit when examining something but at the same time ensures that only one hemisphere of the patient's brain receives the visual information. Zaidel's strategy was to test the abilities of each hemisphere, using a variety of stimuli that had been used previously with children and aphasic patients. His goal was to obtain data that would allow comparisons of the abilities of the right hemisphere of split-brain patients with the abilities of the two other groups.

Other studies of language function have been undertaken by Gazzaniga and his associates, working with patients operated on by Donald Wilson of Dartmouth Medical School (e.g., J.W. and P.S.) as well as others (e.g., V.P. and V.J.). Although some of their research has involved the use of an eye tracking device that tracks eye movements and coordinates the position of the image with the eye movement so that retinal position is maintained, much of it has used the traditional approach of very brief displays of visual stimuli to the left or right of fixation.

A recent review of research on right-hemisphere language in the different groups of split-brain patients found a surprising degree of consistency in the findings, along with some variability of considerable theoretical interest.[16] For example, the ability of the left hemisphere to control speech has been one of the most dramatic and consistent findings in split-brain research. While this continues to be the case in most instances, two patients, P.S. and V.P., have shown evidence of being able to control speech from the right hemisphere. This ability, while not present immediately following surgery, appeared to develop in the years that followed. J.W. has also demonstrated the ability to respond verbally to stimuli presented in the left visual field, an ability that was first detected 12 years after his surgery.

Overall, split-brain patients have difficulty deriving phonology, or the sounds of speech, from words. For example, patient L.B. was able to match pictures with names that sound alike with his right hemisphere (e.g., picture of a flying bat with a picture of a hat), although he could not perform the same task when he had to match a printed name with a picture (e.g., the printed word "bat" with a picture of a hat). This interesting observation suggests that L.B.'s right hemisphere could not evoke the sound image of a word from its orthographic or printed representation, despite the fact that it could match pictures for rhyming.[17] Patient J.W. was also unable to identify visually presented words that rhyme. Patients V.P. and P.S., however, have shown some ability to recognize printed rhymes, although they appear to be exceptions, both in this regard and, as we noted above, in their ability to verbally identify visually presented words and pictures presented to the right hemisphere.

Because all the patients have demonstrated the ability to match printed words and pictures in the right hemisphere, the inability of most patients to select rhyming words suggests that the right hemisphere moves from the printed word to its meaning without the usual phonological decoding that takes place in the left hemisphere. Patients who show no evidence of controlling speech from the right hemisphere appear to lack the ability in that hemisphere to decode the printed word into its phonological representation. Having control of speech in the right hemisphere, however, does not appear sufficient for phonological decoding. Patient J.W., who has shown evidence of right-hemisphere speech, cannot identify words that rhyme, using that hemisphere.

Zaidel's early tests of grammatical competence with N.G. and L.B. led him to conclude that the right hemisphere possesses competence equivalent to that of a five-year-old child. While equivalent testing has not been conducted with other patients, in general they show an ability to differentiate among nouns, verbs, and function words, and to distinguish grammatical from ungrammatical sentences that is consistent with Zaidel's observation. Additional testing of N.G. and L.B. also led Zaidel to conclude that the right hemisphere had an auditory lexicon, or auditory mental dictionary, that included concrete and abstract nouns, verbs, and some spatial prepositions. Its visual lexicon, however, was less extensive. Patients tested by Gazzaniga and colleagues showed results that were generally consistent with this pattern.

The newest patient to be studied by Gazzaniga, V. J., presents an interesting case of how verbal and written expression may be controlled by different hemispheres.[18] V.J., who is left-handed, shows evidence from visual field studies and naming of objects held in one hand out of view that speech is controlled by her left hemisphere. However, since her surgery was completed, she has complained that she is unable to write with either hand. When letters or words are presented in the right visual field, she can name them but cannot legibly reproduce them with her right hand out of view. When the same stimuli are presented in the left visual field, she cannot name them but can write them with her left hand when she cannot see it. Thus it appears that writing is controlled by her right hemisphere, whereas speech is controlled by her left hemisphere, an interesting variation that has not been observed previously in split-brain patients. Gazzaniga and colleagues speculate that this atypical pattern is related to the fact that V.J. is left-handed.

Zaidel has recently reported on additional findings with the California series of patients that led him to conclude that studies of the disconnected right hemisphere underestimate the language competence of the normal right hemisphere. In addition, he argues that the language of aphasic patients also underestimates the language competence of the normal right hemisphere. The reason for this underestimation, he proposes, is that under normal conditions, the corpus callosum permits linguistic interhemispheric interaction, including a sharing of resources residing in the left hemisphere that effectively increases the competence of the right hemisphere. He proposes that "the psycholinguistic profile of a left hemisphere-damaged patient is determined not only by the lost functions of the left hemisphere and by the residual competence of the right hemisphere, but also critically by the balance of activation in a system of control that incorporates several levels of facilitory and inhibitory circuits."[19] Speech following left-hemisphere injury, then, may be a result not only of the left- and right-hemisphere competencies that remain, but of the complex interaction of the two.

Long-standing evidence recently confirmed in neuroimaging studies using positron emission tomography (PET) has demonstrated that recovery from aphasia may involve right-hemisphere compensation.[20] Zaidel's ideas expand on this and make the case that language following left-hemisphere damage reflects the contributions of both hemispheres in a complex, as yet to be understood, way.

Research on right-hemisphere language illustrates well the power of the cognitive neuroscience approach to brain–behavior relationships, bringing together modern neuroimaging and behavioral techniques and linguistic analysis in the study of clinical and normal populations.[21] Split-brain research has been, and will continue to be, an important contribution to the effort. We will return to the topic of right-hemisphere language in Chapter 7.

Visuospatial Functions in the Hemispheres

On the basis of split-brain studies, the most general statement that can be made about right-hemisphere specializations is that they are nonlinguistic functions that seem to involve complex visual and spatial

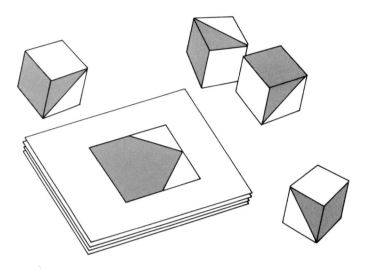

FIGURE 2.5 A block-design task. The subject is asked to arrange the colored blocks to match the pattern shown on a card.

processes. The perception of part–whole relations, for example, seems to be superior in the right hemisphere. In one task, patients viewed line drawings of the separated pieces of geometrical shapes that had been cut up. The task was to decide which of three solid alternatives felt with one hand, but not seen, was represented by the fragmented figure. The left hand was far superior on this task; the right hand showed chance performance in six of seven patients. In another study, arcs (sections of circles) were presented to either the left or the right visual field of commissurotomy patients. After each presentation, they were asked to choose which circle from a set of different-sized circles would be formed by the arcs they saw. The patients performed much better when their judgments were based on arcs presented to the left visual field (right hemisphere).[22]

One of the most dramatic demonstrations of right-hemisphere superiority in visuospatial tasks was recorded on film by Gazzaniga and Sperry while they were testing W.J., the first patient of the California series. W.J. was presented with several cubes, each containing two red sides, two white sides, and two half-red and half-white sides divided along the diagonal. His task was to arrange these blocks to form squares with patterns identical to those shown on a series of cards. Figure 2.5 illustrates the task.

The beginning of the film shows W.J. readily assembling the blocks with his left hand to form a particular pattern. When he tries to form a pattern with his right hand, however, he experiences great difficulty. Slowly and with considerable indecision, the right hand arranges the blocks. At one point, the left hand moves into the picture and begins to assemble the blocks in the correct pattern. It is gently but firmly removed from the table by the investigator, while the right hand continues to fumble, unaided by the more skillful left.

Other evidence pointing to right-hemisphere superiority in visuospatial ability comes from differences in the abilities of the two hands of the split-brain patient to draw a figure of a cube. Invariably, the left hand produces a better drawing. Examples are shown in Figure 2.6.

What is the basis for the right hemisphere's superior abilities in these visuospatial tasks? Two possibilities suggested themselves to investigators. First, the right hemisphere could be dominant for the expression of visual understanding, just as the left hemisphere is dominant for the expression of language understanding, although both halves of the brain might be equally skilled in perceiving spatial relationships. This view emphasizes an asymmetry in the ability to perform the complex motor acts required by the tasks. An alternative

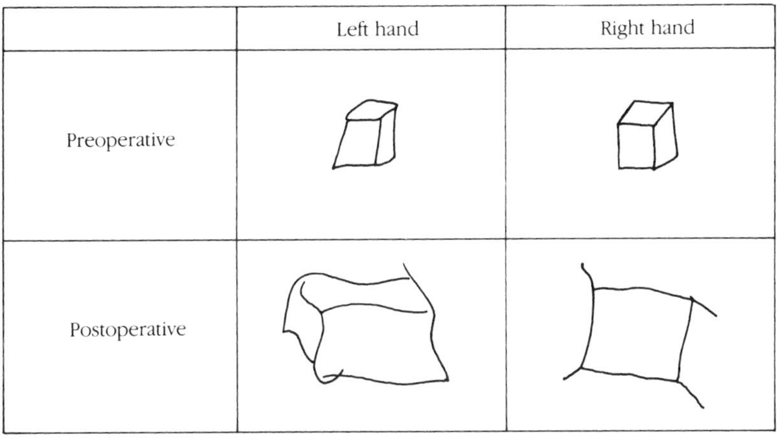

	Left hand	Right hand
Preoperative		
Postoperative		

FIGURE 2.6 Cube drawings by a right-handed patient before and after commissurotomy. Preoperatively, the patient could draw a cube with either hand. Postoperatively, the right hand performed poorly. [From Gazzaniga and LeDoux, *The Integrated Mind*, Fig. 18, p. 52 (New York: Plenum, 1978).]

interpretation holds that there are true differences in perceptual abilities between hemispheres.

Laura Franco and Roger Sperry tested each hand of right-handed commissurotomy patients and normal control subjects on matching unseen objects by touch with geometrical shapes presented in free vision. They found that the left hands of the split-brain subjects performed consistently better than did the right hands. Furthermore, this left-hand (right-hemisphere) superiority increased as the shapes became less geometrical and more free form. When the sets of objects to be matched consisted only of free-form contours, the right hand (left hemisphere) performed barely above choice level. Normal subjects did equally well with either hand on these tasks.[23]

One can argue that left-hemisphere difficulty increased as the objects became less describable verbally or, perhaps, less structurally constrained. In either case, the results showed that matching such objects by touch and visual perception requires the involvement of the right hemisphere, for it seems that simply disconnecting the two half-brains results in a severe breakdown in the performance of the preferred right hand. What seems most important in solving the matching tasks is not the tactile manipulation and sensations from the fingers of the hand, but knowing what kind of object to feel for—the right-hemisphere superiority is not just in spatially related hand activities but also in visual mental manipulations. We will discuss some further implications of this issue in Chapter 13.

Information Processing in the Two Hemispheres

As research into the specialized functions of the two hemispheres continued, the pattern of results suggested a new way to conceptualize hemispheric differences. Instead of a breakdown based on the type of tasks (for example, verbal or spatial) best performed by each hemisphere, a dichotomy based on different ways of dealing with information emerged.

According to this analysis, the left hemisphere is specialized for language functions, but these specializations are a consequence of the left hemisphere's superior analytic skills, of which language is but one manifestation. Similarly, the right hemisphere's superior visuospatial performance is assumed to be derived from its synthetic, holistic manner of dealing with information. Much of the early work that led to this reanalysis of hemispheric differences was conducted by Jerre Levy and her colleagues working with the California series of patients.

One of the first suggestions that the two hemispheres have different information-processing styles came from a study in which split-brain patients were asked to match small wooden blocks held in the left or the right hand with the appropriate two-dimensional representation selected from drawings of blocks shown in "opened-up" form. Overall, the left hand was considerably better than the right at this task, but the most interesting finding was that the two hemispheres appeared to use different strategies in approaching the problem.

An analysis of errors showed that the patterns the right hand (left hemisphere) found easier to deal with were the patterns that were easy to describe in words but difficult to discriminate visually. For the left hand (right hemisphere), the reverse was true. Thus, the left hemisphere appeared to make its matches on the basis of verbal descriptions of the properties of the blocks and the two-dimensional patterns. It seemed unable to fold up the two-dimensional representation mentally so that a match could be made on the basis of overall appearance.[24]

Other work has shown that the two hemispheres differ in the kinds of information they pick up from visual stimuli. For example, pictures that can be matched either by their functions (such as a cake on a plate matched with a spoon and a fork) or by their appearances (such as a cake on a plate matched with a hat with a brim) are handled differently by the two hemispheres. See Figure 2.7 for examples of the stimuli that are flashed briefly in the left or right visual field. When given ambiguous instructions simply to match similar stimuli, the left hemisphere of the split-brain patient matches by function and the right hemisphere matches by appearance.

Levy concluded that the left hemisphere's strategy in dealing with incoming information is best characterized as analytic, whereas the right hemisphere appears to process information in a holistic manner.[25] There are other ways to interpret the differences we have just considered, but the analytic–holistic distinction has been the most influential in moving thinking about hemispheric differences away from the verbal–nonverbal dichotomy.

Additional experiments using these same stimuli have looked at the pattern of responses when two different stimuli were presented simultaneously to patients, one in each visual field. These studies took advantage of the completion effect. Completion is the tendency for split-brain patients to see as whole what are really partial figures falling at the visual midline. It was first noted when patients showed the ability to identify accurately a square flashed briefly in the center of the visual field. Because the left half of the square is projected to the right hemisphere and the right half to the left hemisphere, the fact that the patients reported seeing a normal square meant that the left hemisphere had "completed" the partial figure presented to it. The right hemisphere also perceived a normal square, for the left hand would draw a complete figure when a patient was asked to sketch with that hand what he or she saw.[26] Studies have also shown that composite figures, made up of the left half of one figure and the right half of the other, also show the completion effect. Such figures are known as chimeric figures, after Chimera, a mythical monster made up of parts of different animals.

Jerre Levy and Colwyn Trevarthen constructed chimeric figures from drawings shown in Figure 2.7 and asked subjects to point to a

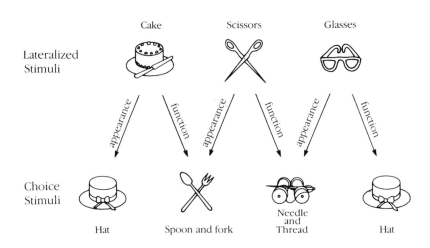

FIGURE 2.7 Function and appearance matches by split-brain patients. The stimuli in the top row are visually presented to one hemisphere at a time. The patient is instructed to pick the best "match" from the choice stimuli. When the left hemisphere sees the stimuli, it tends to match by function. When the right hemisphere sees the stimuli, it tends to match by appearance. [Adapted from Levy and Trevarthen, "Metacontrol of Hemispheric Function in Human Split Brain Patients," Fig. 1, p. 302, *Journal of Experimental Psychology*, 2, 1976 (American Psychological Association). Reprinted by permission.]

FIGURE 2.8 Chimeric figures constructed from the stimuli shown in Figure 2.7.

similar picture from an array viewed in free vision.[27] Sample chimeric stimuli are shown in Figure 2.8. Function and appearance matches for stimuli to both the left and right hemispheres were included among the choices on each trial, allowing the investigators to see whether each hemisphere had a preferred "mode" for making matches as demonstrated earlier. Once again, with ambiguous instructions, responses to left-hemisphere stimuli were overwhelmingly based on function, whereas responses to right-hemisphere stimuli were based on appearance.

The investigators then specifically instructed patients to perform matches on the basis of only function or appearance. In general, function instructions elicited function matches to left-hemisphere stimuli, and appearance instructions elicited appearance matches to right-hemisphere items. A large number of responses, however, deviated from the expected pattern. In some cases, the appearance instruction resulted in a response to the right-hemisphere stimulus, but the subject made a function match. Similarly, function instruction sometimes resulted in a response to the left-hemisphere stimulus that was based on appearance. In these cases, the hemisphere appropriate to the instructions responded, but in an "inappropriate" way. The reverse also occurred: The hemisphere inappropriate in terms of the instruction sometimes controlled the response, using the "appropriate" processing strategy. For example, the right hemisphere might respond under the function instruction, making its decision on the basis of function, or the left hemisphere might respond under the appearance instruction, with the response based on appearance.

These results showed that a given hemisphere does not always do the tasks for which it is thought superior, nor in performing a task does it always process information in the manner expected of it. Levy has explained this observation in terms of an interaction between higher cortical processes and brain-stem "arousal" that she referred to as "metacontrol." In Levy's view, each hemisphere processes a given set of instructions; based on these evaluations, signals are sent to the brain stem, biasing control to either the left or right hemisphere. Thus, the control of hemispheric dominance, that is, which side is "in charge," is mediated by a system that is highly sensitive to task instructions but is distinct from that determining the actual processing by a hemisphere once it is in charge.[28] According to Levy, dissociations occur precisely because the underlying mechanisms governing hemispheric arousal are different from those involved in the task processing.

Separated Awareness and Unifying Mechanisms

Under certain conditions, each hemisphere of a split-brain patient appears to function as an independent processor, producing results reminiscent of the behavior of two separate individuals. As Sperry has observed:

> Each hemisphere . . . has its own . . . private sensations, perceptions, thought, and ideas all of which are cut off from the corresponding experiences in the opposite hemisphere. Each left and right hemisphere has its own private chain of memories and learning experiences that are inaccessible to recall by the other hemisphere. In many respects each disconnected hemisphere appears to have a separate "mind of its own."[29]

Yet, casual observers do not notice anything unusual about most split-brain patients shortly after commissurotomy. In fact, a patient who recovered from the operation without complications could probably go through a routine medical checkup a year or two later without giving away his surgical history to anyone not already acquainted with it. Speech, language comprehension, personality, and motor coordination are remarkably preserved in patients without a corpus callosum and other commissures.

What keeps the two separate hemispheres acting as a unit during the everyday activities of these patients? A variety of unifying mechanisms, some of which we have already considered, seem to compensate for the absence of the cerebral commissures. Conjugate eye movements, as well as the fact that each eye projects to both hemispheres, play an important role in establishing unity of the visual world. The eye movements initiated by one hemisphere to bring an object into direct view serve to make that information available to the other hemisphere as well. Much of the conflict that would result from having the two hemispheres view different halves of the visual field is thus avoided.

Information from the touch modality provides another means by which each hemisphere is made aware of stimulation from both sides of the body. Up to now we have considered only the crossed, or contralateral, nerve fibers that allow each hemisphere to control the hand opposite to it. However, a much smaller number of same-side, ipsilateral, fibers allow each hemisphere to exert some limited control over the hand on the same side of the body. Ipsilateral sensory information is generally incomplete and inadequate to enable a patient to verbally identify an object held in the left hand; however, the ipsilateral pathways do provide partial information.

Cross Cuing

Another mechanism that contributes to the apparent unity of everyday behavior is cross cuing. Cross cuing is the use of whatever cues are available to make information accessible to both hemispheres. Generally the patient does not consciously attempt to trick the investigator. Instead, there is a natural tendency to use whatever information is available to make sense of what is going on.

Cross cuing can be quite subtle. A good example was observed in a patient who was able to indicate verbally whether a 0 or a 1 had been flashed to either hemisphere.[30] The same patient was unable to verbally identify pictures of objects flashed to the right hemisphere, a finding suggesting that he lacked the ability to speak from the right hemisphere. The investigators hypothesized that the left hemisphere in this patient would begin counting "subvocally" after a digit was presented to the left visual field and that these signals were picked up by the right hemisphere. When the correct number was reached, the right hemisphere would signal the left to stop and report that digit out loud.

When the digits 2, 3, 5, and 8 were added to the experiment without warning, the subject was very surprised. With a little practice, however, he was able to give the correct answer for all the numbers presented to the right hemisphere, but with some hesitation when the number was high. In contrast, responses to the same digits presented in the right visual field (to the left hemisphere) were quite prompt. These findings supported the idea of left-hemisphere subvocalization. The larger the number of potential digits, the longer the list of numbers the left hemisphere had to go through before reaching the correct one.

Information Sharing Between the Disconnected Hemispheres

Yet another way information is made available to both hemispheres is by commissures located in the lower regions of the brain. The human split-brain operation severs only the nerve bundles connecting the cortical levels of the brain. These are the major fibers connecting the hemispheres, but other, smaller subcortical commissures remain intact. These other commissures connect paired structures that are part of the midbrain. They are shown in Figure 2.2.

One such structure, the superior colliculus, is involved in the location of objects and the tracking of their movements. The colliculus is believed to process the "where" aspects of the visual world, as opposed to the "what," or finely detailed, aspects of vision. The left and right superior colliculi communicate through the commissures connecting them, so each hemisphere is provided with information about the location of objects regardless of where the objects fall in the visual field. Such crude location information could explain the phenomenon of visual completion mentioned earlier and possibly other data pointing to the ability of split-brain patients to integrate information about location-based attention, orientation, and movement between the two visual half-fields.

In a study designed to investigate such integration, the stimulus consisted of a three-by-three grid located either to the left or to the right of the subject's point of fixation.[31] On each trial, a target digit was presented briefly in one of the nine cells; the subject's task was to indicate whether the target was odd or even. On within-field trials, before the onset of the target, an X (spatial cue) appeared for 150 milliseconds in one of the nine cells or was superimposed on the fixation point. When it appeared in one of the nine cells, it occurred either in the cell corresponding to the position of the target digit to follow or in a different cell. On between-fields trials, two grids appeared, one in each field, with the X appearing in a cell in one field and the target presented subsequently in a cell in the other field. Figure 2.9 illustrates this task.

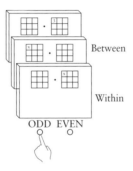

FIGURE 2.9 Example of stimuli illustrating valid cues for within- and between-field conditions. An X cues the subjects on the probable location of a digit to be judged odd or even.

Earlier work in neurologically normal subjects showed that reaction time is shorter when the spatial cue indicates the target's subsequent location and longer when the spatial cue directs the subject's attention to an incorrect location. Would this effect be found in split-brain patients when the task required access to information from both hemispheres (between fields)? The results were quite clear: For each of the two split-brain subjects tested, reaction time decreased when the subject had prior information about the target's spatial location in both the between-fields and within-field conditions and increased when an invalid cue was presented. Another experiment showed that specific information about the location of a stimulus presented in one visual field is not available to the other hemisphere.

The investigators suggested that these data provide evidence for distinguishing between stimulus information needed for explicit identification of spatial location and stimulus information needed to direct visual attention. They argued that different neural pathways are involved in these two functions and that commissurotomy does not disrupt the access of either hemisphere to information needed to direct visual attention.

The issue of what kinds of information may be shared between the two hemispheres in split-brain patients has attracted a good deal of attention. In particular, consideration has been given to the possibility of implicit transfer between the hemispheres. Implicit transfer is said to occur if there is some automatic or unconscious influence of a stimulus in one hemisphere on a decision made in the other. The preponderance of evidence suggests that although subcortical pathways can mediate the direction of visual attention, very little additional information can be shared through them, implicit or otherwise.[32] However, there does appear to be some variability among patients in what kinds of information can be transferred, and no doubt this area of research will continue to be the focus of a considerable activity until this variability is understood.

What Do the Cerebral Commissures Really Do?

We started this chapter with an account of the mystery surrounding the function of the corpus callosum. Are we now any nearer to understanding it? A simple answer would be to say, "Yes, we know that the cerebral commissures transfer information obtained by one hemisphere over to the other hemisphere." Although this is true, it is not a particularly revealing or complete answer. At the very least, we want to know the nature of the information that is transferred and how it is used by the hemispheres.

At this point, the role of the callosum and other commissures can perhaps best be seen as that of a conduit through which the hemispheres exchange information and perhaps handle the problems associated with conflicts among independent processing modules. Because the commissures are simply bundles of nerve fibers, they cannot in and of themselves control anything. But they can serve as channels through which synchronization of hemispheric function occurs and duplication or competition of effort is prevented.

Perhaps this integration is accomplished by the callosum simply serving as a sensory "window," providing a separate and complete representation of all sensory input in each hemisphere. It is more likely, however, that more complex, processed signals normally traverse the commissures, informing each hemisphere about events in the other and, to an extent, controlling their respective operations. This type of communication would allow the whole brain to supersede individual hemispheric competencies.

Early in the course of evolution and in the development of bisymmetric bodily organization, the continuous transmission of sensory information from one side to the other may have been the one essential function of interhemispheric pathways. It seems likely, however, that with the development of asymmetries in brain function, the role of these pathways became more profound.

Some investigators have speculated that there is a delicate balance between the hemispheres, with one or the other taking over, depending on the task and other as yet unspecified factors. In this view, the corpus callosum and other commissures play an important role in achieving interhemispheric harmony in the normal brain, serving to integrate the specialized functions of the left and right hemispheres into unified behavior. We will delve further into models of callosal function in Chapter 13 and will discuss the role of the corpus callosum (and its absence) in development in Chapter 10. In Chapter 10 we will also consider what is known about the relationship between the size of the corpus callosum and hemispheric asymmetry.

Special Insights from the Study of Commissurotomy Patients

· · · · · · · · · ·

Our review of data from split-brain subjects has led us to the conclusion that hemispheric specialization is not an all-or-none phenomenon but represents a continuum. Recent work with split-brain patients has revealed that each hemisphere is capable of handling many kinds of tasks but often differs from the other hemisphere in both approach and efficiency. Almost any human behavior or higher mental function, however, clearly involves more than the actual specialties of either hemisphere and utilizes what is common to both hemispheres.

As compelling as the split-brain data are, however, it is important to remember that the factors that produced the epilepsy in the first place and the epilepsy itself may have produced changes in the patient's brains, making them fundamentally different from those of normal subjects. Norman Geschwind noted that some commissurotomy patients probably suffered epilepsy as a result of brain lesions occurring in utero. Such prenatal lesions have been shown to result in significant reorganizations of the brain that differ from those occurring after birth. Geschwind also pointed out that long-standing epilepsy may itself produce major changes in brain organization. Perhaps the epilepsy has modified the use of brain pathways, thereby making the patients different from the unaffected adult population.

Summarizing his views on this issue, Geschwind observed that "many of the arguments in the literature between different investigators as to the effects of callosal section probably do not reflect a real difference in the adequacy of the data, but simply arise because the investigators have been studying patients in whom the patterns of brain development and connections are simply not equivalent."[33] Some researchers would dismiss split-brain research because of the problems in interpreting results. A better approach, we think, is to continue to learn what we can about the brain from the study of split-brain patients, remembering that such research will be but one approach taken by cognitive neuroscientists as they seek to understand hemispheric asymmetries and their role in mind–brain relationships.

PART II

Exploring Asymmetry in the Normal Brain

Chapter 3

Psychology and Physiology

Building the Link
Through Neuroimaging

Perhaps the most direct way to investigate differences between the hemispheres is to measure the anatomy and activity of the brain itself. Although an obvious approach, it is a very daunting task, the complexity of which can be appreciated by considering the many aspects of brain structure and activity that can be "measured" by using different methods.

The activity of the brain involves various chemical and electrical processes along a continuum from microscopic (i.e., individual neurons) to macroscopic (regional activity involving specific brain structures). The electrochemical communication that takes place at the microscopic level between large numbers of individual neurons results in global patterns of electrical and magnetic activity that occur at the macroscopic level and can be recorded at the scalp by using electrodes and specialized recording devices. The communication between neurons takes place via a number of different chemical substances called neurotransmitters, and different neurotransmitters define, in effect, different networks of neurons in the brain. Techniques have been developed to identify specific neurotransmitters and, through them, "map" different neural pathways in the brain. Finally, the metabolic processes of neurons require that blood bring oxygen and glucose to brain tissue and remove waste products.

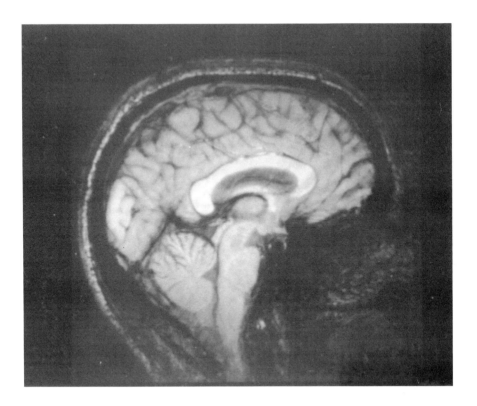

FIGURE 3.1 Nuclear magnetic resonance (NMR) scan. A computer-reconstructed image of a cross section of a normal brain, using data derived from the NMR of hydrogen in the water molecules of a subject's head. [Courtesy of Dr. Hoby Hetherington, Center for Nuclear Imaging Research, University of Alabama at Birmingham.]

Thus, measurements of blood flow as well as differences in the metabolism of specific nutrients can provide useful measures of macroscopic brain activity in each hemisphere or within smaller regions of the brain.

Recent technical developments have allowed increasingly sophisticated "imaging" of much of this activity as well as more precise visualization of brain structure in living and mentally active subjects. The rapidly growing field of "functional neuroimaging" is capturing the imagination of those who view such research as looking at the mind at work. Others feel that expectations for what can be achieved with brain imaging may be exaggerated. We will review some of the current work examining cerebral organization with imaging technology and try to present a balanced view of the potential of this exciting work.

Neuroimaging techniques can be divided into several categories, the most fundamental being the distinction between "structural" and "functional" scanning techniques. Structural neuroimaging refers to scanning techniques that show brain structure or anatomy, such as computerized tomography (CT) and standard magnetic resonance imaging (MRI). Structural scans typically show cross sections of the brain and may literally look as if one sliced through the brain and took a picture (Figure 3.1). Functional neuroimaging refers to techniques that provide views of some particular aspect of brain activity, for example, cerebral blood flow, glucose metabolism, or oxygen consumption; these techniques are best known by their acronyms—PET, SPECT, and fMRI. Functional neuroimaging may be further subdivided into the methods that measure brain metabolism and those that measure brain electrical activity ("brain waves") and magnetic activity. Although the latter methods historically grew out of a different approach to monitoring brain function known as electrophysiology, they are also now considered neuroimaging techniques.

In this chapter, we will first discuss techniques that measure aspects of brain metabolism (metabolic neuroimaging) and then those that measure aspects of brain electrical activity (electrophysiological neuroimaging). In both cases, the methods are used to study the pattern of activity in the brain while subjects perform some task or mental operation. They are thus attempting to assess the cerebral organization of mental functions, including asymmetries in this organization, in a fairly direct way. The investigation of anatomical asymmetries between the hemispheres will be discussed at the end of the chapter.

Functional Neuroimaging:
Metabolic Techniques

· · · · · · · · · ·

Probably the most influential development in the study of brain and cognition in recent times has been the rapid growth of technology that allows imaging brain activity while a subject performs a mental task.

The background for this was set in the late 1960s when consistent regional increases in cortical blood flow were observed in patients during speech production. Cerebral blood flow was measured by Niels Lassen and his colleagues by injecting a radioactive chemical or tracer (xenon-133 gas in saline solution) into the carotid artery and monitoring its buildup and subsequent washout or clearance from brain regions, using multiple detectors placed outside the head. Neuroimaging technologies have improved significantly since then and now also include methods that do not require the use of any injected tracers. Most techniques, however, still depend on cerebral blood flow as an indicator of brain activity.

The flow of blood through brain tissue varies with the metabolism and activity in the tissue. Changes in activity in various regions of the brain are reflected in the relative amount of blood flowing through those regions because cerebral flow is responsive to minute changes in neuronal activity. Thus it is possible to identify and study the interaction of various areas of the brain during ongoing human behavior by measuring regional changes in blood flow. Today's metabolic neuroimaging technologies—positron emission tomography (PET), single photon emission tomography (SPECT), and functional magnetic resonance imaging (fMRI)—still primarily assess cerebral blood flow when the experiment is attempting to measure brain activity during a task. Other aspects of cerebral metabolism can also be studied by these techniques.

There are several factors that determine the kinds of questions any functional neuroimaging method can address and that lead to the practical differences in their use. These are primarily (1) the period of time over which the cerebral activity is measured (temporal resolution); (2) the smallest region of the brain in which the activity can be measured (spatial resolution); (3) how much of the brain is viewed; (4) the point in time, with respect to the behavior or cognitive task in question, that the scan is performed (this is sometimes, but not always, related to temporal resolution; as we will see, it is possible to use tracers that are incorporated into brain tissue while a subject is performing a task but to conduct the scan itself afterward); and (5) how quickly and how many times the scan can be repeated as mental conditions are varied. Contemporary functional imaging techniques vary considerably with respect to these factors, creating large differences in the kinds of mental states that can be studied as well as in the data obtained sometimes for seemingly equivalent conditions. For example, if one is using a technique that takes 5 minutes to obtain an image, it may be appropriate to study the average brain activity associated with a continuously repeated task (e.g., listening to a tape recorded series of words during the 5 minutes), but it would not be appropriate to attempt to make distinctions such as how brain activity differs during hearing a word and during the pause between words. An investigator would need to use a method with a much faster "temporal resolution" to study the latter issue. There is often a trade-off, however, between such factors as temporal resolution, spatial resolution, and how much of the brain is being analyzed or "viewed." (Figure 3.2 illustrates the great range and variability in temporal and spatial resolution among the neuroimaging techniques, including electrophysiological methods.) With this in mind, we turn now to a brief overview of the major techniques.

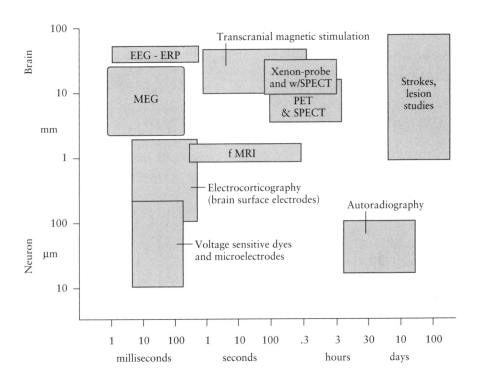

FIGURE 3.2 A graphical summary of the spatial and temporal domains covered by various neuroimaging techniques. The vertical axis represents a large range of distances or sizes, from the molecular scale to the whole brain, plotted logarithmically. The horizontal axis represents a large range of time, from milliseconds to days, also plotted logarithmically. The shaded areas identified show the approximate range of distance and time scale covered by the different neuroimaging techniques. [Courtesy of Dr. Ernest Stokely, Department of Biomedical Engineering, University of Alabama at Birmingham.]

Cortical Blood Flow Measures

The xenon-133 gas clearance technique was the method first used to show changes in regional brain blood flow during different tasks and mental states. Originally used in patients in whom the risk of injection into the carotid artery was clinically justified, this technique was modified to the point where subjects needed only breathe a special air–xenon mixture for 60 seconds and have their blood flow monitored by placing their heads next to a machine housing the special detectors.* This method accurately measured absolute blood flow levels (in terms of milliliters of blood per minute per 100 grams of brain tissue) but did so only in the outer cortical regions of the brain. Nevertheless, the results of studies during different kinds of physical and mental activities were impressive. Many classic predictions about brain areas involved in psychological functions were corroborated. The cortical regions of each hemisphere involved in vision, for example, showed increased blood flow if the subject looked at a moving pattern. Speech stimuli increased blood flow in the auditory cortex on each side.

It is of interest to note that in these early studies, the investigators reported that they were impressed by the similarity in the blood-flow patterns in the two hemispheres, even during highly lateralized activities such as speech.[1] The most striking changes during tasks and mental activity appeared to take place along the anterior–posterior dimension of the brain, rather than left to right. Differences between the hemispheres were nevertheless found. In an early study, Jarl Risberg compared the blood-flow pattern of right-handed male volunteers during two tasks, one a verbal analogies test and the other a test of perceptual "closure." In the closure task, the subjects had to view very sparsely drawn pictures and figure out what they represented.[2] Small but highly significant hemispheric differences in blood flow of about 3 percent were found in the two conditions. As expected, the mean left-hemisphere flow was greater during the verbal analogies task, and the mean right-hemisphere flow was greater during the picture-completion task. Risberg was able to measure which regions within each hemisphere contributed the most to interhemispheric blood-flow differences. The largest differences were found in the frontal, frontotemporal, and parietal regions for the verbal tests. In

---

*The low level of gamma radiation emitted by the isotope is not considered harmful and washes out of the bloodstream within 15 minutes.

the resting state, differences between corresponding regions of the hemispheres were very small.

A great many studies using this technique have been conducted, many of which have bearing on hemispheric asymmetry and some of which we mention in other chapters. It has been replaced, however, for the most part by techniques that produce three-dimensional images of brain activity and cover the internal structures of the brain as well as the cortical surface. (One such technique, xenon SPECT, combines the advantages of the original xenon-133 blood-flow method with new three-dimensional scan capability and will be discussed later.)

Emission Tomography (PET and SPECT)

Emission tomography is a visualization technique that yields an image of the distribution of a radioactively labeled substance in any desired cross section of the body or head. The two major categories of emission tomography are SPECT and PET, which differ in terms of the nature of radioactive emissions used and the equipment needed to record them.

SPECT In SPECT, biochemicals of interest are labeled with radioactive compounds that emit gamma rays in all directions. These substances, called radiopharmaceuticals, are injected into the bloodstream of subjects. As the radiopharmaceuticals reach the brain, detectors surrounding or rotated about the head pick up their emissions, and computer programs are used to "reconstruct" what the distribution of the labeled substance must have been to generate the pattern of emissions sensed by the detectors. So far, SPECT procedures have been used to measure cerebral blood flow and blood volume in three-dimensional cross sections of the brain.

HMPAO SPECT Studies of Cerebral Blood Flow Most current brain SPECT uses the radiopharmaceutical ^{99m}Tc-hexamethylpropyleneamine oxime (HMPAO) as the tracer that is injected intravenously and crosses into brain tissue (and gets trapped) at a rate proportional to the cerebral flow rate. Emission tomography scanning of the gamma photons emitted by the compound allows the investigator to visualize the distribution of the HMPAO tracer, which reflects cerebral blood flow at the time of injection. Because the amount and location of the tracer trapped in brain tissue is based on cerebral blood flow at the time of injection, this technique allows investigators to "lock in" the brain activity state at that time. As a result, it has been possible to capture the cerebral blood flow during an epileptic seizure by injecting HMPAO during the seizure and scanning the patient later.[3] Color plates 1 and 2 show that precisely localized seizure activity onset.

In a similar fashion, the effects of stimulation or mental activity can be "locked in" while the subject is performing a task and then scanned afterward. This property was recently used to study subjects while they performed a task involving mental rotation of pairs of cube arrays such as the example shown in Color plate 3. The subject was asked to decide whether each pair was the same, but just oriented differently, or was truly different.[4] A subject was injected while lying in a darkened room and performing the task presented on a screen. A half-hour later, the subject was scanned while relaxing and lying still. Color plates 5 and 6 show the scan results. The scan showed much greater activity in posterior visual cortex in both hemispheres as well as in the right parietal region relative to a scan of the same subject injected with HMPAO during rest.

These results are similar to those shown in previous studies of cortical blood flow conducted during performance of this task,[5] and they serve both to reinforce the previous findings and to validate this intriguing use of HMPAO SPECT. The lock-in-a-state property of the HMPAO SPECT technique is quite useful for studying tasks or states (e.g., sleep) that cannot be easily done while the subject is in a scanner. It also affords a better opportunity to study patients who cannot normally be scanned without sedation, such as autistic children. Injecting HMPAO prior to sedation and scanning should allow investigators to visualize the cerebral activity as it was before sedation.

The same locked-in property of the HMPAO tracer that makes it very useful for pursuing certain questions also limits such SPECT scans to the study of only one or two conditions at a time because it takes many hours for the tracer to clear from the head. Most current imaging studies of multiple tasks or conditions are investigated by using the much more costly PET procedure or the newest fMRI techniques described later. Before we turn to those methods, there is another new SPECT technique that bears mentioning.

Xenon SPECT New SPECT technology has made it possible to produce three-dimensional images of cerebral blood flow after inhaling an air–xenon mixture for 60 seconds. Rapid consecutive images then show the clearance of this tracer from cerebral tissue; the rate of clearance is based on regional blood flow rate. A program calculates a final image, representing absolute regional cerebral blood flow (rCBF) in terms of milliliters per 100 grams of brain tissue per minute.

Because the xenon-133 washes out rapidly, multiple scans can be conducted in one session. This rapid clearance makes the technique more suitable for activation studies involving multiple conditions. Xenon SPECT is also more sensitive than HMPAO SPECT to the rCBF changes typically accompanying stimulation and cognitive task experiments. Color plate 7 shows a subject undergoing a xenon SPECT scan. Color plates 8 and 9 show the results of two task conditions.

PET Positron emission tomography utilizes the properties of the special radiation generated by positron-emitting substances, which generate pairs of photons traveling in exactly opposite direction. The technique takes advantage of positron emissions by what is called coincidence counting—simultaneous detection of each pair of photons by opposing detectors set at positions 180° from each other allows great precision in mapping the distribution in the brain of the substance in question.

The advantage of PET is that it can theoretically trace many biological compounds because they can be directly "labeled" (i.e., become positron emitters), using special cyclotron procedures. The technique can produce regional three-dimensional quantification of glucose and oxygen metabolism in the living human brain, as well as that of several neurotransmitters, each of which can be made to be positron emitters.

Positron emission tomography has been used quite extensively to study higher mental function. Because the incorporation and scanning of positron emitter glucose compounds takes about 30 minutes, too long a period during which to maintain a reliable mental state or most task conditions, most PET studies of mental activity have used positron-labeled water ($H_2{}^{15}O$) to measure blood flow via a washout technique similar in principle to the original xenon-133 clearance method we described earlier. $H_2{}^{15}O$ water "clears" from the brain extremely quickly (actually decays and becomes nonradioactive); thus new studies can be performed every few minutes.

Because regional cerebral blood flow can be measured quickly and repeatedly with PET, some PET researchers have attempted to isolate and study complex mental functions through ambitious, multistep activation conditions in which the subject is given a series of tasks that form a hierarchical sequence progressing from a simple sensory-motor function to a complex task. The brain activity associated with the high-level cognitive function by itself can then presumably be isolated by subtracting the activity seen in images of the simpler control conditions. This approach, not surprisingly, is known as the subtraction method.

For example, one study attempted to distinguish brain areas activated by specific language functions by repeated PET scans during a four-level progression of tasks in seven normal subjects.[6] The base state was visual fixation on a symbol (+) presented on a video monitor. Observation of single nouns was the second level. Vocal repetition of cue words added motor output. In the final condition, the subject had to respond to a presented object noun with a verb describing some use of the object, thus adding a semantic-processing demand to the condition.

By subtracting the blood-flow pattern measured during one task level from that of another task level, the investigators tried to isolate some of the changes induced by relatively specific mental activity. The investigators found that vocalization produced bilateral flow increases in the sensory-motor strip and several frontal-lobe regions. The semantic task caused an asymmetrical activation of the lower left frontal lobe compared with the control condition (vocal repetition alone). Despite the attempt to isolate the activity due to stimulation from that of cognitive processes, the investigators still found some lateralized activity in association areas of the left hemisphere associated with "just looking" at words. The researchers suggested that the subjects were reflexively performing some linguistic analysis of the stimulus cue words even though there was no language task demand per se. The level of activity did not change in these areas of the left hemisphere during vocal repetition or during the semantic task, a result supporting the idea that the subjects had already automatically done some form of linguistic analysis during passive presentation of the cue words. This type of finding raises important issues of what constitutes an appropriate control condition for many higher level tasks.

A great deal of scientific literature has been published in the last few years involving PET studies of subjects performing various sensory-motor and cognitive tasks. We will review many of these in Chapters 7 and 8 because they have a significant bearing on classical neuropsychological models of brain organization. Other PET studies will be discussed in Chapter 11 when we consider asymmetry's role in pathology.

Before leaving the discussion of PET, we wish to mention one additional study that has implications for the analysis of neuroimaging data in general. The experiments we have discussed so far have all been based on analyzing increases or decreases in regional metabolism or

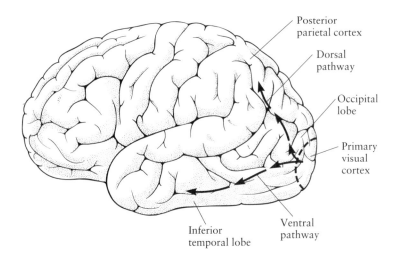

FIGURE 3.3 The dorsal ("parietal stream") and ventral ("temporal stream") pathways from the primary visual cortex. The posterior parietal cortex is thought to mediate the analysis of location and motion of visual stimuli. The inferior temporal lobe is thought to mediate object identification and the analysis of form and color.

blood flow. Although this is the most obvious way to look at changes occurring during tasks, it is not the only way—and perhaps not the best. Some investigators have postulated that, in addition to typically necessitating increases in activity in specific regions, proper cerebral performance depends on the interaction of specific brain regions with one another. Thus, the extent to which regions function together or change together (as opposed to what goes up most) can indicate the areas most involved in the task.

A PET study by James Haxby and associates at the National Institutes of Health used the ^{15}O-water PET technique to examine regional cerebral blood-flow changes while volunteers performed both a face-matching task and a dot-location–matching task.[7] The investigators used these conditions because both animal and clinical human neuropsychological data suggest that there are two visual systems in the brain, one dedicated to object vision and involving mostly occipital and temporal regions, and one dedicated to spatial location and including more occipitoparietal pathways (Figure 3.3).

When analysis was performed in the more traditional manner, in which a control task was simply subtracted from the more complex cognitive task condition, the investigators indeed found what they predicted: Face recognition appeared to activate the occipital and temporal region, whereas the location task activated the occipital and parietal areas. This activation pattern occurred in both hemispheres.

However, when a correlation analysis was conducted, examining the extent to which regions changed together during each task, another finding emerged: The posterior regions subserving face matching and dot-location matching had functional interactions that were much stronger in the right hemisphere than in the left. They concluded that the bilateral activation seen in the simple regional-increase analyses may in fact be due to changes that originate in the right hemisphere but, because of the corpus callosum, also activate the left hemisphere.

This conclusion suggests that perhaps many imaging studies examining task effects on brain activity miss real hemispheric asymmetries in function because of the brain's tendency to show symmetrical increases in activity even though the task is really initiated by one side much more than the other. Newer approaches, such as the analysis of covariance in activity just described, may offer ways to get around this limitation on imaging studies of hemispheric asymmetries.

Functional Imaging of Cerebral Activation, Using MRI

The image shown in Figure 3.1 is a good example of the structural imaging capabilities of nuclear magnetic resonance imaging, or MRI. (Originally called NMR, the "nuclear" is usually left out of the name to make it sound less intimidating.) Magnetic resonance imaging uses a strong magnetic field and radio waves to induce changes in water molecules that can be measured and used to "reconstruct" anatomical detail in any imaginary plane through the head. The use of MRI has more recently extended into the realm of functional imaging as well.

A recent development has allowed indirect but rapid visualization of cerebral activation during stimulation or mental activity with MRI. Because the measurements are based on changes in the level of blood oxygenation, it was originally called BOLD (blood oxygenation-level dependent) MRI, but it is now typically referred to as functional MRI (or fMRI). Because active areas of the brain become slightly engorged with oxygenated blood and because the magnetic properties of oxygenated blood are different from those of deoxygenated blood, special sequence MRI scans can identify cerebral regions that are activated during stimulation, motor activity, and cognitive activity. Color plate 10 shows activation images superimposed on the structural MRI of a volunteer subject performing a hand movement task with the right hand and then with the left hand.

The use of fMRI to investigate cerebral organization and localization of function is growing dramatically. In just the last few years, this technique has revolutionized the study of activated brain function in normal subjects because it can provide data with a temporal resolution of several seconds, can scan activation during any task multiple times, and/or can provide almost continuous information about cerebral activity changes occurring during changing study conditions. These capabilities should allow investigators to examine factors such as strategy changes within individual subjects.

Some examples of recent findings include a report that men activate only a left-hemisphere region during a rhyming or phonological task, whereas women activate both hemispheres.[8] Another study showed that dyslexic children have a deficiency in properly activating the posterior visual cortex.[9] We will be referring to these and a number of other fMRI studies, as appropriate, in later chapters.

As inviting as it appears, however, fMRI does have some drawbacks. One is that the technique is seriously affected by even the smallest movement on the part of the subject, so much so that many studies of even cooperative subjects have to be discarded. Functional magnetic resonance imaging investigators spend considerable effort trying to improve methods to correct for any head-movement artifacts.

Another drawback is that fMRI does not measure rCBF levels in the absolute sense but only shows where rCBF changes between a control condition and an activation condition. Thus, fMRI would not easily reveal the defects in a patient's blood flow associated with stroke, dementia, or head injury, nor would it give you quantitative measures of rCBF in either the resting or activated state. At this point it is not possible, using fMRI, to say how much activity there was in a brain region at rest or during a control condition and how much there was during the experimental task. The investigator may conclude only that there was an increase or decrease in blood flow. These changes are usually termed "activation" or "deactivation," respectively, and are used to declare that the region(s) so involved play a role in the task.

Another concern regarding the use of fMRI follows from the much easier access to neuroimaging technology that fMRI has provided to an increasing number of investigators. Because almost all major hospitals and institutions connected with hospitals have at their disposal a basic MRI unit that can be converted to perform some minimal fMRI scans, there are now many hundreds of places where such studies can be conducted. The increase in fMRI studies reporting various findings regarding localization of function has been great and has been criticized by some as fostering a new "phrenology."*[10] We will return to such issues, which extend beyond fMRI to the other imaging technologies as well, later in this chapter.

Functional Neuroimaging:
Electrophysiological Techniques

Increasingly fine spatial or anatomical resolution is available from PET, SPECT, and fMRI techniques, but many scientists feel that the length of time involved for the images they produce is still too long to resolve the rapidly shifting patterns of activity associated with cognitive processes. Some feel that the answer lies in using electrophysiological measures of brain activity as a complement to the metabolic imaging techniques described in the previous section. As we will see, these methods, although having coarse spatial resolution, have exquisite temporal resolution (in the 1- to 10-millisecond range) and appear to be very sensitive to changes in mental activity.

The EEG

In 1929 the Austrian psychiatrist Hans Burger discovered that patterns of electrical activity could be recorded from electrodes placed at various points on the scalp. These patterns were called the electroencephalogram (EEG), literally meaning "electrical brain writing." Although the EEG is monitored from the scalp, Burger was able to demonstrate that

---

*Phrenology is the long-discredited study of the relationship between mental faculties and the shape of the skull that was advocated by Franz Gall.

some of the activity it records originates in the brain itself and is not simply due to scalp musculature.

Several different rhythms of activity have been identified as constituents of the EEG record. The first one discovered is also the most famous: the alpha rhythm. Alpha activity is a rhythmic cycling of electrical activity occurring from 8 to 12 times per second. It is the predominant activity present in the EEG when the subject is resting quietly with closed eyes. Burger, in the course of his original discovery, reported a decrease in the amplitude of the dominant (alpha) rhythm of the EEG during mental arithmetic.[11] Other rhythms that are part of the EEG are also identified by Greek letters—beta, theta, etc.

Devices to record the EEG soon became commonplace in clinical settings as investigators demonstrated that brain abnormalities such as epilepsy and tumors are accompanied by distinctive patterns of electrical activity. Its potential as a research tool was also quickly recognized, and innumerable studies looking for EEG correlates of personality, intelligence, and behavior were undertaken.

David Galin and Robert Ornstein were two of the first investigators to study EEG asymmetries in detail and to relate them to the nature of the task performed by the subject while the EEG was being recorded.[12] They recorded EEG activity from symmetrical positions on either side of the head while subjects performed verbal tasks, such as writing a letter, and spatial tasks, such as constructing a memorized geometrical pattern with multicolored blocks. Results were analyzed in terms of the ratio of right-hemisphere EEG power (R) to left-hemisphere EEG power (L). Electroencephalogram power is simply the amount of electrical energy being produced per unit of time. They found that the R/L power ratio in the verbal tasks was significantly greater than in the spatial tasks.

Although at first glance surprising, because one would expect the opposite, a further analysis of Galin and Ornstein's results showed that the predominant rhythm in the EEG records was alpha. Because alpha reflects a resting brain state, less alpha activity would be expected to follow greater involvement in a particular task. Thus, the left hemisphere should show relatively less alpha when a subject is performing a language task in contrast with the amount of alpha activity present when the subject is doing a spatial task like the block-design problem. This is precisely what was found.

Electroencephalographic measures of hemispheric asymmetries in activity have been popular with many investigators because the equipment required is fairly accessible and can be used on a wide variety of subjects, including infants. In addition, EEG is a continuous measure over time and can be used to study ongoing activity in the brain while the subject performs long, complex tasks. Although the latter feature of the EEG measure is quite useful in some studies, it is difficult to see changes in the EEG that relate to the occurrence of specific stimulus events.

The Event-Related Potential

A careful analysis of the EEG reveals that specific changes do occur in response to the presentation of a stimulus such as a flash of light, but they are hidden by the overall background activity of the brain. To make visible the change in response to a specific stimulus, a computer is used to average the waveform records following repeated presentations of the same stimulus. Electrical activity that is random with respect to the stimulus presentation will be canceled out by this process, whereas electrical activity occurring in a fixed time relation to the stimulus will emerge as the potential evoked by the stimulus event.

The event-related potential (ERP) consists of a sequence of positive and negative changes from a baseline and typically lasts about 500 milliseconds after the stimulus ends. Each potential can be analyzed in terms of certain components or parameters, such as amplitude and latency (the amount of time from the onset of the stimulus to the onset of the activity). The nature of the stimulus (auditory, visual, somatosensory) is one of the factors that affects the precise form of the evoked potential. In addition, the region of each hemisphere generating maximum activity differs for each type of stimulus. Figure 3.4 shows typical ERPs to stimuli in different modalities.

In the 1970s, psychologist Dennis Molfese and colleagues collected extensive data on ERPs to speech and nonspeech stimuli.[13] In one study, they found that the amplitude of part of the ERP to speech stimuli was greater in the left hemisphere than in the right hemisphere. This difference was seen even when the subject merely listened to the stimuli and did not try to identify them. Nonspeech stimuli, however, produced activity of larger amplitude in the right hemisphere.

A number of studies have also looked at how asymmetries are affected by the task the subject is performing while the ERP is recorded. In one such study, subjects were presented with a sequence of synthetically produced spoken syllables that could differ in initial consonant ("ba" versus "da") or in pitch (high or low).[14] In one-half of the trials, subjects were instructed to listen for each occurrence of "ba," regardless of its pitch. In the other half, the subjects were in-

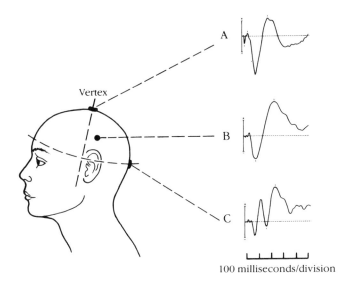

FIGURE 3.4 Typical evoked potentials for (A) auditory, (B) somatosensory, and (C) visual stimulation. The dotted lines indicate the approximate location on the scalp from which the most pronounced peaks are recorded. [Adapted from Thompson and Patterson, eds., *Bioelectric Recording Techniques* (New York: Academic Press, 1974).]

structed to listen for high-pitched syllables, independent of their names. Evoked potentials to the high-pitched "ba" were recorded from the left and right hemispheres in each case. This procedure enabled the investigators to study the effect of two different mental activities on ERP asymmetry while maintaining exactly the same stimulation conditions (which is considered an elegant and effective way to conduct functional neuroimaging studies in general). Results showed a difference in the ERPs produced during the naming and pitch-discrimination tasks, but only in the left hemisphere. The researchers suggested that there are hemispheric differences in the ability to identify a syllable but no differences in the ability to determine the pitch of the syllable.

Probe-Evoked Potentials During Mental Activity

Standard ERP experiments were limited to recording responses to short, usually simple stimuli. The probe-evoked potential is a more recent development that greatly expanded the applications of ERP methods to studying brain–behavior relationships involving more complex mental activity. Instead of examining the response to repeated stimulation against a resting-state background, the experimenter asks the subject to perform a task during which some irrelevant probe stimulus (for example, a click or a light flash) is repeatedly introduced. What is of interest is to what extent the ERP, which is normally excited by the probe stimulus, is suppressed by activity or the task the subject is performing.

It is presumed that the brain can do well on only a limited number of simultaneous tasks. Thus, the more complex the background task, the greater the reduction of the brain's normal response to some intermittent probe stimulus. Probe-evoked potentials can be recorded from different regions of the brain simultaneously. The change in the amplitude of the probe-evoked potential is thought to be determined by how demanding the task is and by what areas are involved in the task performance.

In one study using this approach, the relative engagement of temporal and parietal regions of the left and right hemispheres was monitored during an arithmetic task and a visuospatial task by recording ERPs to a probe tone presented through earphones.[15] In all conditions, the subjects viewed the same series of stimuli, consisting of fragmented segments next to a whole geometrical shape, with numbers printed inside each fragment and inside the complete shape. In the visuospatial run, the subjects signaled with a finger movement if the fragments would create the intact geometrical shape presented next to them. In the arithmetic trials, the subjects signaled if the numbers inside the fragments added up to the number inside the completed shape.

The amplitude of the ERPs to the tone probes varied according to which task the subjects were performing. Probe-evoked potentials were significantly reduced, relative to controls, in the left temporal area during arithmetic calculations. The visuospatial task resulted in greater probe reduction in the right parietal region. These results confirm, of course, left-hemisphere involvement in "serial-analytic" operations, such as those involved in speech and calculation, and right-hemisphere involvement in certain visuospatial processes. In addition, this study is a good example of an experimental design in which instructions to the subject are varied in tasks involving identical stimuli and identical responses, thus allowing investigators to better isolate the changes in brain function that result from differences in psychological or mental function.

How Far Can Scalp Recordings of Brain Electrical Activity Take Us?

A number of neuroimaging investigators feel the EEG is an ideal complement to PET, SPECT, and fMRI because when used together the investigator can have both high temporal resolution (from EEG) and the high spatial resolution of the metabolic scans. However, the spatial detail provided by conventional EEG recordings has been so coarse that it has only been possible to interpret them with respect to underlying functional anatomy at the level of entire cortical lobes. Several laboratories are now attempting to improve spatial resolution by making EEG recordings with high-density electrode arrays, by performing processing that improves spatial detail, and by registering these data with other images of brain structure and function.

In recent years Alan Gevins and colleagues have taken EEG and evoked-response measurements to a new level of sophistication by recording from as many as 125 scalp electrodes placed over a subject's entire head. Through complex computer analysis of the EEG changes in all electrode locations associated with various stages of repeated task conditions, Gevins has reported a number of findings regarding cerebral regions activated by different cognitive operations.[16] Most of these findings are reported in terms of the "covariance" of multiple cerebral regions with each other during stimulation, response, or decision-making. The regions that change together in an EEG are identified as part of the neural "network" involved in the task or particular task stage.

This work has promoted several innovative concepts, including a search for correlations in cerebral activity changes rather than a simple identification of locations of maximum activity change. (We discussed the concept of searching for regional correlations in task-related activation in the earlier discussion of PET.) However, many electrophysiologists maintain that scalp recordings are not sufficient to isolate brain electrical activity with any precision and that different techniques are necessary to make inferences about such activity in multiple cerebral regions. The development of magnetoencephalography was spurred by such considerations.

Magnetoencephalography

Neural activity not only generates electrical fields but also produces magnetic fields. In recent years it has become technologically possible to record and isolate the magnetic fields that accompany the electrical fields generated by neuronal activity within specific regions of the brain. Magnetic fields created by the activity of single neurons are extremely small, but under certain conditions the magnetic fields of a number of simultaneously active neurons combine to produce fields that are sufficiently strong to be measured at the surface of the head. Such a recording is called a magnetoencephalogram (MEG), the magnetic counterpart of the EEG.

Calculations based on MEG measurements permit three-dimensional localization of the cell groups generating the measured field. Thus, a major advantage of this technique over the EEG is its ability to better localize within the brain the source of the activity being recorded. Special superconducting coils are needed to pick up the very weak brain magnetic fields, and measurements routinely are done within elaborate magnetically shielded rooms. The heart of a MEG probe is a sensing instrument called the superconducting quantum interference device (SQUID), which is immersed in liquid helium. By either moving a single probe or using multiple probes placed in different positions, the MEG procedure creates "isocontour maps," that is, charts with concentric circles representing different intensities of the magnetic field. From such maps, a three-dimensional location of the neurons generating the field can be calculated. Figures 3.5 and 3.6 illustrate the equipment and isocontour maps.

Researchers initially attempted to use MEG to establish the location and depth of the electrical currents underlying discharges in epileptic tissue with greater accuracy than was possible with EEG alone. They were very successful; for example, in one patient epileptic activity was localized to an exact region 10 to 11 millimeters beneath the subject's scalp.[17]

Evoked Fields

Response to external stimulation can be measured with MEG by using an analogue of the evoked or event-related potential discussed earlier. We have seen how a repeated auditory, somatosensory, or visual stimulus will generate a measurable response or change in averaged EEG waveforms. The same stimulus results in a characteristic waveshape in the magnetic field recorded over specific cerebral regions, the source of which is much more localizable than the source of an ERP. For example, the source of magnetic-field patterns evoked by repeated clicks (evoked fields, or EFs) has been clearly localized to the auditory temporal cortex of each hemisphere.[18]

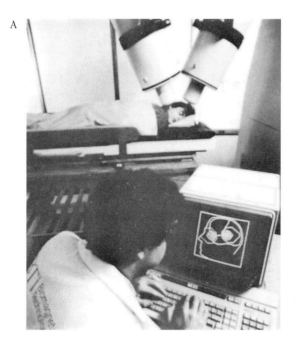

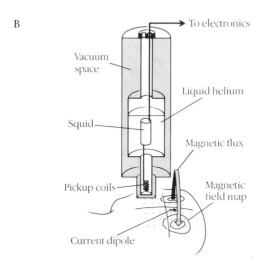

FIGURE 3.5 A. A patient undergoing a brain scan, using a 14-channel neuromagnetometer. The process tracks the electrical function of the brain by detecting magnetic fields generated by the electrical current within the brain. [Courtesy of Biomagnetic Technologies, Inc., San Diego, CA.] B. Brain magnetic fields are measured by using a superconducting amplifier (SQUID; see text) coupled to special coils. The liquid helium keeps the system at a low temperature, necessary for superconductivity. [Courtesy of Dr. Jackson Beatty, University of California, Los Angeles, CA.]

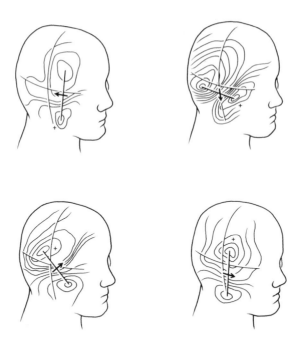

FIGURE 3.6 Examples of isocontour maps displaying the magnetic fields generated by epileptic activity in a patient's right hemisphere. Such MEG recordings allow precise localization of the sources of the seizure activity. This patient's recordings indicated multiple sources within the right temporal lobe. [From Beatty, Barth, Richer, and Johnson, "Neuromagnetometry," Figs. 2–10, p. 38, in *Psychophysiology,* ed. Coles, Donchin, and Porges (New York: Guilford Press, 1986).]

Further study determined the sources of activity within a hemisphere associated with stimulation of the ear either on the same (ipsilateral) side or on the opposite (contralateral) side of the head. The magnetic evoked fields to left- and right-ear stimulation were recorded in the right hemisphere in eight subjects, and the resulting source coordinates were projected onto the structural MRI images of each subject's head. Not only did MEG show that the activity source fell in the vicinity of the auditory cortex in each subject, it also showed that the source was slightly different for ipsilateral and contralateral stimulation, a result indicating that adjacent but separate regions in the right auditory cortex are activated by left- and right-ear stimulation. The investigators suggested that these results point out the potential precision and applicability of MEG in the study of human sensory-motor and cognitive processes.[19]

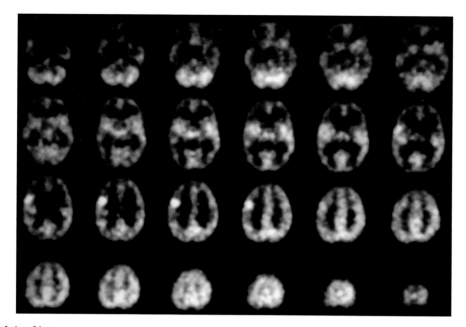

Color Plate 1. SPECT images of cerebral blood flow capturing a seizure onset in an epilepsy patient. Use of the tracer Tc-99m HMPAO allows areas of high blood flow to be identified. Brain images are horizontal cross sections, starting at a lower level of the brain (upper left-hand corner) and proceeding to the top of the brain (lower right-hand corner). Images in the third row show seizure onset, indicated by high blood flow (bright spots) on the left side. This region of high flow corresponds to the patient's right motor cortex, because the image orientation is as if viewed from the patient's toes (right hemisphere is on the left side of the images).

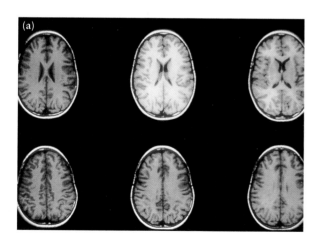
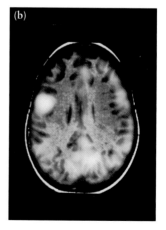

Color Plate 2. (a) MRI scans of the same patient show no anatomical or structural abnormalities in any region, including the region showing seizure onset on the SPECT scans above. (b) Superposition or fusion of SPECT scan image (blood flow) with the MRI scan (anatomy) at the same brain level. [Courtesy of Dr. James M. Mountz, Department of Radiology, University of Alabama at Birmingham.]

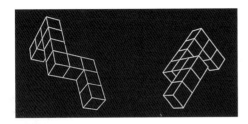

Color Plate 3. Mental rotation task example. (Mentally rotate either of the two figures to see if they are identical.)

Color Plate 4. Subject performing task during Tc-99m HMPAO injection, prior to SPECT scanning. The tracer distributes in the brain, depending on the regional cerebral blood-flow rate at the time of injection. It remains "locked" in place for several hours, thereby allowing a subsequent scan to show the levels of brain activity during the task.

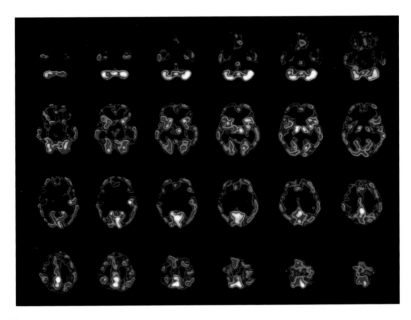

Color Plate 5. SPECT scan images of a normal subject injected with Tc-99m HMPAO while at rest, eyes closed. The darker colors represent lower blood-flow rates and the lighter colors represent higher rates. The horizontal (transverse) cross sections start at a lower level of the brain (upper left-hand corner) and proceed to the top of the brain (lower right-hand corner). The image orientation is as if viewed from the patient's toes (right hemisphere is on the left side of the images).

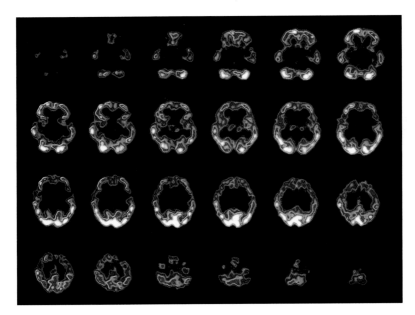

Color Plate 6. SPECT scan images of the same subject injected while performing the mental rotation task. There is a marked increase in blood flow in the occipital regions (visual cortex) and parietal regions of the brain (lower portion of the images in rows 3 and 4). Although the increase is bilateral, it is more pronounced in superior (higher) parietal regions of the right hemisphere, as seen toward the end of row 3 and the beginning of row 4. (The right hemisphere is on the left side of the images.)

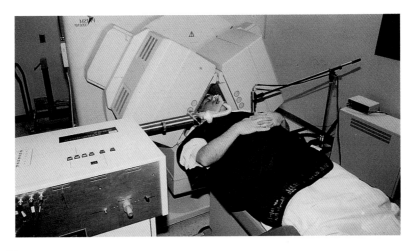

Color Plate 7. Subject undergoing a xenon-133 SPECT scan. The probe positioned over a lung measures the gas input into the bloodstream. The three detector heads of the scanner rotate and measure the clearance rate of the gas from cerebral tissue, thereby allowing quantitative calculation of cerebral blood flow. Speakers located behind the scanner and a projection screen in front allow presentation of mental tasks.

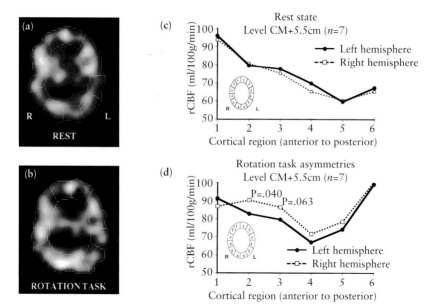

Color Plate 8. (a,b) Xenon-133 SPECT images of a subject at rest and while performing the mental rotation task. A program subdivides the images and identifies the maximum blood-flow rate in each sector. The task resulted in an increase in activity in occipital and in right parietal and temporal cortex. (c,d) Graphs showing the mean cerebral blood flow (rCBF) in six regions of each hemisphere for seven subjects. rCBF in the two hemispheres is highly coupled at rest. During the task, rCBF increases bilaterally but shows a right greater than left asymmetry.

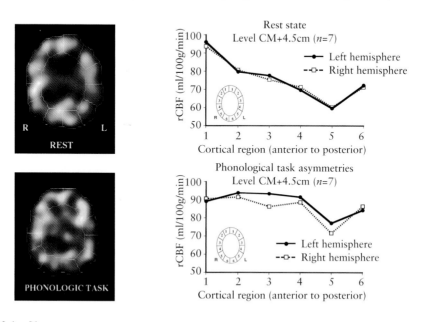

Color Plate 9. Same as Color Plate 8, but showing the results of a phonological target task (identifying words containing the "br" sound from among a tape-recorded series of words). The images show an increase in activity during the task in the posterior left frontal region (Broca's area). The graphs show bilateral increases, as well as a left greater than right asymmetry, in the group data.

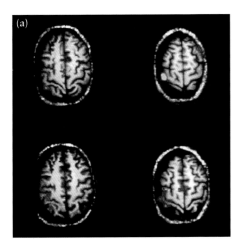 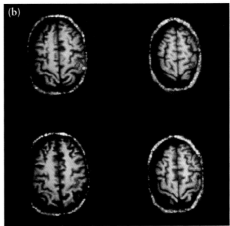

Color Plate 10. Functional MR images (four horizontal slices) depicting motor cortical activation patterns produced by a hand extension/flexion task. (Right hemisphere is on right side of the images.) (a) Right-hand task: Contralateral activation is seen in left-hemisphere motor areas. (b) Left-hand task: Contralateral activation is seen in right-hemisphere motor areas. [Courtesy of Dr. Donald Twieg, Department of Biomedical Engineering, University of Alabama at Birmingham.]

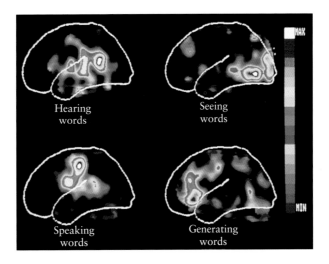

Color Plate 11. Left-hemisphere images, showing the results of a hierarchical series of PET scans of regional cerebral blood flow (rCBF) intended to isolate brain regions active during different stages of language processing. *Top:* Results of subtracting a simple visual fixation control condition from passive listening to words (left) or passive word viewing (right). *Lower left:* Results of subtracting the passive word viewing condition from repeating the words out loud. *Lower right:* Results of subtracting repeating words out loud from generating a verb in response to a noun. [Courtesy of Dr. Steven Petersen, Neuro Imaging Laboratory, Washington University, St. Louis.]

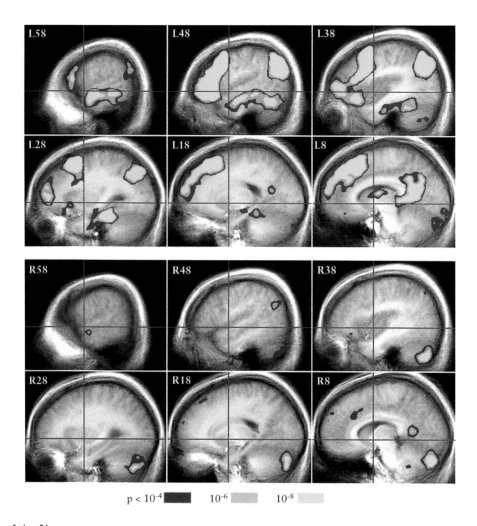

$p < 10^{-4}$ ■■■ 10^{-6} ▨ 10^{-8} ▨

Color Plate 12. fMRI activation map of the semantic decision-tone decision study of Jeffrey Binder et. al. (1997). Subjects had to identify, within a spoken series, animals that are both native to the United States and used by humans. A tone decision task presented at a similar rate was used as the control condition. Matching left (top half of figure) and right (lower half of figure) sagittal sections are shown. Activated regions for a group of 30 normal, right-handed subjects are shown superimposed on group-averaged anatomical brain images. Probability values for the activations are coded at the bottom. Left temporal lobe activation is seen extending through frames L58 to L28. The left angular gyrus is activated over a large region (L58 to L28). Left prefrontal activation involves the entire inferior frontal gyrus (L58 to L38), middle frontal gyrus (L48 to L28), and much of the superior frontal gyrus (L18 to L8). L8 shows activation near midline regions of the frontal lobe (anterior cingulate) and behind the corpus callosum. Cerebellar activation is lateralized to the right side (R38 to R8). Small language activation foci are noted in the left anterior thalamus and caudate, left medial cerebellum, right post callosal region, and right angular gyrus. [Courtesy of Dr. Jeffrey Binder, Department of Neurology, Medical College of Wisconsin.]

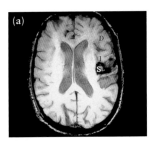

Color Plate 13. Images of a stroke and possible mechanism of recovery. (a) MRI scan shows left hemisphere infarct (S) that resulted in right hemiplegia and aphasia. (Left hemisphere is on the right side of each image.) (b) SPECT scan on left shows that blood flow and/or neuronal activity is reduced outside the infarct in much of the left side. When the patient recovered from his aphasia and the scans repeated 1 year later, the SPECT looked like the image on the right, suggesting the recovery involved resolution of some disconnection effects of the lesion (diaschisis).

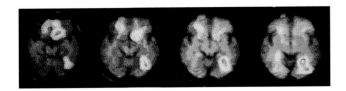

Color Plate 14. PET scans of face recognition task, showing activation of posterior right hemisphere regions. [Courtesy of Dr. Justine Sergent, Montreal Neurological Institute.]

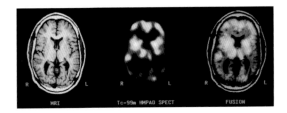

Color Plate 15. MRI and SPECT of autistic 12-year-old child. The MRI scan is normal. Tc-99m HMPAO SPECT scan shows blood flow abnormalities in occipital, parietal, and some temporal regions that are worse in the left hemisphere. (Left hemisphere is on the right side of each image.) Final image is a fusion of the MRI and SPECT scan. [Courtesy of Dr. James Mountz, University of Alabama at Birmingham.]

Color Plate 16. Examples of stimuli used in the PET study of local versus global processing shown in Color Plate 17. The L, D, and P represent the global level, and the D, F, and N represent the local level.

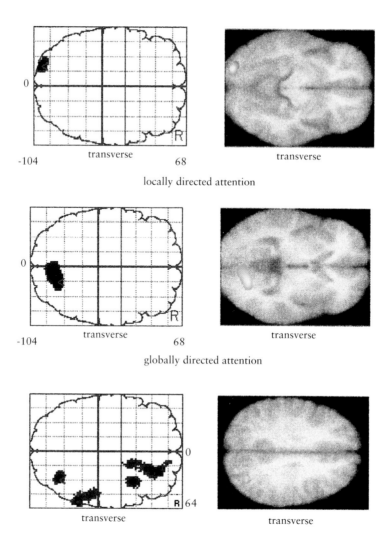

Color Plate 17. PET activation results of directing attention to local versus global attributes of stimuli. (Sample stimuli are shown in Color Plate 16.) Areas of significant relative rCBF increases are shown as through-projections onto transverse representations of standard stereotactic space, a method that adjusts for anatomical variability among subjects. The activation pattern is also superimposed on the group mean MRI scans. Red arrows indicate the local maximum within the area of activation. There is right-hemisphere activation centered on the lingual gyrus during globally directed attention and left-hemisphere activation centered on the inferior occipital cortex during locally directed attention. (Stimulus size only affected the degree of rCBF increase in early visual processing areas on both sides.) During globally/locally divided attention, a positive correlation was observed between relative rCBF in the temporal–parietal junction (red arrow) and the time that attention was sustained to either the global or local level. Other positive correlations were observed in the right temporal cortex, the right orbitofrontal cortex, and the right prefrontal cortex. [Courtesy of Dr. Gereon Fink, Wellcome Department of Cognitive Neurology, University of London.]

Magnetoencephalographic research is currently being extended to study both basic physiology and more complex mental function. Because of technical complexities and costs, most MEG instrumentation has typically consisted of 7 or 14 channels contained within one or two holding assemblies, a factor limiting the regions of the brain that can be studied simultaneously. New MEG instrumentation, however, provides many more channels and even includes a version that covers the whole head with over 100 separate SQUID assemblies. These instruments are allowing better studies of interhemispheric processes during complex cognitive activity, including the measurement of hemispheric asymmetries.

Issues Raised by Techniques Measuring Brain Activity

Studies using PET, SPECT, and fMRI to measure cerebral blood flow and metabolism, and EEG and MEG measures of brain electrical activity all offer investigators the opportunity to study relationships between brain activity and behavior. They have been of great value in validating physiologically some of the insights about brain function gleaned from psychological research with both brain-injured and normal subjects. They are also beginning to contribute new findings about cerebral organization, including hemispheric differences, not previously evident from clinical studies.

Measures of brain activity during task performance have raised some questions about the most exaggerated claims for hemispheric asymmetry. There is little evidence to support the notion that either one or the other hemisphere turns on to perform a specific task all by itself. Each of the measures we have discussed points to the involvement of many areas of the brain in even the simplest task. These findings remind us that hemispheric differences are but one of several different organizational schemes in the brain. There are asymmetries in activity between the hemispheres, to be sure, but they can be very subtle, a fact that should lead us away from thinking about hemispheric specialization in overly simple terms.

Limitations of Neuroimaging Research

Functional neuroimaging has become a powerful tool for the study of brain–behavior relationships. Being able to visualize activity in the living brain without interfering with it has opened the doors to studies of a multitude of questions concerning both normal and abnormal brain function. The possibilities seem enormous, apparently limited only by financial resources and by our ability to ask the right questions and make careful observations.

Some individuals, inspired by the early successes of seeing on screen the involvement of brain regions in tasks exactly as predicted by a hundred years of neuropsychological research, are quick to predict that we will soon have "maps" of how the brain generates most mental operations. Upon hearing this, one might start worrying that brain imaging may soon be able to expose one's innermost thoughts. This is, however, an unwarranted concern. As exciting as this field of research is, expectations for what can be achieved with functional neuroimaging need to be tempered by an appreciation of its limitations, both practical and conceptual. First, one must remember that most neuroimaging involves measuring the distribution of a tracer that, in turn, represents the relative level of some aspect of cerebral metabolism. The regional metabolism thus being traced is also only a reflection of the amount of activity in different cerebral regions and does not, in and of itself, represent the actual physiological mechanism behind the mental activity being studied. Nor does locating the region of greatest activity during a task or mental operation explain the brain processes behind the mental process. Neuroimaging provides, at best, a relatively crude map of where some events associated with a particular task take place.

It must also be remembered that all metabolic neuroimaging represents a cumulative or time-averaged "snapshot" of brain events taking place within the total time period it takes the imaging tracer to properly distribute and/or the scanning procedure to measure the distribution. As we have discussed, the interval is at best approximately one minute for current PET and SPECT scans of blood flow and is considerably longer for most other PET and SPECT procedures. Thus, activity changes occurring over shorter intervals are lost or averaged out. The temporal resolution of fMRI is considerably faster, approximately 5 to 20 seconds, but it still remains very slow relative to neuronal communication speeds and changes in brain electrical activity. Electroencephalography and MEG, though sensitive to these faster events, suffer from other drawbacks.

In addition, there are more serious conceptual problems involved in "timing" and localizing "thoughts" with functional imaging. Neuroimaging attempts to capture a mental operation in a snapshot—or, as technology progresses, in a series of snapshots. This procedure may work, in a limited fashion, for basic sensory-motor functions or even some specific task conditions. However, it will probably never be adequate to characterize the cerebral activity associated with a personal stream of thought, much less provide the brain-imaging investigator with information sufficient to "read" the thought.

Researchers have to rely on averaging many repetitions of the same task or on using many subjects performing the same task to separate some aspect of cerebral activity that is common to the task from a plethora of activity associated with individual differences and much other "noise." In addition, even the simple attempts by PET researchers to isolate specific mental operations through the subtraction techniques we described earlier are fraught with many assumptions and interpretation problems.[20] Is a complex mental operation really the simple sum of simple steps that we can study in isolation? Does adding a new "stage" not affect the operations taking place in prior "stages?" Do experiences really have definable beginnings and ends? We do not really know when thoughts begin or end or whether a mental event can really be the same when repeated.

Finally, all imaging experiments aimed at establishing the brain activity underlying mental processes are naturally guided by current psychological theory and by the investigator's own view of how to partition and isolate mental operations. The actual organization of mental processes—as well as the underlying cerebral processes—is, of course, not governed by our conceptualizations of them. Even though we normally assume that poor models get thrown out or modified by the actual empirical results, for psychology and neuroimaging, the situation is so complex and the number of variables in images so vast that "expected" findings can be fairly easy to tease out or "see" in the data. It is also easy to fall into the "psychologist's fallacy"—to design an experiment based on a certain view of mental function whose results will reinforce that view simply because the experimental design highly constrained the results in that direction.

These considerations are not meant to discredit functional neuroimaging research nor to imply that its potential for studying both normal and abnormal brain function is less than vast. Functional neuroimaging research should, in fact, help redefine some of our psychological distinctions—through associations and disassociations in brain activation findings—in a manner similar to the way in which classical neuropsychological research advanced. We wish merely to acquaint the reader with some of the important constraints that make the endeavor of studying the left and the right brain with this new technology an even more challenging one.

Anatomical Asymmetries in the Two Hemispheres

A 1968 report by Norman Geschwind and Walter Levitsky demonstrated unequivocal anatomical asymmetries in the two hemispheres of the human brain in the regions important for speech and language.[21] Published in a journal widely read by scientists in a number of different disciplines, their paper generated a great deal of excitement among those interested in hemispheric asymmetry of function.

Geschwind and Levitsky were not the first investigators to notice such asymmetries in the brain. Asymmetries had been reported sporadically as far back as the second half of the nineteenth century, at which time the differences generally were considered trivial and insufficient to account for functional differences between the left brain and the right brain.

By the late 1960s, however, the time was ripe to reconsider the possibility that functional asymmetries between hemispheres might have a physical basis on a nonmicroscopic, anatomical level.

Measuring the Hemispheres

The asymmetries found by Geschwind and Levitsky were in the lengths of the temporal plane (planum temporale), the upper surface of the region of the temporal lobe behind the auditory cortex. Of the 100 brains measured at postmortem, 65 were found to have a longer temporal plane in the left hemisphere than in the right, 11 had a longer temporal plane in the right hemisphere, and the remaining 24 showed no difference. On average, the temporal plane was one-third longer on the left than on the right. Figure 3.7 shows the location of these asymmetries.

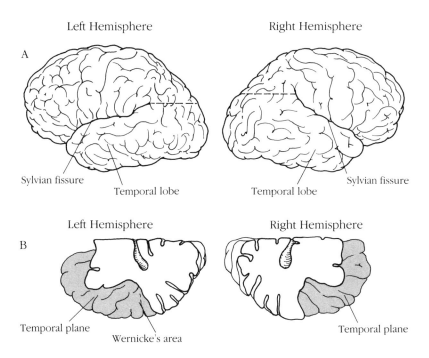

FIGURE 3.7 Anatomical asymmetries in the cortex of the human brain. A. The sylvian fissure, which defines the upper margin of the temporal lobe, rises more steeply on the right side of the brain. The dotted lines represent the plane of section for B. B. (viewed from above) The temporal plane, which forms the upper surface of the temporal lobe, is usually much larger on the left side. This region in the left hemisphere is considered part of Wernicke's, a region involved in language. [From Geschwind, "Specializations of the Human Brain," *Scientific American,* 1979. All rights reserved.]

Although the size of these asymmetries is impressive, their location is more significant. The temporal plane is part of Wernicke's area, a region named after Karl Wernicke, who first noted that damage to this area frequently results in a variety of aphasic symptoms. Geschwind and Levitsky suggested that the asymmetries they observed were compatible with the functional asymmetries believed to be controlled by this region.

Several studies using various procedures to measure the temporal plane have confirmed Geschwind and Levitsky's observations.[22] Seventy percent of 337 brain specimens (including the 100 brains studied by Geschwind and Levitsky) showed asymmetry favoring the left hemisphere in length or area of the temporal plane.

Other anatomical studies have shown that Heschl's gyrus in the temporal lobe, which forms the primary auditory cortex, is larger on the right because there are usually two gyri on the right and only one on the left.[23] Thus there are two complementary asymmetries involving the temporal lobes, although the area involved in the Heschl's gyrus asymmetry is much smaller than that in the temporal plane asymmetry. There has naturally been some speculation that these two asymmetries may reflect the functional dissociation of the left and right temporal lobes in language and musical functions, although there is no direct evidence for this.

Neuroanatomists have also found differences between the hemispheres in the dendritic trees of neurons in several left- and right-hemisphere cortical regions. These findings included a substantial difference between microanatomical samples from Broca's area and the homologous (same location on the other side) region of the right frontal lobe: There were far more branches in cells from Broca's area. Although this study involved just a small number of brains, the only exception to this finding involved the cells taken from a person who had been left-handed.[24]

Does the Left Get Bigger or the Right Get Smaller?

In a reevaluation of the anatomical data used by Geschwind, neurologist Albert Galaburda and associates found an interesting relationship between the degree of asymmetry and the size of each temporal plane. Geschwind previously had assumed that the asymmetry he observed was a result of greater or more rapid development of the left side. He predicted that symmetrical brains resulted from a less developed left side.

Galaburda, however, found that the left planum (temporal plane) remains roughly constant in size (corrected for variability in total brain size) but that the right planum is larger in symmetrical and smaller in asymmetrical brains.[25] Thus, symmetrical brains tend to have two large plana, whereas most asymmetrical brains have a large left and a small right planum. Galaburda speculated that whatever factors play a role in the development of these asymmetries act by controlling the extent of development of the right side in most individuals.

There is a plausible mechanism for the developmental changes that would result in the reduction in size of a neuroanatomical structure. Present knowledge about cortical development includes the fact that the cortex generates more neurons than it finally keeps.[26] Also, it is now almost generally accepted that neuronal loss or degeneration of neuronal connections is part of the organizing mechanisms of the brain during development.[27] The ultimate purpose for neuronal overproduction and subsequent "pruning" must be to set up an optimal anatomy matching environmental requirements; thus it cannot altogether be predicted in advance. Although the reasons are not known, it appears that most individual variation and environmental factors affecting anatomical hemispheric asymmetry are expressed through differences in right-hemisphere development. The relationship between total brain size and asymmetry observed by Galaburda has also been observed in studies of rodents, an observation indicating that this may be a general principle governing the relationship of asymmetry and brain space.[28]

Anatomical Neuroimaging of the Living Brain

The anatomical studies considered up to this point have involved measurements taken from brains examined at postmortem. Several neuroimaging techniques have made it possible to study anatomical asymmetries in the living brain. Such techniques are particularly valuable because they permit investigators to correlate anatomical findings with performance measured in living subjects.

Cerebral Angiography

One technique takes advantage of the fact that the paths of the large blood vessels in the brain reflect the anatomy of the surrounding brain tissue. In particular, the middle cerebral artery courses through the language-critical region of the temporal lobe. For many years, neurologists have used a procedure known as cerebral angiography to visualize this major blood vessel to determine whether the brain regions surrounding it have been damaged. A dye injected into the internal carotid artery in the neck (the same artery used in the Wada procedure) flows into the middle cerebral artery, making the artery visible when a skull X-ray is taken. Marjorie LeMay and her colleagues have shown that left–right asymmetries consistent with those found in post-mortem brain measurements may be observed with the angiographic procedure.[29]

Computerized Tomography

Another technique used to examine anatomical structure in the living brain is computerized tomography (CT scanning). In a CT scan, an X-ray source is revolved in a plane around the head as detectors continuously monitor the intensity of the X-ray beam passed through to the other side. A computer stores this information and then uses it to reconstruct an image of a slice of brain. Figure 3.8 shows a representative CT scan.

This technique has been used for many years to pinpoint the locations of lesions in cases of brain damage. LeMay and her colleagues have also used CT scan data to study asymmetries, with some success.[30]

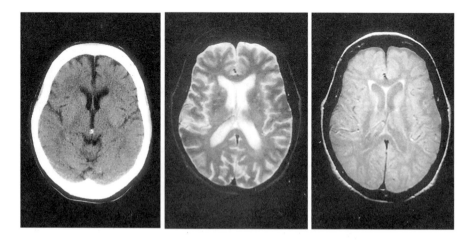

FIGURE 3.8 Examples of a horizontal (transverse) cross section of the brain generated by a CT scan (A) and MRI scans (B,C). The two MRI scans demonstrate the different images obtained by adjustments in the calculations of the effects of the radiofrequency pulses used.

Magnetic Resonance Imaging (MRI)

We mentioned standard MRI and gave an example of its structural imaging capability in Figure 3.1 earlier in this chapter, before we turned to our discussion of the functional MRI technique and its applications. Magnetic resonance imaging is capable of generating fine cross-sectional images of brain structure without using X-ray or gamma ray radiation. In standard (anatomical) MRI, nuclear magnetic resonance of hydrogen atoms in water molecules is induced and recorded by a combination of radio waves and a strong magnetic field. Relative tissue density throughout the brain can be very accurately calculated, and a fine pictorial image can be generated by computer.[31] Figure 3.8 shows an MRI example next to a CT scan.

This technique has also been used for over ten years now to pinpoint the locations of lesions and other brain injuries. Magnetic resonance imaging shows a much clearer distinction between gray and white matter than CT does. It is also used in conjunction with many functional neuroimaging studies to provide the anatomical information used to help make precise judgments about the location of patterns of activity seen on the functional scans. Finally, it has been used as the technique of choice in recent years to study macroscopic anatomical asymmetries in the human brain.

Neurologist Helmuth Steinmetz has led a team investigating the relationships between hemispheric anatomical asymmetries as measured by MRI and several behavioral measures. In a 1991 study, they showed that planum temporale asymmetry is correlated with hand dominance. Using 26 left-handed and 26 right-handed healthy volunteers, they found that left-handers had a significantly lesser degree of leftward planum temporale asymmetry than right-handers. This anatomical difference was significant for left-handedness when measured by hand–motor lateralization tests and not for stated handedness. In addition, a family history of left-handedness was a factor in left-handers, in whom those with at least one left-handed first-degree relative contributed most of the overall anatomical difference between handedness groups.

This study was one of the first demonstrations of a relationship between anatomical asymmetry and a behavioral measure in living subjects. The investigators suggested that the reduction in leftward asymmetry in left-handers corresponds to the reduced functional asymmetry for language in left-handers demonstrated in other research.[32]

Steinmetz and colleagues have also looked for relationships between the size of the corpus callosum, handedness, and sex. They could not find an influence of handedness on MRI-based anatomical measurements of the corpus callosum, measured as a whole or for specific measurements of any of seven subdivisions of the callosum. They found, however, that part of the corpus callosum showed a statistically significant larger proportional size in women, independent of handedness. There was also a trend toward larger absolute callosal areas in women.[33]

A number of other investigators have used MRI and other anatomical techniques to investigate the relationship of brain structure and asymmetry to handedness, gender, and learning disabilities, among other variables. The data obtained are rarely clear-cut, reflecting the complexity and variability of what is being studied. We will return to this topic as appropriate in later sections. We turn now to the problem of interpreting any anatomical asymmetries that may be found.

What Can Anatomical Asymmetries Tell Us?

Evidence for structural or anatomical asymmetries has, in many ways, been more controversial than that for physiological activity because it was originally difficult to relate such findings to functional differences, that is, to show that such asymmetries are responsible for behavioral or functional differences.

Much of the interest in techniques that can measure asymmetries in the living brain concerns the basic problem of interpreting anatomical asymmetries. Are the asymmetries that have been identified related in a meaningful way to behavioral or functional differences? Most of the original data on anatomical asymmetries came from postmortem measurements, where often nothing was known about the kinds of functional asymmetries that may have existed before death. In many cases, even the handedness of the individuals was not known. Despite this, some investigators gathered enough premorbid information to find several suggestive relationships between handedness, gender, and several findings of anatomical asymmetry in postmortem cases. Some of these findings have been confirmed or modified by neuroimaging studies of healthy volunteers.

New high-resolution structural neuroimaging procedures that permit measurements in the living brain offer us a way to collect much crucial information. Behavioral and functional neuroimaging tests designed to reveal the distribution of functions between the hemispheres can be used, along with measurements of brain asymmetry in the same individuals, to examine the significance of differences in anatomical variability on the normal structure–function relationships common across individuals. It is clear, however, that investigators have only begun the process of studying how anatomical asymmetries, functional asymmetries, and cognitive abilities are related.

Physiology and Psychology:
Building the Link

The biological measurements and neuroimaging techniques discussed in this chapter offer investigators the opportunity to study relationships between mental processes, behavior, brain anatomy, and brain activity. These techniques have at least partially validated some of the theoretical insights about brain function and hemispheric asymmetry developed in the brain-damage clinic.

Some researchers have claimed that physiological tools offer the ultimate resolution of questions that deal with the connection between mind and brain; others argue against overreliance on such measures on both philosophical and practical grounds. Clearly, certain concerns must be confronted in the attempt to establish relationships between physiological processes and psychological functions. Although these concerns are important for the study of hemispheric asymmetries, their significance extends beyond any specific area of research and has applicability to the study of brain–behavior relationships in general.

One issue is the problem of selecting from among the various physiological measures available those that will prove most informative. Like all other tissues in the human body, the brain is dependent on complex metabolic processes for its functioning. A great deal of the brain's biochemistry, however, is unique and involves communication between neurons. Biochemical processes operating in each cell generate electrical potentials, and biochemicals operating between cells effectively transmit electrical impulses between groups of neurons. Technological advances are providing ways in which to measure or image various aspects of this activity, but we do not know what aspects come closest (if at all) to representing the physiological mechanisms underlying the mental activity we are investigating. The measures we now have available may not be indicative of the true organizational principles or processing strategies of the brain.

Another issue involves the concept of localization of function in general. How much does attributing some psychological activity to a specific area of the brain contribute to insights about that activity? Certainly, findings on localization have been of tremendous clinical value. Furthermore, relationships between location and function may help establish the components of a complex behavior or task in terms of more basic processes. As a hypothetical example, it may be demonstrated that the memory of how to get somewhere involves linguistic processes in the left hemisphere as well as imagery processes in the right hemisphere. It is not clear, however, how far this kind of approach can take us. Ultimately, it is likely that dividing the brain in terms of "where" will not completely answer the question of "how."

Discovering brain–behavior and brain–mind relationships is not only an experimental problem and certainly not only one of localization of function. The problems are at least equally conceptual in nature: What are we trying to explain? How are we defining things? In what sense does some neurophysiological activity accompanying a mental event explain something about the event? What would constitute a satisfactory "explanation" about some mental or behavioral event?

Investigators have become more sophisticated, at least with respect to localization issues. They now talk of the "state of activity in the system," rather than "where." They realize most psychological functions should be associated with activity changes in multiple areas or defined pathways of the cerebrum. They also realize that these may be flexible and time varying, perhaps even probabilistic. More conceptual development will have to do with the nature of our questions and definitions, including a better appreciation of the levels of explanation involved.

Are We Asking the Right Questions?

There is an old anecdote about three distinguished panelists on a television show who were asked about what they thought was the greatest invention of all time. The first said it was the wheel. The second said it was the printing press. The third had to think about it for a minute and then said, "Well, I do believe it's the thermos bottle." The interviewer and the other panelists looked somewhat incredulously at the man and all asked "Why?" The third panelist proceeded to explain, "Well, on a summer morning you put some cold lemonade in the thermos and then hours later, in the middle of a sweltering afternoon at the ball game, you open it and out comes cold lemonade. On the other hand, on a winter morning you put some hot cocoa in the thermos and then hours later, when you are freezing at the skating rink with your kids, you open it and out comes nice hot cocoa." There was a brief pause and then he added, "How does it know?"

Clearly, the humor in this story revolves around the way in which the third panelist viewed temperature and the functioning of the vacuum bottle. After thinking about what the bottle does, his question was how the bottle knows whether to keep something hot or to keep it cold. To us, this is a silly question because we view variations in temperature as variations in a single process that a thermos bottle simply keeps stable. But perhaps many of the questions we now ask about the brain are not so different from the third panelist's question about the thermos bottle. "How does the brain 'recognize' objects?" "Where do sensations come together?" and "How is consciousness produced?" may be very poor questions when viewed from a potentially more appropriate conceptual framework. Time will tell, but it may be worthwhile to remember this story when thinking about some of the questions people are asking about brain function now that they believe they have the tools needed to understand it.

For now, it does seem that the interaction of psychology and physiology should be fruitful for the study of both mind and brain. Physiological injuries of the sort studied by neuropsychologists have had an impact on the way we break down mental functions. Physiological imaging of the sort described in this chapter has the potential to reorganize it further. Psychological questions are also guiding at least some investigations into anatomy and physiological processes. The growth of cognitive neuroscience as an academic discipline reflects the increasing emphasis on such integrative approaches to brain research, as well as an optimism regarding its eventual success.

Chapter 4

Behavioral Approaches
to Asymmetry

Research with normal subjects is an essential component of the cognitive neuroscience approach to the study of brain–behavior relationships. There are at least three reasons for this. First, use of normal subjects avoids the limitations placed on clinical and split-brain research by the scarcity of subjects. Research can be conducted on a much larger scale than would otherwise be the case. More questions can be asked, and experimentally answered, than would be possible if research opportunities were limited to relatively small groups of patients. Second, work with neurologically normal subjects offers investigators greater freedom in the kinds of experiments that can be devised. Stimuli and tasks can range from the very simple to the very complex, allowing investigators to study the full range of human abilities, including those at the very highest levels of complexity. Third, and perhaps most important, work with normal subjects permits the study of asymmetries in the same system one is ultimately trying to understand: the normal human brain.

The investigation of hemispheric asymmetries in normal subjects has been carried out in a number of ways, the newest of which have been described in the preceding chapter. There is a large and still growing literature, however, that employs older methodologies to address a variety of interesting questions in neurologically intact subjects. In this chapter we will review these methodologies with an emphasis on what they have contributed to our understanding of the nature and extent of hemispheric differences and the way the two hemispheres work together.

Techniques Used in Behavioral Studies

Visual Half-Field Presentation

One of the first and most extensively employed techniques used to study asymmetries in the normal brain takes advantage of the natural split in human visual pathways. This split neatly divides our visual world into two half-fields, each of which projects to one hemisphere. By flashing material very briefly either to the left or to the right of the point on which a subject is fixating, investigators are able to lateralize stimuli, that is, to present them to one hemisphere only. Visual stimuli flashed briefly in the left visual field project first to the right hemisphere; stimuli flashed in the right visual field project initially to the left hemisphere.

As explained in Chapter 2, in split-brain patients this initial lateralization to one hemisphere or the other is maintained because the connections between the hemispheres have been cut. In a normal subject, however, the connections are intact and can transfer information between hemispheres. Nevertheless, differences can be detected in a person's performance on certain tasks, depending on whether the stimuli are presented to the right or the left visual field. At the core of this technique is the assumption that performance will be superior when a stimulus is presented initially to the hemisphere specialized for processing it.[1] Figures 2.3 and 2.4 illustrate the nature of visual half-field presentation.

Dichotic Listening

While visual half-field presentation allows investigators to use visual stimuli to study asymmetry, a procedure known as dichotic listening has enabled investigators to study differences and similarities in the way the two hemispheres handle speech and other types of auditory information. With the dichotic technique, subjects hear pairs of auditory stimuli presented simultaneously, one stimulus to each ear. Psychologist Doreen Kimura at the University of Western Ontario was the first to demonstrate that normal subjects report words presented to the right ear more accurately than words presented to the left ear under conditions of dichotic presentation and to develop a model to explain why the ear asymmetry occurred.[2]

Unlike the retina, which sends projections contralaterally to the brain from one-half of its surface and ipsilaterally from the other half, each ear sends information from all its receptors to both hemispheres. Ipsilateral fibers project from a given ear to the hemisphere on the same side, and contralateral fibers project to the hemisphere on the opposite side. Thus, complete information about a stimulus presented to one ear is represented initially in both hemispheres, and each ear performs equally well when tested alone. Kimura noted physiological evidence, however, that ipsilateral pathways are weaker, less numerous, and more slowly conducting than contralateral fibers. She proposed that when two items are presented simultaneously, one to each ear, the pathway from each ear to the ipsilateral hemisphere is inhibited or suppressed; consequently, information presented to each ear projects primarily or exclusively to the contralateral hemisphere.[3] Figure 4.1 illustrates the operation of these pathways as proposed by Kimura.

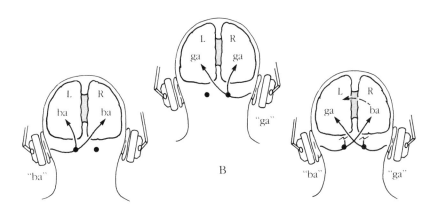

FIGURE 4.1 Kimura's model of dichotic listening in normal subjects. A. The syllable "ba" is correctly reported when presented to the left ear alone; it reaches the left and right hemispheres via ipsilateral and contralateral pathways, respectively. B. The syllable "ga" is correctly reported when it is presented to the right ear alone. C. In dichotic presentation, ipsilateral pathways are presumed to be suppressed. The syllable "ba" is accessible to the left (speech) hemisphere only through the commissures; "ga" is usually reported more accurately. Following commissurotomy, the patient reports hearing only "ga."

Under dichotic listening conditions, the stimulus to the left ear may reach the left hemisphere in one of two ways: over the suppressed ipsilateral route or over the contralateral pathways to the right hemisphere and then across the cerebral commissures. The stimulus to the right ear, however, has a simpler task. It gains access to the left hemisphere along the contralateral route. As in the case of stimuli presented in the left or right visual field, it is assumed that performance will be superior if stimuli are presented initially to the hemisphere specialized for processing them. Thus, the right ear advantage that Kimura observed with dichotically presented words would reflect, presumably, the specialization of the left hemisphere for processing those stimuli.

The dichotic listening test has also been used with split-brain patients. The findings fit nicely with what has been found in normal subjects. Split-brain patients identify words or consonant–vowel syllables equally well in either ear because the ipsilateral and contralateral projections are subcortical and not affected by the surgery. When speech stimuli are presented dichotically to split-brain patients, however, a dramatic, highly exaggerated version of the ear asymmetry found in normal subjects occurs. In fact, the patients frequently have to be coaxed into guessing about the identity of left-ear items, because they report that they hear only one stimulus.[4] This would be expected, because the left-ear stimulus projects only to the right hemisphere as a result of ipsilateral suppression. Because the right hemisphere is unable to produce speech, and because the fibers connecting two hemispheres have been severed, subjects are unable to accurately identify the left-ear stimulus above a chance level.

Why Does Lateralized Presentation Result in Asymmetric Performance?

Even if there are functional differences between the hemispheres in normal subjects, why are they reflected in differences in performance for the two visual half-fields or two ears under dichotic presentation? It is important to remember that despite the initial lateralization or one-sided presentation, both hemispheres have access to all incoming information regardless of the visual field or ear that first receives it. In the case of visual stimuli, for example, very brief presentations to one side of the fixation point ensure that a stimulus is initially projected directly to only one-half of the brain, but the connections between the hemispheres can transmit information about the stimulus to the other side almost instantaneously. Why, then, do we find differences in performance between the visual fields?

Several models of hemispheric asymmetry have been offered to account for these differences. The first, often referred to as the direct access model, assumes that information will be processed by the hemisphere that first receives it, regardless of the differences in ability that may exist between the hemispheres. In this model, the first hemisphere to receive a task will be the one to handle it, although it may not be the one best equipped to do the job. The direct access model predicts an advantage in performance for information that reaches the appropriately specialized hemisphere, because processing by that hemisphere presumably would be better than processing by the other hemisphere.

The callosal relay model, however, assumes that information is always processed by the hemisphere best equipped to deal with it. Material presented initially to the nonspecialized hemisphere, according to this model, would have to reach the specialized hemisphere via the commissural fibers before processing could take place. If this transfer results in some loss of clarity of information, then an advantage should be found for stimuli reaching the specialized hemisphere directly. Some evidence for loss of information following callosal transfer is found in animal research. In monkeys, for example, cells in one hemisphere sensitive to the shape of a stimulus respond more vigorously when a stimulus is presented in the contralateral visual field (input is sent directly to that hemisphere) than when it is presented in the ipsilateral field (information must cross over from the other side of the brain).[5]

In both the direct access and callosal relay models, asymmetries emerge in tasks where the hemispheres do not have equal capacities to begin with. And in both, information presented directly to the hemisphere specialized for a specific function would be expected to produce better performance—that is, more accurate or faster responding than one in which information goes first to the other half. They differ, however, in their view of the participation of the nonspecialized hemisphere and in the role played by the cerebral commissures.

A third model, emphasizing the role of attentional bias in determining the outcome of behavioral tests involving lateralized input, has also been proposed and will be discussed in some detail later in this chapter. Although few investigators see the attentional model as a complete explanation of hemispheric asymmetries found in behavioral studies (and hence a substitute for the direct access and callosal relay models), there is widespread acknowledgment that it plays a role in determining the outcome of at least some behavioral studies.

In What Ways Do the Hemispheres Differ?

During the last 25 years, a great many studies have used the techniques of dichotic listening and divided visual field presentation with normal subjects. As in the research with split-brain patients, there has been a gradual evolution of ideas about the nature of hemispheric asymmetries as new data suggest different interpretations of earlier work. Special effort has been made to identify the underlying basis for hemispheric asymmetries, that is, a common thread that can explain (as well as predict) the outcome of a large number of laterality studies using a wide range of stimuli and tasks.

The Nature of Information: The Verbal–Nonverbal Distinction

Much of the early work on the left brain and the right brain in normal subjects led investigators to believe that the two hemispheres differ basically in terms of the nature of the stimuli they are best prepared to deal with. A typical visual task involved the lateralized presentation of stimuli that the subject was asked to identify. A similar procedure was employed with dichotic stimuli as well: Two items were presented simultaneously, and the subject was asked to report what was heard. Sometimes the basic task was modified so that the subject was required to recognize a specific stimulus rather than to identify each item, and sometimes the experimenter was interested primarily in how quickly a subject could respond to a stimulus instead of how accurate the response was. Often, both speed and accuracy were measured in the same study.

Stimuli were said to show a left-hemisphere advantage if performance was superior when items were presented to the right ear or in the right visual field. A right-hemisphere advantage was assumed if performance was superior when items were presented to the left ear or in the left visual field. Differences in performance between sides frequently were quite small, just a few percentage points better in identification or a few milliseconds faster in response; but anywhere from 70 to 90 percent of the right-handed subjects tested in a typical study showed the asymmetry.

Most of the early studies showing a right-side advantage used stimuli that were language-related in a very obvious way.[6] Word and even single letters produced a right-visual-field advantage. Dichotically presented spoken digits and words also resulted in a right-ear advantage. The advantage, however, was not limited to meaningful spoken utterances. Studies have shown that meaningless consonant–vowel syllables such as "da" and "ka" also produce a right-ear advantage and that speech played backward produces a right-ear superiority in recognition as well. Taken together, the results of these studies suggest that stimuli do not have to be meaningful to produce a left-hemisphere advantage, but should be language-related or verbal in some way.

The picture for the right hemisphere is more difficult to summarize and is less consistent from study to study.[7] Among the visual stimuli that have produced left-visual-field advantage are faces and spatial arrays of dots. The dichotic listening studies that result in a right-hemisphere advantage are also diverse, and have employed stimuli such as melodic excerpts and environmental sounds, for example, a barking dog and a whistling train. All these "right-hemisphere" stimuli share the attribute of being nonverbal, and some investigators have argued that the distinction between the functions of the two hemispheres lies along this verbal–nonverbal dimension. In this view, all language-related stimuli are dealt with primarily in the left hemisphere, with the right hemisphere specialized for handling certain types of nonverbal stimuli. This conclusion appears to be a neat summary of the data we have reviewed so far. However, later work produced results that were inconsistent with this simple scheme for explaining the underlying basis of hemispheric differences.

Operating on the Stimulus: The Information-Processing Approach

Consider the following now-classic experiment. A subject is given a short list of letters to memorize and then briefly views a familiar object in the left or the right visual field. The subject's task is to decide whether the first letter of the name of the object is among the letters in the memorized list. Which visual field would lead to a faster response? Or suppose that the subject views single letters instead of pictures and has to decide whether the letter was among those that had been memorized. What could be predicted about the speed of response in this case?

It would be reasonable to expect a left-visual-field superiority in the first case and a right-visual-field superiority in the second. Pictures, after all, are nonverbal stimuli, and letters clearly fall in the verbal domain. In fact, the results obtained were the complete reverse. Picture stimuli resulted in faster performance when they were presented to the left hemisphere, and the letters were responded to more quickly when they were projected initially to the right hemisphere.[8] Why?

What seems to be more important than the nature of the stimulus is the nature of the mental operations performed by the subject in response to the stimulus. In the picture task, the subject was asked to identify each picture and recover the initial letter of its name, a clearcut language function that is analytic in nature. The single-letter stimuli, however, are verbal in nature but in this task did not have to be approached as verbal stimuli. The subject could readily perform the task holistically by matching the mental image of the letter against the images of the set of memorized letters. Theoretically, the subject could do this without ever knowing the name of the letter presented.

This kind of explanation emphasizes the task to be performed by the subject rather than the nature of the stimulus per se. Additional evidence for information-processing differences between the hemispheres comes from interesting studies using the two Japanese writing systems, Kana and Kanji.[9] The Kana system is sound based, with each symbol representing the sound of a syllable. Kanji, in contrast, is ideographic, with each character representing a meaning as well as a sound. Examples are given in Figure 4.2. Analysis of the errors made by Japanese aphasic patients suggests that different strategies are used for the two types of symbols: visual processing for Kanji, as opposed to phonological, or sound-based, processing for Kana.

When sets of Kana and Kanji nonsense words were prepared and presented briefly one at a time in either the left or the right visual field in normal Japanese subjects, results showed a significant right-field superiority for identification in the Kana task and a left-field (but not significant) superiority for the Kanji task. The investigators concluded that Kana and Kanji characters are processed differently in the two hemispheres; furthermore, Kanji processing is particularly complex because both visual and verbal functions likely play a role, depending on the specific task. Whether Kanji would show a left- or a right-visual-field

MEANING	KANA	KANJI
INK	イ ン キ (INKI)	墨
UNIVERSITY	ダイガ゙ク (DAIGAKU)	大学 (GREAT LEARNING)
TOKYO	トウキヨウ (TOKYO)	東京 (EAST CAPITAL)

FIGURE 4.2 The two forms of writing in Japan. Kana is syllabic, with words articulated syllable-by-syllable. Kanji is ideographic, with each character simultaneously representing a sound and a meaning.

superiority might depend on, among other things, the strategy used by the subject and the mode of response (verbal or nonverbal).

The experiments just cited are among many that led to an emphasis on left- and right-hemisphere modes of processing information. The idea that the left hemisphere is specialized for analytical processing in which fine discriminations of various sorts are required, while the right is specialized for holistic processing, is one that has received a great deal of attention. Other processing dichotomies such as global versus local have also been proposed as candidates for the underlying processing asymmetry between the hemispheres.[10]

Although these ideas have been criticized for being too vague to be rigorously tested, they have been important in moving thinking away from the earlier, overly simple view that looked solely at the verbal or nonverbal nature of a stimulus as the determining factor underlying hemispheric asymmetry.

Representation of Information: The Role of Spatial Frequency

Justine Sergent and colleagues have emphasized the role of the physical characteristics of the stimulus and the conditions under which it is presented in determining the outcome of visual half-field experiments.[11] Stimuli in such experiments, for example, are typically presented quite briefly and off to the left or the right of the fixation point, conditions that would presumably result in degraded representations of information in the two hemispheres. Sergent suggested that the unequal ability of the hemispheres to operate on these degraded representations is responsible, at least in part, for visual-field asymmetries that are observed, and that differential processing of the "spatial frequency" components of a stimulus underlies the relative ability of the two hemispheres to deal with it.

The concept of spatial frequency can be illustrated by a simple grating of alternating black and white stripes; the spatial frequency of the grating is a function of the number of light–dark changes (bars) in the stimulus over a given spatial interval (see Figure 4.3). Any complex visual stimulus can be represented as an array of many such intensity variations, some higher (more bars) and some lower (fewer bars). Incoming visual information is broken down by the brain into discrete neural signals that represent these intensity variations. This processing is believed to be done by "channels" or filters sensitive to different spatial frequencies; the output of these channels reflects the array of spatial frequencies in the stimulus. Among the factors that decrease the availability of higher spatial frequencies relative to lower spatial frequencies are increases in size, distance from fixation, and amount of blur, as well as decreases in brightness and exposure duration.

Sergent has argued that the right hemisphere is more sensitive to low spatial frequencies and the left hemisphere more sensitive to high

FIGURE 4.3 Three sine-wave gratings, illustrating the concept of spatial frequency. The frequency increases from left to right. [After Sekuler and Blake, *Perception* (New York: McGraw-Hill, 1994).]

ones, and that one can influence the pattern of brain asymmetry observed by varying the spatial-frequency components of a stimulus. Sergent also argued that the two hemispheres are equivalent in their ability to process spatial-frequency information at a sensory level—differences emerge between the hemispheres at a later stage of cognitive processing. Thus, stimuli such as faces or letters might be processed more effectively by one hemisphere or the other, depending on their spatial-frequency characteristics.

A recent review of ten years of research on spatial frequency in relation to hemispheric asymmetry is generally supportive of the model as an explanation for a wide array of data, including recent EEG investigations of spatial frequency.[12] The authors concluded, however, that the evidence points to the existence of hemispheric asymmetry at both early perceptual and later cognitive levels of processing, and that the pattern of asymmetry differs at the two stages. At the early stages, the right hemisphere is superior for the whole range of spatial frequencies, whereas at later stages there is a left-hemisphere advantage for high spatial frequency and a right-hemisphere advantage for low spatial frequency.

Thus, the reviewers argue, the relative activation of the two hemispheres changes over the course of stimulus processing, supporting a dynamic view of asymmetry. While it remains to be seen how powerful the spatial-frequency model will ultimately prove to be as an explanation of hemispheric differences, it has clearly been responsible for focusing attention on important aspects of stimulus processing that had long been neglected, including the idea that the two hemispheres may become differentially involved at different stages of processing.

What Are Behavioral Tests Actually Measuring?

Divided-visual-field and dichotic listening studies have served as the basis for much of our current theorizing about the nature of the left brain and the right brain in normal subjects. There is a striking correspondence between many of the hemispheric differences demonstrated in normal subjects through these techniques and the ideas gleaned from the brain-damage clinic by several generations of neurologists and neuropsychologists. Important issues about the techniques themselves and about the nature of hemispheric asymmetry remain unresolved, however.[13]

Comparing Wada Results with Behavioral Testing

Behavioral tests typically underestimate the incidence of left-hemisphere speech in right-handers relative to that determined with sodium amobarbital (Wada) testing. Studies generally find that approximately 80 percent of right-handed subjects show a right-ear or right-visual-field advantage for the identification of spoken or written words. Sodium amobarbital testing, in contrast, indicates that more than 95 percent of right-handed individuals have left-hemisphere language. What causes this discrepancy?

One likely possibility is that the tests are not a pure measure of brain asymmetry and that other factors are involved in determining the magnitude and direction of the asymmetries that are observed while using them. Perhaps individual differences in the neural pathways connecting the eyes and ears to the brain play a role in the outcome of the studies, with some subjects showing less evidence of asymmetry, not because of differences in brain organization, but because of variations in the pathways that transmit information to the brain.

Differences in the tasks themselves may also affect the outcome in ways not yet understood. As an example, consider the study in which patients whose speech centers were previously determined by the amobarbital test were presented with pairs of dichotically presented words that differed only in the first consonant (e.g., coat/goat, pig/dig). The stimuli were constructed so that the two words in a pair fused and so that subjects generally experience and report only one stimulus per trial—either the left- or right-ear item. Ninety-five percent of subjects showing left- or right-hemisphere speech representation with Wada testing had right- or left-ear advantages, respectively. (Subjects with bilateral speech were divided about evenly between those with right-ear advantages and those with left-ear advantages.) This percentage is much higher than what is typically found in more standard dichotic testing situations in which fusion does not occur.[14]

We should also note that the discrepancy between the results of Wada testing and behavioral measures of asymmetry may be due in part to the possibility that each is tapping a different aspect of functional asymmetry. The Wada test is used to determine the hemisphere that controls speech output. Perhaps divided-visual-field and dichotic listening tasks, which are basically tests of perception and not production, reflect functions that are less lateralized.*

Attentional Bias as a Contributor to Asymmetry

The strategies that subjects adopt in these tasks also contribute in a major way to performance. In dichotic listening, for example, subjects can actively shift their attention to either the left-ear or the right-ear stimulus. If the left-ear items are at a disadvantage because of hemispheric asymmetry, then some subjects may adopt a strategy where they direct their attention to the weaker ear, thereby producing a smaller right-ear superiority than might be found otherwise. Other subjects, in contrast, may focus their attention on the clearer of the two stimuli on any trial, without trying to identify both of them. These subjects would show a larger right-ear advantage than one would expect. M. P. Bryden has made a convincing case for the importance of attentional effects in dichotic listening. Nevertheless, he concluded that, across large numbers of studies, the expected ear asymmetries emerge, even when investigators include controls for attentional factors.[15] Bryden has also advanced similar arguments for the study and interpretation of visual-field asymmetries.[16] Thus, in Bryden's view, attentional shifts cannot fully account for asymmetries but may contribute to the variability that is observed.

Marcel Kinsbourne has taken a different approach to the role of attention in behavioral studies of hemispheric asymmetry and has proposed that the asymmetries observed in dichotic listening and tachistoscopic studies are a reflection of covert shifts in attention to one side

---

*The terms *lateralized* and *lateralization* are frequently used to refer to the division of functions between the hemispheres, as well as to the restriction of information to one hemisphere.

of space following the activation of one hemisphere.[17] He argued that the hemisphere specialized for a particular task becomes differentially active, or "primed," when appropriate material is presented to a subject and that this priming "spills over" to the centers controlling attention to the opposite side of space.

Kinsbourne and his colleagues have shown that tasks not normally displaying a visual-field asymmetry can be made to show a right-side advantage if subjects are asked to rehearse subvocally a short list of words while they view the laterally presented stimuli. The rehearsal is presumed to activate the left hemisphere and produce a shift in attention to the right side, a process resulting in more accurate performance in that visual field.

Similarly, the right-ear advantage in speed of responding to certain dichotically presented syllables becomes a slight left-ear advantage when the subject is required to compare a brief melody presented immediately before each syllable pair with a melody presented immediately after. An attentional view would claim that the musical stimuli "primed" the right hemisphere, thereby producing a shift in attention to the left ear, which would cancel out the shift to the right ear that ordinarily occurs when speech is presented.

A number of studies have provided support for the activation-orienting hypothesis, as the attentional model is also known, although few investigators believe it is a complete explanation for asymmetries observed in lateralized testing.[18]

Test–Retest Reliability

Another concern, one that has implications for the two preceding problems as well, is that repeated testing of the same subjects does not always produce the same results. A test is reliable to the extent that repeated administrations yield similar results. Some studies have found the reliability of the dichotic listening and tachistoscopic tests to be lower than one might expect.[19] For example, some subjects who, when first tested, show a right-ear advantage for dichotically presented speech shift to a left-ear advantage when tested a week later. Presumably, the organization of an individual's brain is a stable characteristic and does not change over time. Signs of variability within an individual may mean that the laterality tests are tapping functions, such as the formation of strategies to be used in performing the tasks, that can shift over relatively brief intervals of time.

What Do the Tests Tell Us About the Nature of Asymmetries?

Are hemispheric differences absolute or relative? Does a difference in performance for stimuli presented in the two visual fields mean that only one hemisphere is capable of performing the task? Or does it mean that one hemisphere is simply better at the task than the other? Each of these questions, as well as many others along similar lines, is important to our understanding of hemispheric asymmetry. We noted earlier in this chapter two models of hemispheric functioning—the direct access model, in which each hemisphere processes stimuli presented to it, regardless of its inherent ability, and the callosal relay model, which assumes that the hemisphere best equipped to handle a particular task will be the one to do so. Yet another set of possibilities exists—those involving interaction between the hemispheres in performing a given task. The interaction could take several different forms, but all would involve contributions from each hemisphere to produce the final outcome.

Testing Models of Hemispheric Function

How can these models be differentiated? Eran Zaidel has played a major role in providing the theoretical rationale for differentiating among the possibilities.[20] He notes, for example, that a comparison of the performance of split-brain patients and normal subjects should be helpful in distinguishing between direct access and callosal relay models in a given task. If a task requires callosal relay, a split-brain patient would be expected to show a very large asymmetry, relative to what is found in normal subjects, because callosal transfer is not possible. A direct access task, however, in which the hemisphere first receiving stimulus information is responsible for processing, should produce an asymmetry in the split-brain patient that is comparable to that found in normal subjects (assuming, of course, that the split-brain patient is provided with an opportunity to respond nonverbally).

Another approach that Zaidel suggests to differentiate between the two models is the "processing-dissociation" criterion. Here, Zaidel proposes that the experimenter vary a stimulus dimension that would not be affected by callosal transfer. In an experiment involving word stimuli, for example, varying the words along a concrete–abstract dimension would satisfy the requirement because there is no reason to believe that there would be any difference in the efficiency of callosal transfer of words that differ in degree of abstraction. If the experimenter obtained visual-field differences that varied along this dimension, Zaidel argues, the findings would suggest that the two hemispheres processed the stimuli directed to them in different ways and hence would provide support for the direct access view.

Yet another approach is to vary the hand used to respond in a task measuring speed of response, or reaction time—half of the trials would involve response with the left hand and half with the right hand. In the simplest case, direct access tasks should show faster performance when the subject responds with the hand controlled by the hemisphere to which a stimulus is presented (that is, left visual field, left hand should be faster than left visual field, right hand; right visual field, right hand should be faster than right visual field, left hand). Callosal relay tasks, however, should show faster responding for the hand opposite the hemisphere responsible for processing, regardless of the hemisphere to which the stimulus was presented, because that hand is principally controlled by the hemisphere undertaking the task.

On the basis of the criteria just considered, the identification of consonant–vowel syllables in dichotic listening would be classified as a callosal relay task. In contrast, some lexical decision tasks in which individual concrete English words or nonwords are presented one at a time in the left or right visual fields for classification as "word" or "nonword" appear to be direct access tasks that can be performed by either hemisphere.

Zaidel notes, however, that the majority of tasks likely require interhemispheric cooperation or interaction. Marie Banish has focused attention on the various forms these interactions may take and has conceptualized them along a continuum, ranging from the situation where information is presented to both hemispheres yet one hemisphere takes control of processing, to one where neither hemisphere dominates but both contribute to different aspects of processing, to a situation where the hemispheres act in a manner that cannot be predicted at all from what is known about how information is processed when it is presented to one hemisphere at a time.[21]

As an example of the kinds of behavioral experiments that have been conducted to study hemispheric interaction, consider the work that has been done to study the form of interaction where one hemisphere takes control of processing.

Metacontrol

In the work with split-brain patients reviewed in Chapter 2, Jerre Levy and Colwyn Trevarthen distinguished between the ability of each hemisphere to perform a specific task and the degree to which each hemisphere assumes control of processing and behavior. They demonstrated that the hemisphere that assumed control for a task was not always the hemisphere with a greater ability for that task; they used the term *metacontrol* to refer to the neural mechanisms that determine which hemisphere will be in charge.

Joseph Hellige has argued that the concept of metacontrol is particularly important when trying to understand processing in the intact brain.[22] In many situations, both hemispheres are capable of performing a task, at least to some degree, but do so in different ways. When the same information is available to both hemispheres, what determines how the information will be processed?

Hellige has approached this problem experimentally by using selected tasks that can be performed by both hemispheres but in qualitatively different ways. He and his colleagues presented stimuli in three different conditions: right visual field, left visual field, and bilateral (both visual fields simultaneously). By comparing the performance on bilateral trials with performance when stimuli are presented to only one hemisphere, Hellige reasoned, it is possible to determine whether the qualitative pattern of results on bilateral trials matches that of one of the other two conditions.

In several such studies, the mode of processing on bilateral trials has been identical to that observed in presentations to one hemisphere but not to the other. Moreover, the mode of processing found in bilateral trials was not always the mode used by the hemisphere with greater ability for that task, a finding reminiscent of the commissurotomy studies of Levy and Trevarthen. Individual differences among subjects were also observed. In general, 75 to 85 percent of right-handed subjects showed the same pattern of results in any given study. The remaining 15 to 25 percent showed a mode of processing in bilateral trials similar to that of the other hemisphere. Whether these variations represent meaningful differences in metacontrol among subjects is not clear at this point. Hellige has written, "An important challenge facing cognitive neuropsychologists is to account for the emergence of unified information processing from a brain consisting of a variety of processing subsystems. The left and right cerebral hemispheres may be characterized as two very general subsystems with different processing properties and biases. Understanding interhemispheric interaction and the conditions for metacontrol can provide important clues about the emergence of unified information processing."[23]

Criteria for Assessing Interhemispheric Interaction

Banish has noted that investigations of interhemispheric interaction require two conditions in order to assess the presence of such interactions. First, the experiment must include two types of trials—one in which different information is presented simultaneously to the two hemispheres (the bilateral or bihemispheric condition) and a control condition in which the same information is presented to one hemisphere (the unihemispheric condition where stimuli are presented to one visual half-field at a time). Second, some aspect of the task must produce different results on the unihemispheric task that differ from those on the bilateral task. She offers the following illustrative example.

Suppose females were better than males in determining whether shapes presented in the left and right hands, out of the field of vision, were the same. Although one might be tempted to conclude that these data supported the idea that females had better interhemispheric transfer than males, the conclusion would be premature because appropriate controls were not included. For example, females might have more sensitive palms than males, and that could account for the difference that was observed between males and females, independent of any difference in interhemispheric transfer. Only by employing a unihemispheric control, in this case by presenting both shapes to one hand, would it be possible to evaluate whether any difference between males and females may be attributed to interhemispheric processing as such. If the differences favoring females were greater in the bihemispheric condition relative to the unihemispheric condition, Banish argues, then inferences about interhemispheric transfer would be appropriate.[24]

Research using behavioral techniques have raised, if not resolved, very important questions regarding the nature of hemispheric specialization and interaction. The role of the corpus callosum, which we addressed in a preliminary way in Chapter 2, has also been the focus of a good deal of attention in more recent behavioral studies, in keeping with the growing interest in interhemispheric interaction. In Chapter 10, we will consider the role of the corpus callosum in brain development, as well as the ways in which behavioral studies can help inform ideas about the role of the corpus callosum in the intact brain.

Can Degree of Asymmetry Be Measured?

Yet another issue that is of theoretical significance in behavioral studies is whether the size of the asymmetries found in experimental testing of different subjects can tell us anything about the degree of hemispheric asymmetry in those subjects. Is it possible that differences among subjects in the size of the asymmetry can tell us something about the extent to which processing is limited to one hemisphere in those subjects? Is a subject with a large right-ear advantage for a given task more lateralized, that is, more dependent on processing by a given hemisphere, than a subject with a smaller right-ear advantage?

The issue of how to compute measures of lateralization from scores on behavioral tests is important and complex. In tests where percentage correct is the dependent variable, some investigators use difference scores (left minus right, or variations thereof) as the index of lateralization. Such scores are not independent of overall performance, however, and others have claimed that a laterality measure should be independent of how well someone does. Still others have argued that information on overall performance may itself be related to lateralization. The most appropriate measures of lateralization, and what those measures might mean about underlying patterns of asymmetry, are among the many questions that remain unresolved at this point.[25]

Must There Be a Single Dichotomy?

Finally, as noted earlier, considerable effort has been directed toward characterizing the nature of the underlying differences between the hemispheres. Implicit in this approach is the idea that hemispheric differences can all be related to a single, fundamental dichotomy, for example, analytic/holistic. Studies that do not "fit" with the predictions of a given dichotomy pose a problem for it and can result in a reformulation or reevaluation of that dichotomy.

Joseph Hellige has argued that this approach may be fundamentally flawed, however, and that consideration should be given to the possibility that specific processing components or modules may become lateralized to one side of the brain independently of the other, or even in keeping with a totally different organizing principle that will not result in a neat classification scheme.[26] Investigators will no doubt continue to look for the organizing principle that offers the best explanation of the greatest amount of data, and it is that one, whatever form it may take, that is likely to prevail. Hellige reminds us, correctly, that we are far from having this key issue resolved.

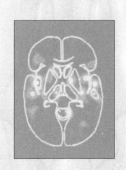

PART III

Handedness, Sex, and the Brain

Chapter 5

The Puzzle
of the Left-Hander

An overwhelming majority of human beings almost exclusively use their right hands for writing and other skilled, unimanual activities. Cross-cultural studies put the incidence of right-handedness at about 90 percent. A variety of indirect evidence suggests that this has been the case since prehistoric times.[1] Drawings of people found on cave walls and inside Egyptian tombs typically show the subjects engaged in activities involving the right hand, and an analysis of paleolithic tools and weapons suggests that they were made with, and for, the right hand.

A study of hand tracings believed to have been made by Cro-Magnon people showed over 80 percent to be of the left hand. If we assume the artists traced their own hands, these data also point to a very strong preference for the right hand in skilled activity. A study of 1,180 works of art spanning a 5,000-year period, from pre-3000 B.C. to 1950, showed that depiction of right- and left-hand use showed no significant change or trends over time, with left-hand use averaging 7 to 8 percent. Perhaps the most ingenious evidence of all for right-hand preference in early humans comes from an analysis of fossilized baboon skulls with fractures. On the basis of the locations of the fractures, the investigator concluded that the injuries were the result of blows inflicted by early humans wielding clubs with their right hands.

Why are most human beings right-handed? Conversely, why does a significant percentage of the population use the left hand, despite subtle and sometimes overt social pressure to conform to the handedness pattern characteristic of the majority? We mentioned in earlier chapters that handedness is related in complex ways to the distribution of functions between the left brain and the right brain. Any analysis of brain asymmetry must deal with this problem if it is to be complete. What factors determine handedness? In what ways do left-handers and right-handers differ?

In this chapter, we will consider modern theories proposed to account for variations in handedness and studies designed to examine possible differences between left-handers and right-handers. To provide a historical context for recent work, we will briefly review some of the older ideas about handedness.

Historical Notions of Left-Handedness

Is There Anything Sinister About Being Left-Handed?

Webster's Third International Dictionary lists several definitions of the adjective *left-handed,* including the following:

> **a:** marked by clumsiness or ineptitude: awkward;
> **b:** exhibiting deviousness or indirection: oblique, unintended;
> **c:** obs.: given to malevolent scheming or contriving: sinister, underhand.

Left-handers are frequently referred to as "sinistrals," and *Roget's Thesaurus* lists left-handed as a synonym for unskillfulness. In other languages as well, the terms for left or left-handed have almost always contained at least one derogatory meaning, ranging from "clumsy" or "awkward" to "evil." The French word for left, *gauche,* also means "clumsy"; *mancino* is Italian for left as well as for deceitful. The Spanish idiom *no ser zurdo* means "to be very clever." Its literal translation is "not to be left-handed." Other examples abound.

Anthropologists have provided us with a number of examples of how symbolic associations with left and right are part of different cultures.[2] For example, the involuntary twitching of an eyelid is thought to be significant by the native people of Morocco. For them, twitching of the right eyelid signifies the return of a family member or other good news, whereas twitching of the left eyelid is a warning of an impending death in the family. In another part of the world, the Maoris of New Zealand at one time believed that a tremor during sleep meant that a spirit had seized the body. A right-side tremor meant good fortune, whereas a left-side tremor meant ill fortune and possibly death.

The Bible, too, reflects a striking bias against the left hand or left side.[3] One example from the New Testament that is especially striking is the Vision of Judgment in St. Matthew, Chapter 25:

33 And he shall set the sheep on his right hand, but the goats on the left.

34 Then shall the King say unto them on his right hand, Come, ye blessed of my Father, inherit the kingdom prepared for you from the foundation of the world: . . .

41 Then shall he say also unto them on the left hand, Depart from me, ye cursed, into everlasting fire, prepared for the devil and his angels: . . .

46 And these shall go away into everlasting punishment: but the righteous into life eternal.

Michael Barsley, author of *Left-Handed People,* has argued that the Vision of Judgment has been responsible for "fixing the prejudice against left-handers [more] than any other pronouncement, and that this prejudice has come down through the ages, adopted by inquisitors, judges, soldiers, artists, teachers, nurses, and parents as the supreme example of the association of sinistral people with wickedness and the Devil."[4] Whether or not Barsley is correct, it is clear that the association of left with bad is of very long standing. What is the origin of this bias? At this point, we can only speculate.

The late Carl Sagan has suggested one possibility in *The Dragons of Eden,* his book on the evolution of intelligence.[5] Sagan notes that in preindustrial societies, both now and in the past, the hand has been used for personal hygiene after defecation. This use of a hand is both unaesthetic and potentially harmful because it can spread disease, but these drawbacks can be reduced somewhat by using only the other hand to eat and to greet others. Right-handed individuals would perform activities like eating and throwing weapons with the right hand, leaving toilet hygiene to the left. Sagan suggests that the left hand became associated with excretory activities, which have a long history of negative associations in human cultures. Thus, the chain linking left with bad was forged. This explanation assumes that human beings begin with a preference to use the right hand for activities requiring fine control. We must still explain the basis for that preference. Speculation abounds on this issue, but, thanks to the tools of modern science, we now stand a good chance of resolving the question in a satisfactory way.

Nineteenth-Century Theories of Handedness

Let us first consider some of the ideas proposed in the nineteenth century to account for handedness. One popular theory was known as "visceral distribution." Proponents argued that the asymmetrical placement of visceral organs, such as the liver, puts the center of gravity of the human body slightly to the right of the midline, and, as a consequence, human beings are better able to balance on the left foot. This stance leaves the right hand free, so over time the muscles on the right side became better developed. This notion, however, does not explain why some people are left-handed, unless we assume, incorrectly, a reversal in the orientation of their viscera.

Social-evolution explanations of handedness were also popular in the nineteenth century. There are several variations on this general theme, the most common being the sword-and-shield theory.[6] According to this theory, attributed to English essayist and historian Thomas Carlyle and others, most soldiers hold their shields with their left hands to protect their hearts when they are engaged in battle and use their right hands to hold their weapons. As a consequence, during eons of armed conflict, the right hand gained in manipulative ability and came to be used for other unimanual activities as well. There is no attempt to explain left-handedness or the apparently high incidence of right-handedness in humans before the invention of the shield.

The idea of cerebral dominance emerged in the last quarter of the nineteenth century, and with it came yet another theory of handedness. D. J. Cunningham, a Scottish anatomist, summarized this view in 1902 in a Huxley Memorial Lecture: "Right-handedness is due to a transmitted functional preeminence of the left brain. Left-brainedness is not the result but, through evolution, it has become the cause of right-handedness."[7] As it is stated, this view would not easily account for left-handers with left-hemisphere speech, who comprise about 70 percent of all left-handers. In addition, it fails to explain the reasons for the "transmitted functional preeminence" of the left brain.

The Difficulty of Determining Handedness

Before we consider more modern theories of handedness, it is important to consider how handedness is actually assessed. We might assume that the best way to find out whether a given individual is a left- or a right-hander is simply to ask. Unfortunately, this direct approach does not always work. Few people use one hand exclusively for all unimanual activities, and simple self-classification does not indicate how someone weighted various activities when making the determination. Another approach is to ask people which hand they use for specific activities. The researcher can then compute a handedness preference based on the same weighting scheme for everyone.

One widely used questionnaire to measure hand preference is known as the Edinburgh Handedness Inventory. Subjects are asked to indicate their preferred hand, if any, and strength of the preference for writing, drawing, throwing, cutting with scissors, brushing teeth, cutting with a knife without a fork, using a spoon, holding a broom (upper hand), holding a match while striking, and holding a lid while removing it from a box. The questionnaire yields a laterality quotient that ranges from −100 for extreme left-handedness, through 0 for equal use of the two hands, to +100 for extreme right-handedness.

When this inventory was used in a study of over 1,000 undergraduates at the University of Edinburgh, most showed a consistent preference for one hand; few showed no preference.[8] Those showing right preference, however, tended to show their preferences more strongly than those showing left preference. That is, the distribution of positive and negative scores was different. The positive scores were clustered toward the high end of the range, whereas the negative scores were more evenly distributed over the range of values. Findings like these have led some investigators to speak of right-handers and non–right-handers, rather than right-handers and left-handers.

Regardless of the terminology used, the way in which subjects are classified into different handedness groups is critical for the outcome of research investigating handedness as a variable. Most studies use questionnaires in an attempt to classify subjects in terms of the direction of handedness on the basis of their scores. Problems arise, however, because handedness is not a simple all-or-none dimension—a decision, most likely arbitrary, must be made about where to place the boundaries between handedness group categories.

Other studies, however, do not form groups on the basis of test scores but use the actual scores in the handedness measure. In this way, information about the degree of consistency of hand preference is retained, along with information about the direction of preference. Despite this refinement, different types of questionnaires may yield different classifications in the same group of subjects. It should not be surprising, then, that experiments investigating the effects of handedness sometimes yield conflicting results. Differences in the way subjects are classified may account for much of the conflict among studies.[9]

What Determines Handedness?

Is handedness, like eye color, blood type, and general body build, genetically determined? Do environmental influences determine hand preference? Or, as is often the case with complex human behaviors, do genetic and environmental influences each play a role? The probability of two right-handed parents having a left-handed child is 0.09. It rises to 0.19 if one parent is left-handed and to 0.26 if both are left-handed.[10] Relative to those with two right-handed parents, individuals having one left-handed parent are 2.3 times more likely to be left-handed; those having two left-handed parents are 3.4 times more likely to be left-handed.

The problem with interpreting these data as evidence supporting the role of heredity is that environmental factors as well as genetic factors can account for these differences. Two left-handed parents could provide a child with different experiences relevant to the determination of handedness, just as they might provide specific genes. Nature (genes) and nurture (experience) are confounded in these figures, making it impossible to sort out the contribution of each from the numbers alone. In the following sections, we will consider a variety of ideas about how handedness is determined, including ones that consider the possible role of factors that may operate during prenatal development and at the time of birth.

The Environmental View

Robert Collins has taken an extreme environmental position, arguing that handedness is transmitted from one generation to the next through cultural and environmental biases. Collins based his conclusions in large part on his work with paw preference in mice, which showed that individual mice demonstrate consistent paw preferences in reaching for food in a glass tube. These preferences are not subject to genetic selection: It is not possible to breed right-pawed mice over several generations by mating mice that show a right-paw preference. The offspring of such animals will show the same paw-preference distribution found among mice in general: 50 percent left preference and 50 percent right preference. Collins also showed that young mice that have not yet shown a preference for either paw become predominantly right-pawed if they are presented with the glass tube placed toward the right side of the cage, thereby making it easier to reach with the right paw than with the left paw.[11]

Extended to human handedness such a view would hold that right-handedness is a learned response to a right-handed world and that left-handedness occurs when this response is not learned as a result of a physical defect, faulty education, emotional problems, or the like. An environmental model of handedness determination must account, however, for the fact that right-hand preference has been found across all cultures studied and over all time periods for which evidence is available. It would have to explain why environments biased in favor of the left hand do not occur.

Genetic Models

Genetic models of handedness may be evaluated by formulating specific predictions of how handedness might be transmitted from generation to generation through the action of genes. A good fit between the predictions of a specific model and actual data would support the position that genetic factors can account for most of the variations in handedness found among people.

One of the first genetic models of handedness to be formulated hypothesized that handedness is a consequence of the action of a single gene that has two different forms, or alleles. One allele, R, was dominant and coded for right-handedness. A second, l, was recessive and coded for left-handedness. An individual inheriting the R allele from each parent would be right-handed, as would someone with an Rl genotype (R from one parent, l from the other). Left-handers would be those individuals who inherited the l allele from each parent.

This model, however, cannot account for the fact that only 26 percent of the offspring of two left-handed parents are left-handed. The model predicts that all offspring of such parents should be left-handed, because the l allele is the only one that left-handed parents can transmit to their offspring. There have been attempts to rescue this model by introducing additional complexity such as the concept of variable penetrance, which proposes that all individuals with the same genotype do not express that genotype the same way. Proponents have argued that as a result of variable penetrance some individuals with the Rl genotype would be expected to be left-handed, although they would transmit the R allele to one-half of their offspring. Nevertheless, this kind of model does not provide a good fit to the data.

Marion Annett, of the University of Hull in England, has proposed a different kind of genetic model of handedness.[12] She hypothesized that there is no gene for left- or right-handedness as such, but that there is a dominant gene (rs^+) responsible for the development of speech in the left hemisphere, which, in turn, increases the chances of greater skill in the right hand. Annett refers to her theory as the "right shift" theory. She proposed a recessive form of the gene (rs^-), which results in the absence of systematic bias to one side, for either speech or handedness. With rs^-, chance factors would operate independently on the direction of lateralization for speech and handedness.

If both alleles occur equally often in the population and if mating is random with respect to this gene, then 50 percent of the population will be rs^{+-}, 25 percent rs^{++}, and 25 percent rs^{--}. Persons in the first two groups would show a right shift (left-hemisphere language and right-hand preference). The rs^{--} group, however, would lack any right shift; and in Annett's view, environmental effects would determine their hand preference. In the absence of any strong environmental bias, one would expect about half of this 25 percent to be left-handed and half right-handed. The percentage of left-handed persons predicted by Annett's model is quite close to the number of left-handers actually found in the general population.

Although we will have more to say about the relationship between handedness and cognitive abilities later, we should mention here that Annett has specifically proposed such a relationship. She suggested that the rs^{++} genotype may lead to poor performance with the left hand and to spatial deficits, whereas the rs^{--} person may be susceptible to reading disabilities. The rs^{+-} genotype would be optimal, according to Annett, and could account for the continued presence of both rs^+ and rs^- in the population.

Handedness, Hormones, and the Immune System

A possible relationship between handedness and the body's immune system has been the subject of a great deal of interest and controversy since it was first proposed in the early 1980s. The idea emerged when Norman Geschwind commented at a scientific meeting that those interested in studying the genetics of dyslexia should look for the presence of other conditions as well in the family history of dyslexic individuals.* In the audience were a number of parents of dyslexic children, who came up afterward to tell Geschwind about their family histories of immune disorders and migraine. These informal reports were subsequently confirmed in a series of studies that demonstrated an unexpected link between left-handedness and disorders such as migraine, allergies, thyroid problems, and other disorders believed to be autoimmune in origin.

These observations led Geschwind and colleague Albert Galaburda to develop a far-reaching theory of lateralization in which a common factor, testosterone, is responsible for both left-handedness and susceptibility to immune disorders.[13] Geschwind and Galaburda proposed that testosterone, to which both male and female fetuses are exposed during uterine development, slows the growth of parts of the left hemisphere during fetal life, so that corresponding regions on the right develop relatively more rapidly. Because male fetuses are exposed to greater quantities of testosterone, they argued, males will show a greater degree of shift to right-hemisphere participation in handedness and language and will more likely have augmented right-hemisphere skills. In addition, the delay in left-hemisphere development may, in some cases, result in a

---

*Dyslexia is the term used to describe reading disability unaccompanied by other problems such as sensory impairment. Dyslexia is discussed in greater detail in Chapter 11.

permanent developmental learning disorder, the incidence of which is higher in males.

At the same time testosterone is affecting the development of the left hemisphere, Geschwind and Galaburda believed that it may also affect the development of the immune system, thereby increasing susceptibility to subsequent immune disorders. Hence, testosterone could be responsible for both the apparent association between the incidence of left-handedness and the incidence of immune disorders.

Geschwind and Galaburda's ideas are intriguing and suggest a host of interesting possibilities. They note that in some cases, the more rapid development of the right hemisphere mediated by testosterone may lead to special skills. Autistic individuals, for example, occasionally show very superior artistic ability (we discuss this phenomenon in greater detail in Chapter 11). Geschwind and Galaburda argue that the effects of testosterone on the left hemisphere would account for the disabilities the person showed, and the accompanying enhanced development of the right hemisphere would account for the "island" of superior performance.

Such a mechanism could even explain certain types of superior performance in persons not showing cognitive deficits. In a study of a large, male-predominant group of mathematically gifted children, the subjects had twice the rate of allergies and twice the rate of left-handedness as the general population.[14] Could the testosterone hypothesis account for this as well? Geschwind and Galaburda tentatively suggested that it could— depending on the precise timing and levels of testosterone present in utero, the deleterious consequences of a slowing of left-hemisphere development might be avoided while the advantages of right-hemisphere enhancement might be realized.

The Geschwind and Galaburda model is far reaching and has generated a great deal of interest and further research. M. P. Bryden, Ian McManus, and Barbara Bulman-Fleming have undertaken the enormous task of reviewing the literature bearing on the Geschwind and Galaburda model in the ten years since it was first proposed and have concluded that the data do not support the model in its strong form.[15] As an example, they point to inconsistencies in the association between handedness and immune disorders that is predicted by the model. The data show that some disorders such as allergies, asthma, and colitis show left-handers to be at greater risk, whereas other autoimmune disorders such as arthritis and myasthenia gravis show the reverse pattern, with right-handers more at risk. They also conclude that other predictions that follow from the model, such as a relationship between atypical lateralization and giftedness, are not generally supported by existing data.

An entire issue of *Brain and Language,* a major journal in cognitive neuroscience, was devoted to the review and to replies from both critics and supporters of the views presented. It is clear from reading these articles that the scientific community is divided on the issue of the usefulness of the Geschwind and Galaburda model. Few would disagree that the strong form of the model is not supported—too many predictions explicitly made by the model are not borne out by the data. It is equally clear, however, that several unexpected phenomena predicted by the model have been confirmed empirically and still require explanation.

Birth Stress and Left-Handedness

The incidence of left-handedness in twins is 15 to 18 percent, about twice that found in the singleton population.[16] Twins also show a disproportionately high incidence of neurological and other disorders, which is believed to be a consequence of brain damage resulting from intrauterine crowding during fetal development and delivery. It is a logical next step to suggest that the elevated incidence of left-handedness in twins is due, at least in part, to these factors.[17]

Paul Bakan and associates have extended this hypothesis to non-twins and have asserted that all left-handedness is essentially pathological in origin and that trauma occurring at birth, or birth stress, can account for most of it.[18] They suggested that left-handedness is the result of left-hemisphere motor dysfunction following perinatal hypoxia, or reduced oxygen supply at birth. According to Bakan, sinistrality runs in families because of an inherited tendency for difficult births or abnormal pregnancies, and not because handedness per se is genetically determined.

The studies relevant to Bakan's hypothesis do not yield a consistent or particularly supportive pattern of results. However, all have been based on retrospective data, that is, information about the presence or absence of birth stress obtained from subjective reports of mothers or subjects many years after the fact. To reduce the errors inherent in retrospective reporting, Murray Schwartz undertook a longitudinal, prospective study that began tracking children at age two and includes hospital records as well as maternal reports to assess birth stress.[19] Of all the stress/risk factors and complications examined by Schwartz, only one showed a statistically significant relationship to subsequent sinistrality. The data fall far short of supporting the hypothesis that all left-handedness is the result of birth stress.

Less extreme views of the role of pathology have been taken by others, however. Paul Satz, for example, suggested that pathological factors can account for a good deal of the elevated incidence of left-handedness among certain clinical populations, as well as some left-handedness in the population at large.[20] The remaining left-handers are, in his view, "natural" left-handers, whose left-handedness is genetic in origin.

Satz and his colleagues became interested in other changes—what they called the syndromes of pathological left-handedness (PLH)—that may occur in individuals who are left-handed because of early brain injury. One of these is a shift in hemispheric specialization for speech. Left-handers with a history of early brain damage are three times more likely to have speech controlled by the right hemisphere than are left-handers without early brain damage. Another component of PLH, according to Satz, is impaired visuospatial ability, because injury to the left hemisphere may shift language functions to the right hemisphere, thereby disrupting and displacing the visuospatial functions that otherwise would develop there. A third component is failure of the right side of the body to develop fully. In support of this Satz and colleagues cited their research showing that epileptic patients whose seizures began before age two had a shorter right foot if the lesion was located in the left hemisphere, whereas patients with early right-sided lesions had a shorter left foot.

Overall, existing evidence appears sufficient to support the position that some left-handedness is pathological in origin, although few researchers would take the extreme view that all, or even most, left-handedness can be explained in this way.

How Is Handedness Related to Language Lateralization?

In what ways does the brain organization of left-handers differ from that of right-handers? Both clinical and behavioral studies have helped answer this question. In Chapter 1, we noted that sodium amobarbital testing has shown that over 95 percent of right-handers have speech localized to the left hemisphere, with 70 percent of left-handers showing the same pattern. Of the remaining 30 percent, most show evidence of bilateral speech representation.[21] From these figures, one might conclude that the majority of left-handers are just like right-handers in terms of speech representation.

Other clinical data, however, suggest that the picture is more complex. Several studies have reported that the prognosis for recovery from aphasia following stroke is better in left-handers than in right-handers.[22] Many investigators believe that recovery from massive damage to the speech hemisphere is a function of the extent to which the remaining, undamaged hemisphere can take over. If this is so, language functions may be bilaterally represented in more than just those left-handers identified by the sodium amobarbital data. Left-handers with speech controlled predominantly by one hemisphere may have the other hemisphere available "in reserve" to a much greater extent than right-handers.

Behavioral studies with normal subjects generally confirm this picture of complexity. Dichotic listening and lateralized tachistoscopic studies that compare the performance of groups of left- and right-handers show less evidence of asymmetry in left-handers.[23] As a general rule, any asymmetry found in right-handers will be smaller and perhaps in the opposite direction when studied in left-handers. When data from individual subjects are examined, we find that left-handed subjects show smaller asymmetries than right-handed subjects, although there are some left-handers with strong left or strong right superiorities. These findings mesh nicely with the clinical evidence pointing to greater bilaterality in left-handers.

The Role of Familial Sinistrality

The brain organization of left-handers appears to be more complex than the sodium amobarbital data would lead one to expect. Other clinical work has suggested that some of the variability between left-handers may be accounted for by determining whether a given left-hander has first-degree relatives (parents, siblings, or children) who are themselves left-handed. Left-handers with histories of familial sinistrality (left-handers in the immediate family) showed similar frequencies of language disturbances occurring after damage to either the left or the right side of the brain. In nonfamilial left-handers, language disturbances were almost nonexistent after right-hemisphere lesions. Clinical data have also suggested that left-handers and right-handers with a family history of left-handedness show better recovery from aphasia. The clinical data, however, are not completely consistent in demonstrating the effects of familial sinistrality.[24]

Studies with normal subjects have looked at the effect of familial sinistrality on performance in lateralized tests. A number of studies support the idea that left-handers with left-handed relatives differ from those without. Unfortunately, studies are not consistent in their findings about the nature of that difference.[25]

Hand Posture

Jerre Levy and MaryLou Reid identified another variable—hand posture—which they believed might help sort left-handers into different groups on the basis of brain organization.[26] Some left-handers write in an inverted or hooked position, holding the pen or pencil above the line of writing. Other left-handers, as well as almost all right-handers, hold their writing instruments below the line of writing.

Levy and Reid argued that the inverted hand posture means that the speech hemisphere is ipsilateral to the preferred hand. Thus, the speech of a left-handed inverter would be controlled by the left hemisphere. The speech of a right-handed inverter (these individuals are rare) would be controlled by the right hemisphere. The speech of non-inverted writers would be controlled by the hemisphere opposite the preferred hand. Their view conflicts with conventional wisdom, which suggests that hand posture is due only to training.

Some evidence supporting these ideas has come from visual half-field tests. Unfortunately, however, other studies including clinical data, present a picture too filled with inconsistencies for hand posture to be a useful predictor of brain asymmetry.[27]

Is Footedness a Better Measure of Asymmetry?

While handedness is clearly the most obvious human asymmetry, most people also have a preferred, or dominant, eye, ear, and foot. Depending on what is being studied, eye preference can refer to the eye that shows relatively better performance on standard tests of visual acuity, or the eye that is used to sight down a telescope or along a pistol. Ear preference can also be measured in terms of acuity—in which ear is hearing more sensitive, or in terms of which ear is chosen when subjects cannot use both ears simultaneously, as in pressing a watch against an ear to hear its ticking. Footedness refers to the preferred foot for tasks such as kicking a ball or grasping a small object with the toes.

Data have generally shown that the relationship of eye and ear preference, as defined above, to hemispheric asymmetry is not particularly strong.[28] This outcome should not be surprising because the neuroanatomy of visual and auditory systems is such that, under normal conditions, preference for the left or right eye or ear does not simply reflect preferential use of one hemisphere. The picture for footedness, however, is different. A recent report has suggested that footedness may actually be a better predictor of language lateralization than handedness.

This surprising finding emerged in a study by Lorin Elias and M. P. Bryden.[29] Using self-report questionnaires to assess handedness and footedness, the investigators developed a subject sample in which there were equal numbers of right- and left-handed males and females in each footedness group, and equal numbers of people with uncrossed (right-handed/right-footed and left-handed/left-footed) and crossed (right-handed/left-footed and left-handed/right-footed) lateral preferences. A dichotic listening test previously shown to correlate highly with speech lateralization was administered to each subject to assess hemispheric asymmetry. The results showed that footedness was a far better predictor of language lateralization than handedness.

Overall, left-footed subjects showed nonsignificant left-ear advantages, whereas right-footed subjects showed significant right-ear advantages. When the same subjects were classified on the basis of handedness alone, however, left-handed subjects did not differ from right-handed subjects in their pattern of ear asymmetry. Similar findings have been found by several other investigators. Lainy Day and Peter MacNeilage argue that foot preference is an indicator of a habitual asymmetry involving body posture—using one foot to kick or stomp requires having the other leg bear the weight of the body temporarily.[30] They have emphasized the relationship of postural asymmetries to hemispheric specialization for language as opposed to the relationship of manual skill asymmetries (handedness) to hemispheric specialization. In most human beings, they observe, the postural asymmetries and skill asymmetries are homolateral (i.e., on the same side), so handedness is useful as a predictor of hemispheric asymmetry. In those cases where they are not homolateral, however, the importance of postural asymmetries becomes evident and footedness becomes a more useful predictor.

Further work will no doubt help clarify how footedness fits into the unfolding picture of hemispheric asymmetry.

Handedness and Cognitive Abilities

Do left-handers differ from right-handers in ways other than brain organization? The search for the relationship between handedness and brain asymmetry has led many investigators to consider the consequences of this relationship for other functions. The pathological model of left-handedness, for example, leads readily to the prediction that minimal brain damage will result in lowered ability on various tests of higher mental functions. The Geschwind and Galaburda model predicts overrepresentation of left-handers in populations of those with learning disabilities and in those who are exceptionally gifted intellectually. How do the data bear on these predictions?

Evaluating the Case for Deficits in Left-Handers

Studies that compare the performances of left-handers and right-handers on tests of higher mental functions have yielded little in the way of data to support predictions of inferior performance by left-handers.[31] Despite the meager collection of empirical evidence documenting performance differences between left-handers and right-handers, however, the association of left-handedness with deficit persists. This belief is most likely a result of the higher incidence of left-handedness among mentally retarded and reading disabled individuals. This association, although the subject of controversy, suggests that some of the left-handedness in these groups selected for deficits is pathological in origin.[32] The same damage that produces the impairment also might be responsible for the shift to left-hand usage. It does not follow, however, that a similar relationship holds for unselected groups of subjects obtained outside of the clinical setting.

Another theoretical approach to the relationship between handedness and cognitive ability has been taken by Levy.[33] She noted that many left-handers show evidence of some language ability in the right hemisphere in addition to language ability in the left hemisphere. What, she asked, are the consequences of this for the visuospatial functions typically controlled by the right hemisphere in the right-hander? She proposed that language and visuospatial functions compete for available neural tissue within a hemisphere and that language functions predominate at the expense of the others, "crowding-out" visuospatial centers. Thus, she predicted that left-handers should do more poorly than right-handers on visuospatial tasks but should perform similarly on verbal tasks. Levy's idea continues to be an intriguing one, although the empirical support for it is quite mixed.

Leonardo da Vinci Was a Lefty

In contrast to the ideas just presented, some investigators have suggested that the more bilateral distribution of language function that appears to characterize left-handers may actually result in superior abilities. The argument has been made that creativity might be enhanced in individuals whose brains permit a greater interplay between verbal and nonverbal abilities by virtue of their being housed within the same hemisphere. Proponents of this idea are eager to mention that Leonardo da Vinci, Benjamin Franklin, and Michelangelo were all left-handed.

Overall, occasional studies have reported superior performance by the left-hander, but these studies do not paint a picture any clearer than do those pointing to deficits in left-handers.[34] A possible exception is research on mathematical ability, which we will discuss in Chapter 6 in the context of sex differences. This research presents a compelling case for a higher incidence of left-handedness among the mathematically gifted.

It is interesting to note that the incidence of left-handedness is considerably higher among artists than among the general population. For example, in one study comparing college undergraduates with less than two years of art training with students enrolled in an art-degree program, 20 percent of the artists, but only 7 percent of the nonartists, were left-handed. Mixed-handedness occurred in 27 percent of the artists and in only 15 percent of the nonartists.[35] The meaning of these findings is uncertain, however. They clearly pose problems for Levy's cognitive deficit model of left-handedness, unless one argues that the deficit in visuospatial ability predicted by Levy occurs in only a subset of left-handers. Another possible interpretation is that interest in and experience with art leads to greater utilization of the left hand.

Despite the suggestion of deficits in left-handers and the amply justified reprisals mentioned, it is evident that any differences in the cognitive abilities of left- and right-handers in general are very small and of little practical importance. Individual variation within a group is much greater than the statistical difference between groups. No doubt, however, the issue of differences in cognitive functioning and handedness, regardless of how small, will continue to be pursued because of its significance to theories of brain variability and organization.

The Controversy Over Longevity

This chapter has dealt with basic issues related to hand preferences—their origins, their implications for human abilities, and their relation to hemispheric asymmetry of function. Recently, psychologists Stanley Coren and Diane Halpern have presented a controversial set of findings suggesting that left-handers, by virtue of living in a world designed primarily by and for right-handers, are more prone to accidents that may have a negative impact on longevity.[36]

Coren was initially intrigued by his own preliminary data showing that the proportion of left-handers diminished from 13 percent in 20-year-olds to less than 1 percent in 80-year-olds. Were these differences in the incidence of left-handedness as a function of age real, and if so, what did they mean? In subsequent work, Coren and Halpern obtained information about cause of death and hand preference in a large sample of recently deceased people from next-of-kin who did not know the purpose of the study. They found that females lived an average of almost six years longer than males, but a much larger difference was found as a function of handedness. The mean age of death for right-handers in their sample was 75.34 years; for left-handers, it was 66.20 years.

Earlier in this chapter we reviewed evidence suggesting that some left-handedness is pathological in origin. Perhaps the pathological factors producing left-handedness produce other conditions that affect mortality as well. Coren and Halpern, however, proposed yet another possible explanation—a higher rate of accidents among left-handers. When cause of death was examined in their next-of-kin study, left-handers were found to be six times more likely to die from accident-related injuries than right-handers.

Coren and Halpern's work relating left-handedness, accidents, and mortality has been highly controversial, and a number of investigators have claimed that their data are flawed by methodological problems.[37] Specifically, psychologist Kenneth Hugdahl and others have argued that differences in the mean age at death of left-handers and right-handers are an artifact of the relationship between age and the incidence of left-handedness found in the population as a result of cultural pressure.[38]

According to this view, the differences in the incidence of left-handedness between younger and older persons are due to changing social norms—older persons are more likely to have been exposed to stronger pressure to shift from left-hand to right-hand use. Thus there are fewer left-handers, proportionately, among older persons—not because of early death (the elimination hypothesis), but because older persons were more likely to have had right-hand use imposed on them in childhood (the modification hypothesis.)

Hand switching does not appear to completely account for the distribution of handedness across the age span, however, and issues of handedness and its implications for mortality continue to be discussed and debated.[39] Coren, meanwhile, has continued to focus his attention on data showing that left-handers are more susceptible to accident-related injuries resulting from the fact that left-handers must deal with tools, equipment, and traffic patterns that are designed for the safety and convenience of right-handers. His most recent work has examined whether the probability of skeletal injuries of the kind that result from accidents is different for left- and right-handers.[40] The findings based on large samples of young adults were supportive of the hypothesis that left-handedness predisposes an individual to such injuries. Coren suggests that incorporating handedness on mandatory forms used to report accidents could help isolate accident "hot spots" for left-handers in the work environment and eventually lead to redesign of those environments to make them equally available and safe for use by both left-handers and right-handers.

Chapter 6

Sex Differences in Cognition and Asymmetry

Consider the following simple experiment. In one condition, subjects are asked to mentally run through the alphabet and count the number of letters, including the letter *e*, that when pronounced contain the sound "ee." In a second condition, subjects are asked to count the number of letters that contain curves when they are printed as capitals. In both conditions, the subjects must perform the task "in their heads." Writing or speaking out loud is not permitted. Participants are told to do each count as quickly as possible because the results are scored for speed as well as for accuracy.

Which task is harder, counting sounds or counting curves? The outcome of this study, it turns out, depends on whether male or female subjects are being tested. Males are more accurate and slightly faster in the shape task; females do better in the sound task.[1]

This study is one of many pointing to sex differences in certain human abilities—in this case, verbal and spatial skills.[2] Considerable evidence suggests that females, on average, are superior to males in a wide range of skills that require the use of language, such as verbal fluency, speed of articulation, and grammar. Women also tend to be faster than men at tasks involving perceptual speed (the ability to rapidly identify matching items), manual precision, and arithmetic calculation. Males, on the other hand, perform better, on average, in tasks that are spatial in nature, including maze performance, picture assembly, block design, mental rotation, and mechanical skills. In addition, males do better than women in mathematical reasoning and in finding their way through a route, and are also more accurate in guiding or intercepting projectiles. Figure 6.1 shows some of these differences.

It is intriguing to note that the types of abilities that differ by sex appear to be roughly the same ones that differentiate the hemispheres in terms of function. Are sex differences in cognitive abilities related in some way to sex differences in the organization of the brain? Are there differences between men and women in hemispheric asymmetry? In this chapter we will review the fascinating and frequently conflicting evidence bearing on sex differences in brain organization and how they might be related to cognition.

The Case for Sex Differences in Asymmetry

Some Clinical Evidence

If the hemispheres of the brain are organized differently in men and women, one would expect to find some evidence of those differences reflected in the effects of brain injury. Herbert Lansdell, working at the National Institutes of Health, was among the first investigators to note that the consequences of damage to one-half of the brain appeared to differ for males and females.[3] Lansdell was interested in studying the effects of the removal of part of the temporal lobe on one side of the head in patients operated on to alleviate epileptic seizures. A wealth of earlier research had led him to predict greater deficits in visuospatial tasks after operation on the right hemisphere and greater deficits in verbal tasks following left-hemisphere surgery. His predictions were borne out, but only for male patients. These unexpected findings led Lansdell to speculate that some physiological mechanisms underlying visuospatial and verbal abilities might overlap in the female but be located in opposite hemispheres in the male brain.

Later work has pointed to the same conclusions. For example, psychologist Jeannette McGlone reported data from 85 right-handed adults

FIGURE 6.1 (*Right*) Tasks for which there are sex differences in performance. [From D. Kimura, "Sex Differences in the Brain," Scientific American, Inc., 1992. All rights reserved.]

Problem-Solving Tasks Favoring Women

Women tend to perform better than men on tests of perceptual speed, in which subjects must rapidly identify matching items—for example, pairing the house on the far left with its twin:

In addition, women remember whether an object, or a series of objects, has been displaced:

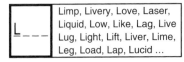

On some tests of ideational fluency, for example, those in which subjects must list objects that are the same color, and on tests of verbal fluency, in which participants must list words that begin with the same letter, women also outperform men:

L - - -	Limp, Livery, Love, Laser, Liquid, Low, Like, Lag, Live Lug, Light, Lift, Liver, Lime, Leg, Load, Lap, Lucid ...

Women do better on precision manual tasks–that is, those involving fine-motor coordination–such as placing the pegs in holes on a board:

And women do better than men on mathematical calculation tests:

77	$14 \times 3 - 17 + 52$
43	$2(15 + 3) + 12 - \dfrac{15}{3}$

Problem-Solving Tasks Favoring Men

Men tend to perform better than women on certain spatial tasks. They do well on tests that involve mentally rotating an object or manipulating it in some fashion, such as imagining turning this three-dimensional object

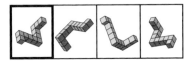

or determining where the holes punched in a folded piece of paper will fall when the paper is unfolded:

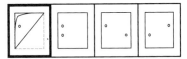

Men also are more accurate than women in target-directed motor skills, such as guiding or intercepting projectiles:

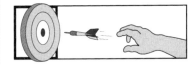

They do better on disembedding tests, in which they have to find a simple shape, such as the one on the left, once it is hidden within a more complex figure:

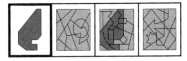

And men tend to do better than women on tests of mathematical reasoning:

1,100	If only 60 percent of seedlings will survive, how many must be planted to obtain 660 trees?

with damage to the left or the right side of the brain.[4] Most had suffered a stroke, although some were tumor cases. Each patient was given a battery of psychological tests, including the Wechsler Adult Intelligence Scale (WAIS) and an aphasia test, to determine whether the pattern of verbal and nonverbal deficits that emerged was a function of both sex and side of damage.

The results for language impairments were striking. Aphasia after damage to the left hemisphere occurred in males three times more frequently than in females. Even when patients showing signs of aphasia were excluded from the analysis, deficits in higher verbal tasks in the remaining patients continued to be more common and more severe in males.

In contrast, performance on the nonverbal subtests of the WAIS did not show any significant differences due to sex or side of damage. When performance on the nonverbal tests was compared with performance on the verbal tests, however, differences by sex and side of lesion again appeared. The relevant measure is the difference between the score on the nonverbal IQ items and the verbal IQ score. For men, left-hemisphere damage impaired verbal IQ more than nonverbal IQ, and right-hemisphere damage lowered nonverbal performance relative to verbal. Women showed no effect of side of lesion. Their verbal and nonverbal IQ scores were not significantly different for damage to the left or the right side. These data also support Lansdell's speculation that both language and spatial abilities are more bilaterally controlled in females than in males.

Have Sex Differences Always Been Present?

How can these findings of sex differences be reconciled with over 100 years of clinical investigations of hemispheric asymmetry that did not report sex differences? One possible explanation is that many older studies involved patient populations that were predominantly male. Patients in Veterans Administration hospitals, who are almost exclusively male, have been among those most extensively studied. Patients suffering from war-related brain damage have also been the object of much research; they, too, are overwhelmingly male. Populations having surgery on the temporal lobe are biased as well. Most surgery of this type is done to alleviate epilepsy, a disease that is much more common among males.

Another important factor that can help explain the failure of early work to notice sex differences is simply that no one specifically looked for them. There is tremendous variation from patient to patient (even within one sex) in the effects of unilateral brain damage. Damage to certain regions in the left hemisphere of some right-handed individuals produces a massive disruption of language skills, whereas comparable damage in other individuals has a minimal effect. This variability in the effects of brain damage within groups of males and females makes it difficult to find differences between males and females unless the investigator is working with a large subject population and is specifically looking for those differences.

With these ideas in mind, James Inglis and J. S. Lawson performed an interesting reanalysis of a number of older studies that investigated the effects of unilateral brain damage on verbal and spatial abilities without looking for sex differences.[5] Inglis and Lawson predicted that studies reporting significant verbal and spatial deficits in groups with left- and right-brain damage, respectively, would be found to contain many more male than female patients. Those studies that did not report this pattern of deficits would be expected to contain more female than male patients, they argued, because reduced laterality effects in women would mask the stronger effects found in men. Their reanalysis strongly supported these hypotheses and has provided additional evidence for the importance of sex differences in the study of brain injury and brain lateralization.

Anatomical Evidence for Sex Differences

In Chapter 3 some of the evidence pointing to anatomical differences between the hemispheres was reviewed. Mounting interest in sex differences in lateralization has encouraged investigators to see whether sex is a factor in these asymmetries; findings suggesting that it is have begun to appear.

In one large investigation of brain asymmetry assessed postmortem, brain measurements were reported as the ratio of the length of the right temporal plane to the length of the left temporal plane.[6] Overall, this ratio was less than 1, reflecting a longer plane on the left side. Of those individuals showing a reversal of this pattern, however, most were female. If a reversal is assumed to reflect greater bilaterality of function, these findings are consistent with the other data reviewed so far. Females seem to be less lateralized.

A recent MRI study produced similar results—the planum temporale was 38% larger in males, on average, but no asymmetry was
found in females.[7] Other work has looked at measurement of the Sylvian fissure.[8] Investigators found that although the horizontal component of the Sylvian fissure was larger in the left hemisphere for both
sexes, men had a larger horizontal component in the left hemisphere
than did females. No difference was found in the right hemisphere.
Although some studies have failed to find evidence supporting sex differences in anatomical asymmetries, overall the results suggested a sex
difference in brain anatomy in the regions important in speech and
language.[9]

The corpus callosum is another area of the brain that has been
extensively studied anatomically, most recently for the possibility of
sex differences. A study of brain scans from 146 healthy subjects by
neuroanatomist Laura Allen and neuroendocrinologist Roger Gorski
showed a dramatic sex difference in the shape of the corpus callosum.[10]
Although there were no significant differences in overall size of the corpus callosum as a function of sex, the splenium (the last one-fifth of the
corpus callosum) was more bulbous shaped in females and more tubu-
lar in males. It is not known whether this difference is related to a sex
difference in the number or relative distributions of axons.

Neuroanatomist Sandra Witelson has also investigated the corpus
callosum with regard to possible sex differences as part of an extensive
project begun in 1977 to study the relationship between structure and
function in cognitively normal adults.[11] The brains she has studied
were obtained from people with metastatic cancer who agreed to participate in testing and permit an autopsy to allow study of their brain
in the event of death.

Witelson found that the corpus callosum, as well as the splenium, is
comparable in overall size in males and females when size is corrected
for brain weight. It is important to do this correction, because males
have larger brains consistent with their larger overall size. Witelson did,
however, find that the isthmus, a thin region just in front of the splenium, is relatively larger in females. She also found that the size of the
callosum decreases with chronological age in males but not in females,
and that callosal size varies with handedness in males but not in females. Although the significance of these sex differences is still unclear,
the pattern of relationships is an intriguing one that will no doubt be investigated in future work.

Still further evidence of sex differences in brain structure has been
reported by Witelson, most recently in terms of differences in the number of neurons per unit volume in a specific region of auditory associ-

ation cortex.[12] In the brains of the five men and four women, all right-handed, the number of neurons per unit volume was greater by 11% in women, with no overlap in scores between the sexes. Thus, for this region of the brain, women had a higher density of neurons. While expressing caution because of the small sample size, Witelson noted that these results provide a first step to finding a cellular basis that might underlie the well-known but little-understood sex difference in overall brain size. It is possible that the differences in neuronal density she found may also be related to the way cortical neurons connect, and that these differences in density could have behavioral consequences.

Sex Differences in Cognition:
Linkages to Asymmetry

The existence of sex differences in certain cognitive functions as well as in brain anatomy has encouraged investigators to look for evidence that would demonstrate the existence of functional asymmetries that would differ for men and women.

New Findings from Neuroimaging

A recent and widely cited study by Bennett and Sally Shaywitz and colleagues has demonstrated differential patterns of activity in the brains of men and women during a cognitive task.[13] The research involved the use of fMRI to measure blood-flow changes in the brain in 19 men and 19 women, all of whom were right-handed. Blood-flow data were collected while each subject was tested in several sets of tasks, including one set in which the subjects judged whether pairs of letter strings contained the same pattern of upper- and lowercase letters, for example, BtbT appeared on the top and BtbT appeared on the bottom, and one in which subjects decided whether pairs of visually presented nonsense words rhymed, for example, GOOZ on the top, REWS on the bottom. In both of the examples presented, the subjects pressed a response bulb to indicate a match. No response was required when the stimuli did not have the same alternation of upper- and lowercase letters or did not rhyme.

By comparing the pattern of blood-flow activity obtained in the second set of tasks with that obtained during the first, the investigators calculated the pattern of brain activity specifically resulting from the processing of speech sounds in the rhyming task. For all 19 men studied, the results showed an increase in blood flow in the left hemisphere in the inferior frontal gyrus. For 11 women, blood flow increased about evenly on both sides of the brain in that region, and 8 of the women showed a tendency, smaller than that shown by the men, for more activity on the left side. No sex differences in blood flow were found in other conditions that involved recognition or word comprehension, however, a result suggesting that the difference in blood-flow pattern found between men and women was limited to the processing of phonological information. There were also no differences between men and women in accuracy in any of the tasks. The investigators concluded that brain activation in males is lateralized to the left inferior frontal gyrus region during phonological processing, whereas in females, the pattern is different and engages more diffuse neural systems involving both hemispheres.

The approach used in the Shaywitz's study is one that will no doubt be extended to other components of language processing as well as to other cognitive tasks. However, the premise that investigators can isolate a region of the brain responsible for a specific cognitive operation by subtracting a control condition is one that is not universally accepted. The results are intriguing, however, and no doubt other approaches will be employed to investigate these sex-specific patterns of brain activity further.

The Case from Behavioral Data

A number of researchers doing traditional behavioral studies of laterality have looked at the possibility of sex differences, either as the main purpose of the research or as an incidental part of it. The results have been highly variable, with a large proportion showing no significant differences in laterality measures between males and females. Three recent analyses of a large number of these studies have concluded, however, that despite considerable variation among studies, overall they support the conclusion that males show greater evidence of lateralization of function.[14]

In conducting one of these analyses, Daniel Voyer looked at a total of 396 comparisons of laterality effects in males and females drawn from 266 different studies.[15] The studies primarily involved dichotic listening and divided visual field techniques with a variety of verbal and nonverbal stimuli. Using metaanalysis, a technique that allows an investigator to consider the outcome of a large number of experiments at the same time, Voyer concluded that the data support the existence of sex differences in lateralization—specifically, for greater lateralization in males.

Are Sex Differences in Laterality Real?

Although many studies have found evidence of sex differences in hemispheric asymmetry, others have not. This situation, which is especially true of behavioral studies, but is also true of anatomical and neuroimaging studies as well, has led some investigators to question the reality of sex differences in laterality in the first place. Some have argued that this area of research is inherently plagued by bias in the reporting of results.

Investigators are much more willing to report differences between groups (and journal editors are much more eager to accept such studies) than they are to publish negative or "no-difference" results. Critics have suggested that journals contain a biased sample of the studies that are actually carried out and that the majority of studies that do not find evidence of sex differences are never published. This situation has been referred to as the "file drawer" problem.

Those who believe that sex differences in laterality are real counter this argument with one that challenges the statistical sensitivity of studies that fail to find evidence of sex differences. They note the tremendous variability in lateralization within a given sex and point out that this variability makes it very difficult to detect real, but small, differences between the sexes.

Are there sex differences in the distribution of verbal and spatial functions between the hemispheres? Much of the evidence reviewed in the preceding sections suggests that there are. A variety of findings suggest that males tend to be more lateralized for verbal and spatial abilities, whereas women show greater bilateral representation for both types of functions. But what about bias in the report of findings? Aren't there studies (most of which we do not know about because they are never published) that fail to find these purported sex differences?

Our review of the lateralization literature in general has given us a healthy respect for the file drawer problem and the scientific chaos it can create. The frequency as well as the consistency of reports of sex differences in cerebral organization, however, lead us to accept their reality, at least as a working hypothesis. The strength of the case, in our opinion, rests on the diversity of methodologies (clinical studies, behavioral research, neuroimaging) that point to the same conclusion: Females are less lateralized than males. A review of those studies that do not support this conclusion shows that most of them report no differences between the sexes. It is rare to find a study that reports sex differences in the direction of greater lateralization in females. This consistency in the direction of asymmetries that are reported suggests that there are true sex differences that are small in magnitude and easily masked by individual variability or other factors that may not be controlled.

The Origin of Sex Differences

Assuming that sex differences in laterality are real, it is natural to ask how such differences might have arisen. The speculations that have been offered come in two forms—first, some hypotheses about the origin of sex differences in cognition, and second, some ideas about the brain organization that presumably underlies them.

A number of investigators have suggested an evolutionary basis for sex differences in cognitive abilities.[16] The hunter–gatherer theory makes the case that in evolutionary history it was the male who was more likely to be involved in hunting and navigation, a task leading to selective pressure on abilities such as orienting oneself in relation to objects or places, and performing the mental transformations necessary to maintain accurate orientation during movement. Females, as primarily foragers, would seek food closer to home base and would have evolved greater sensitivity to small changes in the appearance of infants and the immediate familiar environment. The superiority of females on many types of verbal tasks would fit nicely into this analysis if one assumes that language became a valuable tool for communication in the context of the forager role.

But how might these differences in cognitive functioning relate to hemispheric asymmetry? Jerre Levy has offered a suggestion in terms of a model of neural structure in which the "optimal" brain organization depends on the particular skills being selected for.[17] She has proposed that greater bilateralization of function may facilitate the skills needed by females, because those skills appear to require a blending of the specializations of the hemispheres that may be best achieved by their representation within each hemisphere, along with good communication between them. Stricter separation of function, however, would be needed to ensure the high level of visuospatial skills needed for hunting. The cognitive crowding hypothesis, which we briefly discussed in Chapter 5, is based on the idea that two or more cognitive abilities primarily controlled by the same hemisphere will compete for available neural tissue. If it is assumed that verbal skills displace spatial skills when they share the same "neural space," the optimum neural arrangement to ensure a high level of spatial ability would be separation of spatial–verbal functions across the two hemispheres.

Hormones and Cognitive Function

In Chapter 5 we discussed a theory by Geschwind and Galaburda that proposed a relationship between prenatal levels of testosterone and brain organization resulting in particular patterns of handedness.[18] Although these ideas are highly controversial, they have stimulated research on another issue—the differences in brain organization between males and females.

A great deal of evidence points to the profound effect of sex hormones on mammalian development, both physical and behavioral, although much remains to be learned about their effects on brain organization and cognitive functioning in humans.[19] As background for the discussion to follow, we should note that sex hormones are secreted by the testes in males, by the ovaries in females, and by the adrenal glands in both males and females. Both males and females produce the hormones found in both sexes, with the relative concentrations of these hormones varying by sex and life-cycle stage. Females have greater concentrations of female hormones, estrogen and progesterone, whereas males show greater concentrations of male hormones, the androgens (testosterone is an androgen).

Early in life, the action of sex hormones establishes sexual differentiation; if the testes of a genetically male organism do not produce androgens or if the hormones cannot act on the developing tissue, the organism will develop as a female. It is also well established that sex hormones organize gender-specific behaviors early in life. If a rodent with functional male genitals is deprived of androgens right after birth, it will show enhanced female sexual behavior and reduced male sexual behavior as an adult. The reverse is also found; if androgens are administered to a female directly after birth, her behavior as an adult is more characteristic of a male. In this section we will review findings suggesting an important role for sex hormones in human cognition, both during development and in later life.[20]

Effects of Prenatal Hormones

Studies relating prenatal hormones and cognitive behavior in humans have been relatively recent and few in number. Nevertheless, the results are intriguing. Studies of children with a genetic disorder known as congenital adrenal hyperplasia (CAH) have provided evidence bearing on the cognitive effects of hormones present early in life.[21] In CAH the adrenal glands produce abnormally high quantities of androgens, beginning in the third month of fetal life. Researchers have found that the effects of early androgen exposure can be seen later in life in behavioral differences between CAH girls and their unaffected sisters, even when the hormonal balance is restored to normal. One such difference is enhanced spatial ability in the CAH girls.

Other research has looked at the relationship between prenatal sex hormones and cognitive function in male subjects whose mothers had taken diethylstilbestrol (DES) while pregnant.[22] Diethylstilbestrol, a synthetic form of estrogen, was commonly used in the 1950s as a treatment, now known to be ineffective, to prevent miscarriage. A control group consisted of male siblings who were not exposed to DES. The DES-exposed group scored lower than their nonexposed brothers on the spatial component of the Wechsler Intelligence Scales, which included measuring the time to find the missing parts of a picture and complete a jigsaw puzzle. Although overall performance and

IQ did not differ between the groups, the researchers believed that exposure to DES in utero changes, very subtly, the way men approach spatial tasks.

Hormone Levels in Adulthood

Doreen Kimura and her colleagues have conducted a number of investigations relating naturally occurring hormone levels to cognitive performance.[23] Several studies have looked at the relationship of level of testosterone and measures of spatial ability, both between sexes and within a given sex. In general, it is the women with higher levels of testosterone who excel on spatial tests, whereas in men it is those with lower levels. This finding suggests that superior spatial ability may be associated with an optimal level of testosterone, most likely in the low male range.[24]

Other research has shown that the performance of women on certain tasks changes throughout the menstrual cycle.[25] The investigators chose tasks that typically show the largest male–female differences, such as speed of articulation and spatial tests. They found that women performed significantly better at midcycle (when estrogen and progesterone are at their highest levels) than during menstruation (when hormones are low) on speed of reciting a tongue twister, verbal fluency, and a manual dexterity task. Performance on spatial tasks, however, was better during the low-hormone part of the cycle. A control group of nonmenstruating women receiving hormone replacement therapy showed the same pattern of performance, whereas a control group of those not receiving replacement therapy did not show the variation.

Daily fluctuations in the level of testosterone in males have also been shown to affect spatial ability. Overall, men perform worse on spatial tasks in the morning, when testosterone levels are highest, than they do later in the day.[26] There have been reports as well of seasonal fluctuations in spatial ability in men, with improved performance in the spring when testosterone levels are lower.[27]

Sexual Orientation and Asymmetry

Sexual orientation is the most recent biological variable to be related to hemispheric asymmetry. Although the factors responsible for same-sex sexual preference are unknown, there is ample evidence that the factors involved are biological, and perhaps neurohormonal, in nature. We have just considered how hormonally mediated biological sex is related to cognitive abilities and brain organization. In this section, we will consider data pointing to a similar relationship as a function of sexual orientation.

Anatomical studies have been limited, but one study measuring size of the corpus callosum found the cross-sectional area of the anterior commissure to be larger in gay men than in heterosexual men.[28] There is evidence that hand-preference patterns differ as well.[29] Data suggest a higher prevalence of nonconsistent right-handedness (defined as left-hand preference for at least one of 12 manual tasks) among gay men and women than in the general population.

Data on cognitive abilities, however, have been inconsistent. Several papers have reported that gay men show lower spatial ability than heterosexual men do, although a recent study with a sample size substantially greater than that of any prior study found no significant relationship between sexual orientation and spatial ability.[30] The same study also failed to find any differences in handedness. The authors concluded that any association between sexual orientation and either spatial ability or handedness is probably smaller, and more difficult to detect, than previous studies would indicate.

More robust effects of sexual orientation on spatial ability have been found on tasks that involved throwing to a target. In one study by Jay Hall and Doreen Kimura, heterosexual men made smaller errors than gay men.[31] The performance of gay men did not differ from that of heterosexual women. A finger dexterity task that favors women did not reveal any difference between heterosexual and gay men. Hall and Kimura suggested that gay men may show either a male-typical or female-typical pattern, depending on what function is being studied.

Much more remains to be learned about the relationship between sexual orientation, cognition, and brain organization. Because gay and heterosexual males have comparable levels of circulating hormones, any explanation based on hormones must look to differences present earlier in life.

Mathematical Talent: Sex, Handedness, and Immune Disorders

Mathematical talent is one of the newest areas to attract the interest of neuropsychologists looking at possible biological bases for cognition.

It has been defined as a high level of mathematical reasoning ability demonstrated at an early age. One of the most striking characteristics of the mathematically highly talented is that they are much more frequently male than female.

Using the mathematics section of the College Board's Scholastic Aptitude Test (SAT-M) to measure mathematical talent, Camilla Benbow and her colleagues analyzed data from a large group of intellectually talented seventh-graders, with males and females equally represented.[32] The ratio of boys to girls scoring 500 on the SAT-M was about 2 to 1, increasing to about 4 to 1 for students scoring 600; and to 13 to 1 for those scoring 700.*

Both nature and nurture explanations have been offered to explain this sizable sex difference. Benbow has argued that the data supporting socioeconomic explanations such as differential course taking in school, social attitudes, and gender stereotyping are weak, and that biologically based approaches are more likely to be fruitful. As part of her continuing efforts to understand the mechanisms underlying sex differences in mathematical ability, Benbow has looked at handedness as a variable. When she limited her subject sample to those with the very highest scores, she found frequency of left-handedness, as measured by a questionnaire, to be twice the figure found in the general population. She also noted that about 50 percent of these extremely precocious students were either left-handed, mixed-handed, or were right-handed with left-handed family members. Benbow proposed that this evidence supports the idea that bilateralization, rather than greater specialization of the hemispheres, is associated with extreme mathematical ability.

The incidence of allergies was also very high in this population; over 50 percent of the extremely precocious students had allergies, twice the frequency found in the general population. Benbow related both the allergy data and the handedness data to the Geschwind and Galaburda idea that higher testosterone levels in utero slows the development of the left hemisphere while simultaneously affecting immune development.

More recently, Benbow and her colleagues have obtained EEG recordings of brain activity from gifted and average male and female

---

*To put these scores in context, a score of 600 on the SAT-M falls in the seventy-eighth percentile for twelfth-grade males, and a score of 700 falls in the ninety-fifth percentile.

adolescents in two conditions involving word pairs and chimeric face pairs.[33] For word stimuli, subjects were asked to choose which of two words, for example, vomit or smile, conveyed the more pleasant sentiment, whereas for the chimeric face stimuli they were asked to judge which of two faces appeared to be the happiest. Previous work had shown that when a chimeric face is created by using one smiling side and one neutral side, the left side smile–right side neutral composite is subjectively judged to be happier than its mirror-reversed counterpart. This has been related to greater right-hemisphere engagement during the task, despite the fact that the stimuli are presented in free vision.

The results revealed an interesting pattern of brain activity that differentiated the gifted and average subjects. In the word task, gifted subjects activated frontal regions to a greater extent than control subjects, who tended to activate temporal regions. This pattern was true for both male and female subjects. During the chimeric face test, however, a pattern of brain activity unique to gifted males was observed. When judging which of two chimeric faces was happier, gifted males exhibited significant inhibition of left-hemisphere electrical activity. The authors interpret this result in terms of a pattern of disengagement that allows the right hemisphere to play a predominant role in analyzing the face composites for their affective context. They go on to speculate that such inhibition may minimize undesirable cross talk between the cortical areas in the right hemisphere and other areas of the brain. Female subjects in both groups were more bilaterally engaged during face processing.

In terms of overall response, gifted subjects, and males in particular, were more likely to choose the left side smile–right side neutral face as happier, again presumably reflecting greater right-hemisphere activation in the task. In fact, the degree of right-hemisphere involvement in the chimeric task in gifted males and females was predictive of their general intelligence and of measures of nonverbal intelligence in particular.

These data, then, provide an interesting glimpse of the way in which patterns of brain activity in the intellectually gifted differ from those of average ability. Although Benbow and her colleagues continue to believe that these sex-related patterns of cortical activity result from prenatal exposure to high levels of testosterone, the data themselves do not provide any independent support for that linkage. Much more work remains to be done before the bases of mathematical talent are fully understood.

The Significance of Sex Differences

From a theoretical standpoint, the significance of sex differences in brain organization is considerable. If sex differences are real, what is (or was) their adaptive advantage? How does brain organization relate to patterns of higher mental function? Do sex differences in child-rearing practices affect brain asymmetries? These are a few of the many important questions that remain unanswered.

Particularly interesting is the issue of how ability is related to extent of lateralization. Does greater lateralization for a given function imply superior performance for that function? Is the spatial ability of males better than that of females because males seem to rely more on one hemisphere to process spatial information? There is, of course, no logical reason to expect that greater lateralization necessarily leads to superior ability. In fact, we have to assume the opposite to explain the superior verbal ability of females. According to behavioral tests and clinical data, women appear to be less lateralized for language functions, yet as a group they are superior to men in language skills. And, as we have just seen, mathematical talent may be related to greater bilateralization of function as well.

There may be a relationship between lateralization and ability that is different for different tasks. If this is the case, it would be fascinating to know why the brain organizes itself so differently for the optimal functioning of different abilities. At this point, we can only speculate about the relationship of lateralization and ability. For example, assume that complex visuospatial capability preceded the evolution of language in humans (which is a reasonable assumption). One can then postulate that in men only the left hemisphere became involved in language, leaving visuospatial functions intact in the right, whereas in women language was established in both hemispheres, crowding visuospatial capability. If this in fact occurred, "more lateralized" would be better for visuospatial function, whereas "less lateralized" would be better for language.

Psychologist Diane Halpern has proposed an alternative way of conceptualizing sex differences in cognitive abilities that may not only more accurately capture the nature of such differences, but may be helpful in thinking about the brain mechanisms that underlie them.[34] Instead of focusing on the type of task to be performed (e.g., verbal or spatial), Halpern has proposed a process model in which cognitive tasks are analyzed in terms of what the subject does to perform the task. Specifically, Halpern predicted that females will show superior performance on tasks that require rapid access to and retrieval of information from memory, and that males will show superior performance when maintaining and manipulating a mental representation is required. The findings of her preliminary studies to test this hypothesis are encouraging and suggest that this reconceptualization of sex differences in cognition may be useful in accounting for a variety of data.

Although most investigators would probably agree that theoretical questions of the sort we have just considered are significant, undoubtedly there would be less agreement concerning the practical meaning of sex differences in brain organization and cognitive function. There is also concern, not without foundation, that data on sex differences in cognition may be misused and politicized in harmful ways.

It is essential to remember that sex differences in higher mental functions are typically on the order of one-fourth of a standard deviation. In other words, there is a great deal of overlap in the distribution of ability across men and women. Some women have better spatial abilities than most men, whereas some men have better verbal skills than most women. Awareness of the extent of the overlap in ability should temper any suggestion that sex be used as a major criterion for determining career options and educational opportunities. The need for curricula and methods of instruction better geared to individual abilities is clear. What is equally clear is that neither sex, nor handedness, nor any other single variable or simple combination of variables can be used as a shortcut to assessing those abilities. Diane Halpern summarized the situation as follows:

> Knowledge about individual and group differences in how people think, learn, and remember is essential for understanding human cognition and developing educational programs and theories that can identify cognitive weakness and capitalize on cognitive strengths. The real enemy is the potential for misuse of knowledge, not the knowledge itself.[35]

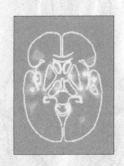

PART IV

From the Clinic to the Laboratory

Integrating Neuropsychology and Neuroimaging

Chapter 7

Language, Voluntary Movement, and Perception

Contemporary Neuropsychology

In Chapter 1 we reviewed from a historical perspective how the concept of brain asymmetries developed from data on brain-injured patients. In this chapter, we will continue our review of the insights into brain function gleaned from studies of the effects of various injuries to the cerebral hemispheres. This pursuit is the realm of clinical, experimental, and cognitive neuropsychology. Before the days of CT scans and other brain-imaging methods, neuropsychologists emphasized the use of their clinical skills to predict the location of damage in patients showing various functional or behavioral disturbances. Modern neuropsychology still does this to an extent, when neurological and physiological techniques show questionable findings; but the emphasis is on comprehensive assessment of any mental and behavioral dysfunction accompanying evidence of brain damage, usually for clinical purposes but often also for theoretical insight.

Modern neuropsychology attempts to extend our understanding of psychological processes by examining the ways in which they break down. Sometimes a behavior thought to be a unitary mental process turns out to be a complex interaction; at other times, investigators discover that what were thought to be separate mental activities actually arise from the same brain mechanisms. Memory, language, and emotion are among the psychological processes that have been studied.

Information obtained from the brain-damage clinic must be interpreted very carefully. Neuropsychologists studying brain–behavior relationships must rely on lesions occurring naturally or on lesions created by surgeons for medical reasons. These are usually less than ideal for answering specific questions an investigator might wish to ask. Natural lesions, such as those caused by stroke, do not respect anatomical boundaries. A lesion may destroy an area of the brain involved in some psychological process, it may disconnect areas contributing to this process, or it may do both.

There are other confounding problems as well. In Chapter 1 we mentioned the brain's tendency to adjust its operations as best it can in the presence of damage. As neurologist John Hughlings Jackson pointed out a century ago, the abnormal behavior observed after a brain lesion reflects the functioning of the remaining brain tissue. This remaining tissue may compensate for the damage and thus minimize the deficit. However, it may also react adversely and operate more poorly, thus adding to the deficit—a situation thought to arise primarily through "diaschisis," the effects a lesion can have on more remote areas of the brain by destroying nerve fiber tracts and normal interconnecting pathways.

Cognitive Neuropsychology

The advent of cognitive neuropsychology, introduced in Chapter 1, has not changed the importance of the problems discussed above, but it has more explicitly connected them to the assumptions underlying the cognitive neuropsychological approach. In Chapter 1 we briefly described an assumption of cognitive neuropsychology, namely, that of the "modularity" of mental processes, which holds that mental activity is the result of the coordinated activity of many different "modules," each of which engages its own form of processing independently of the activity in others.

Several other assumptions are also implicit in the approach taken by cognitive neuropsychologists.[1] These include the following ideas:

> *Neurological specificity or isomorphism:* the assumption that there is a correspondence between the organization of the mind and the organization of the brain

Transparency: the assumption that impaired performance following brain injury will provide us with a basis for determining which mode of the system is disrupted

Subtractivity: the assumption that the performance following brain injury reflects the previous intact cognitive apparatus minus those systems that have been impaired; subtractivity also assumes that the mature brain does not produce new modules

The first two assumptions are, for the most part, implicit in all neuropsychological research, both past and present, that seeks to establish brain–behavior relationships from the effects of brain damage. With regard to the subtractivity assumption, cognitive neuropsychology is somewhat more explicit in regard to how brain injury affects the hypothesized modular organization of the brain. A very literal (or strong) form of the subtractivity assumption implies that brain injury does not affect the normal function of modules not directly damaged by the injury; therefore, performance following brain injury reflects the normal operation of all undamaged modules.

This last statement is almost certainly an oversimplification, because at least some undamaged brain is likely to adjust some aspect of its normal operation. Most cognitive neuropsychologists agree with this conclusion; however, they insist that what matters is not that old modules can be put to new use but that new modules should not come into existence following brain injury.[2] They believe that if the brain can truly reorganize its structure and generate new modules following injury, then it is not possible to learn much about normal brain function from clinical disorders. However, all indications are that most neural destruction, once it occurs, is permanent and that compensation and recovery must depend on changes in spared brain. It is relatively safe, therefore, to assume that an injured brain functions only with spared preexisting modules, although these may modify their operations as recovery progresses and new strategies are developed over time.

The modularity concept is not accepted by all neuropsychologists and is constantly undergoing modification. We will mention some of the revised views later, including a distinction between modular and "central" processes when we discuss memory in Chapter 8. Some neuropsychologists do not invoke "modular" to describe any function, preferring to model cerebral organization and hemispheric differences in terms of more subtle shifting gradients of specialization.[3] Other neuropsychologists are now emphasizing computational and computer modeling approaches that invoke a great deal of "connectionism" in the brain and, in effect, run counter to some of the assumptions of modularity.[4] The use of parallel distributed processing (PDP) models is an example we will discuss later in Chapter 13. Despite these questions, changes, and challenges, however, the concept of modularity continues to serve a useful purpose—a well-defined model that is a starting point for evaluating what is and what isn't compartmentalized in the brain.

A discussion of neuropsychological disorders involves many concepts and definitions that have been developed over the years by investigators. We will not attempt to trace these developments but will present certain concepts as established while citing newer studies in greater detail.* We will briefly discuss some of the more general concepts of brain structure–function relationships gleaned from the study of brain injury and from neuroimaging studies of normal brain activity, concentrating on how newer data has furthered our understanding of functions within each cerebral hemisphere.

Disorders of Speech and Language

Language is a complex, multifaceted skill that encompasses the formation of sounds, the development of sophisticated rule systems, and the existence of a vast quantity of meaning and significance information. Linguistics, the formal study of language, has developed many concepts that deal with the structure of a language and apply to all languages.

Linguists have defined four major components of language: phonology (dealing with producing and processing speech sounds); syntax (involving the rules of word order and form, or grammar); semantics (the processing of meaning); and pragmatics (involving intonation in speech, practical significance, and context).

The term *aphasia* has become the general heading for a broad class of speech and language dysfunctions caused by neurological damage. We will review here the major categories of aphasia with respect to how they arise from damage to different areas of the brain and the extent to which they shed light on the organization of linguistic processes. The study of the aphasias also provides classic examples of the theoretical

*The interested reader is referred to some of the excellent texts that review clinical neuropsychology in general.[5]

controversies that can arise when psychological theories are formulated from clinical data.

The Aphasias

The two major categories of aphasia are expressive (motor) aphasia and receptive (sensory) aphasia. Not all investigators, however, adhere to this distinction.

Expressive aphasia, also known as Broca's aphasia, is a deficit involving primarily the patient's own speech; the patient's comprehension of the speech of others remains relatively intact. This type of aphasia is associated with damage to the frontal regions of the left hemisphere controlling speech output, particularly the region called Broca's area. Broca's area, shown in Figure 7.1, is located just in front of the primary

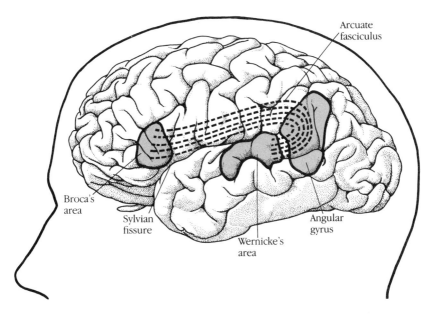

FIGURE 7.1 Areas of the left hemisphere associated with speech and language in humans. The arcuate fasciculus is a nerve-fiber bundle beneath the cortex, connecting Broca's and Wernicke's areas. [Adapted from Geschwind, "Language and the Brain," Scientific American, Inc., 1972. All rights reserved.]

motor zone for speech musculature (lips, tongue, jaw, and so on). These speech motor areas, however, are spared in cases of classic Broca's aphasia; that is, there is no paralysis of the speech apparatus.*

A patient with Broca's aphasia speaks very little. When speech is attempted, it is halting—the patient has difficulty getting the words out. There is an absence of small grammatical parts of speech and proper inflection. Such speech is often called telegraphic or agrammatical speech. For example, in response to a picture showing a woman washing dishes, an overflowing sink, and some children tipping a stool as they attempt to get a cookie jar, a Broca's aphasia patient might say, "Sink . . . water . . . b . . . boy . . . boy fall . . . step . . . ." In severe cases the patient will often be able to vocalize only one or two words over and over again in any attempt to speak or describe something.

When a patient does say a word, it is usually pronounced reasonably well. The ability to name objects is poor, but prompting helps significantly. These facts help justify the view that the deficit is not simply at the level of articulation. Most Broca's aphasics seem to understand spoken or written language, so the problem is considered to be at the motor output stage of language rather than in comprehension. Patients also seem to be aware of most of their errors. Some investigators have argued, however, that the comprehension of Broca's aphasics is not as intact as many have believed. When the syntactic structure of a sentence is more complex, comprehension seriously falls off. Patients seem unable to properly utilize the information conveyed by complex grammatical structure.

Receptive aphasia, also known as Wernicke's aphasia, is a disturbance in which the patient has great difficulty comprehending speech. It is associated with damage to the posterior region of the first temporal gyrus, or Wernicke's area (see Figure 7.1). The speech of a patient with receptive aphasia is much more fluent than that of an expressive aphasic, but, depending on the extent of damage, it may vary from being slightly odd to completely meaningless. Patients often use inappropriate words (paraphasias) or nonexistent words (neologisms). In some cases, the patient's output sounds like complete jargon or "word salad," although the rhythm and flow of speech seem to be preserved. One patient, when asked how he was, responded, "I felt worse because I can no longer keep in mind from the mind of the minds to keep me from mind and up to the ear which can be to find among ourselves."[6]

---

*Impairment of speech (such as slurring) due to partial paralysis of the speech musculature is called dysarthria.

In severe cases, it may consist mostly of meaningless utterances yet sound fluent, as in the following exchange [examiner's interjections in brackets]:

Examiner: How did you get sick?
Patient: Eeh, oh malaty? Eeeh, favility? Abelabla tay kare. Abelabl tay to po stay here. [stay here?] Aberdar yeste day. [yesterday?] and then abedeyes dee, aaah, yes dee, ye ship, yeste dey es dalababela. Abla desee, abla detoasy, abla ley e porephee, tee arabek. Abla get sik? [get sick?][7]

Such patients often seem unaware that their speech is defective or meaningless and continue to talk as if nothing were wrong.

Reading and writing are comparably impaired. There are aphasic patients who will go through the motions of reading a book out loud but produce only gibberish. Some investigators believe that Wernicke's aphasia results from damage to verbal or semantic memory stores, as distinct from a defect in syntactic and articulatory mechanisms involved in Broca's aphasia.[8]

Beyond the Expressive–Receptive Distinction

Although relatively pure forms of expressive and receptive aphasia do occur, the division of aphasia into these two categories implies a more clear-cut distinction than is generally the case. Patients often show symptoms attributed to both types of aphasia, and some investigators feel the distinction is too artificial—not truly representing how language is organized in the brain. We will review some of these criticisms later but must first consider several other categories of aphasia. Beyond the expressive–receptive distinction, investigators have labeled other forms of aphasia, according to both patterns of brain damage and patterns of language deficits. Some of these categorizations are controversial, yet many neuropsychologists and speech pathologists argue that they truly represent distinct, recurring clinical syndromes.

Besides the receptive aphasia named after him, Wernicke predicted another type of aphasia that he claimed would arise from a lesion interrupting the neural pathways connecting the centers for speech production (Broca's area) and speech comprehension (Wernicke's area). This aphasia, now labeled conduction aphasia, is characterized by a patient's inability to repeat aloud what is heard. In addition, spontaneous speech may be meaningless, fluent jargon (as in Wernicke's aphasia), but unlike comprehension in Wernicke's aphasia, comprehension of spoken and written material remains largely intact.

These symptoms can be explained as arising from a disconnection of the receptive and expressive language centers of the brain. In fact, damage to the neural tract called the arcuate fasciculus, connecting Broca's and Wernicke's areas (see Figure 7.1), has been implicated in such cases.[9] Stuart Dimond has claimed that the arcuate fasciculus, along with some subcortical structures (the thalamic region), is involved in integrating the input and output aspects of speech.[10] He also suggested that these neural tracts and associated structures form a storehouse of linguistic information and may act as language generators.

The anatomical model for conduction aphasia was elaborated further by Norman Geschwind to explain several other combinations of symptoms observed in aphasic patients.[11] The transcortical aphasias involve lesions that spare the speech areas and their main interconnecting pathways but, in a variety of ways, isolate these areas from the rest of the brain. Depending on whether brain damage isolates Wernicke's area (transcortical sensory aphasia), Broca's area (transcortical motor aphasia), or both (transcortical mixed aphasia), there are various degrees of comprehension and spontaneous speech problems. Such patients, however, are able to repeat quite well what is said to them. Transcortical aphasics, in extreme cases, may echo everything they hear, a condition known as echolalia. This sparing of repetition ability is what distinguishes transcortical aphasia from Broca's, Wernicke's, or conduction aphasia, where repetition is disturbed. Several additional aphasia types should also be mentioned.

Word deafness results from a lesion disconnecting Wernicke's area from auditory inputs. Comprehension is impaired for spoken language only; the ability to hear sounds in general is not affected. Comprehension of writing is normal, as is verbal and written expression, although the patient's speech may eventually also suffer because the patient lacks adequate feedback from his own speech.

Anomic aphasia involves difficulty in naming objects. Although this condition is present in most aphasics, a "purer" or isolated form results from damage limited to the cortical area at the junction of the temporal, parietal, and occipital lobes—the area called the angular gyrus (see Figure 7.1). A purely anomic patient will have normal comprehension and be able to speak almost normally in spontaneous casual conversation. When confronted with objects, however, or when trying to think of a word or a name, the patient will falter badly. It has been suggested that this impairment is a result of disruption of associations involving different sensory modalities (and, hence, different regions of the brain) that are part of the naming act.

Global aphasia refers to severe impairment of all language-related functions. Comprehension as well as production of speech are defective or absent in global aphasia. Communication may be attempted with a symbol system—for example, by learning to use plastic objects to stand for words—but even this approach is difficult and sometimes unsuccessful. Global aphasia results from widespread damage to the left hemisphere involving most of the areas thought to play a role in language.

Theoretical Issues Arising from Aphasia Classification

The view that there are discrete cerebral centers performing specific aspects of language processing has been called the localizationist–connectionist view (or localizationist–associationist, in the sense that most modern concepts that attribute functions to specific areas of the brain also place importance on the interactions between these areas in any complex mental activity.) It has served to categorize the variety of language disorders seen in clinical settings and, to an extent, to predict the kind of disorder one might expect to see after specific types of brain damage. Evaluating a patient's language disorder can also do the reverse, that is, predict where the damage might be.

The localizationist approach has been criticized, however, by investigators who claim it is overly simplistic in its "flow diagram" view of the brain and the organization of language, placing too much emphasis on independent components or depots interconnected by neural wiring.[12] Such criticisms can be traced back to the nineteenth-century holistic view of brain function, when neurologists such as Jackson argued that all aphasia is associated with defective comprehension, that is, that sensory aphasia underlies all others.

Cognitive neuropsychologists have not faulted the idea of independent components itself; rather, they have placed an emphasis on the need to reorganize our conceptions of what the components or "modules" really are.[13] Most neuropsychologists have agreed, however, that the actual situation is more dynamic than the traditional connectionist view, involving simultaneous interactions of many areas for any language function. The evidence mentioned for comprehension deficits in Broca's aphasia supports such a viewpoint, as does a great deal of contemporary neuroimaging research.

Neuroimaging Studies of Language

Functional neuroimaging studies have, in general, confirmed and extended, rather than contradicted, language findings based on clinical data. We mentioned in Chapter 3 blood-flow studies and new PET procedures that literally visualized aspects of brain activity associated with language. The multistage subtraction technique employed in the PET studies of Marcus Raichle, Michael Posner, and associates isolated the cerebral activity associated with several stages of language processing, demonstrating the important role of the left temporal lobe and other left hemisphere structures in speech and language that was predicted by clinical studies. Their studies included an experiment in which brain activity during semantic analysis was localized to the left frontal lobe when subjects generated appropriate action verbs in response to nouns[14] (see Color plate 11).

A series of fMRI studies of language-related versus nonlanguage auditory processing by Jeffrey Binder and colleagues reported results that differed from the PET studies of the Posner and Raichle group.[15] One experiment employed a semantic monitoring task, in which subjects responded when they considered an animal name heard in a series of tape-recorded names to be both (1) found in the United States and (2) used by people as pets, clothing, or food. The control task consisted of determining whether tone sequences contained two occurrences of a specific tone and was designed to control for simple auditory stimulation and various attentional and linguistic functions. Both conditions were alternated within the same fMRI scanning session. Subtraction of the control task from the semantic monitoring task revealed activation of the frontal region as well as posterior association cortex (see anatomy in Figure 7.2) of the left hemisphere during semantic monitoring (Color plate 12).

The earlier PET research, as previously noted, had suggested an almost exclusive left frontal localization for semantic processing. The authors of the fMRI study argued that the PET study results are at odds both with clinical data and numerous lesion studies indicating

FIGURE 7.2 (*Right*) Neuroanatomical locations. A. Primary sensory and motor areas of the brain. The remaining areas (unshaded) are often termed "uncommitted" or "association" cortex. B. Major landmarks of the lateral surface of the cerebral hemisphere, cerebellum, and brain stem. C. Deep brain structures. The basal ganglia (caudate nucleus, putamen, globus pallidus) surround the thalamus but are not shown in this illustration.

A

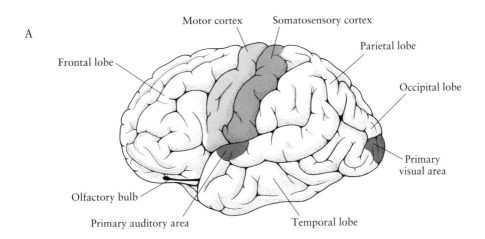

B

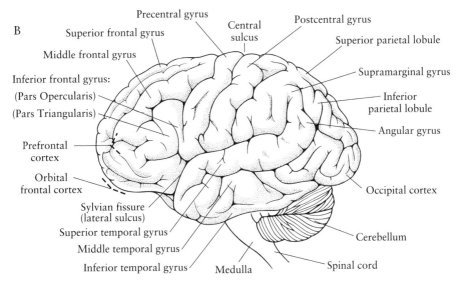

C

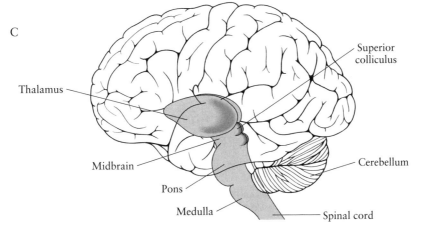

major semantic knowledge deficits after posterior temporal and temporal–parietal lesions of the left hemisphere, and with their own findings. They cited studies indicating that the frontal areas serve as an "executive" component of the language system that facilitates access to posterior semantic memory stores.* The frontal regions may be more continuously active than the posterior information storage regions, the authors further suggested, thus making them more readily apparent on functional imaging studies of intact brains.[16]

Although the argument for both frontal and posterior involvement in semantic processing may be correct and both imaging studies attempted to isolate higher level language stages involving semantic processing, the two imaging studies did not really study identical processes. It can be argued, for example, that the fMRI study did not really separate or control for phonological analysis with the pure tone control task; thus the results combine both phonological and semantic aspects of language processing more than the results of the PET study did. At the same time, the results of the fMRI study do make more sense when viewed in the context of clinical data. Such issues currently abound in the interpretation of functional neuroimaging studies and in attempts to reconcile new findings with the older clinical literature. The inconsistencies or controversies raised often appear to be resolvable if attention is paid in future research to experimental design and differences in conceptualization.

The Enigmatic Role of Broca's Area

Several neuroimaging studies have found a surprising degree of activation in Broca's area during tasks that at first glance seem to involve primarily perception and comprehension of speech stimuli, rather than speech production, which is the more traditional view of this region's role in language.[17] Some studies reported activity in Broca's area during tasks involving distinguishing speech sounds such as "br" versus "pr," as well as during consonant–vowel syllable discrimination and rhyming tasks.

One PET study attempted to identify the cerebral structures associated with phonological processing by having subjects monitor the occurrence of different phonemes in pseudowords, and in lexical–semantic

---

*These issues, relating to memory processes, are discussed in some detail in Chapter 8.

processing by having subjects evaluate concrete nouns on the basis of meaning. The control task involved monitoring changes in pitch. The investigators reported that phonological processing led to activation of the left superior temporal gyrus and parts of Wernicke's area, and to some activation of Broca's area. Lexical–semantic processing led to activation in left middle and inferior temporal regions, inferior parietal, and superior prefrontal regions, in addition to those areas activated by phonological processing alone.[18] (Figure 7.2 will assist the reader in identifying some of the anatomical regions discussed here.) Another PET study concluded that Broca's area was activated during lexical processing of single words, that phonological processing activated the middle temporal gyrus, and that semantic or conceptual processing activated Wernicke's area (left superior temporal gyrus).[19]

Despite some inconsistencies in precisely what aspect of speech perception activates Broca's area to the greatest extent, the number of studies reporting involvement of Broca's area appears to provide some support for the motor theory of speech perception, which proposed that perceiving speech involves accessing the same cerebral system used for producing speech. We will discuss this idea in greater detail when we consider several models attempting to account for hemispheric asymmetries in Chapter 13. The PET group headed by Richard Frackowiak has conducted a great number of studies of language and memory function and concluded that Broca's area serves an important role in the phonological processing stage of speech perception, along with a region in the inferior parietal cortex that serves as the "phonological store" or repository of phonological-code-related memory.[20]

Neuroimaging Sentences and Stories

In a PET study of sentence-level language processing, B. M. Mazoyer and associates had native French speakers listen to a story in French, a story in a foreign language (Tamil), lists of French words, a French story in which every content word was replaced by a pseudoword, and a French story in which every content word was replaced with a grammatically appropriate but semantically unrelated word (semantic anomaly condition). The investigators reasoned that the foreign language story would result in only acoustic processing, that French word lists would result in acoustic, phonological, and lexical processing, that pseudoword sentences would involve acoustic, phonological, prosodic, and syntactic processing, and that only the good French story would engage semantic or conceptual processing.

Despite the heroic attempt to create conditions which, with appropriate subtractions, would identify and separate many stages of sentence processing, the study failed to show consistent regional brain activity with several of these stages, including syntactic processing. They concluded that the large network of areas in the left hemisphere activated by meaningful material correspond to those areas identified in lesion studies, but that this network of activity is barely evident during languagelike but meaningless input.[21]

Despite this, they concluded that Broca's area was activated during lexical processing of single words, that phonological processing activated the middle temporal gyrus, and that semantic or conceptual processing activated Wernicke's area (left superior temporal gyrus). In addition, the investigators suggested two different memory roles for the left and right temporal poles (anterior tips of the temporal lobes). After subtracting the lexical and phonological component of continuous speech, the activity remaining in the left temporal pole appeared to be associated with linguistic content, whereas activity in the right temporal pole was for prosodic and pragmatic aspects.

Partly because they failed to find consistent activity associated with some of the proposed stages in language processing, the authors rejected the serial model of speech-sound processing in which individual specialized brain regions successively activate to process the phonological, lexical, semantic, and other aspects of the stimulus. Instead, it is was proposed that there is coordination of a network of areas, operating in parallel, each of which may be specialized in one aspect of speech processing.

A more recent PET study was able to find a consistent activation associated with syntactically complex sentences compared with less complex sentences. The study involved comparison of comprehension of several different sentence structures, including center-embedded relative clauses ("The juice that the child spilled stained the rug") versus right-branching relative clauses ("The child spilled the juice that stained the rug"). They found that blood flow in the vicinity of Broca's area (particularly in the pars opercularis) was greater during judging the meaningfulness (semantic plausibility) of syntactically more complex sentences. The researchers suggested that this activation may be related to the greater memory load associated with processing center-embedded sentences.[22]

How Distributed Is Lexical Knowledge?

A series of PET studies by Hanna and Antonio Damasio and colleagues has revealed the intriguing possibility that retrieval of different classes of words is, in effect, mediated by different parts of the left hemisphere. The Damasios have been particularly interested in what neural structures become active when a word that denotes a person or object is recalled and is either silently verbalized or vocalized, that is, "when an item from the lexicon of a given language is retrieved and explicitly represented in the mind."[23] Although they agreed that the traditional language areas around the Sylvian fissure (including Broca's and Wernicke's areas) figure prominently in reconstruction and phonemic representation of word forms, they felt that additional neural sites, in many regions of the brain, support conceptual knowledge and that the general location of these sites depends on distinct conceptual categories. They based their claim on naming studies of visually presented items in 127 patients with discrete lesions in various parts of the two hemispheres as well as on a PET study conducted with the same tasks in normal subjects.

The clinical study task required the naming of 327 visually presented items representing three word groups—(1) unique persons (photographs of well-known people), (2) animals, and (3) tools—and was used to test retrieval of words denoting entities belonging to three distinct conceptual categories. The animal and tool categories were both nonunique, basic object categories, that is, they did not represent instances of a specific well-known animal as did the faces of the people. Results from the clinical data showed a disruption of word retrieval category that was, in fact, dependent on lesion location within the left temporal lobe. Abnormal retrieval of words for persons was correlated with damage clustered in the left temporal pole; abnormal retrieval of words for animals was correlated with damage to the inferior temporal region; and abnormal retrieval of words for tools correlated with damage to more posterior sections of the inferior temporal region extending back to the junction with occipital and parietal lobes. Although there were some instances of combined defects, for example, "persons/animals," or "animals/tools," there were almost no instances of a combined "persons/tools" defect, a result further validating the greater anatomical separation for these two classes indicated by the lesion data.[24]

Positron emission tomography studies of normal subjects completely supported the clinical data, showing the greatest blood-flow activation in the three separate regions of the left hemisphere during naming tests involving the three categories of items. The person-naming task also activated the right temporal pole, a result that was not unexpected on the basis of other evidence for a right hemisphere role in face recognition. The authors suggested that this activation emphasizes the difficulty of separating recognition and naming processes in normal subjects. The Damasios hypothesized that the left temporal lobe regions identified in these studies play an "intermediary" role in lexical retrieval, serving to promote access to the knowledge representations involving different sensory modalities and neural networks throughout the two hemispheres (we will discuss a related issue, the idea of cerebral "convergence zones" in Chapter 8). In keeping with this view of an intermediary role for the temporal regions identified in the Damasio study, preliminary studies of concept retrieval involving conceptual categories similar to those used in this experiment indicated that the cerebral regions most strongly associated with two of the categories are in the right hemisphere.[25]

Language Beneath the Cortex

Neurologist Jason Brown has proposed an alternative to the standard cortical localizationist view. Synthesizing the work of several earlier theorists, he described the organization of the brain in terms of evolutionary layers modified by maturational growth.[26] Speech and language emerge in Broca's and Wernicke's areas simultaneously from more primitive linguistic stages operating below. Thus, cortical lesions do not so much disconnect the cortical flow of information necessary for language as force the language system to operate at a more primitive, incomplete level.

Some support for such a hierarchical view of language organization comes from evidence that certain subcortical structures, particularly the thalamus, play an important role in language.

Subcortical Aphasia: The Role of the Thalamus

Lesions to brain structures deep within the brain, especially the thalamus, can result in language disturbances. The thalamus is also divided into right and left halves. Damage to the left thalamus has been reported to affect verbal fluency, creating word-finding hesitation as well as perseveration (repeating the same sound or word several times).[27] As mentioned in the discussion of conduction aphasia, it has been suggested that the thalamus is an integrating center between frontal and posterior cortical language areas.

Neurosurgeon George Ojemann reported on the effects of electrical stimulation of the thalamus, using a procedure similar to the cortical stimulation tests described in Chapter 1. Left thalamic stimulation typically led to speech arrest or to problems with object naming coupled with perseveration of the initial syllable of the word a patient was attempting to say. Ojemann also reported that there was a general slowing, slurring, and distortion of speech. He suggested that the thalamus has two general functions in speech: (1) to serve as an alerting mechanism to direct attention to verbal information in the environment as well as to retrieve verbal information properly from verbal memory; (2) to control, at least in part, some of the physical substrates of speech, such as respiration and the speech musculature.[28]

Left Hemispherectomy

Hemispherectomy, or removal of one-half of the brain, is a rare operation and, despite the name, usually involves removing only the cortex or outer layer of the hemisphere. It is sometimes performed in infants suffering from serious cerebral birth defects. Because of their age, such children often recover and develop remarkably well after the operation. We will discuss childhood hemispherectomy in Chapter 10.

Hemispherectomy is performed very rarely in adults, usually for removal of malignant tumors. The operation is almost never performed on the dominant hemisphere, because of the very severe consequences. Nevertheless, left hemispherectomies offer investigators the opportunity to examine the functions of the right hemisphere in isolation. Neuropsychologist Aaron Smith and others have extensively studied such patients.[29] Several patients made significant recoveries, although they initially showed markedly impaired language function. They were eventually able to produce short, relatively grammatically correct sentences. Most left-hemispherectomy patients show a surprising amount of verbal comprehension, although their voluntary speech, reading, and writing abilities remain severely impaired.

An important case example that contributes to our understanding of how the two hemispheres may interact involves a patient who underwent surgery to remove most of a damaged right hemisphere.[30] The patient's language improved after the surgery! This outcome suggests that the damaged right hemisphere hindered the potential of the left hemisphere. It is very probable that normal communication between the hemispheres involves a substantial number of inhibitory signals, an exchange that serves to coordinate function and prevent unnecessary duplication or competition. When one hemisphere is damaged, its inhibitory effects on the other may become pathological or, at least, inappropriate for recovery of function. The extent to which such pathological inhibitory effects take place makes interpretation of the effects of focal brain damage that much more difficult. It is also possible that understanding pathological inhibition eventually may allow surgeons to develop a rationale for when to remove damaged brain tissue for therapeutic reasons.

Reading and Writing

Disorders of reading and writing accompany some types of aphasia, especially aphasias resulting from posterior lesions. We mentioned, for example, how some Wernicke's aphasics go through the motions of reading aloud but produce only jargon. Reading and writing, however, can be selectively impaired; that is, a reading deficit or a writing deficit can be the primary problem after certain brain injuries even though speech production and comprehension remain relatively intact.*

Most reading and writing disorders involve either direct damage to the left angular gyrus or damage to adjacent regions. As mentioned in the discussion of anomic aphasia, the angular gyrus is located at the junction of the parietal, temporal, and occipital lobes and is thought to integrate the sensory, auditory, and visual information processed by these regions, respectively. This central position adjoining the major sensory and language comprehension systems of the brain seems to make the left angular gyrus fundamentally important to reading and writing.

---

*Our discussion of reading and writing disorders here concerns only those acquired following injury, after a person has developed the skills. Developmental disorders in children will be discussed in Chapter 11.

Investigators have subdivided disorders of reading and writing into two main categories: alexia with agraphia (inability to read and write) and alexia without agraphia (inability to read, but with writing spared). Alexia with agraphia almost always involves damage to the angular gyrus. In addition to deficits in reading and writing, it is often accompanied by some aphasic deficits, such as difficulties in word finding and naming. Alexia without agraphia is a rather astonishing condition to observe, for patients with this disorder can write a sentence properly, either spontaneously or from dictation, but when this writing is shown to the patients, they cannot read it.

Alexia without agraphia has been explained as a "disconnection" between certain visual processing areas of the brain and the angular gyrus. It seems to arise when lesions damage the left occipital lobe and a part of the neural tracts forming the corpus callosum. The lesion to the corpus callosum disconnects the intact right occipital lobe from the left angular gyrus, leaving little, if any, visual information flow to the language processing areas.[31] Thus, these patients cannot read, although they can still see. Writing is preserved because the angular gyrus is intact and because writing can proceed with only minimal visual feedback.

A more controversial form of alexia, labeled deep dyslexia, has been described and is believed to demonstrate some right-hemisphere reading skills.[32] (The nature of right hemisphere language skills will be discussed in the next section.) When asked, for example, to read aloud the printed word *table,* some alexic patients with left-hemisphere damage will respond with *chair.* This type of error is called paralexic and involves a wrong response that is nevertheless meaningfully relative to the target word. It has been proposed that brain lesions have entirely inactivated the normal reading mechanisms of the left hemisphere in such patients. The right hemisphere, having some semantic skills, understands the word and communicates some meaning information to the left hemisphere. The semantic information conveyed by the right hemisphere is not enough to distinguish among synonyms or closely related words, however, and thus the paralexic errors are made by the speaking left hemisphere.

As part of the evidence that supports this theory, researchers have found that patients who make paralexic responses in attempting to read do so to concrete words such as object nouns, whereas they show little or no response to abstract words. As we will see, there is evidence that right-hemisphere comprehension abilities, although limited, do include concrete words.

The Role of the Right Hemisphere in Language

Semantic processing, the comprehension of word meanings, is severely disrupted in patients with damage to posterior regions of the left hemisphere, like that found in Wernicke's aphasia. No similar disruption can be demonstrated with right-hemisphere lesions. However, as mentioned in our discussion of split-brain patients in Chapter 2, investigators have demonstrated that the right hemisphere can show comprehension of certain words, especially object nouns. Some research with normal subjects suggests that the extent to which a word's meaning is understood by the right hemisphere depends on how concrete (as opposed to abstract) it is.[33] Thus, correct comprehension of words such as *justice, harmony,* and *hate* seems to depend more exclusively on left-hemisphere processing than does comprehension of words such as *table, car,* and *hospital,* which the right hemisphere can also understand.

The right hemisphere's ability to understand certain words, however, probably does not contribute much to our speech and language skills in the intact brain, because the left can do the same and more. But does the right hemisphere make any unique contributions to our language communication skills? The answer, based on observing many patients and several studies with normal subjects, appears to be yes.

The multistage PET studies of language organization led by Michael Posner and Marcus Raichle in the late 1980s, which we described in part in Chapter 3, included a final stage, involving accessing meaning, when subjects thought of and spoke a verb representing an appropriate use for each noun they heard or read. A blood-flow scan was generated during this task, from which was "subtracted" the image obtained during the previous stage of the experiment when subjects just spoke the nouns aloud. The cerebral activity associated with the resulting image represented, according to the investigators and the logic of subtraction, the pure mental activity associated with accessing meaning. This turned out to involve blood-flow increases in the left hemisphere only, mostly in frontal regions.[34] We discussed earlier an fMRI study that also found posterior left activation in a somewhat different but nevertheless "semantic" task. Another fMRI study, attempting to replicate the tasks of the PET study, found that frontal areas of both the left and right hemispheres were activated during the semantic task.[35]

An independent and very different study, performed at about the same time and involving visual field testing, may help explain when semantic tasks activate the right hemisphere. Atsuko Nakagawa examined the effects of a variety of semantic primes, varying from very strong to very weak associations, on the subsequent recognition of words presented to the left and right visual fields. *Pound* would be a common or strong associate for *hammer,* whereas *drop* would be a very weak associate for *hammer.* The study showed very different patterns of priming by the two hemispheres. Priming by only the strong, frequent associations made a difference in left-hemisphere performance, whereas the right hemisphere benefitted from even the weakest associations.[36] Posner has suggested that the unilateral left frontal activation seen in the verb generation task of his original PET studies is due to the fact that subjects had very little time, were very focused, and responded with very common verb associations to each presented noun. The fMRI study, however, presented words at a slower rate, allowing subjects to come up with less common associations at least part of the time and resulting in right-hemisphere frontal activation as well as left.[37] Although there are other possible explanations for the difference between these studies, this interpretation fits well with other evidence indicating a right-hemisphere dominance for less literal, more metaphorical aspects of word meanings and language.

Intonation

Communicating through speech and language involves many subtle nuances such as intonation patterns and emotional tone that are not an obvious part of the structure and content of sentences.

Many left-hemisphere-damaged aphasic patients can discriminate the purpose of an utterance and, despite their problems with verbal output, attempt to use the correct pattern to produce a statement (as opposed to a question).[38] Patients with right-hemisphere damage, however, often speak with a flattened intonation; they also have difficulty judging the emotional tone of the speech produced by others.[39] Right-hemisphere-damaged patients have been known to add parenthetical phrases to their speech to emphasize their feelings—for example, "I am angry (and mean it)."[40] This behavior occurs after the patients realize that their speech is not sufficiently forceful or emotional to evoke the desired response.

Neurologist Elliot Ross has developed a model of how lesions of different areas of the right hemisphere result in the disruption of the rhythmic and intonational aspects of language ("prosody") in a manner analogous to the way in which left-hemisphere lesions disrupt the syntactic and semantic aspects of language. Thus, Ross claimed that there is a "conduction aprosodia" and a "transcortical sensory aprosodia" and so on.[41] This model, although supported in part by the general evidence for a right-hemisphere role in intonation, remains controversial in terms of its finer distinctions.

Melodic Intonation Therapy

The preservation of intonation and singing that often occurs in aphasic patients (see Chapter 1) has been exploited in therapy designed to teach such patients phrases through song. The program, called melodic intonation therapy, has been successful with certain patients who have reasonably good comprehension but poor speech production, such as Broca's aphasics. Word sequences are first incorporated in a song, and the melody is deemphasized gradually until the patient can speak the phrase without singing. It is presumed that the intact right hemisphere learns the phrases this way and, as a result, develops more language production skills that compensate, to a degree, for the left-hemisphere deficit. The program's developers claimed that some aphasic patients, after not having had any meaningful speech for over a year following a stroke, are able to carry on short, meaningful conversations after a month or two of therapy.[42]

Metaphor and Humor

There are several other language-related skills in which the right hemisphere appears to be involved. For example, right-hemisphere-injured patients, but not left-hemisphere-injured patients, tend to be overly literal in their interpretation of words, stories, and cartoons. Given a choice, they often pick literal interpretations of metaphorical statements ("sour grapes") and popular sayings ("A penny saved is a penny earned."). They also very frequently pick totally inappropriate endings to cartoon strips, as if the humor is in a surprise ending.[43]

We see again that the right hemisphere contributes in important ways to language communication. In addition to possessing some comprehension abilities, as discussed earlier, it truly complements left-hemisphere speech and language processing through more subtle, but definitely important, communication skills. Emotional intonation, aspects of metaphor, and some qualities of humor seem to depend on right-hemisphere abilities. The extent to which the right hemisphere enriches other language skills remains to be determined.

The Right Hemisphere in Recovery from Aphasia

Partial or complete recovery from initially severe deficits after stroke or head injury is not uncommon. Reports generally show that most improvement occurs during the first 6 to 12 months, depending on a number of factors such as age, cause, and severity of the original symptoms. The fact that recovery does take place raises a number of issues concerning the mechanisms responsible for it and the plasticity of the central nervous system.

One of the hypotheses offered to explain the recovery of language after left-hemisphere damage is that structures of the intact right hemisphere become more involved in language processing. Wernicke was probably the first to propose this idea, which has continued to be entertained by investigators to this day. In the late 1800s it was observed that recovered aphasics who had sustained left-hemisphere injuries relapsed after new lesions developed in the right hemisphere.[44]

Related findings were obtained by Marcel Kinsbourne, who studied the effect of intracarotid injection of barbiturates (the Wada procedure) in three patients recovering from aphasia due to left-hemisphere lesions.[45] Although injection into the left carotid artery did not worsen speech, right carotid injection resulted in arrest of speech in two of the three patients.

More recent work has examined recovery by using more direct physiological measures of brain activity. One probe-evoked potential study showed greater than normal participation of the right hemisphere during a language task in patients who had recovered from aphasia.[46] Some cerebral blood-flow data also supports increased participation of the right hemisphere in recovery from aphasia.[47] Related issues were also noted in Chapter 2 in our discussion of the language capabilities of the disconnected right hemisphere in split-brain patients.

Another possible mechanism for recovery of function has to do with the resolution of "diaschisis." We briefly mentioned diaschisis earlier in discussing how brain tissue that is not directly affected by an injury or stroke may nevertheless react adversely and operate more poorly. It is thought that this adverse response occurs because the injury interrupts neural pathways and information that normally stimulates the area involved. Functional neuroimaging scans have recently shown this to indeed be the case in cerebral regions outside the lesion in some stroke patients: Some areas of the brain outside of the stroke area are less than normally active despite an adequate blood supply. Thus, diaschisis immediately poststroke may account for some of the patient's deficits and, as the area recovers, may also account for the recovery of those deficits.[48] Color plate 13 shows SPECT scan images of cerebral blood flow in an aphasic patient one month after a left-hemisphere stroke and one year later, when the patient had made a significant recovery.

The "resolution of diaschisis model" and the "unaffected hemisphere taking on new functions model" are competing but not necessarily mutually exclusive explanations of recovery. Both probably occur in many cases.

Disorders of Purposeful Movement

Our daily activities involve many movements that have become almost automatic. We perform many complicated acts without having to think about how to do them, from picking up a pen, to drinking from a cup, to putting on perfume. Patterns of complex learned movements are organized in terms of both position and timing and follow intricate sequences established through experience. Apraxia is the inability to perform certain learned or purposeful movements despite the absence of paralysis or sensory loss. This breakdown in movement can occur in a number of ways.

Kinetic (or motor) apraxia is most frequently associated with lesions of the premotor area of the frontal lobe on the side opposite the affected side of the body. It affects the finer movements of one upper extremity, such as properly holding a pen or placing a letter in an envelope. Kinetic apraxia may be regarded as a breakdown in the program or "memory" of the motor sequences necessary to perform some basic act.

Ideomotor apraxia is usually due to damage in the parietal lobe of the left (dominant) hemisphere, but it seems to have bilateral effects behaviorally. Patients are unable to perform many complex acts on command, although they may perform them spontaneously in appropriate situations. The difficulty is especially noticeable when patients are asked to use pantomime, for example, when asked to "Pretend you are brushing your teeth." Given the actual objects and appropriate context, patients will usually perform much better. The main disturbance seems to be in voluntary recall of some action, not in its actual execution. Therefore, it seems that the motor memory of the action is not disturbed, as it is in kinetic (motor) apraxia. Ideomotor apraxia is considered to be a result of the interruption of pathways between the center for verbal formulation of a motor act and the motor areas of the frontal lobe necessary for its execution.

Ideational apraxia involves an inability to formulate an appropriate sequence of acts or to use objects properly. Patients seem to know how to perform isolated movements, such as striking a match, but will do them inappropriately. For instance, given a candle and a book of matches, they may strike the candle against the matchbook cover. Sometimes complex sequences are done out of order: Patients may start the hand motions involved in writing before picking up a pen.

The patients' appreciation of what they are doing often seems to be defective, so it has been suggested that such apraxia is a form of agnosia, a deficit in knowing or perceiving the object properly. The assigned locus of damage in such disorders is controversial. A classic view was that ideational apraxia arose from lesions in the parietal lobe of the left (dominant) hemisphere or in the corpus callosum. It is most frequently found, however, in cases of diffuse bilateral damage, such as that following disruption of the oxygen supply to the brain (anoxia).

Constructional apraxia involves a loss in the ability to reproduce or construct figures by drawing or assembling. There seems to be a loss of visual guidance or an impairment in visualizing a manipulative output, although basic visual and motor functions appear to be intact. It is seen in certain cases of damage to the occipital and parietal cortex, and perhaps to pathways between them.

Although the incidence of deficits called constructional apraxia by various investigators seems to be the same for either left- or right-hemisphere lesions, later reviews show that there are characteristic differences in the quality of performance on constructional tasks between left- and right-hemisphere-injured patients.[49] For example, when the left hemisphere is damaged, patients draw pictures that preserve the overall configuration of objects but tend to lose detail; this result supports the view of the right hemisphere as better at perceiving overall spatial relationships. When the right hemisphere is damaged, patients draw pictures that include much detail but lack an overall coherence. Proportion and spatial relationships are often quite poor.

The Role of the Hemispheres in Apraxic Disorders

As noted earlier, ideomotor apraxia and, possibly, ideational apraxia much more often involve lesions of the left hemisphere than of the right. The anatomical model for ideomotor apraxia explains it as a disconnection between posterior brain areas for verbal formulation of an act and those areas of the frontal lobes that generate the motor output.

There is a high incidence of apraxia in aphasic patients, but the fact that the two disorders can occur relatively independently suggests that apraxic disturbances involve motor memories that in some cases can be separated from the speech system. It is intriguing to speculate, nevertheless, that there is a similarity in the mechanisms required to produce speech and those required to produce fine motor movements of the limbs. A recent PET study provided some further evidence for this.

The study compared PET scans of subjects preparing and executing a right-hand finger movement with scans of the subjects just executing the movement. In both conditions subjects viewed a drawing of a right hand on a screen. The "execute only" condition was a simple reaction-time task in which one of the fingernails in the drawing was briefly marked and a short tone was sounded. Subjects were to respond quickly with a movement of the same finger on their own hand. The time intervals between stimuli and the finger marked varied so that the subjects could not anticipate the next move they were to make.

In the "prepare and execute" condition, after one of the fingernails was briefly marked, the subjects were asked to prepare to move the appropriate finger of their right hand, but not to execute the movement yet. Three seconds later a short tone would tell the subjects to move the finger they had prepared to move. Time intervals between trials were constant, so that subjects could anticipate the time of the next movement and prepare the appropriate finger movement itself. Comparing the two conditions (subtracting the blood-flow activation pattern during "execute only" from the pattern during "prepare and execute") showed activation in a lower part of the left parietal lobe and an unexpected activation of part of Broca's area. The investigators concluded that Broca's area is not specialized only for the motor functions of speech but possibly for mental preparation of simple movements.[50] We will return to the topic of the similarity in the mechanisms required to produce speech and those required to produce fine motor movements in Chapter 13.

Constructional apraxia, as we have seen, appears to be not one but many different disorders involving either or both hemispheres.

Neuropsychologist Arthur Benton has provided some perspective on constructional apraxia in the context of distinguishing among various kinds of visual deficits.[51] He separated visuoconstructive, visuoperceptive, and visuospatial deficits and argued that the right hemisphere is most involved in the latter two disorders. For visuoconstructive tasks—those involving block designs and construction and figure drawing—both hemispheres are usually involved, although in different ways, as demonstrated in our brief discussion of constructional apraxia. For visuoperceptive tasks—those involving separating a figure from a complex ground, recognizing deformed objects, discriminating between faces—the right hemisphere plays a greater role than the left. Finally, for visuospatial tasks—those involving judgments of depth, line orientation, and matching simple patterns—the right hemisphere plays an almost exclusive role.

Imaging Imagined Movement

Neurophysiologist Per Roland showed in early PET studies that simple finger movements resulted in blood-flow increases confined to the contralateral sensorimotor hand region (within areas S1 and M1 of Figure 7.3). In contrast, performing a complicated finger sequencing task resulted in increased activity within the supplementary motor area (SMA, see Figure 7.3) and bilateral premotor areas (PMA, see Figure 7.3), in addition to the contralateral sensorimotor hand area activated during simple movements. Imagining the complex finger task produced blood-flow changes within the SMA, but not within the primary sensorimotor cortex. Roland proposed that the SMA is a higher order "supramotor" center involved in the generation and programming of complex movements.[52] This view is supported by patients with lesions of the SMA who have bilateral ideomotor apraxia for limb movements.[53]

Roland's proposal has also been supported by fMRI studies comparing simple motor tasks, complex motor tasks, and motor-task imagery.[54] Subjects performed simple finger tapping, complex finger sequence tapping (e.g., a 2431 sequence required tapping the middle finger, followed by the little finger, the ring finger, and finally the index finger), and imagined performing the complex task to a specific four-digit sequence. The simple task resulted in only the expected contralateral hemispheric activation, whereas the complex tasks showed some additional activation of SMA, bilateral activation of premotor cortex, and even some ipsilateral activation of primary sensorimotor cortex,

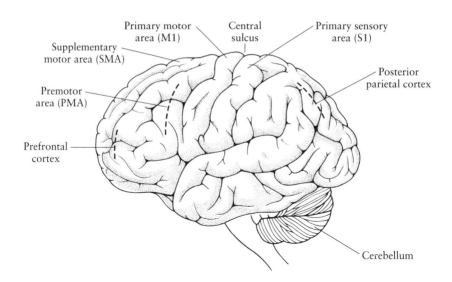

FIGURE 7.3 Cerebral areas involved in the planning and execution of voluntary movement.

that is, on the same side as the hand movements. The findings were consistent with Roland's hierarchical model of voluntary motor control in which the SMA and premotor cortex participate to a greater extent during complex sequential motor acts. During imagined complex movement, the largest changes were in the SMA, demonstrating, according to the authors, the sensitivity of the technique to higher order mental processing in the absence of motor activity.

Several other PET and fMRI studies have corroborated and expanded on these findings. Studies of subjects involved in tasks that alternated between performing a series of movements and just "thinking about" performing the same movements have indicated that the posterior region of the SMA may be involved in planning or imagining movements, with the remainder involved in the selection and execution of movements.[55] In addition, it was shown that part of the primary cortical motor area itself (M1, Figure 7.3) was activated during simulations (approximately one-third of that activated during actual task performance.) The authors suggested that the contribution of primary cortical motor areas to the imagining of a movement may indicate that primary cortex intervenes in the transition from intention to execution of a motor task or that it may have a role in the memorization process.[56]

In one of the first studies to show brain activity in certain motor and visual areas of the brain during mental simulation of a complex skill, David Ingvar and colleagues conducted a study of cerebral blood flow of tennis players imagining that they were playing tennis.[57] Blood flow increased in areas adjacent to sensorimotor cortex, in the cerebellum, and in regions adjacent to primary visual cortex. Thus, although the primary motor cortex itself did not activate, higher level motor regions (premotor cortex and SMA) thought to be involved in initiation and motor sequence planning were active during the imaginary movement activity, as were higher level visual areas. This fascinating finding has led to many follow-up studies and serves to remind us of the recently emerging general theme that many complex, even abstract, mental operations appear to require activation of cerebral structures involved in more basic motor, sensory, and perceptual processes.

Imaging Asymmetries in Motor Activation

An asymmetry in the activation induced by left- and right-hand movements was reported years ago by investigators using probe-based xenon-133 cortical flow measurements: nondominant (left) hand use showed significant increases in blood flow in the right motor cortex, but dominant (right) hand use showed barely perceptible increases in the left hemisphere. It was suggested that this occurred because dominant hand movement was highly automatic but that left-hand use required more effort or planning.[58] This asymmetry in the extent of activation of primary sensorimotor cortex during dominant and nondominant hand finger movements has been confirmed by newer techniques.[59] In addition, a recent fMRI study reported on the extent of activation of hemispheric regions ipsilateral to the hand doing the movement. Along with the very noticeable activation of contralateral primary motor cortex (M1) during finger movements of each hand, left-hand finger movements resulted in some activation of the primary sensorimotor cortex in the ipsilateral (left) hemisphere. The study suggested that nondominant hand movement is more complex than dominant hand movement, requiring the participation of ipsilateral cortical motor areas in addition to the contralateral areas.[60]

A recent PET study evaluated the effects of left and right thalamic lesions on glucose metabolic activity in each hemisphere in two patients in whom these lesions had produced impairment in visuospatial movement control. The patient with the right thalamic lesion exhibited marked misreaching for both hands in both visual fields, whereas the patient with a similar lesion in the left thalamus had a reaching deficit more confined to the right hand and right side of space. Scan analysis showed that metabolic activity was reduced in a large region outside of the lesion in both patients, but that the patient with the right lesion also had reductions in activity in some areas of the intact hemisphere. The investigators suggested that visuospatial motor control is lateralized to the right and that lesions of parts of the right thalamus may result in significant bilateral hemispheric effects, both in terms of regional metabolic activity and motor function.[61]

Another PET study reported a hemispheric asymmetry during learning new hand movement sequences. In addition to primary and supplementary motor area activation, the study showed increased activity in prefrontal cortex and right medial temporal regions during the initial phase of learning a hand movement sequence. The increased activity in frontal and right temporal regions disappeared after the movements were well learned.[62]

Perceptual Disorders

Our interaction with the external world depends on intact sensory and perceptual processes in the two hemispheres. We are all aware that damage to the peripheral organs of our senses, such as our eyes or ears, effectively destroys the use of a sensory modality. In a similar fashion, damage to areas of the brain receiving neural information directly from a sensory organ leads to blindness, deafness, and so on. However, there are many other more subtle injuries to our perceptual systems, injuries that result in symptoms such as not understanding what one is seeing. We will review how some of these disorders have been categorized and what has been learned from them about the workings of the left brain and the right brain.

Agnosia

Agnosia is usually defined as failure of recognition that is due neither to impairment of the sensory input nor to a naming disorder of the kind seen in aphasia.* For example, agnosic patients would not be able to tell what they are looking at, although one could demonstrate that the patient could see the object and have no trouble naming it if they held it. Definitions of agnosia suffer from an inability to carefully specify the difference between sensory loss and "higher level" loss of recognition, because in fact there is no clear-cut dividing line. For the most part, the distinction is based on some of the practical differences observed in patients with various kinds of perceptual problems.

Visual object agnosia, as mentioned, is a failure to recognize objects for reasons that cannot be attributed to a defect of visual acuity or to intellectual or language impairment. Certain cases of mixed sensory and perceptual loss have also been called agnosia. The decision as to whether a visual deficit is purely a sensory or a higher level perceptual problem is often very difficult to make. Most cases fall somewhere in between. Most severe agnosias for objects occur after bilateral damage to parietal–occipital regions of the brain or after damage involving these areas in the left, dominant hemisphere coupled with damage to interhemispheric pathways. The latter situation is thought to mimic bilateral damage by disconnecting any remaining intact visual processing areas from the language centers of the left hemisphere. A patient with visual agnosia may still be able to recognize objects tactually, although extensive parietal damage often leads to problems in both modalities.

A distinction has often been made between "associative" object agnosia and "apperceptive" object agnosia. In associative agnosia a patient demonstrates form (or shape) and detail perception as evidenced by the ability to copy a drawing, for example, but the patient is still unable to recognize or identify objects. In apperceptive agnosia the patient is not only unable to recognize objects but also demonstrates problems in form perception and copying. So defined, apperceptive agnosia appears as a more basic deficit in perception, perhaps of vision, than associative agnosia, which appears as a deficit in a later stage in object recognition.

Auditory agnosia is a condition in which patients with unimpaired hearing fail to recognize or distinguish what they hear. These sounds may include musical tones or familiar noises, such as a telephone ring or running water. They may also be limited to speech sounds, but such an auditory agnosia—known as word deafness—is usually considered to be a type of aphasia, as noted earlier in this chapter. Auditory agnosia

---

*The patient's failure technically should also not be due to a general intellectual impairment, such as that seen in dementia.

is associated with damage to regions of the temporal lobe in the left, dominant hemisphere, although these disturbances are more severe when the injury is bilateral.

Astereognosis is a breakdown in tactile form perception (stereognosis). The patient cannot recognize familiar objects through touch or palpation, even though sensation in the hands appears to be normal. This condition usually results from damage to regions in the right parietal lobe adjacent to the somatosensory projection areas. It is thought that such damage interferes with tactile–kinesthetic memories that have been acquired and stored over the years and built up into perceptions of form, size, and texture.

The Right and Left Hemispheres in Perception

Of the agnosias just discussed, only astereognosis results from right-hemisphere lesions alone. Further evidence from the clinic, however, as well as from functional neuroimaging studies, does suggest several interesting differences in hemispheric contributions to perception. Some of this evidence comes from the study of patients with a selective agnosia for faces.

Prosopagnosia We can recognize a familiar face almost instantly, despite the infinite number of expressions and orientations it can have, and we can distinguish it from hundreds of similar faces in a crowd. Patients with prosopagnosia, however, will not be able to recognize a previously known face and, in some cases, have difficulty recognizing their own face in a mirror. The patients have no trouble, however, recognizing that the face is in fact a face. Originally thought to be a right-hemisphere deficit, prosopagnosic symptoms were later described as involving lesions to both hemispheres.

Arthur Benton shed some light on the controversy by distinguishing between two forms of failure to recognize faces.[63] One is agnosia for familiar faces, or true prosopagnosia, and the other is a defect in discriminating between unfamiliar faces or in learning new faces. Benton claimed that true prosopagnosia is largely due to right-hemisphere deficits but also involves the left hemisphere. The parietal–occipital regions of both hemispheres must sustain damage for the deficit to clearly manifest itself. Defective discrimination of new, unfamiliar, faces, however, a much more common disorder, can result from just posterior right-hemisphere damage.

These findings naturally raise the question of whether there are specialized mechanisms for facial discrimination and what their relationship to other right-hemisphere abilities might be. It is frequently speculated that facial recognition is accomplished so quickly because it involves some global or holistic analysis as opposed to feature-by-feature processing.

PET Studies of Face Recognition Justine Sergent used PET scanning of cerebral blood flow to identify the cerebral activation specific to face recognition.[64] To do so, a face-recognition condition was compared with a condition requiring the processing of another property of faces—categorizing by gender—that is not typically affected in brain-injury patients suffering from face-recognition problems, or prosopagnosia. Two other experimental conditions—viewing simple patterns and viewing common objects—were also employed, along with a baseline condition that involved fixating a monitor screen.

Compared with the baseline condition, cerebral blood-flow changes in the simple-pattern condition were found in the primary visual cortex in the occipital lobe (striate cortex) of both hemispheres. Activation of the primary visual cortex did not change in any of the five experimental task conditions.

Categorizing faces by gender resulted in activation in right-hemisphere posterior regions just outside the visual cortex. The face-identification task produced additional activation in right temporal lobe regions, the activation extending deep into the temporal lobe toward the hippocampus. Cerebral activation during an object-recognition task occurred in the left posterior temporal cortex and did not involve the right-hemisphere regions specifically activated during the face-recognition task (Color plate 11).

Sergent's study thus provided the first evidence from normal subjects regarding the important role of central temporal regions of the right hemisphere in face recognition. Because there is conflicting data and opinion regarding the role of the left hemisphere in face recognition, she and her colleagues conducted an additional study, using divided visual-field presentation of faces. They found a right-hemisphere advantage only during the first lateralized presentation of each face. Once subjects were familiarized with the faces, there was an overall left-hemisphere advantage in the task. The investigators concluded that conflicting evidence for a left-hemisphere role in face recognition is based on data gathered in artificial experimental settings involving repeated presentation and over-familiarization with testing stimuli.[65] Normal, everyday facial recognition, they contend, depends essentially on the right hemisphere, as shown in the PET results. These data are clearly consistent with Benton's suggestion that hemispheric differences in face processing are based on the familiar–unfamiliar distinction.

One of the more surprising findings of this study was the extent to which object recognition and face identification involved activity in separate cerebral regions. The organization of the cortex dissociates objects from faces, utilizing different regions—and probably strategies and physiological mechanisms—to deal with the kind of information that is gleaned by humans from these two types of visual stimuli.

These findings are consistent with clinical neuropsychological data that associates visual object agnosia mostly with left-hemisphere lesions. So, should the roles of the left and the right hemispheres in visual perception be characterized in terms of object recognition and analysis of new faces, respectively? Other evidence indicates this is too simple a view as well as one that does not identify more general principles in hemispheric specialization that are really behind these differences.

New Views of Visual Agnosia A recent examination of several prosopagnosic patients, none of whom had damage in the posterior left hemisphere, showed that they were all defective at recognizing objects seen from an unusual perspective—identifying a bucket or a hat viewed from the top, for example—whereas they recognized the same objects perfectly well when viewed from more typical perspectives.[66] This finding suggested that the contribution of the right hemisphere to object recognition becomes much more crucial when perceptual operations involving corrections, transformations, or rotation of the stimulus have to be performed.

Some related observations are found in the descriptions of visual agnosia categories by neuropsychologist Elkhonon Goldberg.[67] Goldberg identified apperceptive agnosia as a loss in the ability to recognize an object as the same object when it is viewed under different conditions.* The patient does not necessarily have a problem in identifying what an object is (for example, "It is a hat.") but will not be able to identify it as "the same hat" if the object is viewed from another orientation or perspective (Figure 7.4).

In contrast, the skill impaired in typical left-hemisphere damage induced visual agnosia is recognizing the object as a member of a generic

---

*Apperceptive agnosia, as stated earlier, has also been used to describe disruption of an early, more sensory stage in object recognition, occurring before meaning and understanding are achieved.

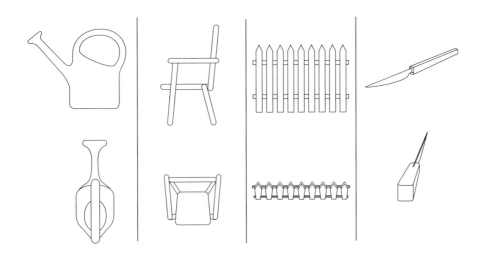

FIGURE 7.4 Usual versus unusual (noncanonical) views of objects. Some agnosia patients have difficulty recognizing objects viewed from an atypical perspective.

category. Goldberg suggested that, because face recognition is clearly a matter of specific physical identification (i.e., to identify the specific John Smith as opposed to Bob Taylor), it is therefore more dependent on right-hemisphere function.[68]

We will return in Chapter 13 to some of these distinctions, and how they may reflect even more general differences in hemispheric function, when we consider several theoretical models of cerebral lateralization.

A Cognitive Neuropsychological Perspective

Some cognitive neuropsychologists view distinctions, such as that between apperceptive agnosia and other agnosias, as only a starting point. They believe that a richer type of theory is necessary to account for some of the issues raised by modern studies of agnosia. They have pointed out, for example, additional ways in which failures in object recognition could occur. One patient may be unable to perceive the shapes of objects properly. Another patient may perceive shapes without a problem but fails to form an integrated representation that combines specific and global features of the object. Yet another patient may recognize and even mime the use of seen objects but be unable to verbally identify them. Thus, complex abilities such as object recognition are organized as a number of separable functional components or modules, any one of which may be impaired selectively.[69]

Cognitive neuropsychologists have constructed a model of object recognition that accounts for some of the deficits in agnosic patients in a somewhat different way. Visual recognition of objects is thought to proceed through a sequence of three types of representation: (1) an initial representation or "primal sketch" in which brightness changes and the two-dimensional geometry of the object is generated; (2) a "viewer-centered representation" in which the spatial locations of the object's surfaces, as visible from the viewer's position, are internally generated (this representation lacks generality because it describes the object only from the observer's viewpoint—sometimes called a "2½-dimensional" sketch); and (3) an "object-centered representation," or truly three-dimensional, representation is generated.[70]

Object recognition is effected by comparing viewer-centered and object-centered representations to stored structural descriptions of known objects. The object's semantic representation, or "meaning," is accessed when the visual representation of a seen object corresponds to a description of an object in the stored structural descriptions of known objects.

Thus, cases of agnosia in which the patient has a severe impairment of form perception and inability to copy seen objects would involve impairment of the ability to construct the viewer-centered representations. Patients who have problems identifying unusual views of objects would have impaired object-centered representations (Figure 7.4). Impairment of object-centered representation formation would, however, not interfere with the ability to recognize objects from a more standard or prototypical view, because the separate viewer-centered representation module would be intact.[71]

The latter case, that of impaired object-centered representation, essentially describes the situation Goldberg discussed as apperceptive agnosia and linked to right-hemisphere damage. The former case, that of impaired viewer-centered representation, is a more severe situation in which the patient's visual processes appear to be disturbed at an earlier and more elementary stage. It is the situation more traditionally described as apperceptive agnosia—and one that is not specifically associated with damage to any one hemisphere.

It is interesting to note how, despite some differences in approach and even definitions, a good deal of modern research in neuropsychology is yielding similar distinctions about how cerebral processes are organized. As work progresses, including that based on a more modular view of brain organization, we expect to see new distinctions, some reorganization of questions, and hopefully new and accurate findings about the cerebral processes involved in perception.

Because there is a very close relationship between the cerebral systems used in perception and those involved in memory storage, we will return to the topic of perception when we discuss amnesia and human memory in the next chapter. A recurring contemporary theme in understanding the functional neuroanatomy of higher level cognitive operations, whether they involve perception of language, visual perception of objects or retrieval of memory, is that the perceptual or mnemonic process invokes domain-specific cortical structures closely related to those initially involved in the sensation, perception, and identification of those events.

Visual Imagery

Visual imagery involves the ability to mentally recreate objects or visual scenes without any direct sensory input. Interest in the brain mechanisms subserving visual imagery has grown in recent years as neuroimaging* technology has provided methods to study brain activity during mental functions that previously could only be examined by personal introspection or indirect laboratory tests of mental manipulations.

One of the first questions investigators have addressed is whether visual imagery involves the same mechanisms as those involved in visual perception. Part of the interest in this question comes from a long-standing debate about the nature of mental images. Are mental images really "depictive representations" that are coded in the brain in some spatial manner, for example, as an array of active cells with space between them that in some way codes the physical distances of the image? Or are mental images more like language, involving

---

*The various uses of the word *image* can get confusing. We try to use *imagery* or *imagining* to refer to mental functions and *imaging* to refer to brain scanning. Thus brain "imaging" can be used to study mental "imagery"!

"propositional representations" that simply specify some or all of the relationships among points or objects in the image, as in "the ball is lying on top of the table at the far right corner"?

The way in which "real" visual information flows from the eye to higher level processing areas of the brain is important to investigators interested in understanding the cerebral mechanisms of "imagined" visual information. It is well known that the primary visual areas in the occipital lobes of the brain receive input from the retina of the eye in a very orderly manner—there is a point-to-point representation, or "mapping," of every region of the retina in the primary visual cortical area called V1. Thus a pattern of stimulation on the retina of the eye results in neural activation in a geometrically similar pattern in area V1. The physical preservation of the initial spatial pattern of activity continues through several stages of visual processing, becoming less apparent in higher visual areas, and disappearing in higher level association cortex.

Is there activity in primary visual cortex during mental imagery that corresponds to the pattern of activity seen when subjects are actually viewing the object? Some evidence for this has been reported in cases of brain injury where removal of part of the primary visual cortex resulted in a reduction of the visual angle of any scene the patient could mentally recreate.[72] Neuroimaging evidence of activity in area V1 during imagery has also been reported in some PET studies[73] but remains somewhat controversial.

Stephen Kosslyn, a leading figure in visual perception and imagery research, claims that V1 shows activity during several types of mental imagery conditions—his PET studies with collaborators have reported this and so have several SPECT studies performed by an Austrian group in which subjects judged sentences like "A grapefruit is bigger than an orange."[74] Physiologist Per Roland and colleagues of the Karolinska Institute in Stockholm, who have conducted PET studies of visuospatial and motor-related cerebral activity for many years, insist that only higher level visual areas in the temporal–occipital and parietal–occipital regions are active during imagery. They have never seen area V1 activated without real sensory input.[75]

Although there is disagreement regarding the primary cortical projection area of the eyes, most investigators agree that some areas of the brain involved in visual perception show activity during mental imagery, particularly the higher level visual processing centers located at the junction of the occipital with the parietal and temporal regions. It is intriguing, although perhaps not entirely surprising, to see activity during mental imagery in cerebral areas normally involved in visual perception.

Imagery and the Hemispheres

The role of the two hemispheres in mental imagery has also been a controversial issue. Although the visuospatial, presumably nonverbal, nature of mental imagery might initially suggest a greater role for the right hemisphere, evidence for the lateralization of imagery processes is far more complex. The preponderance of clinical evidence, in fact, suggests a greater incidence of imagery deficits following left-hemisphere damage.[76] Psychologist Martha Farah has presented considerable evidence for a left-hemisphere role in imagery, including studies of a split-brain patient who could do a task involving judgments about the appearance of lowercase letters only when the initial capital letter stimuli were presented to the left hemisphere.[77] Recent studies of brain-injured subjects have reported that the ability to generate a mental image of a previously presented item is most disrupted by damage to posterior regions of the left hemisphere.[78] A number of neuroimaging studies, involving both PET and SPECT cerebral blood-flow scans, have reported greater activation of left-hemisphere regions, particularly the left temporal–occipital area, during experiments involving image generation, imagined mental walks, and imagined hand movements.[79]

It has become clear, however, that imagery tasks are highly variable, most involving multiple components or steps, and that at least some mental imagery conditions involve the right hemisphere. Stephen Kosslyn has presented experimental evidence to show that imagery is not a single mental process but a collection of at least four distinct subabilities: image generation, image maintenance, image scanning, and image transformation.[80] He has also suggested that images are built up by arranging parts and that two different processes can be used to arrange them. One process uses stored descriptions to arrange parts and is more effectively performed by the left hemisphere. The other process uses stored memories of precise distances and positions ("metric relationships") to arrange parts and is more effectively performed by the right cerebral hemisphere.[81] In an experiment supporting this model, subjects who had initially memorized descriptions of how parts were arranged in a visual array could later form images of the composite pattern more accurately when they were cued in the right visual field (left hemisphere). In contrast, when subjects memorized individual segments on a screen and were to mentally "glue" them into a single pattern, they later could form images more accurately when cued in the left visual field (right hemisphere).[82]

Demands on hemispheric processes become even more complex when various manipulations of the mental images are required of subjects. As mentioned in Chapter 3, neuroimaging experiments involving mental rotation and other complex manipulations of objects in the "mind's eye" have shown substantial right-hemisphere involvement.[83]

Chapter 8

Attention, Memory, Music, and Emotion

The Neglect Syndrome

A patient in a rehabilitation hospital wakes up in the morning and proceeds to shave his face. When he puts the shaver down to go to breakfast, one notices that he shaved only the right side. While eating breakfast, the patient starts to look feverishly for his coffee cup until someone points out that it is just slightly to the left of his dish. At lunch or dinner, he may leave the food on the left half of his plate untouched while asking for more, only to be reminded that there is still food on the plate. If asked to draw a clock, the patient will draw a circle correctly but then crowd all the numbers into the right half. If asked to draw a person, he will draw only the right side of the body, leaving out the left arm and leg. If questioned, the patient states that the drawings look all right to him.

This phenomenon, known as neglect or hemispatial inattention, is observed in stroke or accident victims who have fairly extensive damage to the posterior (parietal or parietal–occipital) regions of the right hemisphere.[1] It sometimes occurs after similar damage to the left hemisphere, but much less frequently and in milder form. The impression one gets in observing such patients is that they behave as if the whole left side of space, and

Model   Patient's Copy

FIGURE 8.1 Drawings by a neglect patient.

sometimes even the left side of their own body, does not exist.* Figure 8.1 shows drawings made by a patient with neglect.

Several questions have long been asked about the syndrome. Why is there such blatant inattention to one-half of space? To what extent is it related to damage in the visual system? Why are patients with damage to the right hemisphere much more likely to show long-lasting neglect symptoms than patients with equivalent damage to the left

*We will consider a more extreme form of this disorder, in which the patient denies the disability, in Chapter 14.

hemisphere? The answers are still not clear, but the phenomenon of neglect provides some valuable clues about the working relationship between the left brain and the right brain.

Although they may be initially unaware of it, many neglect patients are actually blind in their left visual fields. Because information from the left half of visual space is initially processed in the visual area of the right hemisphere, damage there can produce a hemianopic (literally, "half-blind") observer who cannot see any object to the left of the point of fixation. This half-blindness, however, does not solely explain the inattention of neglect patients.

Many examples can be found of patients who are blind to half of the visual field but do not show neglect of that side of space. Patients in whom damage is restricted to the optic nerve pathways or to the primary visual areas of either hemisphere typically compensate for their half-field blindness through eye and head movements. Patients with damage to the left hemisphere who are blind in the right visual field rarely display the kind of persistent functional neglect of one-half of space shown by right-hemisphere-injured patients.

Moreover, some neglect patients are not hemianopic at all. In testing situations, they can accurately report simple visual stimuli flashed alone in the left visual field. However, when stimuli are presented simultaneously in both visual fields, experimentally or in everyday situations, they will report only the items in the right half of visual space. Input from the right field reaching the undamaged left hemisphere appears to interfere with the brain's ability to process input from the left field coming into the damaged right hemisphere. The left half of the stimulus is "extinguished" by the right, but the patients see the left half of the pattern clearly if it is presented alone. The extinction effects seen in these patients may explain at least part of the patient's inattention to the left half of the world.

What happens to extinguished left-field information? Is it truly lost? Or is it present in the nervous system but unavailable to conscious experience? Some investigators have found that, under certain circumstances, patients are able to report what appeared in the left field even when there was simultaneous stimulation in the right. If forced to guess from among several choices, they perform much better than chance, although they may never acknowledge having actually seen the pattern in the left visual field.[2] In a somewhat different line of research, patients who normally extinguished the left-field stimulus when two discrete patterns were presented did not do so when a single large pattern crossing the midline between the left and right fields was used, even though relying only on the information in the right half of the drawing would not have provided them with enough information to recognize it.[3]

Information in the left field is apparently not processed to the same extent as that in the right but is nevertheless available at some preconscious level. Some have speculated that neglect is basically the result of limited visual capacity (due to right-hemisphere damage) coupled with a left-hemisphere tendency to rationalize what it sees. There is some parallel to this in work with split-brain patients, discussed in Chapter 2, where it has been shown that the left hemisphere often "completes" partially drawn figures or may confabulate about what is in the left visual field.

Other explanations have been proposed for the asymmetrical nature of the neglect syndrome. One possibility is that mechanisms controlling selective attention or even arousal are lateralized to the right hemisphere. Another is that the right hemisphere is more spatially adept in general and thus, in its absence, the left does a poor job of comprehending space.

Attentional theories of neglect postulate an asymmetry in the extent to which each hemisphere controls orientation to stimuli in extrapersonal space, that is, to events occurring outside the body. Marcel Kinsbourne proposed that each hemisphere has a directional field of attention into contralateral space that can also inhibit the other hemisphere. The directional tendencies of each hemisphere thus oppose each other but are not equal in strength, the left hemisphere having the stronger directionality (into right space).[4] Severe neglect of events on the left occurs after right-brain damage because the normal directionality advantage of the left hemisphere into right visual space becomes even more exaggerated.

Kenneth Heilman has suggested that the right hemisphere is dominant for attention and arousal.[5] The left directs attention contralaterally, but the right is able to direct attention to both contralateral and ipsilateral space. Evidence for this model consists of an assortment of findings from the EEG literature, blood-flow studies, and other physiological experiments showing activation of the right parietal region during task conditions involving orienting or attending to events in both the left and the right sides of space. Left hemispatial neglect occurs, according to this view, because right parietal damage leaves only the attentional mechanisms of the left hemisphere intact, and these direct attention only to the right side of space.

Positron emission tomography studies of cerebral blood flow during shifting attention in normal subjects provide some of the strongest supporting evidence for this model. In one such study, a line of boxes ran across a screen viewed by subjects, who were to respond to a target that flashed within one of the boxes.[6] While maintaining central fixation, subjects were asked to shift their attention and covertly follow the target as it shifted from box to box (left to right or right to left) in either the left or right visual field. In the control condition, subjects were asked to maintain fixation and ignore any shifting of the target.

Analysis of the PET results revealed that shifting attention within either visual field activates the right parietal lobe, but that the left parietal lobe is activated only when the right visual field is attended. Furthermore, two separate areas of activation could be distinguished within the right superior parietal lobe, one showing increased blood flow during attention shifts in the right visual field and one showing increases in activity during attention shifts in the left visual field. Psychologist Michael Posner, the designer of the experiment, stated that it is not known whether this separation is a general property of right hemisphere organization, or whether it is a special property of the mechanisms involved in shifts of attention.[7]

Using tests of visual scanning and tactile exploration, Sandra Weintraub and Marcel Mesulam found that many right-hemisphere-injured patients not only show neglect of the left side of space but also demonstrate significant neglect of events in the right—they miss considerably more items on the side ipsilateral to the lesion than do left-hemisphere-damaged patients. Weintraub and Mesulam argued that these data provide pivotal support for the model that the right hemisphere is involved in the distribution of attention within both sides of space.[8]

Our initial discussion of hemianopia and extinction has emphasized the sensory and perceptual components of neglect. The studies and models just reviewed emphasize the role of attention and of exploratory factors, such as those measured by visual-scanning and manual exploration tests. Some investigators have expressed the opinion that thinking about neglect in perceptual and even attentional terms does not capture all its manifestations nor perhaps the real basis of the problem.[9] An anecdote about a neglect patient serves to illustrate this point.

An Italian neglect patient was asked to imagine entering a well-known plaza in Milan, called the Piazza del Duomo, from the north end and to describe what he saw. The patient had been very familiar with the plaza before his stroke. He proceeded to describe all the buildings to the west—that is, to the right—of where he would have entered, but he failed to mention any of the buildings to the east. He was then asked to imagine entering the plaza from the south and to describe what he saw. The patient proceeded to describe all the buildings in the eastern half of the plaza.

This story suggests that neglect can be independent of real sensory events, because it even affects the recall of images from memory. Can neglect be an attentional disorder or a disorder in higher perceptual processes? There is no final answer yet, but additional insights may be forthcoming from new investigations into memory and its relationship to perception, a topic we will discuss in the next section.

Amnesia and Localization of Memory

Concepts of localization in the brain have long included the idea that specific storage sites exist for human memories. The search for the engram, the storage unit of memory, has continued for decades. Karl Lashley, following extensive experiments with rats whose brains were lesioned in a systematic fashion with respect to location and size, concluded that memory was critically affected by the amount of cortex removed (principle of mass action) but not by the area removed; that is, all areas of the cortex were equally important for memory (principle of equipotentiality).[10] Lashley was unable to reduce significantly a rat's performance on a learned task following removal of small areas of brain tissue from any of a great many regions of the brain. However, in destroying a rather large portion anywhere in the brain, he significantly affected the rat's memory of what it had learned.

Human clinical data over the years have provided evidence that aspects of what we loosely term memory are organized in both diffuse and focal ways in the brain. Electrical stimulation studies by Wilder Penfield and his associates, some of which are described in Chapter 1, were used to support the concept of the localization of long-term memories.[11] Interesting responses were obtained from stimulation of points in the temporal lobes, including the hippocampus and the amygdala (see Figure 8.2), structures deep within the temporal lobes. Patients at times reported experiencing vivid visual or auditory memories, as though they were being lived over again. However, excision of the whole area did not seem to erase any memories. This and other evidence has led to the view that most memory impairment after brain damage to a particular region is not so much a removal of localizable

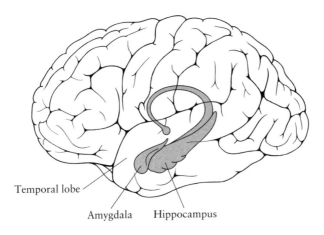

Temporal lobe

Amygdala   Hippocampus

FIGURE 8.2 Areas of the human brain involved in memory disorders. Certain memory processes appear to be associated with structures on the inner surface of the temporal lobes, such as the hippocampus and amygdala.

engrams as an interference with mechanisms involved in forming or retrieving memories.

Most neurological disorders affecting higher mental function have some impact on memory. Diffuse neurological damage, such as that often observed in accidental head injury, typically results in prominent memory disorders. Memory loss in these and many other kinds of patients involves amnesia for events prior to the accident (retrograde amnesia) and loss of new learning capacity (anterograde amnesia). Retrograde amnesia usually diminishes in an orderly fashion, with oldest memories coming back first. Both types of memory loss typically diminish simultaneously during recovery. Ultimately, it is only the recall of certain events after the accident that may seem to be lost.

Alzheimer's dementia is a disease that most frequently affects the elderly. There is diffuse degeneration of cerebral tissue and an accentuation of the degeneration in the posterior temporal lobes, losses that result in a very prominent memory disorder.[12] Although the "senile" symptoms of this disease involve most intellectual functions, deficits in orientation and memory are the most obvious impairments. Dementia patients usually retain older memories—that is, memories of people and events they encountered earlier in their lives—until the later stages of their disease.

Isolated Memory Disorders

In addition to the memory loss that can frequently occur in neurological disorders affecting other functions, striking disorders of memory can occur in isolation, that is, out of proportion to any other deficit of higher function. Such isolated disorders are associated with damage to relatively specific areas of the brain, notably, the temporal lobes, the hippocampus, and several other structures deeper within the brain (see Figure 8.2). Patients with some damage to these structures can appear normal under casual observation and may have normal intellectual capacity. Their defect is primarily in acquiring and retaining new memories.

Most amnesic syndromes do not convincingly show a true obliteration of long-term memories. When older memories are affected, there is evidence that the defect is in accessing the memories, for most do, indeed, "come back" when patients recover. Prompting or cuing an amnesic patient can also bring back many memories.

Partitioning Memory

Different physiological processes are thought to underlie two basic forms of memory representations, short-term memory and long-term memory. Material in short-term memory can be retained only for a brief period of time and can contain a very limited amount of information.[13] Remembering a telephone number for a few seconds is an example. One is always very conscious of information in short-term memory. Material in long-term memory, in contrast, is stored over a long duration and can represent very large amounts of information. We are normally not aware or actively conscious of this information unless it has been activated and probably reintroduced into short-term memory.

The concept of "working memory" was proposed to describe what must take place during most mental tasks. Mental arithmetic, reading, problem-solving, and reasoning in general all require not only some form of temporary storage but also an interplay between information that is stored temporarily and a larger body of stored knowledge.[14] Thus, working memory corresponds to the activated information in long-term memory, the information in short-term memory, and the decision process that manages which information is activated. The decision-making system that selectively activates information in long-term memory and "swaps" information in and out of short-term memory as needed to perform a task is believed to involve the frontal lobes.

Cerebral blood-flow studies with PET have tentatively identified cortical regions that may make up the verbal and visuospatial short-term working memory systems.[15] Scans were recorded during a short-term memory task with letters and compared with a similar nonverbal task. Activated regions involved Broca's area and the left inferior parietal cortex. The investigators identified the left inferior parietal region as the "phonological store" or memory area by comparing these results with a rhyming task not involving any memory demands in which only Broca's area was activated. In the tests of visuospatial memory, scans were conducted while subjects memorized line drawings and were compared with a control task. Predominantly right-hemisphere structures were activated during these "visuospatial sketchpad" operations, including the right occipital, parietal, and prefrontal cortices. Subtraction of another control condition not involving any memory demands led the investigators to conclude that the short-term visuospatial memory "buffer" is in the right angular gyrus region. (We will return to some of this evidence when we discuss false memories later in this chapter.)

The pattern of impairments and sparings of memory observed in brain-damaged patients has led investigators to "divide up" memory processes in a number of additional ways. These include episodic versus semantic, explicit versus implicit (tacit), conscious versus unconscious, and declarative versus nondeclarative. These distinctions do not necessarily conflict with one another, but each emphasizes somewhat different aspects of memory. Most were devised to account for certain dissociations in what is typically affected (first term in each pair) versus what was spared (second term in each pair) in most amnesic patients. Much of neuropsychological memory research has been concerned with confirming or disproving such distinctions.

Episodic Versus Semantic Memory; Cortical Versus Hippocampal Lesions Many memory researchers have agreed to recognize two types of long-term memory: episodic and semantic. Episodic memory records information about specific events within the context of other events in a person's lifetime—for example, having the memory of learning to play soccer when in first grade. Semantic memory concerns our permanent knowledge of the world; that is, it primarily concerns facts, concepts, rules, and meanings.* It contains the information necessary for

---

*In this context, the term *semantic* has a broader definition than it has in linguistics, where it refers to word meanings. Semantic memory refers to a more general kind of knowledge encompassing perceptual codes, motor skills, and other "how" and "what" information.

perceptual recognition and complex motor skills, including speech (for all of us) and playing the piano or typing (for some of us).

The cerebral cortex is thought to subserve much of semantic memory. The loss of meaning information in certain aphasias and the loss of object recognition in certain agnosias can be viewed as loss of semantic memories resulting from damage to the language regions and the perceptual regions of the brain, respectively. Thus, the memory loss associated with damage to cortical regions can be relatively specific, as in Wernicke's aphasia, where left temporal lobe damage appears to interfere with language knowledge.

In contrast with the role of the cortex in semantic memory, the hippocampus (and associated structures) is thought to be primarily involved in episodic memory, because bilateral hippocampal lesions that occur in conjunction with deep damage to the middle of the temporal lobes produce a severe loss for new episodic information.[16] Patients with such damage quickly forget events in their daily lives: where they are, what they had for lunch, where they put their checkbooks, or if, in fact, they wrote a check. Their verbal skills, however, may remain intact, and they are able to have normal conversations, at least about events that occurred before their injuries. When damage is restricted to the hippocampus, patients can learn to perform new tasks, such as playing a new card game. They will be able to use their knowledge of the rules and play correctly when tested at a later time, without remembering how or when they learned the game.

Explicit Versus Implicit Memory Most direct or "explicit" testing of memory in amnesic patients reveals profound deficits in the conscious recollection of events, faces, new facts, and so on. However, careful testing of a patient's performance generally reveals that previously presented information does in fact have some permanent, although unconscious, impact on the patient.

"Implicit" tests of memory make no reference to the past but evaluate whether there is any evidence for memory for an item or any evidence of training by inferring it from performance. For example, after not being able to remember any words presented in a prior testing trial, a patient may be asked to come up with endings to word stems, for example, to complete "sho____". Amnesic patients will often use an ending that creates a word related to one of the words they were exposed to (but could not "remember") in the prior memory test. They may say "shower," for example, because they have just previously been exposed to the word "bath," instead of coming up with many other equally probable endings.

This effect is called semantic priming, because the meanings or categories of previously presented information influences, or "primes," choices made on subsequent tests. Other types of priming effects are also commonly tested, including a simple form of priming in which the primers are the actual words that may later be useful for completing word stems—for example, presenting "shower" before a task involving completion of "sho___".

Implicit forms of memory are also revealed by an amnesic patient's ability to perform a skilled task or play a game learned in a prior testing session, despite the fact that the patient may not recollect that the session ever took place, as described earlier. Other neuropsychological disorders, such as neglect and aphasia, have also come under scrutiny in terms of the explicit–implicit testing distinction. Because the explicit–implicit distinction appears to yield similar results across multiple disorders, it is now thought to hint at a general organizing principle of the brain. Many researchers feel that explicit and implicit testing basically reveal conscious and unconscious cerebral processes, respectively.

Conscious Versus Unconscious Memory; Modular Versus Central Processes In almost all cases, amnesia is now described as an impairment only of conscious recollection of recently acquired information, not as a global failure to retain it. The level of brain function that is damaged in these patients can best be revealed by carefully analyzing these disorders in terms of interruptions of unconscious versus conscious stages of the task performance.

Neuropsychologist Morris Moscovitch has elaborated a theory of memory that encompasses the conscious–unconscious distinction. Moscovitch distinguished "modular" and "central" processes in the brain. Modular processes apply to more automatic and often elementary stages of cerebral operations. The actual processes involved may be quite complicated but are "shallow" in the sense that they are stages that occur automatically without conscious effort or modification. Modules operate strictly within one domain (e.g., visual input), deal with a limited type of information, and have an output not amenable to conscious manipulation.[17]

In the case of memory, multiple modules are thought to represent the input stages of different sensory modalities. These input modules are modified by stimulation: Specific aspects of events create "records" in the input modules via modification of neural circuitry in response to stimulation. The hippocampus, damage to which, as we have said, plays a major role in producing amnesic disorders, is also considered to be modular in organization and operation. The hippocampal retrieval process is automatic and results in the often-described experience of a memory automatically "popping" into one's mind once some cue is provided. We do not have conscious access or awareness of most of the process leading to this. The fact that no conscious strategies or modifications are involved is one reason Moscovitch considered the hippocampal system modular, with "shallow" output.

Most tasks, however, including any real recollection of past events, do involve conscious strategies and assessments of which we are often aware. These are thought to involve the "central systems" of the brain, most notably, the frontal lobes. Moscovitch contended that patients with frontal-lobe lesions provide a dramatic demonstration of how memory might operate if it relied only on the "shallow" output of the hippocampal system. Such patients appear to confabulate extensively because the stories they generate have no temporal order or spatial context. The stories are not pure fabrication, however, but appear to be because they are often completely out of context, in terms of both when and where events took place, and are mixed up in terms of the order of events.[18]

Many other investigators agree that the frontal lobes play a crucial role in guiding conscious memory-retrieval operations. We mentioned earlier, for example, that the frontal lobes are thought to control what information in long-term memory was brought into short-term memory to form working memory.[19] Whether the frontal-lobe functions in memory represent modular processes or not is partly a question of definition that should be resolved as cognitive neuropsychologists refine their approach and conceptualizations on the basis of new experimental findings.

Hemispheric Differences in Memory

Differences have been reported for many years in the kinds of memories lost after production of either left or right temporal lobe lesions. The most striking asymmetries related to memory function were observed in cases involving surgical removal of one temporal lobe. These unilateral temporal lobectomies were performed to remove tissue responsible for epileptic seizures or tumors. Left, or dominant, temporal lobectomy led to difficulty in the learning and retention of verbal material. This deficit was always evident, whether the material was presented visually or through auditory means, and occurred when memory was tested either by straight recall or by recognition procedures.[20]

Right temporal lobectomy led to difficulties with nonverbal material, whether visually or auditorily presented. ("Nonverbal material" involves stimuli that are difficult to name or encode verbally, such as abstract patterns.) In addition, patients with right temporal lobe removals have difficulty with maze learning, whether by visual or proprioceptive (exploratory touching) means.

Thus, memory deficits resulting from lateralized lesions, such as unilateral temporal lobe removals, seem to involve loss in specific semantic memory skills. They are often coupled with some impairment of the contextual (episodic) information involving the hippocampus, however, because this structure deep in the temporal lobe may also be damaged.

Analysis of split-brain patients has supported the evidence from lesion studies of some differences in the memory processes of the two hemispheres. As mentioned in Chapter 2, cutting the corpus callosum alone seems to have negligible effects on a patient's memory when tested in a conventional manner. However, when the hemispheres are tested separately, there is a clear difference in the kinds of information each can learn and remember. With lateralized testing procedures, it is primarily language information that is retained best by the left hemisphere and primarily visuospatial information that is retained by the right hemisphere. Cerebral blood-flow studies have also shown greater right temporal lobe activation during recognition tasks involving visuospatial information.[21] These differences, of course, are expected on the basis of other data we discussed in previous chapters concerning what types of information each hemisphere is best equipped to deal with.

Other studies undertaken from a cognitive neuropsychological perspective have also shown asymmetries in how memory is affected by hemispheric lesions. For example, short-term phonological memory storage appears to be selectively impaired by damage to the lower ("inferior") region of the posterior left parietal lobe.[22] Short-term visuospatial memory has been shown to be selectively impaired by lesions of specific areas in the posterior right hemisphere.[23] Additional data bearing on recent models of memory function are presented in the next section.

Stages in Memory Formation and the Hemispheres: Neuroimaging Studies

The earlier listing of attempts at partitioning memory included the declarative–nondeclarative distinction. This classification scheme is an effort at modifying the older episodic–semantic dichotomy, which did not always appear to account for all the ways in which memory broke down. Declarative memories are memories of specific facts and events and are, in effect, explicit memories. Declarative memory thus encompasses all episodic memory but also includes some semantic knowledge in the sense of memory for faces, words, objects, and so on. Nondeclarative memory underlies stimulus–response habits (conditioning) and various motor and cognitive skills that have essentially become automatic. It is, in effect, implicit memory and is revealed by implicit testing procedures such as those examining the indirect effects of testing sessions on subsequent sessions. Unconscious motor skills and priming effects are examples.

Neuropsychologist Larry Squire and colleagues, who have promoted the declarative–nondeclarative distinction, conducted PET scan studies of normal subjects at several stages of memory testing. According to Squire, the results of these studies indicate that declarative and nondeclarative memories are associated with neuronal activity in different brain locations and in different hemispheres.

The PET study provided direct evidence for the importance of the right posterior cortex, just outside the primary visual (or striate) cortex, in word priming. Priming was measured by having subjects rate words in terms of likes and dislikes, followed by the presentation of a word stem completion task in which the stems could be completed by using words from the previous task.[24] The cerebral blood flow in a region of right extrastriate cortex during word stem completion with prior priming was significantly lower than that during a control condition in which subjects without prior priming also completed word stems.

One explanation for the reduced activity during priming is that, for a time after a perceptual stimulus has been presented, less neural activity is required to process the same stimulus. Squire proposed a physiological or neural role for the key psychological feature of priming—that less information is needed to perceive and identify a stimulus the second time it is presented.

The investigators also measured explicit memory by using word stems as cues to recall previously presented words. They found activation of the right hippocampal regions during this recollection task. In addition, the overall increase in cerebral blood flow was significantly greater during the cued recall condition than during priming. This study thus found that recollection resulted in activity distinctly different from the priming experiment.

Squire maintained that these studies strongly support the idea of multiple forms of memory and the position that declarative and non-declarative memory are indeed associated with distinct and separate neural processes. Priming effects, he believed, can be supported by right posterior cortex functions that operate prior to the analysis of meaning. Later stage memory processes involve the hippocampus and more widespread cortical areas and result in truly conscious recollection—the item is remembered declaratively, that is, in relation to the item's meaning and in relation to the context in which the item was presented.

Although many memory researchers prefer to interpret these findings in terms of the explicit versus implicit memory distinction, Squire's general findings seem to have been upheld. Several recent PET studies have essentially replicated the finding of reduced blood flow in the right posterior cortex for words that had previously been studied (primed) relative to the blood flow recorded for items that had not been studied when subjects performed a word stem completion task.[25]

Electrophysiological studies of event-related potential (ERPs) in normal subjects also point to different brain systems for explicit and implicit memory.[26] Event-related potentials related to memory (word recall or recognition) had a different amplitude, latency, and scalp distribution than do ERPs related to word stem completion priming or perceptual identification priming. In one study the ERP associated with recollection was largest at a latency of 500 to 800 milliseconds, whereas the ERP associated with priming was largest at a latency of 400 to 500 milliseconds. The ERP related to priming was greater at posterior electrode placements. A very recent study examined the time course of cortical activations during word stem completion using ERPs recorded from a high-density, 64-channel array of electrodes. The investigators concluded that their results not only confirmed the PET findings but indicated that the reduced right-hemisphere activity was truly the result of more efficient input processing of the word stem ("bottom-up" processing) as opposed to a result of an overall reduction in the difficulty of cognitive operations necessary to generate the target word ("top-down" processing.)[27]

Taken together, the combination of several metabolic studies and electrophysiological data make a very strong case for the reality of a posterior right hemisphere mechanism underlying memory priming effects. The idea that prior information can reduce the extent of neuronal activity involved in processing a target is an attractive general model for priming.

Attempting to Recall Versus Actual Recollection

In a follow-up study of cued recall (explicit memory), R. L. Buckner and colleagues gave subjects three-letter word beginnings and asked them to remember words that had been studied previously (either in the auditory modality or in a different typographic case). They observed no evidence of hippocampal activation in either condition, but they found that areas in prefrontal cortex showed blood-flow increases in both conditions.

Psychologist Daniel Schacter has suggested that frontal activations, which have been observed frequently in PET studies of explicit retrieval, are related to the effort involved in trying to remember recently studied items. He also suggested that studies reporting an absence of blood-flow activation in the hippocampus indicate that trying to retrieve a past event is not sufficient to activate the hippocampus—the memory has to be successfully retrieved. Schacter conducted an experiment to specifically separate "effort-to-recall" from the "actual recollection."[28] One condition was designed to yield high levels of recall during a later memory test by presenting 20 words several times and having subjects count the number of meanings associated with each word. Another condition was designed to yield low levels of recall on a later test by presenting a series of 20 words only once and having subjects make a simple nonsemantic judgment about each word.

Positron emission tomography scans were conducted during two subsequent test sessions. In one, subjects were to complete three-letter word stems that could be completed with words from the low recall condition. In the other, the word stems were designed to be completed with words from the high recall condition. The success rate was much higher for the latter condition, as expected. Subtraction was performed on the resulting scan images, using the logic that brain regions that are specifically associated with the conscious recollection of a word should show significant blood-flow increases in the high recall minus low recall comparison, whereas regions that are specifically associated with the effort involved in trying to retrieve a recently studied word should show blood-flow increases in the low recall minus high recall comparison. Results showed that effort to retrieve target words was associated with blood-flow increases in left frontal regions, whereas the conscious recollection of studied words was associated with blood-flow increases in the hippocampal formation in both hemispheres.

At first glance, these findings appear to be inconsistent with the model proposed by Moscovitch, in which hippocampal processes were called unconscious and automatic. Actually, Schacter's results support the role proposed by Moscovitch for both the frontal lobes and the hippocampus; the frontal lobes are involved in the conscious effort of memory retrieval and the hippocampus provides the memory once the proper cue is given. Schacter's PET study showed that the memory had to be successfully retrieved, not just attempted, for the hippocampus to show activity. Moscovitch used the word *conscious* to refer to the awareness of efforts to recall, whereas Schacter used the word to refer to the actual recollection itself.

Hemispheric Asymmetries in Encoding and Retrieval

On the basis of data from a number of PET studies, psychologist Endel Tulving has proposed a functional neuroanatomical model of encoding and retrieval of episodic memory in which the right and left prefrontal lobes play different roles. A PET study by Shitij Kapur and associates focused on episodic memory encoding: Cerebral blood flow was measured while subjects engaged in a "shallow" or "deeper" encoding activity.[29] Shallow encoding involved simple repetition of presented nouns, whereas deeper encoding was achieved by requiring subjects to decide whether the noun represented a living or nonliving thing, thus elaborating the word with some semantic information. Relative to shallow encoding, deeper encoding was accompanied by prominent left prefrontal activation and resulted in higher recognition of the studied material. The prefrontal activation was asymmetric: Encoding conditions showed no significant difference in right prefrontal regions.

Another PET study focused on episodic memory retrieval.[30] Subjects listened either to novel sentences or to comparable sentences that they had learned the previous day. All other conditions were held constant between the two types of scan. Subjects recognized the "old" sentences without difficulty, and their experience of recognition was accompanied by increases in blood flow in several cerebral loci, including dorsolateral prefrontal cortical regions (i.e., upper, side view surface toward the front of the frontal lobe) in the right hemisphere. On the basis of these and several other studies, Tulving has proposed a hemispheric encoding/retrieval asymmetry (HERA) model of episodic memory. According to this model, the left and right prefrontal lobes are part of an extensive neuronal network that subserves episodic remembering, but each hemisphere plays a different role within the network. Left prefrontal cortical regions are more involved in retrieval of information from semantic memory and in simultaneously encoding novel aspects of the retrieved information into episodic memory. Right prefrontal cortical regions, on the other hand, are involved in episodic memory retrieval.

Evidence for similar hemispheric asymmetries in memory for objects has come from other recent PET studies. A study that examined the functional anatomy of object location memory revealed an interesting hemispheric effect relating to encoding versus retrieval.[31] Cerebral blood flow was measured while normal volunteers encoded (memorized) and then retrieved the locations of eight objects presented on a computer screen. In control conditions designed to separate object-location memory into its component processes, subjects were asked to simply encode, and then to retrieve, eight distinct locations represented by identical white boxes on the screen. In analyzing the data, the researchers found an increase in blood flow in the right hippocampal region when they subtracted the simple "retrieving location" condition from the "retrieving object-location" condition. In contrast, when they subtracted the simple "encoding location" condition from the "encoding object-location" condition, no significant changes were observed in the hippocampal region, but there was bilateral activation in the frontal lobes (anterior fusiform gyrus). They also noted that the two encoding conditions activated left-hemisphere regions to a greater extent, whereas the two retrieval conditions activated right-hemisphere regions.

The investigators noted that their results with visual stimuli appear to mimic Endel Tulving's and Timothy Shallice's models of asymmetries in frontal activity in the encoding and retrieval of verbal material.[32] In the present study, when the "retrieving object-location" condition was subtracted from the "encoding object-location" condition, significant changes in blood flow were observed only in the left hemisphere. In contrast, the reverse subtraction (retrieval minus encoding) yielded significant foci of activation only in the right hemisphere.

In reviewing some of the functional neuroimaging data on memory, it is clear that evidence converging from different studies and especially different technologies (e.g., PET and electrophysiology) forms the most convincing case for the appropriateness of the some of the distinctions, divisions, and stages of memory operations made by memory researchers. Functional neuroimaging has confirmed some of the findings on memory that were based on brain damage and neuropsychological data. Neuroimaging studies are also providing new and different information to investigators, such as the ways in which priming effects and stages of memory encoding and retrieval may break down along hemispheric lines.

Memory and Perception: The New Synthesis

In the 1960s physiologists David Hubel and Thornton Wiesel discovered that many neurons in the visual cortex respond only to extremely selective aspects of visual stimuli, such as a specific line orientation, and that there is a hierarchical organization of these neurons leading to ever increasing specificity of response. Their observations have led to a relatively unidirectional information processing view of perception and even brain function in general. In this view, "early" or "low level" sensory neurons pick out relevant details from a myriad of real world data and send summaries up to "high level" neurons. The information gets refined and integrated as it proceeds up this chain of hierarchical processing. The final product, which is stored in memory, consists, in some way, of the "distilled yet complete essence of an experience," something like a finished movie.[33]

This view, although perhaps accurate in its account of the earliest phase of the analysis of sensory data, suffers from several problems. One is that it seems to assign the art of "perceiving" to something like a little person (or "homunculus") looking at the finished movie. Another is that, if each experience is individually coded in totality and separately stored, then our mental library would have to be impossibly vast.

There is an alternative view: Instead of storing every possible image at high brain centers, the brain attempts to reconstruct them by reactivating sensory fragments in different patterns. Current perspectives emphasize the close relationship between the locus of storage and the locus of the processing systems that are engaged during the perception, processing, and analysis of the material being learned.[34] The contributions to memory of a given brain structure are usually closely related to its nonmnemonic functions.[35] For example, lesions of the lower posterior temporal cortex, an area important for visual discrimination, impair visual recognition and associative memory.[36] Lesions of the superior temporal cortex, an area important for auditory discrimination, impair auditory recognition memory.[37]

Several PET studies have attempted to image the extent to which sensory cortex is activated during imagining and recall and have indeed reported significant increases in activity in brain regions considered to be devoted entirely to sensory processes.[38] Subjects were asked to imagine or visualize events, with eyes closed. Cerebral blood-flow increases were observed not only in higher level association areas of the brain but also in primary sensory cortex, regions known to perform early stage processing of input from the sense organs. These data support the view that recollection of events involves some cerebral activity in the regions utilized in the original sensory analysis and perception of the event.

Perceptual Convergence Zones and Memory

Neurologist Antonio Damasio has expanded on the preceding idea by suggesting the existence of a specific type of hierarchical cortical organization that could be efficiently utilized in reconstructing memories. He proposed the term *convergence zones* for regions that combine the constellation of details needed to distinguish one object from another as opposed to storing memories of individual objects. For prosopagnosia, Damasio suggested that patients have lost convergence zones for any unique visual image (of a face, and in many cases, of specific car types). The lower zones that link the smaller number of features one needs to tell that a face is a face remain unchanged. Higher zones that link diverse features such as gait, voice, face, and name are also intact. What is damaged are intermediate zones that distinguish one face (or car) from another.[39]

On the basis of his brain-lesion data from many patients, Damasio proposed that similar hierarchies of convergence zones cover the cerebral cortex—convergence zones for generic knowledge feeding into zones for more specific knowledge. Convergence zones store only information that links knowledge fragments, not the fragments themselves. The fragments—for example, the color of the eye or the shape of the nostril—remain scattered in the separate sensory cortices. To recall an image, convergence zones must reactivate the various fragments. Damasio noted that this idea reconciles the fluidity of mental images with the limited storage capacity of the brain.

Imaging True and False Memories

The inaccuracies in recollection, distortions of memory, and illusions have been common themes in the psychological literature, involving both normal subjects and brain-injured patients. Modern analysis of memory distortions is usually traced to Bartlett, a British psychologist who, in the early 1930s, discussed how people sometimes misremember stories they recently studied.[40] This issue has obvious implications both for the nature of recall and for more practical activities such as eyewitness identification. David Schacter and colleagues at Harvard and Massachusetts General Hospital recently reported a provocative difference in their PET scan studies of veridical ("accurate") versus illusory ("false") memory recollection.[41] In one condition, subjects were asked to remember a list of words that was read to them and were then scanned as they listened to another list of words from which they had to identify as "old" any word they had heard before. In another condition, the second list included words that were semantically related to items in the first list, for example, "candy" and "chocolate" were presented in the first list, "sweet" in the second. As before, subjects were told to respond "old" only to words they had heard before.

Although the scan results showed many similarities between brain activity during veridical versus illusory recollection, there were some interesting differences in the two blood-flow patterns. Both veridical and illusory recognition was associated with left hippocampal–medial temporal activation, as expected on the basis of previous studies of episodic memory. Veridical recognition was distinguished by additional blood-flow increases in the left temporal–parietal region (left angular gyrus) previously implicated in the retention of auditory–phonological information, that is, the same area identified in PET studies of short-term verbal memory.[42] False recognition, however, showed a greater degree of frontal activity. This, the investigators postulated, may have reflected the subject's effort to monitor or make a decision about the sense of familiarity induced by the false target items, to resolve a conflict between two opposing tendencies: to call a word "old" because they had a sense that the word had been presented or to call it "new" because they failed to retrieve a "trace" of the actual phonological processing.* Additional clinical evidence for this hypothesis comes from the study of a patient who had suffered a stroke of the right frontal lobe and exhibited a tremendous rate of false recognition on any item related in any meaningful way to something that had been presented to him before.[43]

It is, of course, interesting that one of the main differences between veridical and illusory recognition memory found in this study involved the presence of activity in a region associated with the initial phonological processing of word stimuli. This finding tends to support the

---

*Note that the role of the frontal lobes is similar to that proposed by Moscovitch (notes 17 and 18), and was discussed earlier in this chapter.

general idea we have been discussing, that memory involves retracing many of the same steps involved in perception. It is also natural to wonder whether imaging studies such as this can ever be used to verify or call into question the testimony of individuals in cases where the passage of time could have faded the actual event. Although a fascinating thought, the variables are far too great and current techniques too dependent on multiple subject analyses for the idea to become viable anytime soon. Besides, as Schacter mused in an interview about his study, what if the memory of sensory details fade and one is left only with the gist of what happened, just as with the false memory condition of the PET experiment.

Music and the Hemispheres

In Chapter 1 we presented evidence for the role of the right hemisphere in music. Patients who had suffered left-hemisphere strokes that affected their speech were often unaffected in their ability to sing. Conversely, right-hemisphere strokes often resulted in the loss of musical abilities while leaving speech unimpaired.

Early research was consistent with the idea that most aspects of musical perception are right-hemisphere functions. Pre- and postoperative testing of musical skills was performed on patients undergoing excision of either the left or the right temporal lobe to remove epileptic tissue. It was found that removal of the right hemisphere significantly increased errors on tests of melodic pattern, loudness, sound duration, and timbre. Left-hemisphere removal did not result in a change in performance. The ability to sing was also investigated in patients undergoing temporary anesthetization of the right hemisphere with the Wada procedure. Singing was grossly disturbed, and, although rhythmic elements were preserved, melody was reduced to a monotone.[44]

Evidence from other clinical cases, however, has suggested that the right-hemisphere predominance in music is not always complete. Additional studies using sodium amobarbital have revealed a more complex picture: As expected, interference with singing followed right-side injection; however, interference, although less severe, also followed left-side injection.[45] A review of the literature on musical perception following brain damage by Robert Zatorre showed that deficits in the processing of patterns of pitches and in the processing of timbre differences accompany right-side damage most consistently.[46] Left-side damage, regardless of whether or not there is aphasic impairment, causes problems with the naming or identification of familiar tunes.

Musicians who have sustained left-hemisphere stroke have shown documented impairment of at least some of their skills. Composer Maurice Ravel suffered a stroke (presumed to be in the left hemisphere) and developed a Wernicke's type of aphasia while at the peak of his career. Many of Ravel's musical skills remained intact; he could recognize melodies, pick up the smallest mistakes in performed music, and judge how well a piano was tuned. In contrast to these preserved skills, however, Ravel experienced a substantial loss in ability to label notes and recognize written music. He also could not play the piano or write music, even by dictation.

Some neuropsychologists have argued that the cerebral dichotomy in terms of musical expertise revolves around a left-hemisphere mediation of "local" information processing in melodies, and a right hemisphere superiority at a "global" level.[47] A study of melody processing in left- and right-brain-damaged patients found evidence for hemispheric dissociations in processing pitch and rhythm, but with some qualifications: Although the right hemisphere was involved with pitch, especially where melodic contour was important, the left played a role where local cues were significant (e.g., with respect to the structure of musical intervals). Processing temporal or rhythmic variations appeared to favor the left hemisphere, except where global cues were relevant.[48] Thus, the local–global distinction appeared to cut across the right hemisphere–pitch, left hemisphere–rhythm distinction. This result is also supported by a case study of a musician with temporal–parietal damage to the right hemisphere. The patient experienced problems in interpreting music as emotionally or intellectually meaningful, although he retained the ability to process individual elements such as rhythm, melody, and harmony.[49]

Overall, the data on music and the hemispheres suggest that, just as all of the components of language do not appear to be equally lateralized to the left hemisphere, all aspects of musical skill do not reside exclusively in the right hemisphere. Those aspects of musical processing that require judgments about duration, temporal order, sequencing, and rhythm differentially involve the left hemisphere, whereas the right hemisphere is differentially involved when judgments about tonal memory, timbre, melody recognition, and intensity are required.

Modules in Musicians: Evidence from PET Studies of Cerebral Blood Flow

The late Justine Sergent of the Montreal Neurological Institute conducted an ambitious PET imaging study of cerebral blood flow in ten classically trained musicians.[50] The main experimental condition consisted of the presentation on a TV monitor of a little-known score, which each subject played on a keyboard with the right hand while listening to their own performance. In addition, PET scans were conducted during six other "control" conditions that included simple visual fixation of the lighted TV monitor, listening to musical scales, playing scales on the keyboard with the right hand, making simple manual responses to a dot presented on the screen, reading a musical score presented, and listening to its performance.

The scans of all subjects in each of the testing conditions were averaged and then compared as pairs of conditions (task minus control) to isolate the component operations of the successively more complex tasks. Each of the three components of the main experimental task (playing, listening, and reading) engaged specific cortical areas. Activation related to listening to musical scales was detected in the auditory cortex of both hemispheres (as expected from auditory stimuli) and in the superior temporal region of the left hemisphere, regardless of whether the scales were played by or to the subject. Listening to a musical piece activated the same areas but also engaged the right superior temporal region, a result showing bilateral temporal lobe activity not evident in simple scale listening.

Just reading a musical score activated visual cortex in both occipital lobes (as expected of visual stimuli) but did not engage additional areas normally activated by visual processing of words. Instead, an area at the junction of the left occipital and parietal lobes involved in spatial processing was activated. Sergent suggested that, in contrast to word reading, the relevant information in musical notation is derived through analysis of the spatial location of notes on the staff (which is directly related to pitch intervals).

When both reading and listening to a score are done conjointly, areas are activated in the lower parietal lobe of both hemispheres that are not engaged when either condition is done separately. Sergent suggested that these areas perform a mapping between musical notation and its corresponding sounds or melodies. Similar visual-to-sound mapping functions are performed by the parietal lobes in the case of word reading, not in the identical region but in adjacent areas.*

Finally, two additional regions were activated when the main experimental task was performed. One involved the superior parietal lobe in both hemispheres. This activity was thought to represent transformations from the musical notation to the visually guided finger positioning involved in executing the musical piece. The other area of activation involved the region in the left frontal lobe immediately above Broca's area. Because Broca's area plays a critical role in organizing the motor sequencing underlying speech production, Sergent suggested that a similar role is played by the adjacent area during keyboard performance. This study indicated that reading music and performing it results in activation of cortical areas distinct from but adjacent to those underlying similar verbal operations. Sergent felt that this result explains why some musicians suffering from left-hemisphere injury and aphasia also have their musical skills impaired. Sergent also suggested that these findings are consistent both with a modular view of cerebral organization, emphasizing the unique competencies of specific cerebral regions, and with a distributed view, made necessary by the multiple processes involved in musical performance and most other forms of human expression.

Evidence for Cerebral Reorganizational Changes in Musicians

Two recent studies of musicians, one involving functional imaging of cortical activity during finger movement and the other, MRI measurements of the corpus callosum, have generated provocative evidence for developmental and experiential changes affecting brain organization.

In one study, magnetoencephalography (MEG) was used to compare the cortical response to finger stimulation of the left and right hands in nine string players (violinists, cellists, and one guitarist) with that in nonmusician controls. The researchers reasoned that violinists and other string players provide a good model of the effects of different

---

*As based on the damage observed in cases of alexia without agraphia, which was discussed in Chapter 7.

sensorimotor input to the two sides of the brain. During practice or performance, the second to fifth digits of the left hand are continuously engaged in fingering the strings, a task involving considerable dexterity and enhanced sensory stimulation. Analysis of the magnetic source (dipole moment) during stimulation showed that response in primary sensory cortex was shifted and of a greater magnitude for the left hand in the musicians than in the controls.

The shift of the response in musicians away from the finger region and toward the region normally representing the palm of the hand, combined with an increase in signal strength, was interpreted as reflecting an increase in the total cortical representation of their left fingers. Furthermore, there was a correlation between the age at which the string players began studying their instruments and these changes: the earlier they started, the greater the magnitude of the change in the cortex. It was concluded that cortical territory of the left hand expands in string players and is dependent on the age they start practicing.[51]

In the other study, MRI scans of 30 professional classical musicians (keyboard or string players, or both) were compared with scans of 30 nonmusician controls matched for age, sex, and handedness. (The musicians all described themselves as right-handed, but were shown to have a greater degree of ambidexterity than the controls in formal testing of motor skills.) Analysis of the MRI scans revealed that the anterior half of the corpus callosum, measured at the midsagittal plane between the hemispheres, was significantly larger in musicians. This difference was due almost entirely to the subgroup of musicians who had begun musical training before the age of seven. The investigators concluded that, because anatomical studies have provided evidence for a positive relationship between callosal size and the number of fibers crossing through it, these data indicate a difference in interhemispheric communication between musicians and controls. They also suggested that the finding may represent differences in hemispheric symmetry of sensorimotor areas. Their results are also consistent with the view that maturational changes in the corpus callosum extend into late childhood.[52]

Taken together, these two studies provide compelling, although preliminary, evidence for developmental and experiential changes affecting relatively macroscopic measures of brain organization. As Gottfried Schlaug, the senior author of the MRI study suggested, musicians may form a particularly promising group for disclosing relationships between brain structure and behavior.

Emotion

· · · · · · · · · ·

Emotion involves many kinds of human mental states, reactions, and attitudes, some related in terms of the brain mechanisms involved, others not. Emotional information is reflected in our facial expressions and in other less noticeable physiological signs. Emotional information may be conveyed directly in speech, or it may be superimposed in the tone by which other information is conveyed in speech. As in other studies of brain–behavior relationships, the answers to where and how emotional processes take place in the brain depend, to a great extent, on what aspects of emotional behavior one is investigating.

Models of Emotion

Three significant models have been proposed to explain the basis for emotional feelings.[53]

Visceral Feedback The visceral feedback or James–Lange theory proposes that emotion-provoking stimuli induce bodily or "visceral" changes and that the experience of these changes as they occur is essentially the emotion. For example, the "sick feeling in the gut" associated with anguish and certain upsetting situations or the "adrenaline rush" sensations in the upper torso associated with danger or fright are considered to represent visceral changes that we read as emotional states.

Although this theory has been around for 100 years and has been ridiculed or dismissed by many psychologists, some modern research does demonstrate that different bodily reactions can be associated with different emotions[54] and that certain drugs that only affect the body (and do not cross into the brain) may reduce anxiety and fear in humans and animals.[55] Furthermore, there is some evidence that patients with very high spinal cord lesions, disconnecting their viscera from their brain, report experiencing fewer emotional states than patients with lower spinal cord damage.[56]

The visceral feedback or "somatic" theory may not be a comprehensive model of emotion but it does identify an important, often overlooked, aspect of emotional experience. Neurologist Antonio Damasio has recently made a strong case for the importance of the body and bodily sensations in emotion in his book, *Descarte's Error.*[57]

Cognitive Arousal The cognitive arousal or Maranon–Schacter theory proposes that a cognitive state must interact with arousal to produce emotion. Psychologist Stanley Schacter claimed to disprove the James–Lange visceral feedback theory by showing that drug-induced physiological arousal did not produce an emotional state in and of itself. In Schacter's experiment, subjects attributed different emotions to the same arousal state (induced by an adrenaline injection), depending on differences in their mental state at the time, which was manipulated by variations in the way the investigators prepared each subject for the experiment.[58]

This highly cited study has recently been criticized for the broad generalizations made on the basis of very limited methodology, including the use of only one drug.[59] Nevertheless, some neuropsychologists believe that the cognitive arousal theory is consistent with clinically observed effects on emotion of left- and right-hemisphere damage.

Central Theories Central theories of emotion hold that feelings or subjective emotions depend entirely on activity in the central nervous system, that is, on brain activity alone and not on physiological changes in the body. Cannon proposed in 1927 that the thalamus was the critical structure. He felt that signals emanating from the thalamus not only were important for the expression of emotion but also, upon reaching the cortex, were responsible for subjective emotional experience. Since Cannon's time, other brain "centrist" theories of emotion have moved the major organ of emotion to the hypothalamus, another deep brain structure, and then to a larger circuit also involving the hypothalamus, hippocampus, and cortex.

It is highly likely that a comprehensive model of emotion or emotional experience will have to include a role for central brain structures and an assessment of the extent to which our emotional experience depends on our body state. Clearly, the visceral reaction emphasized by the James–Lange theory is determined by the brain also, but this seems to occur in an automatic, almost instantaneous manner. Thus, both the cognitive appraisal and visceral changes associated with an emotion-provoking situation are controlled by the brain. The questions are, "What comes first, the visceral changes or cognitive appraisal?" "What is the relative importance of each?" and "Are specific regions of the brain responsible for emotion-related changes, whether visceral or cognitive?" Most research on hemispheric asymmetries related to emotion has stressed the latter question and has simply looked for any differences accompanying left- versus right-hemisphere damage or evidence for asymmetries in emotional expression and perception in normal volunteers.

Emotional Responses to Hemispheric Injuries

A number of investigations have focused on the emotional behavior of patients with unilateral brain lesions. Left-hemisphere-injured patients have been reported to display feelings of despair, hopelessness, or anger (often referred to as a catastrophic–dysphoric reaction), whereas right-hemisphere damage produces what is known as an indifference–euphoric reaction, in which minimization of symptoms, emotional placidity, and elation are common. A frequently cited study, for example, compared the frequencies of the catastrophic and indifference reactions in 150 patients with unilateral brain lesions. Of the patients with left-hemisphere lesions, 62 percent showed a catastrophic reaction, whereas that response was observed in only 10 percent of right-lesion patients. The incidence of indifference reactions, however, was 38 percent among those with right lesions and only 11 percent among those with left lesions.[60]

Extreme emotional reactions have also been reported after unilateral injection of sodium amobarbital into the carotid artery (the Wada test). Several investigators have observed dysphoric reactions, frequently accompanied by crying, after left-side injections.[61] Indifference–euphoric reactions were found in significantly fewer patients. One researcher described the catastrophic reaction in the following way: "the patient especially when spoken to despairs and expresses a sense of guilt, of nothingness, of indignity and worries about his own future or that of his relatives." After right-side injection, however, indifference–euphoric reactions were more common than dysphoric reactions, with patients sometimes breaking out into peals of laughter as the effects of the sodium amobarbital wore off. The same investigator described the indifference reaction that occurs as "a complete opposite emotional reaction, a euphoric reaction that in some cases may reach the intensity of a maniacal reaction. The patient appears without apprehension, smiles and laughs and both with mimicry and words expresses considerable liveliness and sense of well-being."[62]

Although not all investigators have reported results that are this consistent, the findings we have just reviewed strongly suggest that the two sides of the brain differ in the emotional states they subserve. However, there are two problems with this interpretation. First, the reported emotional changes accompanying insults to either half of the brain might not result from disruption of brain mechanisms underlying emotion but, instead, might be a consequence of the patient's reaction to the deficits resulting from the brain insult. Thus, the catastrophic reaction following left-hemisphere injury or inactivation can be viewed as a reaction to the inability to speak and not as representing the lateralization of emotion per se. Although an analogous explanation to account for a euphoric reaction after right-hemisphere injury is not as intuitively obvious, it is possible, nevertheless, that both the dysphoric and euphoric reactions are secondary manifestations of other deficits and not the direct result of alterations to the lateralized mechanisms subserving emotion.

The second problem deals with the relationship of the two sides of the brain to the emotional states under discussion. For example, damage to one side of the brain might produce emotional reactions through its effects on the same hemisphere, or it might exert its influence on the side contralateral to the damage, perhaps through the destruction of regions that normally inhibit certain activities of the other hemisphere. To understand the nature of hemispheric asymmetry for emotion, it is important to determine which of these two actually occurs.

Psychologist Harold Sackheim and his colleagues looked at cases of pathological laughing and crying in which patients show spontaneous uncontrollable displays of emotion that are uncorrelated with objective events.[63] Their review showed that patients with pathological laughing were three times more likely to have right-side lesions than to have left-side damage, whereas pathological crying was more than twice as frequent in patients with left-side damage. Sackheim argued that pathological laughing and crying often precede the appearance of other deficits and are often the first signs of a lesion. Therefore, they concluded, these data support the hypothesis that the two sides of the brain do differ in subserving positive and negative emotional states.

Sackheim then looked at cases of uncontrollable emotional outbursts of laughing and crying that sometimes accompany epileptic seizures. Of the 91 patients showing outbursts of laughing, a left-side focus was twice as likely as a right-side focus. Many fewer cases of crying were found. In the six cases of crying that were reported, however, a different pattern was observed. Four patients were judged to have a right-side focus, with one left-side, and one indeterminate.

In brain-lesion cases, pathological laughing was strongly associated with predominantly right-side lesions. In the case of epilepsy-induced uncontrollable laughing, however, the epileptic focus was more often left-side than right-side. Similarly, results were reversed in the few cases of pathological crying and epilepsy-induced crying that were studied.

Although the results may appear to conflict, they are actually quite consistent. Seizures are associated with hyperexcitability in the regions included within the focus, whereas lesions involve destruction of tissue. These data suggest that uncontrollable outbursts of laughter may result from excitation within the left half of the brain (as occurs in epilepsy) or disinhibition of the left side resulting from damage to the right (as occurs in the case of brain injury). The conclusions regarding uncontrollable crying are more tentative because of the small number of cases. However, the data that exist are consistent with the idea that uncontrollable crying results from excitation within the right half of the brain, or disinhibition of the right hemisphere following left-hemisphere injury.

The notion of disinhibition, as used here, implies that ordinarily the two halves of the brain exert inhibitory effects on each other in the area of emotional expression, thereby resulting in a normal balance that is free of uncontrollable outbursts of any kind. In the event of damage to one side, however, this mutual inhibition is disrupted and the damaged side no longer exerts the same degree of inhibition on its partner; hence, the other hemisphere is disinhibited.

The model of hemispheric control of emotional experience that emerges from this review is thus one in which the left side of the brain typically subserves positive emotions, whereas the right side typically subserves negative emotions. The model is a useful working hypothesis that helps explain a good deal of the data just reviewed, although it is far from being complete and universally accepted.

The Perception and Expression of Emotion

Clinical Data As mentioned in the discussion of language disorders, clinical evidence has suggested a role for the right hemisphere in the processing of emotional information. Kenneth Heilman and his colleagues, for example, reported that patients with damage in the right hemisphere have greater difficulty picking up on the emotional messages conveyed by speech intonations than do patients with damage in the left hemisphere.[64]

Patients sat in front of pictures of four faces—one happy, one sad, one angry, and one indifferent—and listened to sentences read in different tones of voice. The sentences were neutral; emotional information was conveyed only by the way in which the examiner read the sentences. The patients' task was to point to the face that best illustrated the emotional tone that the examiner was expressing on each trial. Aphasic patients, even one global aphasic, did quite well—often flawlessly—on the task. In contrast, patients with right-hemisphere lesions had great difficulty.

Another study was designed to address the question of whether this failure on the part of right-hemisphere patients was due to an inability to identify emotional expression—that is, a perceptual loss—or to a loss in the concepts of what different emotions mean—that is, a cognitive loss. The investigators required patients with right-hemisphere lesions to discriminate between pairs of sentences that had the same words but were spoken with either the same or different intonations. The patients did not have to identify the emotion but merely had to tell whether the sentences sounded the same or different.

The right-hemisphere patients, like those in the Heilman study, performed more poorly on this task than did aphasic controls. But when right-hemisphere patients were tested on whether they could identify the emotion conveyed by the contents of a story, they performed as well as controls. These results have been interpreted as showing that right-hemisphere patients have not lost the concept or comprehension of different emotions but do exhibit difficulty with standard perceptual cues to emotion.[65]

More recent studies have generally (but not unanimously) continued to support the idea that right-hemisphere damage interferes with the perception of emotion more than does left-hemisphere damage. One study found that right-brain-damage patients were significantly more impaired on discrimination and identification tasks involving emotional words than on parallel tasks involving nonemotional words.[66] Left-hemisphere-injured patients and normal controls did not show the same dissociation. However, another recent study, examining comprehension of emotional tone (or prosody) in various speech stimuli, reported equivalent deficits in left- and right-hemisphere-damaged patients.[67]

Joan Borod, in her review of emotion research, suggested that many apparent discrepancies in the literature can be resolved by more closely examining what "processing mode" (expression or perception), what "communication channel" (facial, prosodic, or lexical), and what "emotional valence" (positive or negative) is being studied.[68] She asserted that, overall, research findings indicate that the right hemisphere is dominant for emotional perception of facial or lexical (i.e., emotional vocabulary) information, independent of whether positive or negative emotions are involved. The situation with studies examining emotional expression is more complex, with positive or negative aspects of the emotion, as well as whether it is facial communication or not, often playing an important role. In general, she felt that the concept of right-brain dominance for both positive and negative emotional expression is supported by studies of the production of appropriate intonation in speech. Conclusions about the site of control of emotional facial expressions, however, depends more on whether one is examining positive or negative emotions, as we will see in the following section.

Behavioral Tests in Normal Subjects Studies with normal subjects also support a major role for the right hemisphere in the expression of emotion. In a study looking at possible asymmetries in the expression of emotion, full-face photographs and their mirror reversals were split down the midline.[69] Composites were put together from two left sides or two right sides. Subjects were asked to rate the intensities of emotional expression evident in a series of such pictures depicting different emotions. Figure 8.3 shows one such face and the composites formed from it.

  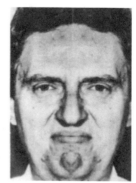

FIGURE 8.3 Comparison of the intensity of emotional expression in composite faces. A. Left-side composite. B. Original face. C. Right-side composite. [From Sackheim, "Emotions Are Expressed More Intensely on the Left Side of the Face," Fig. 1, p. 434, *Science* (1978) 202; American Association for the Advancement of Science.]

Left-side composites were judged to express emotion more intensely than right-side composites. The researchers noted the preponderance of contralateral projections controlling facial muscles and argued that these results point to greater involvement by the right hemisphere in the production of emotional expression. A number of subsequent investigations have produced similar results.

Findings are conflicting, however, when the expressions are divided into positive and negative categories. Some investigators have reported differences in the pattern of asymmetry for positive and negative expressions. Joan Borod and her colleagues, for example, found that negative expressions were consistently and significantly expressed on the left side, whereas positive expressions were not systematically lateralized.[70] Other studies, however, have shown left-side effects for both positive and negative stimuli under certain conditions.[71] Still others reported different facial asymmetries in response to positive and negative emotional arousal: Positive stimuli resulted in more obvious changes on the right side of the face, whereas negative stimuli resulted in stronger left-sided facial expressions.[72]

A Perspective Based on Physiological Measurements Electrophysiologist Richard Davidson has also argued that many apparent discrepancies in the literature are due to a lack of regard for the "multi-componential nature of emotion"—that some investigators do not even differentiate between the perception of emotional information and the production of emotion in the design and interpretation of experiments.[73] Davidson stressed the need to deal with differences in organization within a hemisphere when making generalizations about the differential role of each hemisphere in emotion. He proposed that, taken together, electrophysiological studies indicate that the anterior regions of the two hemispheres are differentially specialized for the experience of positive and negative emotions, with the left frontal region more activated during positive, approach-related emotion and the right frontal more activated during negative, withdrawal-related emotion.[74] The situation is not equivalent, according to Davidson, to the pattern of lateralization present for the perception of emotion, for which posterior regions in the right hemisphere appear to be specialized, irrespective of the valence of the perceived emotion.

Furthermore, Davidson argued, many researchers do not distinguish between posed emotional expressions and spontaneous expressions, nor do they really verify that an intended emotion is truly produced by a laboratory stimulus assumed to normally produce a certain emotion. Finally, he attributed many of the inconsistencies in reports on the emotional consequences of unilateral brain damage to the fact that lesions only alter the probability that certain emotional states will arise in response to environmental factors—the appropriate environmental challenge has to occur for the inappropriate or heightened emotional response or mood to occur.

Davidson's recent work has suggested that individual differences in frontal electrophysiological asymmetries can predict both dispositional mood and reactivity to emotion-inducing stimuli. Quantitative scalp-recorded EEG measures of frontal brain activity in normal subjects appeared to predict variations in the subjects' emotional response to positive and negative emotion-laded film clips. Higher levels of left-sided prefrontal activation at baseline were associated with more intense positive emotion to an emotionally positive film clip. Higher levels of right-sided prefrontal activation were associated with a more intense negative emotion to a negative film clip.[75] General disposition and mood seemed to also be related to baseline prefrontal electrophysiological activation: Left-activated subjects reported greater positive and less negative affect than their right-activated counterparts.[76]

Davidson suggested that activation in the left prefrontal region may be a part of a mechanism that inhibits negative affect. Subjects with greater left-sided electrophysiological activation were found to score highly on personality measures that reflect the tendency to minimize negative affect.[77] Some corroboration for this also comes from PET studies which indicate that the amygdala, a deep brain structure implicated in some emotional and psychiatric diseases, is inhibited by prefrontal activation. Depressed patients exhibited a negative correlation between left prefrontal blood flow and blood flow in the amygdala.[78] A PET study of glucose metabolism also reported a similar negative correlation between left prefrontal metabolism and metabolism in the amygdala.[79]

Concluding Comments: Is the Right Hemisphere Dominant in Emotion?

Overall, there appears to be a good case for believing that the right hemisphere is more involved in both the processing or perception of emotional information than is the left. It also appears to be more involved in some aspects of the production of emotional expression, but this is more controversial, with considerable evidence for a left-hemisphere role in positive, approach-related emotions, as proposed by Davidson. One can only speculate as to why such a dominant right-hemisphere involvement is the case. Joan Borod suggested that "emotional processing involves strategies and functions for which the right hemisphere is superior: strategies termed nonverbal, synthetic, integrative, holistic, and Gestalt, and functions such as pattern perception, visuospatial organization, and visual imaging."[80] Howard Gardner suggested that the right hemisphere's critical role in emotional processing is a spatial one, that is, it has a sensitivity to relationships among emotions that determines which behavior is appropriate for a particular situation.[81]

Kenneth Heilman has suggested that the right hemisphere is more "in touch" with the subcortical systems that are important for arousal and intention.[82] He also argued that the cognitive arousal theory (which he termed the self-attribution model of emotion) is consistent with the finding that patients with right-hemisphere lesions tend to have flattened affects and patients with left-hemisphere disease tend to be depressed and have catastrophic reaction. Because right-hemisphere-damaged patients have difficulty comprehending the intonation of speech and recognizing emotion in facial expressions, these deficits could interfere with developing an appropriate cognitive state to interpret or interact with any physiological arousal occurring in the patient himself. The situation would be further exacerbated by indications that arousal itself is reduced after right-hemisphere damage.[83]

Conversely, patients with left-hemisphere damage should have no trouble interpreting intonation or facial expressions nor in properly interpreting their own physiological states. In addition, they should have increased arousal as a result of the release of right hemisphere arousal mechanisms from left-hemisphere control and thus be susceptible to catastrophic reaction.

As interesting as these speculations are, it is important to keep in mind that the laterality of emotion is far from determined—the data reviewed earlier pointing to a specialized role for the left hemisphere in the expression of positive emotions is just one case in point. To speak of the right hemisphere as the one specialized for emotion clearly oversimplifies what we know about hemispheric asymmetry as well as what we call emotion. Adding even more to this picture of complexity are the data reviewed in Chapter 11, dealing with a possible role of hemispheric differences in psychopathology. We look to future research (and perhaps some reconceptualization of what is being studied) to provide clues about how it all fits together.

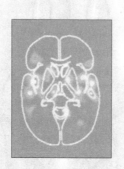

PART V

The Evolution and Development of Asymmetry

Chapter 9

Animal Asymmetries

The Search for the
Biological Origins

If one dates the beginning of the study of hemispheric asymmetry to coincide with Broca's observations, the field of laterality is now approximately 135 years old. For much of this time, investigators have viewed the lateralized brain as the end point of an evolutionary and developmental progression—human beings, but not other animals; older children and adults, but not infants—were believed to possess brains showing hemispheric asymmetry of function. In the last three decades, however, new evidence has called into question these assumptions and has substantially increased our understanding of brain lateralization and its significance.

The study of the evolution of a trait or characteristic across different species is known as phylogeny. Ontogeny, in contrast, is the study of development within an organism over time. In this chapter we will look at evidence bearing on the phylogeny of asymmetry to determine whether animals other than humans show asymmetries that might be related to those found in humans. At the core of questions about asymmetries in animals are the assumptions that laterality is a true biological trait that can be studied in much the same way as other biological phenomena, such as color vision and digestion, and that precursors of human laterality will be found by studying other species.

Research demonstrating the existence of hemispheric asymmetries in animals would have important implications for our understanding of the origin and significance of asymmetry in humans. Some investigators have argued that brain asymmetry is intimately related to higher linguistic abilities. The presence of hemispheric differences in nonlinguistic animals would suggest that this view is too limited. Thus, the asymmetries found in animals may provide clues to the actual evolutionary basis for brain asymmetry in humans. Conversely, convincing evidence for the absence of asymmetries, even in the closest evolutionary relatives of human beings, would be consistent with the view that brain asymmetry is unique to *Homo sapiens* and that it may be fundamentally related to linguistic functions.

Avian Asymmetries:
What the Bird's Brain Can Tell Us

One of the first and most striking asymmetries in animals was discovered in an unlikely place—song production in song birds. To fully appreciate these findings, we must make a brief digression to consider how bird song is produced.

The vocal system of birds essentially consists of a set of bellows that act on an air-driven structure called the syrinx. The position and tension of tissue folds and membranes in the syrinx determine the frequency and amplitude of the sounds produced. The syrinx is divided into a left half and a right half, which are controlled independently by the left and the right hypoglossus nerves, respectively.*

Fernando Nottebohm and his colleagues demonstrated that sectioning the left hypoglossus in adult chaffinches and canaries results in a dramatic change in song.[1] Most of the song components disappear and are replaced either by silence or by poorly modulated sounds. Sec-

---

*Notice that control of the syrinx is same-sided, or ipsilateral, in contrast with the crossed, or contralateral, control we have come to expect.

tioning of the right hypoglossus, in contrast, has minimal effects on song.

Further investigation has shown that the right hypoglossus may come to control song to various degrees, depending on the age at which the left hypoglossus is cut. Canaries with the left hypoglossus cut within two weeks after hatching develop song of normal complexity that is completely controlled by the right hypoglossus. Birds operated on as adults also show some plasticity in that they can learn new song under control of the right hypoglossus; the end result, however, is less accomplished than that produced by intact canaries.

The asymmetries in control of bird song appear to extend to the highest vocal-control stations in the brain, with lesions of the left or right hemisphere producing results similar to those found following lesions of the left or right hypoglossus.[2] Hemispheric differences in the auditory discrimination of song have also been found in songbirds.[3]

Although the similarities between these asymmetries found in songbirds and in human language are striking, the remoteness of the evolutionary relationship between birds and humans as well as some physiological data suggesting that peripheral asymmetries may explain some of the bird song data call for caution in interpreting the evidence.[4] The asymmetries that have been identified remain intriguing, however, and will no doubt be the subject of continued research into the mechanisms underlying them.

Other equally dramatic examples of brain asymmetries in birds have also been identified. Birds are excellent subjects in experiments using lateralized visual stimuli because the optic nerve in each eye crosses over almost completely in the optic chiasm. Thus, stimuli presented to one eye are projected almost exclusively to the contralateral hemisphere. The bird brain also lacks the large corpus callosum connecting the two sides of the mammalian brain, limiting the amount of information transfer between the hemispheres at higher levels of processing.

For both pigeons and chickens, research has shown that visual discrimination learning is faster when the right eye is used.[5] The right eye, and by inference, the left hemisphere, appear to be specialized for categorizing objects, such as food versus nonfood. The left eye–right hemisphere, on the other hand, appear to be specialized for the processing of novelty and topographical information, that is, the location of a stimulus. These asymmetries depend on exposure of the developing chick embryo to light at a critical point in time. The chick embryo is normally oriented in the egg so that its right eye can be stimulated by light—the left eye is usually occluded. Eggs hatched in the dark produce birds that do not demonstrate the characteristic patterns of hemispheric asymmetry we have described. This phenomenon suggests that the development of asymmetries in the chicken is a consequence of both genetic and environmental factors.

As compelling as these results are, however, serious attention to the existence of animal asymmetries as precursors to human asymmetries awaited the demonstration of asymmetries in mammals, and in infrahuman primates, in particular.

Paw Preference: Precursor to Handedness?

As noted in Chapter 5, the most obvious sign of lateralization in humans is handedness. Thus, investigators have looked for paw or limb preferences in animals as evidence of brain lateralization, and they have found that many species do show such preferences.[6] Cats typically use one paw in tasks that involve reaching for an object; mice show consistent preferences in a task in which they must use one paw at a time to reach for food.

Although the pattern of limb preference in a given animal bears some resemblance to hand preference shown by human beings, there is an important difference. Approximately 50 percent of cats, monkeys, and mice show a preference for the right paw, and 50 percent show a preference for the left paw. This result is strikingly different from the breakdown found in human beings—approximately 90 percent right-hand preference, 10 percent left-hand preference.

The 50–50 split in animals has led some investigators to propose that paw preferences are the result of chance factors. According to this hypothesis, the limb first used by an animal is determined by chance, with the additional dexterity gained as a result of the experience increasing the probability that the same limb will be used again. The inability to selectively breed mice for right- or left-paw preference supports the idea that such preferences are not genetically determined.

Hand Preference in Primates

Up until the last decade, most reviews of paw preference in animals reported that there was no population preference for one limb over the other in monkeys. This result proved particularly troublesome for an evolutionary view of asymmetry, because one would expect to find such evidence in the closest evolutionary relatives of humans.

Peter McNeilage, Michael Studdert-Kennedy, and Bjorn Lindblom have reopened this issue.[7] They argued that inconclusive findings about hand preference in nonhuman primates result from the use of inappropriate tasks as well as the use of animals too young to demonstrate a consistent preference. Taking these factors into account, the authors reexamined existing data and reported evidence of a left-hand specialization for visually guided movement (i.e., reaching) and a right-hand specialization for manipulation and bimanual coordination. They concluded that "both the left and right hand preference patterns observed in non-human primates may be precursors of human specialization. However, monkeys and humans would seem to be separated by an evolutionary progression in which the importance of the ability to operate on the environment (including the use of bimanual coordination and the consequent right-hand preference) has so increased that the right hand now normally preempts the left, even for visually guided movement."[8] Their analysis has generated a great deal of controversy. At the same time, it has stimulated increased interest in primate hand usage.

Joel Fagot and Jacques Vauclair have reviewed the large body of data regarding manual lateralization in nonhuman primates and concluded that it is important to distinguish between handedness, defined by a consistent lateralized usage in familiar and highly practiced tasks, and "manual specialization," which concerns lateralized hand usage in novel and relatively complex tasks.[9] This view led them to predict that behaviors that could be classified as "handedness" usually show symmetrical hand biases (either left or right, depending on the individual animal), whereas those behaviors that characterize "manual specialization" show asymmetrical distribution of hand biases in the overall primate group. It is manual specialization, they suggest, that holds the most promise in helping us understand the evolution of lateralization in humans.

Fagot and Vauclair's own research with a group of ten gorillas and six baboons was consistent with these conclusions.[10] While there were no group preferences in a simple reaching task, there was a significant left-hand preference in each of several tasks involving manipulation of a horizontal or vertical sliding window, with almost all animals showing a left-hand preference. Although these results are consistent with the hypothesis that a left-hand specialization would be found for visually guided movement, Vauclair and Fagot note that the continued study of cognitively and motorically complex manual specialization tasks will be needed to determine how manual specialization is related to hemispheric asymmetry in these animals.

Split-Brain Research with Animals

A number of studies have focused on the kinds of deficits in behavior that follow surgical lesions in specific brain structures in primates. In general, deficits following lesions on one side only (unilateral lesions) are less serious than those that follow bilateral brain damage, regardless of which side the lesion is on. Some of these studies, however, have shown greater impairment when the lesion occurs in the hemisphere opposite the preferred hand; others show no relationship to hand preference.[11]

What differentiates studies that have found lesion effects from those that have not? One factor that is likely to be of critical importance is the nature of the stimuli and the task to be performed. Some studies have employed stimuli and tasks that would probably not show an asymmetry in humans. In those cases, why should one be expected in primates? To fairly test the hypothesis of hemispheric specialization in primates, stimuli and tasks are needed that are sufficiently complex to tap the brain asymmetries that may exist in these animals.

In principle, split-brain research is an ideal way to test for hemispheric specialization in animals, allowing the investigator to study separately the abilities of each half of the same brain. Except for possible hemispheric differences, which are the object of the research in the first place, both hemispheres are genetically identical and have been exposed to the same environmental influences.

In contrast to split-brain research with human patients, limited by necessity to persons with epilepsy (generally of long standing), animal studies may be done with healthy animals with two intact hemispheres. Interpretation of any differences that might be found is therefore much more clear-cut. In addition, split-brain research avoids the problem of inferring the function of specific regions of the brain from the effects of lesions in those areas.

As is the case in lesion studies, most of the tasks used to study asymmetries in split-brain animals have been simple and bear little resemblance to those that reveal asymmetries in humans. Hence we should not be surprised by the findings of earlier research that failed to demonstrate any consistent hemispheric differences. Studies that have used more complex tasks, however, have revealed an intriguing pattern of results.[12] Psychobiologist Charles Hamilton has tested rhesus monkeys with stimuli that included lines in different orientations and facial expression and identity (using monkey faces). Geometrical patterns not expected to show lateralized differences were used as control stimuli. Because the monkeys had a complete section of the cerebral commissures and the optic chiasm, it was possible for Hamilton to present stimuli to one hemisphere by presenting it to the ipsilateral eye. The monkeys were taught to discriminate between the members of pairs of stimuli by responding to only one member of the pair.

As expected, the geometrical patterns did not show any evidence of asymmetry and were learned equally well by both hemispheres. Spatial discriminations, however, were processed significantly better by the left hemisphere. Discriminations of monkey faces, in contrast, were processed better by the right hemisphere. Moreover, an analysis of the data from the 25 monkeys who learned both the orientation and facial-discrimination tasks showed convincing support for complementary specialization; of those 25 animals, 16 discriminated oriented lines better with the left hemisphere and faces better with the right hemisphere. This result shows that possible unrecognized asymmetries in surgical or testing procedures did not produce an asymmetry artifactually.

More recent research with rhesus monkeys has suggested that laterality effects are determined by the manner in which a stimulus is processed, analogous to findings in humans.[13] In one task, the simultaneous orientation identification task, two split-brain monkeys had to decide which of two simultaneously presented gratings (visual displays of alternating light and dark bars) was horizontal. In the other task, the temporal same–different task, each monkey had to decide whether or not two successively presented gratings differed in orientation. Both monkeys showed left-hemisphere superiority on the same–different task, but no consistent asymmetry in the identification task. Because the stimuli and form of response were the same in both conditions, the investigators concluded that the asymmetry that was found is related to hemispheric differences in higher order cognitive processing and not early visual or motor processing. Although these findings must be considered preliminary because of the small sample size, they are consistent with an overall pattern of results pointing to asymmetries in primates, some of which are similar to those found in humans.

Anatomical Asymmetries in Primates

Anatomical studies have suggested that the temporal lobe region of some nonhuman primates may reveal structural asymmetries between the hemispheres similar to those found in human brains. One comprehensive study found asymmetries favoring the left hemisphere in humans and, to a lesser extent, in chimpanzees, but no significant differences between sides in the rhesus brain.[14]

Another study examining the brains of a variety of monkeys and apes resulted in a similar conclusion. Sixteen of 28 great apes (orangutans, chimpanzees, and gorillas) showed an asymmetry favoring the left hemisphere; one showed the opposite. In contrast, only 3 cases among 41 monkeys and lesser apes (gibbons) showed a sizable asymmetry.[15] Skull size, rather than brain size, has been studied by another investigator. In this study examining skull length in three species of gorilla, only the mountain gorilla showed evidence of gross asymmetry.[16]

It is tempting to speculate that these asymmetries are related to the ability of the apes, particularly chimpanzees, to learn words, some grammar, and even some abstract concepts through the use of sign language or the manipulation of plastic symbols. Some investigators have suggested the anatomical asymmetries in the great apes are a reflection of their having reached a "prelinguistic" evolutionary stage in which their thought patterns are similar to those of humans, but much more primitive.

It is important to keep in mind that we do not yet have evidence linking anatomical asymmetries in primates to actual asymmetries in function, such as those for speech and language in human beings. In fact, we are only beginning to see evidence of a link between anatomical asymmetries and functional asymmetries in human beings. It is possible that asymmetries in the brains of primates are not related to behavioral asymmetries, just as it is possible that some asymmetries in the human brain may be unrelated to behavioral differences. Underlying much of the interest in anatomical asymmetries, however, is the as yet unproven assumption that such a relationship will ultimately be established.

Pharmacological Asymmetries

Evidence suggesting that the rat may be a useful animal in which to study the possible pharmacological bases of asymmetries comes from the work of Stanley Glick and his colleagues.[17] They found that rats rotate or move in circles at night, and that individual rats show a consistent preference in the direction in which they run. This preference seems to be established very early—the direction in which newborn rats turn their tails predicts their turning preferences later in life.

Glick has shown that a rat's characteristic turning preference is related to a chemical imbalance in the region of the brain called the nigrostriatal pathway, an area that helps regulate movement. The concentration of dopamine, a chemical transmitter released by the neurons in the nigrostriatal pathway that is responsible for circling behavior, is higher by about 15 percent in the side of the brain opposite the direction of the animal's turning preference.

More recently, other investigators have demonstrated a linkage between hemispheric differences in dopamine levels and paw preference in mice.[18] Mice showing a left-paw preference tended to have dopamine levels higher in the left-hemisphere areas of the brain involved in the movements associated with eating, whereas mice showing right-paw preference had higher levels of dopamine in the right hemisphere.

Although the relationship, if any, between pharmacological asymmetries associated with paw preference and those associated with circling behavior remain to be determined, these phenomena in the mouse and rat may reveal functions and mechanisms of brain asymmetry that apply to humans as well. Ernst Mach considered the possibility more than a century ago:

The idea that the distinction between right and left depends upon an asymmetry, and possibly in the last resort upon a chemical difference, is one which has been present to me from my earliest years . . . Human beings and animals that have lost their direction move, almost without exception, nearly in a circle . . . we have here a teleological device to help parents to find their hungry young again when they have been lost.[19]

Behavioral Tests

In many respects the search for asymmetries in animals has followed a progression similar to that of laterality research with human beings. A major difference between the human and animal research, however, lies in the role played by behavioral studies. Behavioral work forms a large part of the literature on human laterality, but, with the exception of research on paw preference, until recently few studies have used behavioral approaches to hemispheric differences in animals.

In one behavioral study, Japanese macaque monkeys were taught to discriminate two different types of vocalizations made by members of their own species. The sounds were prerecorded and presented to the left or right ear in a random sequence. The investigators found that all five of the monkeys tested performed more accurately when the sounds were presented to the right ear. Only one of five monkeys of other species showed ear asymmetry when presented with the Japanese macaque vocalizations.[20] If we assume that sounds presented to the right ear are preferentially delivered to the left hemisphere, these results suggest a hemispheric asymmetry in Japanese macaques for the processing of vocalizations produced by members of their own species.

William Hopkins and colleagues have taken a different approach in their study of language-trained chimpanzees.[21] Their subjects were a small number of chimpanzees who had received language training with geometrical visual symbols over a 12- to 18-year period. The task required the chimpanzees to hold down a response button until a response cue occurred. On each trial, a geometrical symbol, in some cases meaningful and in some cases nonmeaningful but familiar, was presented as a warning stimulus in either the left or the right visual field. The warning stimulus was expected to prime the hemisphere to which it was presented, resulting in greater readiness to respond. Results showed a right-visual-field advantage in priming for the meaningful symbols. Hopkins concluded that

> the data suggest that the manner in which these chimpanzees perceive symbols that have acquired functional meaning may be similar to that observed in human subjects in the processing of words. Further research using traditional lateralized recognition and memory paradigms should help to determine the relations between these simple priming effects and other higher cortical processes.[22]

A small number of studies investigating asymmetries through the use of EEG recordings have also been conducted in animals. Richard Davidson and colleagues have based their work on previous findings in humans suggesting that diazepam, a tranquilizing drug, has an asymmetrical effect on the activity of the frontal lobes and that it plays a role in individual differences in anxiety and fearfulness.[23] They recorded EEG from the scalps of nine infant rhesus monkeys prior to and after injection of diazepam. Fearfulness was assessed on separate occasions by measuring the length of time an infant maintained a tense body posture without any vocalization or head movements (i.e., freezing posture) in the presence of an adult male human. The monkeys showed left-sided frontal activation following injection with diazepam, and the amount of activation was strongly correlated with the level of fearfulness that the animals had previously demonstrated. Thus, animals that showed longer freezing times also had larger frontal change scores following injection with diazepam. These data are particularly interesting because they demonstrate a behavioral correlate—fearfulness—of an electrophysiological measure of hemispheric asymmetry.

Theoretical Implications of Animal Asymmetries

Comparative research with nonhuman species may help to answer two fundamental questions about brain lateralization: Why are there asymmetries in the first place? Why are such asymmetries generally consistent in their direction, that is, why is speech usually represented in the left and not the right hemisphere?

The evidence we have reviewed points to the existence of anatomical, pharmacological, and/or behavioral asymmetries in a wide range of animals. Much work remains to be done, however, to firmly establish the existence of these asymmetries and to determine what their relationship might be to the asymmetries found in human beings. Norman Geschwind, one of the researchers primarily responsible for current interest in the biological foundations of laterality, has speculated on some of the more far-reaching implications of animal asymmetry research.[24]

Geschwind argued that the widespread belief that humans have certain completely distinctive characteristics, such as language and high levels of artistic and musical abilities, would be discredited as more is learned about asymmetries in animals. He was particularly interested in the recent scientific debate as to whether chimps could be taught "true" language. Chimpanzees had been specially trained to communicate with sign language, but there is much controversy over whether this represented language in the same sense as spoken language used by humans.

Geschwind proposed a hypothetical experiment to help resolve the issue. If the chimpanzee's language abilities were impaired by a left-side lesion in the region of the brain comparable to the human language centers and if a bilateral lesion in other locations did not disrupt performance, the results would be consistent with the idea that chimpanzee "language" and human language were similar in mechanism. If the chimpanzee's abilities were impaired as a result of the bilateral lesions in areas not homologous to human language centers, however, and were not impaired with the left-side lesion, he argued, this would be evidence against the linguistic nature of the chimpanzee's performance. We agree with Geschwind that a "positive" outcome to this hypothetical study would be powerful indirect evidence for the linguistic nature of the chimpanzee's performance. However, we believe the failure to demonstrate hemispheric asymmetry in chimpanzees of the same sort found in humans would not necessarily rule out the possibility that chimpanzee language was linguistic in the same manner as human language.

The fact that asymmetries are found in animals that do not seem to possess linguistic abilities does not weaken the argument, Geschwind claimed. He postulated that perhaps there is a forerunner of language that does not involve communication among individuals but is still useful to the individual animal. Geschwind stated:

It is clearly conceivable that such an internal method of coding might have appeared very early in evolution and could have been used by individual non-human animals. The ability to communicate, although of great interest, might be a later "technical" development that enabled transmission of the code from one individual to another, but the essential step in the development of the internal code might have occurred much earlier.[25]

Although these ideas are speculative, they are representative of the problems that neuroscientists wishing to understand lateralization are starting to confront. By extending the search for asymmetries beyond human beings, researchers have begun the process of discovering the answers. Some of those answers may prove surprising. A recent paper reported asymmetry in limb use in two species of toad. The authors conclude, without hesitation, that "Pawedness and motor asymmetries found in natural populations of toad could represent a precursor of handedness in higher vertebrates and thus contribute to our under-standing of the evolution of the brain."[26]

In the next chapter, we turn to another issue critical to an under-standing of lateralization—the ontogeny, or development, of asymme-try in humans.

Chapter 10

Asymmetry
Over the Life Span

At birth, the brain of a human infant is one-fourth the weight of an adult brain. By the time a child is two years old, the brain will have more than tripled its mass and come close to its full size. Accompanying this dramatic change in physical size are equally dramatic changes in a child's capabilities. By the age of two years, the average child has begun to talk and to show the beginnings of many of the higher mental functions that characterize human beings.

In the sections that follow, we will discuss how and at what point the basic differences between the left brain and the right brain found in adults fit into this picture of physical and functional change in childhood. Do these asymmetries emerge over time as the child develops, or are they present at birth or even before? What roles do genetic and environmental factors play in the establishment of asymmetry? Can the pattern of asymmetry be changed and, if so, what are the limiting factors?

These fundamental questions relating to the ontogeny of asymmetry are the focus of research efforts that use many different methodologies reflecting the approach of cognitive neuroscience. The answers have the potential for contributing in important ways to our understanding of language disorders, both in children and in adults. They may also help investigators better understand other problems that have been linked to the division of functions between the hemispheres.

Brain Injury in Childhood:
Laterality and Plasticity

Current interest in the development of lateralization can be traced to the work of Eric Lenneberg, a psychologist who reviewed a variety of evidence in the mid-1960s and concluded that lateralization of function in the brain develops over time but is complete by puberty.[1] His research also led him to conclude that puberty marks a crucial turning point in the ability to learn new languages, without signs of a foreign accent, through mere exposure. Lenneberg believed it was not simply a coincidence that both lateralization and language-learning ability appear fixed at puberty. He saw the former as the biological basis of the latter.

In drawing his conclusions about the time course of lateralization, Lenneberg relied heavily on clinical data collected by the neurologist L. S. Basser.[2] Basser reported that about half of a group of children with brain injury occurring before the age of two years began to speak at the usual time, whereas the other half showed some delay. The results were the same for children with damage to the left or the right hemisphere, suggesting that hemispheric asymmetry for language is not well established by the age of two years. Results from a group of children with injuries occurring after the onset of speech, however, showed the emergence of hemispheric differences. Here, injury to the left side resulted in speech disturbances in 85 percent of the cases; injury to the right side produced disturbances in only 45 percent of the cases.

A third pattern of impairment was found in right-handed teenagers and adults who sustain brain injury. In these groups, aphasia very rarely follows damage to the right hemisphere but occurs more often after damage to the left half of the brain. On the basis of this evidence, Lenneberg concluded that lateralization begins at the time of language acquisition but is not complete until puberty.

Lateralization by Puberty Reconsidered

Lenneberg's influential interpretation of these data has not gone unchallenged. A careful reexamination of Basser's data has suggested that most of the cases in which right-hemisphere damage in infancy resulted in aphasia were really cases of injury to the left as well as the right hemisphere.[3] If this is so, the early childhood data look no different from adult data in terms of the incidence of aphasia after damage to the brain and are consistent with the hypothesis that laterality is complete at birth.

Additional findings confirm this interpretation. Among them is the research of Bryan Woods and Hans Lucas Teuber, who reported 65 cases of children with unilateral hemispheric injury occurring after the onset of speech.[4] They found that 25 of the 34 children with left-hemisphere lesions were initially aphasic, whereas only 4 of the 31 children with right-hemisphere lesions (including two left-handers) were aphasic.

In reviewing earlier studies, the authors observed that there had been a sharp drop in the reported incidence of aphasia after right-hemisphere injury in children seen in studies begun after 1941, coincident with the use of antibiotics for scarlet fever and other infectious diseases. Research had shown that these diseases, if severe and untreated, could produce localized brain lesions as well as diffuse damage to both hemispheres. A child who showed both left hemiplegia and aphasia after such an infection probably would have been classified as a right-hemisphere case, when, in fact, the left hemisphere was most likely also affected. The investigators concluded that the incidence of aphasia after right-hemisphere lesions in children had been greatly overestimated in earlier studies before the use of antibiotics and that the data as a whole supported the idea that the pattern of language functions seen in adults is essentially complete soon after birth.

Thus, clinical evidence suggested that hemispheric specialization for language is present at birth and does not develop over time. This conclusion, however, does not contradict what we know about the ability of the right hemisphere to take over language functions after very early lesions of the left hemisphere. We know that there are dramatic differences in recovery from aphasia in children and in adults, and we will consider the theoretical implications of these findings later in this chapter.

Hemispherectomy in Childhood:
Removing Half a Brain

Occasionally, it is medically necessary to remove most of one cerebral hemisphere. We discussed in Chapter 7 some of the consequences of hemispherectomy in adults. The operation is also done early in childhood when extensive damage to one hemisphere threatens to impair the function of the undamaged side as well.

Adult patients with the right hemisphere removed typically show little or no language impairment, but the removal of the left hemisphere generally results in marked aphasia that improves only slightly with time. In children, the severity of impairment is directly related and the prognosis for recovery of language is inversely related to the age of the child at the time of surgery. Several reports have noted that if surgery is performed early enough in infancy, no signs of lateralized deficits in higher mental functions remain in adulthood. This finding suggests that the remaining hemisphere, whether it is the left or the right, is able to take over for the hemisphere that is removed.[5]

It is possible to draw at least two different theoretical conclusions from these data. One is that no shift of functions has taken place in early hemispherectomy cases because lateralization of function is not present in early infancy. A second interpretation is that hemispheric differences are present early in infancy, but the young brain has a tremendous ability to reorganize itself in the face of damage to specific regions. Studies of the abilities of patients with left and right hemispherectomies suggest that of the two possibilities, the latter "plasticity" explanation is more likely to be correct.

Maureen Dennis and Harry Whitaker studied three nine- to ten-year-olds who had undergone hemispherectomy by the age of five months.[6] One was a right-hemispherectomy patient; the other two had had the left hemisphere removed. Results showed that both discrimination and articulation of the sounds of speech as well as words were normal in all three children. Important differences between the hemispheres, however, appeared in tests of the patients' abilities to deal with syntax—the rules for combining words into grammatically correct sentences. For example, each child was asked to judge the acceptability of the following sentences:

1. I paid the money by the man.
2. I was paid the money to the lady.
3. I was paid the money by the boy.

The right-hemispherectomy patient correctly indicated that sentences 1 and 2 are grammatically incorrect and that sentence 3 is acceptable. The two left-hemispherectomy patients did not make these distinctions.

The researchers concluded that the right hemisphere in the left-hemispherectomy cases does not accurately comprehend the meaning of passive sentences. Other tests led them to propose that the right-hemisphere defect is an organizational, analytical, and syntactical problem rather than one rooted in the conceptual or semantic aspects of language. The results suggest that there are limits to the plasticity of the infant brain and that hemispheric differences are present very early in life. Dennis and Whitaker's conclusions, however, have been criticized on the grounds that the errors produced by the left hemispherectomy patients are typical of those made by young people of low or even normal intelligence who have not had brain surgery.[7]

More recent work has provided additional evidence regarding the consequences of early hemispherectomy.[8] Nine subjects, ranging in age from 7 to 24 years, were studied. Five had undergone left hemispherectomy and four right hemispherectomy, all after an initial period of normal language acquisition. Intelligence tests showed that a majority of them had IQ scores in the borderline normal to mentally retarded range. The investigators used the estimated mental age of each subject obtained from the IQ tests to determine whether performance on a variety of language tests was poorer than what would be expected on the basis of the patients' overall cognitive level.

Results showed that four out of five of the left-hemispherectomy patients showed syntactic comprehension deficits, relative to their cognitive level, compared with one out of four right-hemispherectomy patients. A similar pattern of findings was found in a task requiring the processing of speech sounds (i.e., distinguishing between "ba" and "da"). No deficits were found between the two hemispherectomy groups and normal children in speech production. These results suggested that the right hemisphere is better able to take over control of speech production than syntactic or speech sound processing following early removal of the left hemisphere.

It may well be that data definitively showing the limits of plasticity eventually will be obtained. These limits, however, whatever they might be, would not detract from the very important role plasticity plays in much of the dramatic recovery from aphasia that is found after left-hemisphere damage in children. The ability of a brain to readjust its function relatively quickly makes it hard to distinguish between a system in which lateralization does not exist or exists only in rudimentary form and one in which lateralization is extensive, but where rapid compensation for unilateral damage is possible. Only through the use of very sensitive tests designed to measure subtle differences in performance can we begin to tease apart these alternatives.

The Search for the Beginnings of Lateralization

Clinical evidence dealing with the effects of early brain damage on language functions has played a central role in shaping current thinking about the development of asymmetry. As noted earlier in this chapter, the effects of unilateral brain damage occurring early in life contrast dramatically with the effects of damage occurring later. Language impairments after damage to the left hemisphere generally are less severe and of shorter duration the younger the individual at the time of the injury. Does this imply that lateralization becomes more extensive or complete with age? While this is certainly one possible explanation, another interpretation of these brain-damage findings is that asymmetry is present at birth, but that the plasticity of the brain decreases with age; that is, as the individual grows older, the right hemisphere loses the ability to take over the control of language. In this section we will consider evidence from a variety of sources that will help us determine which of these explanations can best account for the clinical data.

Anatomical Asymmetries in Infants

The presence early in life of anatomical asymmetries between the hemispheres similar to those found in adult brains would be consistent with the hypothesis that hemispheric asymmetry of function is present at birth. Neurologist Albert Galaburda has reviewed the data in this area and has cited several studies showing the presence of gross anatomical asymmetries in the cerebral cortex before birth, as well as studies demonstrating asymmetries in the brains of newborns.[9] He noted that the gross anatomy of the brain does not change significantly after birth, other than overall growth and the formation of fissures in the cortex; hence the anatomical asymmetries found at birth would not be expected to change over the course of development. Indeed, the asymmetries that are observed in the fetal and newborn brain are the same as those found in the adult brain.

As noted in Chapter 3, however, we do not know the precise nature of the relationship between anatomical asymmetry and functional asymmetry. Is the former the structural basis of the latter? If so, are functional differences between the hemispheres present whenever we find anatomical differences? Only when additional information is available to help answer these questions will we be able to interpret the anatomical data with a high degree of confidence. Until then, the evidence will remain suggestive and intriguing, but by no means a complete answer to the issue of whether lateralization of function is present at birth.

Evoked Potentials in Infants

Because electrophysiological recording techniques do not require a deliberate response of any sort from the subject and carry no risk of side effects, they are well suited to the study of hemispheric asymmetries in infants. In one of the earliest studies of its kind, Dennis Molfese recorded event-related potentials (ERPs) from the temporal regions of 10 infants between 1 week and 10 months of age, 11 children between 4 and 11 years of age, and 10 adults from 23 to 29 years of age in response to a series of simple speech and nonspeech sounds.[10]

Overall, the magnitude of the left-hemisphere ERPs to the speech stimuli was greater than that for the right hemisphere in 27 of the 31 subjects tested. For the nonspeech stimuli, however, the amplitude of the right-hemisphere response was greater than that of the left (30 of 31 subjects and 29 of 31 subjects, respectively, depending on whether the stimulus was a piano chord or a noise burst.) The proportion of subjects showing this lateralized pattern of responding was the same at each age level, a result demonstrating that hemispheric differences of the sort found in adults were present in very young infants and children as well. The magnitude of the asymmetries, in fact, was greatest in infants and decreased with the age of the subjects across the age groups tested. To account for this surprising result, Molfese suggested that the ERP asymmetry may decline with age as a consequence of the maturation of the cerebral commissures that connect the hemispheres.

In a longitudinal study that builds upon this early work, Dennis Molfese and Victoria Molfese have attempted to relate the pattern of an individual child's ERPs to speech sounds that are similar, for example, "ba," "da," "ga," to later language and cognitive performance.[11] Intriguingly, they have found that patterns of ERPs recorded shortly after birth at 36 hours of age predicted the performance of the same children on the verbal subscale of the Stanford-Binet Intelligence Test five years later. Event-related potentials recorded from both hemispheres, however, were needed to make the prediction, supporting the idea that the functioning of mechanisms within both hemispheres of the brain are important to later language development.

The investigators suggested that ERPs to speech stimuli may be useful in the early identification of children with potential language problems, so that successful intervention can be carried out at the earliest possible age. We will see in Chapter 11 how impairments in the processing of temporal information has been implicated in a variety of language-based learning disorders.

Dichotic Listening Across the Life Span

A number of studies have looked at the magnitude of ear asymmetries in dichotic listening to see whether there are changes as a function of age. Although there is some inconsistency among such studies, overall the data indicate that auditory laterality first appears early in life and neither increases nor decreases during childhood or throughout adulthood.[12] A right-ear advantage is typically found in the standard dichotic listening test in which subjects report what they have heard when children as young as two to three years of age are tested. Efforts to study dichotic listening in infants, however, clearly require another form of response.

In one study employing what is known as a high amplitude sucking procedure, infants averaging four days of age first learned to suck on a nipple in order to receive dichotic presentation of a pair of consonant–vowel syllables.[13] Each time the infants sucked with a previously specified force, the same pair of syllables was presented. The procedure continued until the infants habituated to the stimuli, as evidenced by a sustained reduction in the sucking rate. At this point, either the left-ear or right-ear stimulus was changed, and the infants monitored for changes in sucking rate. In another condition, the procedure was identical, except the stimuli consisted of two notes selected from four instruments (piano, violin, flute, and oboe).

Because infants typically increase their rate of sucking when a novel stimulus is presented, the investigators looked for changes in sucking rate that varied with the ear to which the changed stimulus was presented. They found that a change in speech stimulus tended to induce a stronger reaction when it occurred in the right ear, whereas a change in music stimulus tended to induce a stronger reaction when it occurred in the left ear. This result was statistically significant, although the separate ear advantages for music and speech stimuli were not. The study is striking in terms of the age at which evidence of complementary specialization may be observed, and it is consistent with the hypothesis that hemispheric asymmetry is present at birth.

The Role of the Corpus Callosum in Development

The brain of most mammals, including humans, is largely underdeveloped at birth and undergoes a major portion of its structural and functional maturation during infancy and early childhood. In addition to its obvious growth, the brain undergoes dramatic changes at the microscopic level. The connections between neurons multiply tremendously in the first few years and are thought to continue changing throughout a person's lifetime. In addition, insulating fatty layers called myelin are laid down around nerve fibers, thereby making them more efficient conductors of electrical impulses. The corpus callosum, the largest tract of nerve fibers in the brain, and other cerebral commissures are included in this picture of rapid development.

The corpus callosum is present at birth but appears disproportionately small in cross section when the brain of a newborn is compared with the brain of an adult. Figure 10.1 shows the growth of the corpus callosum and other cerebral commissures during three stages of human development. The most rapid growth takes place during fetal development. Between birth and the age of two years, however, the corpus callosum continues to grow at a rapid rate, approximately doubling and reaching a size equivalent to that of a corpus callosum at the low end of the adult size range. A recent MRI study demonstrated that growth of the corpus callosum continues into the third decade of life, reaching a maximum size at approximately 25 years of age.[14]

At present, we have only a limited understanding of the role of the corpus callosum in higher cognitive functions; it is no doubt a complex one that may vary as a function of the task to be performed and other conditions. One model of callosal function assumes that the corpus callosum serves primarily excitatory functions that involve generating activation in both hemispheres as well as sharing information between the hemispheres. Another model postulates that the functional role of the corpus callosum is primarily inhibitory, serving to maintain independent processing in the two hemispheres and the separation between

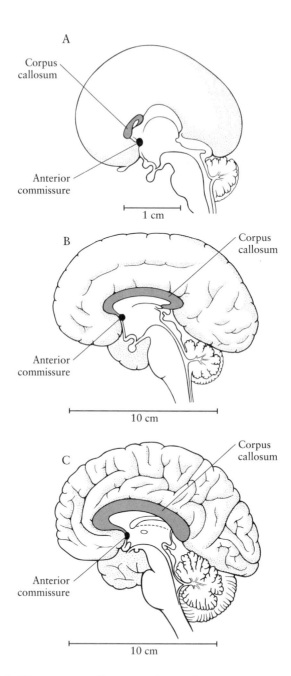

FIGURE 10.1 The corpus callosum and anterior commissure at three stages of human development. A. Fetus (16 weeks). B. Neonate (40 weeks). C. Adult. [From C. Trevarthen, "Cerebral Embryology and the Split Brain," Fig. XI-7, pp. 228–229 in *Hemisphere Disconnection and Cerebral Function,* ed. M. Kinsbourne and L. Smith, Springfield, IL: Charles C. Thomas, 1974.]

them by inhibiting one of the hemispheres when the other engages in a task for which it is specialized.

These two models lead to different predictions concerning hemispheric asymmetry of function and the degree of connectivity attributable to the corpus callosum. The excitatory model suggests that increased connectivity (presumably associated with a larger corpus callosum) should be associated with decreased asymmetry, because interhemispheric sharing of information and interhemispheric activation would tend to mask any hemispheric differences. The inhibitory model, on the other hand, leads to the opposite prediction—greater connectivity would be associated with increased asymmetry of function.[15]

Attempts to directly relate the size of the corpus callosum (and, by inference, its connectivity) and measures of hemispheric asymmetry in individual subjects have been made. One such study examined the relationship between the midsagittal cross-sectional area of the corpus callosum, as measured with MRI, with three behavioral measures of asymmetry, including a dichotic listening test that correlated highly with the results of Wada testing.[16] The size of the asymmetry demonstrated in the behavioral tests was inversely related to callosal size, for example, a larger corpus callosum area was associated with a smaller right-ear advantage. The authors concluded that "as one side of the brain assumes control of the behavior in these tasks, a smaller corpus callosum favors increasing control of the specialized hemisphere, whereas the larger corpus callosum distributes this role more equitably between the two." Similar results have been found in some, but not all, previous studies.[17] Further work is needed to definitively clarify the relationship between callosal size and functional asymmetry.

Agenesis of the Corpus Callosum

What role do the commissures play in lateralization and in the normal development of cognitive functions? What would be the consequences of severing the commissures at birth? Although there are no cases of split-brain surgery performed in infants, cases of a congenital absence, or agenesis, of the corpus callosum provide a unique opportunity to look at these questions.

Until relatively recently, most cases of callosal agenesis came to the attention of investigators as a consequence of other neurological conditions, often accompanied by impaired mental function. The introduction of noninvasive neuroimaging techniques, however, has led to the detection of cases without cross neurological dysfunction such as epilepsy or brain damage. These cases are of great interest because they provide an opportunity to study the functioning of a brain that has developed without the largest interhemispheric pathway.

One of the first questions addressed in research on callosal agenesis is how language is organized in the brain. If the corpus callosum is important in the development of hemispheric asymmetry, perhaps by inhibiting simultaneous activation in related areas in the other half of the brain, then one might expect to find language functions bilaterally represented in acallosal subjects. In fact, most subjects with callosal agenesis show a clear hand preference and small, but reliable, asymmetries in dichotic listening and visual half-field tests, as well as left-hemisphere speech as determined by the Wada test. This, of course, is the pattern found in most subjects with a functioning corpus callosum.[18]

Other results suggest that individuals born without the corpus callosum can have normal cognitive abilities, although they tend to fall at the lower end of the range that is considered normal. They do not show an imbalance between verbal and perceptual functions, nor do they show evidence of the typical disconnection symptoms seen after surgical section of the cerebral commissures. For example, acallosal subjects perform well on tasks involving recognition of material presented unilaterally to either hemisphere, and they show no impairments in divided visual field tasks requiring interfield comparisons.[19]

Despite this overall pattern of normality, however, recent work has identified subtle deficits in individuals lacking the corpus callosum.[20] Maryse Lassonde, Hannelore Sauerwein, and Franco Lepore have studied subjects with complete agenesis of the corpus callosum. They found impairments, relative to normal controls, in tasks requiring interhemispheric transfer of motor and visuospatial skills and in some tasks requiring integration of visual and tactile information across the two sides of the body.

Subtle deficits in cognitive function have also been found in a small group of normal IQ acallosal children by Christine Temple and Joanne Isley.[21] Although these children showed no gross impairments—their speech was clear and well formed and their overall language skills, including reading, were normal—they displayed deficits in tasks involving the production and recognition of rhyme. An example is a task in which the subjects are asked to generate in one minute as many words as possible that rhyme with a given word. Children with agenesis are also impaired in the ability to pronounce nonwords (letter strings that conform to the orthographic rules of language, e.g., gip, sutter) relative to normal children. The investigators concluded that while overall language development may be normal in children with callosal agenesis, there is a consistent deficit in phonological processing. The acallosal subjects were also deficient in certain kinds of visuoconstructional skills that require the coordination of a series of movements, for example, putting pieces of a puzzle together to form an abstract pattern. Temple and Isley concluded that "the results therefore implicate a number of selective cognitive domains in which the corpus callosum may play a critical role in normal performance. The results also indicate that acallosal subjects provide useful evidence about the nature of the modular subcomponents of cognitive skill which may develop in relative independence of each other."[22]

The apparent normality, for the most part, of individuals with callosal agenesis points to the ways in which noncallosal commissural pathways can compensate for the absence of the callosum. The existence of highly selective deficits, however, suggests a role for the corpus callosum in the development and functioning of mental processes. Both sets of findings have the potential for providing important insights into the way in which the brain is organized.

Nature and Nurture in the Establishment of Asymmetries

Nature

Much of the evidence reviewed in this chapter suggests that hemispheric asymmetries in some form are present at or near birth. The earlier the age at which asymmetries are detected, the more confident we may be that they are part of the biological makeup of the organism and independent of experience. Asymmetries occurring later may also be part of an organism's biological makeup, with genetic factors determining the emergence of asymmetries in later stages of development.

Several genetic models have been proposed to account for hemispheric asymmetries. Chapter 5 contained a brief review of this topic in the context of our discussion of handedness. More recently, some investigators have begun to consider other ways, not genetic in the strict sense, in which patterns of lateralization may be inherited.

Research has shown that cytoplasm, the fluid contained in all cells, including the maternal egg, can transmit certain traits from parent to offspring in some species. Such "cytoplasmic inheritance" has been proposed as a possible basis for the transmission of asymmetry from parent to offspring in human beings.

Michael Corballis and Michael Morgan proposed that there is an underlying cytoplasmic gradient operating during embryonic development that favors the left side of the body.[23] This gradient, they claimed, is responsible for physiological asymmetries in humans and animals, which, in turn, are responsible for the functional asymmetries we see.

Why are some people left-handed, and why do some have speech represented in the right or, perhaps, both hemispheres? Corballis and Morgan suggested that the hypothesized gradient is absent in some individuals and that in these cases, environmental factors play a major role in determining which pattern a given individual will show.

Corballis and Morgan's ideas are intriguing ones and are an attempt to place human hand preference and hemispheric asymmetry in a broader biological context. A gradient favoring faster development on the left side is a fundamental one shared by many species, they argued, and handedness and speech lateralization are simply a species-specific consequence of that gradient. Critics of their views, however, have pointed to other examples, in both humans and other animals, in which the right side of the body appears to be favored.[24]

Nurture

What can be said about the role of experience or environmental factors in determining hemispheric asymmetries? At one extreme, we have seen that early damage to one hemisphere of the brain can result in a dramatic reorganization of lateralized functions. The fact that persons with the left hemisphere removed in infancy develop language skills in the right hemisphere is but one piece of evidence pointing to the tremendous plasticity of the brain. The compensation for early removal of one hemisphere, however, is not total. Sensitive tests reveal language deficits, a result suggesting that the basic blueprint for asymmetry is present very early in life and that its traces remain despite damage-induced reorganization. In our earlier discussions of left-handedness, we noted that some investigators believe that left-handedness (and presumably all right-hemisphere or bilateral control of speech) is a result of brain injury, however subtle. We also considered Geschwind and Galaburda's ideas regarding the role of prenatal levels of testosterone on the developing brain. In this section we will consider yet another environmental variable—the quality and quantity of exposure to language itself—and how it may affect the development of lateralization.

Exposure to Language Some evidence pointing to early environment as a factor in asymmetry is based on the study of Genie, a girl discovered at the age of 13½ after having spent most of her life in almost complete isolation, during which time she was punished for making any noise whatsoever. Two years after she was found, she was reported to have made slow but steady progress in language learning.[25]

Of particular interest is Genie's performance on two dichotic listening tests, one composed of familiar words, the other of familiar environmental sounds. Genie was able to correctly identify these stimuli when she was tested one ear at a time. With dichotic presentation, however, Genie showed an extreme left-ear advantage with familiar words and a small left-ear advantage for the environmental sounds.[26]

These findings suggest that the processing of both language and nonlanguage stimuli took place in Genie's right hemisphere. The investigators speculated that her left hemisphere may have begun language acquisition before her confinement but through disuse was no longer able to fulfill its original function. As Genie began to learn language a second time, the right hemisphere assumed control because its functions presumably had been exercised (by visuospatial processes) in spite of her confinement.

The problem with a single-subject study such as this, of course, is that there is no way of knowing the pattern of asymmetry that would have developed in Genie's brain had she had a normal childhood. Perhaps she would have shown right-hemisphere specialization for language and nonlanguage stimuli anyway. Nevertheless, the results are intriguing, especially in light of work looking at hemispheric asymmetry in the congenitally deaf.

Gregory Hickok, Ursula Bellugi, and Edward Klima have examined the linguistic ability of 23 congenitally deaf individuals who sustained unilateral brain damage—13 with left-hemisphere damage and 10 with right-hemisphere damage.[27] All used American Sign Language (ASL) to communicate and were assessed using sign language in several aspects of language use: production, comprehension, naming, and repetition.

The investigators found that left-hemisphere-damaged signers performed significantly worse than right-hemisphere-damaged signers on all measures. In contrast, the right-hemisphere-damaged patients performed poorly on visuospatial tasks, while the left-hemisphere-damaged patients performed well.

The investigators concluded that with regard to hemispheric asymmetry, the neural organization of sign language is indistinguishable from that of spoken language. It is clear from these findings that spoken language is not necessary for hemispheric specialization. Congenitally deaf signers show differential specialization for the processing of ASL and for visuospatial tasks, despite the spatial and manipulative aspects of ASL.

The Bilingual Brain Does the experience of acquiring two languages change the pattern of brain organization? This question has been the subject of controversy.[28] Although a number of studies have concluded that the left hemisphere is dominant for processing both the native language and the nonnative language, other studies claim weaker left lateralization for language among bilinguals and still others have reported differential hemispheric asymmetry for language. Clinical data, however, have not provided any evidence for reduced asymmetry in bilingual subjects for either language. Most notably, crossed aphasia, in which damage to the hemisphere ipsilateral to the preferred hand produces aphasia, is not significantly higher in bilingual subjects than in monolingual subjects. The results from Wada testing show a similar picture—both languages are disrupted only by left-hemisphere administration of the drug.

A recent study using PET has directly addressed the issue of the cortical representation of language in bilinguals by investigating word generation in native speakers of English who were also proficient in French.[29] Presented with different words in English, subjects were asked to find a word similar in meaning, a word that rhymed, and a translation into French. The synonym and translation tasks were also performed in French. Positron emission tomography results showed the greatest blood-flow increases in parts of the left hemisphere for all tasks, regardless of whether they were performed in English or French. No right-hemisphere activation was observed in any condition. The authors, with appropriate caution, conclude that with these tasks and with current methods available to evaluate cortical activation, the data provide no evidence that a language learned later in life is represented differently from the native language.

A very recent study with bilingual subjects has used fMRI to investigate how multiple languages are represented in the brain.[30] The subjects tested were instructed to generate sentences silently describing events of the previous day; immediately before each fMRI scan they were told which language to use in producing this internal speech. The findings led the investigators to conclude that second languages acquired in adulthood are spatially separated from native languages within the frontal lobe language-sensitive regions (Broca's area) although native and second languages acquired early in life tend to be represented in common frontal cortical areas. There was no difference in activity based on age of language acquisition in the temporal lobe language-sensitive regions (Wernicke's area) of the brain. The authors suggest that their findings, which contrast with those reported in the PET study just described, may reflect the greater resolution of the fMRI technique as well as differences in the average age of initial exposure to the second language in the two studies. The average age of initial exposure to the second language in the PET study was 7.3 years, younger than that of the late bilingual subjects in the fMRI study. The PET study, they propose, could be consistent with their data for early acquisition of a second language.

Further investigations involving the tools of cognitive neuroscience are clearly needed to gain a more complete understanding of how multiple languages are represented in the brain.

Some Theoretical Issues

Although investigators are far from having definite answers to the questions about the development of asymmetry, a pattern of findings is emerging. Of great theoretical significance are the observations suggesting that hemispheric differences are present at birth. In apparent conflict with the lateralization-at-birth view is clinical evidence showing that the effects of very early unilateral brain damage do not vary as a function of the side of injury. The latter data, however, are compatible with the lateralization-at-birth position if we take into account the plasticity that allows the young brain to compensate for the effects of damage. In this context, we pointed to the importance of tests that are very sensitive to subtle impairment and could perhaps differentiate between the results of damage-induced reorganization and the absence of lateralization in the first place (presuming damage-induced reorganization is in some way less than optimal).

Research investigating the development of lateralization is challenging for several reasons. A major problem is the difficulty of addressing nature–nurture questions in human beings. Ethical and practical considerations severely limit the kinds of environmental effects that can be studied, and genetic models can be difficult to test in human populations. Compounding these problems is the fact that our measures of lateralization are far from perfect, with many tests apparently sensitive to factors other than brain lateralization. This state of affairs is one for which there are no simple solutions. As more and more investigators appreciate the significance of developmental questions and the care with which they must be investigated, we can expect significant progress toward finding answers.

PART VI

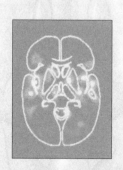

Pathology
and Asymmetry

Chapter 11

Links to Developmental Disabilities and Psychiatric Illness

Research in the area of hemispheric differences has had an impact on many fields involved in the investigation of human function and dysfunction. In Chapters 1, 7, and 8 we discussed the clinical symptoms of injury to the right and left hemispheres. In this chapter we will consider other disabilities in human behavior that have been related to the division of function between the hemispheres. They are considered developmental disabilities because they generally manifest themselves in childhood in the absence of obvious physical damage to the brain. It has been suggested that these disorders may arise from subtle problems in either the left or the right side of the brain, or in the relationship between the two.

Is stuttering the result of competition for control of speech by the two hemispheres in a less than normally lateralized individual? Does incomplete lateralization predispose a child to reading problems, despite otherwise normal intelligence? Why does psychiatric depression seem to respond better to right-hemisphere shock treatment than to left-hemisphere shock treatment? These are a few of the questions investigators have pursued in an attempt to determine the roles of the two hemispheres in pathological processes. In this chapter we will review data from a variety of sources that bear on those roles.

Learning Disability:
Is There a Link to Asymmetry?

Learning disability is an umbrella term for a wide range of difficulties in school despite adequate intelligence, home environment, motivation, and instructional opportunity. It is estimated that 10 to 15 percent of the school-age population in North America and Europe shows evidence of a learning disability of one form or another. *Dyslexia* is the term used to refer to the most common and most extensively studied form of learning disability—a marked impairment in the development of reading skill compared with what would be expected on the basis of intelligence level and education.[1] It is common in school-age children, affecting anywhere from 2 to 8 percent of them.

In general, dyslexia is considered to involve decoding—the ability to read words accurately—rather than reading comprehension per se. The context present in written material can often help dyslexic individuals decode specific words they would have difficulty reading in isolation. Over time, many dyslexic children improve and no longer show obvious signs of reading impairment as adults. However, neuropsychological tests can frequently reveal subtle deficits that remain in phonological coding—the ability to recognize individual phonemes, or speech sounds, in words and to apply the phonological, or sound–symbol, rules of English. For example, the ability to read nonwords, which requires application of the rules of phonology, may be impaired even though there is no problem reading familiar words. Spelling may also be impaired. Recent data suggest a strong genetic component to dyslexia. Thirty-five to forty percent of boys with a dyslexic parent show dyslexia themselves; the figure is 17 to 18 percent for girls. Thus, having an affected parent increases the probability a boy will have dyslexia 5- to 7-fold; girls show a 10- to 12-fold increase in risk.[2]

One of the first investigators to propose a link between brain asymmetry and reading disability was Samuel T. Orton, a physician who had worked during the early decades of the twentieth century with children suffering from reading and writing problems. Orton noticed that these children sometimes wrote in mirror form, reversing the orientation of individual letters as well as their sequence within a word. For example, the word *cat* might be written ƚɒɔ, as it would appear if one viewed it in a mirror. Similarly, these children often reversed letter sequences in reading, so that *saw* was read as *was*. Orton observed that children who made mirror-image reversals in reading and writing also tended to have unstable handedness preferences. He interpreted this finding as a sign of incomplete cerebral dominance. This association between reading disability and incomplete cerebral dominance led him to propose that the two were related.[3]

Because the two sides of the brain are symmetrical about the midline, information about the visual world, he suggested, is represented in mirror-image form on each side. Orton argued that information represented in the dominant hemisphere was oriented correctly, whereas information in the nondominant hemisphere was in mirror-image form. In the absence of sufficiently developed cerebral dominance, the two representations would cause confusion in reading and writing.

Orton's ideas of how representations are laid down in mirror-image fashion in each hemisphere have been shown to be incorrect, but the basic notion that reading disability may be biologically based and in some way linked to hemispheric asymmetry is under active investigation. In Chapter 5 we discussed Norman Geschwind's and Albert Galaburda's controversial ideas relating dyslexia, left-handedness, and other conditions to the differential hemispheric effects of testosterone on the brain during prenatal development. These ideas are but one of the ways in which learning disabilities have been linked to anomalies in brain asymmetry.

Behavioral and Anatomical Evidence of Atypical Asymmetry

A large number of dichotic listening and divided visual field studies have explored hemispheric asymmetry in children with reading disability by comparing normal and poor readers on tasks that consistently show an asymmetry in normal children and adults. M. P. Bryden identified 51 such studies in a review of this work.[4] Of this group, 30 studies claimed to show that poor readers are less lateralized than good readers. No difference between groups was found in 14 studies, and 7 studies reported that poor readers show greater lateralization.

Our discussion of behavioral tests in Chapter 4 identified several factors, such as attentional strategies, that may affect the outcome of behavioral tests. While acknowledging the need to better control for these factors, Bryden ended his review with the conclusion that "there is at least some fire in the smoke of reading ability and laterality. Although almost all possible results have been obtained at one time or another, the general pattern that appears is that poor readers are less lateralized for receptive language than are good readers."[5]

Anatomical evidence pointing to a relationship between brain asymmetry and dyslexia has been reported by a number of investigators. The most widely cited studies are those by Albert Galaburda and colleagues, who performed autopsies on the brains of seven dyslexic persons, the majority of whom died from accidents. The four dyslexic men in this group showed unusual symmetry in the planum temporale.[6] In Chapter 3, in contrast, we considered evidence showing that the planum is larger on the left side of the brain in 65 to 75 percent of the general population. Microscopically, the four brains also showed a large number of neural anomalies in the left perisylvian area. These neural anomalies are believed to occur during the second trimester of fetal development when neurons migrate in the developing brain to reach their ultimate location. The three female brains also showed highly symmetrical plana and displaced neurons.[7] The symmetry was not due to a decrease in the size of the left planum, but to an increase in the size of the right planum.

Anatomical studies using magnetic resonance imaging have also been undertaken with dyslexic subjects. In contrast to anatomical investigations conducted at autopsy, measurements made using MRI with living subjects permit researchers to study greater numbers of subjects who can be tested on various indices of language function. An MRI study conducted by Jan Petter Larsen and colleagues reconstructed and measured the planum temporale in 19 eighth grade dyslexics and control subjects.[8] Seventy percent of the dyslexics showed symmetry of the planum, compared with 30 percent of the controls. The size of the corpus callosum has also been studied, using MRI. An investigation measuring the relative area of the midsagittal, or lengthwise, cross section of the corpus callosum found that female dyslexics had the largest corpus callosum, male dyslexics the next largest area, and normal readers the smallest.[9] The rear portion of the corpus callosum, the splenium, also followed the same size pattern. Thus, alterations in the size of the corpus callosum may also be characteristic of dyslexics. The possible relationship between callosal size and functional asymmetry was considered in Chapter 10.

Not all studies have shown the same pattern of results, however. A recent review of this research has suggested that variables such as the sex, age, and handedness of subjects may account for discrepancies among studies if dyslexic subjects are not carefully matched with control subjects on these dimensions.[10] Brain size may also be an important factor to take into account when looking at comparisons between groups, because the size of one brain region tends to be correlated with the size of other regions. Further research is needed to see whether careful control of these variables will effectively eliminate the differences in brain asymmetry and callosal size that have been reported between learning disabled and normal populations, or whether such differences will continue to be found.

A somewhat different approach to the issue of asymmetry and reading ability has been taken by Christina Leonard and her colleagues.[11] Instead of looking at patterns of asymmetry in reading impaired and normal subjects, these investigators explored the possibility that asymmetries in the temporal plane would be related to language skill in normal children. They demonstrated that anatomical asymmetry of the auditory association cortex measured with MRI in children five to nine years of age could be used to predict the performance of those children on a test that involved the manipulation of colored blocks symbolizing phonemes. The relationship they observed disappeared, however, in older children who were skilled readers.

Perhaps, the authors conclude, "the relationship between phonemic skill and planar asymmetry is strong in early development, but weakens with the impact of cultural forces focused on the development of literacy."[12] While far from definitive by themselves, these findings suggest that efforts to relate various measures of brain anatomy to behavioral measures may be surprisingly revealing.

New Ideas About Learning Disabilities

Recent work by Nina Kraus and colleagues has provided evidence that children with learning disabilities show impairments at a very basic, auditory level in the ability to distinguish between the sounds of similar phonemes.[13] They recorded electrical activity from the brains of children via scalp electrodes as the children watched a video on TV while trains of sounds, for example, "da, da, da, da" or "da, da, da, ga," were simultaneously presented softly into their right ears. The subjects were not asked to pay attention to the sounds and most likely ignored them as they listened to the sound track of the video.

Previous research had shown that a distinctive change in brain electrical activity occurs when a physically different stimulus occurs in a series of repeated stimuli, even in infants or in subjects who are sleeping. Kraus and her colleagues found that the activity recorded from normal children who had no difficulty telling "da" from "ga" changed abruptly in the expected fashion when "ga" followed repetitions of the syllable "da." There was no change, however, in electrical activity in the children who had difficulty telling the two sounds apart. The investigators concluded that the brains of normal children make the distinction between similar speech sounds even before the children are consciously aware of them, whereas those of the learning disabled children do not.

These findings mesh nicely with the earlier work of Paula Tallal, who had demonstrated that children with language-based learning impairments have major deficits in their ability to identify some brief phonetic elements in speech. Most recently, in collaboration with Michael Merzenich and others, Tallal has extended her work to see whether language-impaired children five to ten years of age would show improvements in the identification of those sounds following specialized training.[14]

In one condition, children listened to pairs of syllables that differed in their initial phoneme ("be" versus "de".) Acoustically, these sounds normally differ only in the information present in the first 50 milliseconds of the syllable. On each trial, the child was asked to indicate whether a pre-cued "be" or "de" was the first or second syllable presented. Training consisted of exposing the children to acoustically modified syllables in which the information that differentiated the syllables was stretched out or extended over a longer period of time, or where the intensity of the consonant portion of the syllable was increased relative to the intensity of the vowel. The modified stimuli were adjusted over the course of training, which lasted 8 to 16 hours over 20 days, so that the stimuli gradually moved closer and closer to normal, unmodified stimuli as subjects mastered them.

Tallal and Merzenich not only demonstrated marked improvement in the ability of language-impaired children to recognize brief and rapid sequences of speech stimuli as a result of training, but they also found a dramatic improvement in measures of the children's language comprehension. After one month of daily training with acoustically modified speech, the scores of the language-impaired children significantly improved by approximately two years, with each child approaching or exceeding normal limits of his or her age in speech discrimination and language comprehension.

In drawing conclusions from this work, Tallal and colleagues suggested that "there may be no fundamental defect in the learning machinery in most of these children, because they so rapidly learn the same skills at which they have been defined as deficient."[15] They went on to speculate that the physical differences and the functional response differences observed in the brains of language-impaired individuals may be a consequence of their learning history as children rather than irreversible defects in their brains. Moreover, they noted, the rapid improvement in language processing that followed from relatively limited and simple training suggests that the deficits in the children reflected a "bottom-up" processing problem rather than a deficit in linguistic competence per se.

These ideas are exciting and have generated a great deal of interest. They also pointed to the need for caution in interpreting the link between measures of activity and brain asymmetry and reading disabilities. Differences in brain asymmetry may not be the cause of learning impairments; both, Tallal and Merzenich suggested, may be the result of factors that affect the individual's ability to process rapidly changing auditory information.

Still more data bearing on brain mechanisms underlying dyslexia have been reported recently by Guinevere Eden and colleagues.[16] Eden based her work on evidence that dyslexics exhibit certain visual processing abnormalities in addition to deficits in the processing of speech sounds. Functional magnetic resonance imaging was used to study visual motor processing in six adult male dyslexic subjects. In each of the dyslexic subjects, the presentation of moving stimuli failed to produce the pattern of bilateral task-related activation observed in control subjects. In contrast, presentation of stationary patterns resulted in equivalent bilateral activation in both groups.

The authors concluded that this visual system abnormality is one aspect of a broader disorder that has many components, including a deficit in the processing of speech sounds. They went on to suggest that both the visual system problem and the speech sound problem in dyslexics have in common the processing of temporal properties of stimuli. Abnormalities in temporal processing, then, rather than in language functions per se, may underlie at least some forms of dyslexia. Much further research is needed to test this hypothesis and its relationship to the brain asymmetries that have been observed.

Evaluating the Evidence

Overall, the data just presented are highly suggestive of a relationship between brain anatomy and function and reading disability, although a variety of subject and measurement variables no doubt play an important role in the results found in particular studies. The data do not, however, in and of themselves tell us anything about the nature of that relationship. One possibility is that the anomalous patterns of brain organization observed are in some way responsible for the reading difficulties. Orton, it will be recalled, assumed that weak cerebral dominance caused reading disability.

One could easily argue, however, that some third factor is responsible for the relationship observed and that there is no direct causal link between the differences in brain organization that have been observed and reading skill. Paula Tallal and Michael Merzenich, as just noted, have made such a proposal.

Two additional points should be kept in mind when considering the relationship between brain organization and reading ability. First, most subjects who show little evidence of asymmetry (or even reversed asymmetry) on measures of lateralization do not show evidence of reading problems. Second, many subjects with reading problems have a pattern of brain organization, at least as measured by these tests, that is similar to that of subjects without reading difficulties. Thus, reduced hemispheric asymmetry is neither a necessary nor a sufficient condition for reading problems. Reading difficulties are a complex class of problems to which many different factors may contribute. Similarly, hemispheric asymmetry of function may be but one aspect of a complex of brain functions that provide the neurological substrate for reading.

Stuttering:
The Case for Competition for Control of Speech

Stuttering is defined as a disruption in the fluency of verbal expression characterized by involuntary audible or silent repetitions or prolongations in the production of sounds and syllables. It is estimated that about 1 percent of the population stutters to some degree.

Most people have probably heard the claim that it is unwise for parents to force a child showing a natural preference for the left hand to use the right hand. It has been argued that such attempts have potentially serious consequences for the child's overall adjustment, including increasing the chances that the child will stutter.

Samuel Orton, whose ideas were discussed in the previous section on dyslexia, played an important role in establishing this idea. Orton believed that in some cases stuttering is the result of competition between the hemispheres for the control of speech. In individuals with well-established cerebral dominance, the left hemisphere assumed control, whereas those with poorly established dominance were at risk for stuttering. He argued that forcing children to switch hands against their natural preference could disrupt the establishment of dominance and result in a stuttering problem.

Although there is little evidence to support the idea that forcing a child to switch hands increases the likelihood that the child will stutter, the link between stuttering and atypical patterns of hemispheric asymmetry is one that has some, but far from unequivocal support. One piece of evidence sometimes mentioned is the purported higher incidence of left-handedness and ambilaterality among stutterers than in the general population. Other studies, however, have challenged the figures.[17]

Another interesting approach has involved stutterers who underwent sodium amobarbital testing for an unrelated neurological problem. In one study, all four patients—three left-handers and one right-hander—showed speech impairment following injection on either side. This result contrasts with the typical sodium amobarbital finding, in which transient aphasia follows injection on one side (usually the left) but not on the other. Moreover, in each case, stuttering was reported to have stopped after the surgical removal, for medical reasons, of one of the presumed speech centers. This finding is perhaps the strongest evidence linking stuttering to the bilateral distribution of speech. An attempt to replicate the sodium amobarbital work, however, failed to obtain similar results.[18] The subjects in this study were four right-handers, only one of whom showed any evidence of bilateral representation of speech. The fact that even one of the right-handers showed bilateral speech is important, however, for it is extremely rare in normal right-handers. The sodium amobarbital data can thus be viewed as a partial, but certainly not total, confirmation of the idea that stutterers have speech bilaterally represented in the brain.

Neuroimaging has also been used, with increasing sophistication, to investigate the brain mechanisms associated with stuttering. In one recent study, Peter Fox, Roger Ingram, and colleagues used PET imaging to compare the overall brain activation of ten right-handed male stutterers with that of ten control subjects during three tasks—reading a paragraph aloud, reading a paragraph aloud in unison with a recording, and resting quietly with eyes closed.[19] Previous work had shown that reading aloud in unison with others or with a recording, known as chorus reading, often produces a dramatic, temporary suppression in stuttering.

The investigators found that during solo reading by the control subjects, brain activation was higher on the left side of the brain in the area that controls speech and also in the areas that process incoming auditory information. In contrast, in the stutterers, activation was shifted to the corresponding areas in the right hemisphere. The stutterers were not a simple mirror image of the controls, however. Activation of specific motor regions, some left-sided, some right-sided, and some bilateral, were seen in the stutterers, in addition to activation of the cerebellum, which was twice that of the controls. Activation of the left superior temporal gyrus, seen in the controls and believed to be related to self-monitoring as subjects spoke, was absent in the stutterers.

Chorus reading eliminated stuttering temporarily in the experimental group, and markedly reduced the anomalous patterns in brain activation that were observed. The motor system overactivation was significantly reduced or eliminated and some activation in the left superior temporal cortex was noted. The overall pattern of right-hemisphere activation continued to be demonstrated, however.

The investigators saw their findings as providing evidence for three different theories of stuttering. Exaggerated activity in motor control areas supports the view that stuttering reflects hyperactivity in specific motor areas involved in speech. The absence of the activity in the left superior temporal area, however, is consistent with the hypothesis that stutterers do not get adequate auditory feedback when speaking. And finally, the shift in activation to the right hemisphere in stutterers is predicted by the theory that stutterers have abnormal patterns of hemispheric asymmetry, resulting in hyperactivity of the right hemisphere during speech production.

The Fox and Ingram study highlights the complexity of stuttering. Their data suggest that it is unlikely that a single cause will be found; instead, investigators would be wise to consider the possibility that multiple mechanisms are involved in at least some, and perhaps most, cases.

Autism

Autism is one of the most puzzling of all behavioral abnormalities in children. The classic symptoms of autism include inability to use speech to communicate in a normal way, stereotyped and obsessive movements, and deficient social interaction. The first signs of autism are sometimes noticed when the child is an infant. Such children may be unresponsive to parental handling and do not seem to react to their environment. Other autistic children may develop normally well into the toddler stage, when regression of their sociability, language, and play takes place.

Autism varies widely in severity and prognosis. Intelligent, highly functioning autistic adults may function well enough to live independently and be employed in a sheltered environment. Those with more severe impairment may require lifelong care by their families, in a group home, or in an institution. In most cases, the behavioral deficits associated with autism remain detectable for the life of the individual.[20]

Current approaches to autism focus on its origins in brain dysfunction. Although the nature of that dysfunction is far from clear, several investigators have suggested that the disorder may differentially involve the left hemisphere, no doubt because a salient characteristic of autism is the failure to acquire language normally. Intelligence per se does not seem to be a factor, because even severely retarded (but not autistic) children learn to speak without special training.

Even though autistic children have depressed language skills, they sometimes show considerable artistic or musical ability or extraordinary memory abilities in selected areas. It is not uncommon to find autistic children who are able to tell the weekdays on which a particular date falls over several centuries. The ability to perform elaborate mental arithmetic problems has also been reported. A case history of an autistic girl with extraordinary drawing ability has been documented.[21] At the age of $3\frac{1}{2}$, Nadia was producing lifelike drawings with considerable detail (see Figure 11.1). Like the skills that characterize other autistic children, Nadia's performance was quick and almost without conscious effort. It has been suggested that the nature of these special abilities is a reflection of the contributions of the right hemisphere. Nadia's drawing skills diminished as therapy continued; however, it is impossible to tell whether the change was a consequence of the therapy or would have resulted naturally as she matured.

A limited amount of other evidence is consistent with the hypothesis that abnormal patterns of hemispheric asymmetry are involved in autism. A review of the literature combining the findings of a number of studies on handedness in autism reported that 52 percent of autistic children did not have an established hand preference or were left-handed.[22] Autistic children who had an established hand preference performed better on a variety of cognitive tasks than did children with mixed handedness. These figures point, albeit indirectly, to differences in hemispheric asymmetry between normal and autistic children. In addition, dichotic listening studies have typically reported a left-ear

FIGURE 11.1 Horses were among Nadia's favorite subjects. She drew this merry-go-round horse before she was four years old. [From L. Selfe, *Nadia: A Case of Extraordinary Drawing Ability in an Autistic Child* (New York: Academic Press, 1977).]

advantage or no ear preference for autistic subjects, although the results are not compelling.[23]

A more convincing picture of the relationship between autism and hemispheric asymmetry emerges from studies of electrical activity in the brain. A study comparing EEG activity in autistic subjects with age- and handedness-matched normal controls looked at performance in several verbal and spatial tasks. Results showed that the autistic and control groups did not differ significantly in the pattern of hemispheric activation during the spatial tasks, but the autistic subjects showed greater right-hemisphere activity in the linguistic tasks.[24] Seven out of ten autistic subjects and three out of ten control subjects showed right-hemisphere dominance during the verbal tasks. A subsequent study with autistic subjects recorded cortical auditory-evoked potentials from the left and right hemispheres. Eleven out of 17 subjects showed evidence of right-hemisphere specialization for speech, with right-hemisphere specialization associated with poorer language ability and greater degree of asymmetry.[25]

New neuroimaging techniques have made it possible to look for both structural and functional abnormalities in vivo. Overall, no statistically significant abnormal frontal or posterior brain asymmetries have been reported,[26] although a variety of studies point to a high incidence of regional structural abnormalities in the brains of autistic persons. The subtle abnormalities that are found are consistent with the effects of disturbances in neuronal migration during early central nervous system development, most likely in the first six months of gestational age.

A study combining functional and structural imaging has looked at 13 autistic children.[27] Of that group, 6 had regional abnormalities in either PET or structural images. The PET abnormalities included regions of hypometabolism, or underactivation, in cortical association areas. The structural abnormalities found were suggestive of an abnormality in neuronal migration, consistent with earlier work.

Because the patient's cooperation is needed to successfully complete most neuroimaging protocols, studies of autistic children have typically used mildly impaired individuals capable of lying still in the scanner. A recent SPECT study was able to scan children with more severe cases of autism by taking advantage of the "locked-in" property of the cerebral blood-flow tracer Tc-99m HMPAO, described in Chapter 3. The subjects were injected while awake and then placed under general anesthesia. Although they were scanned during anesthesia, the distribution of the tracer reflected the blood-flow pattern associated with the patients' awake state.

The study found striking abnormalities in cerebral activity in temporal–parietal and frontal regions of these severe cases, despite the fact that all had normal structural MRI scans. Although the impairments were bilateral, the investigators noted that the left hemisphere was affected to a greater degree in most cases.[28] Color plate 15 illustrates a case example.

The cerebellum has also been implicated in autism as a result of studies showing reductions in cerebellar size, including loss of Purkinje neurons, cells that convey information out from the cerebellar cortex to other brain structures. All such abnormalities appear to be bilateral and symmetric, although there have been failures to replicate some of the findings.[29] Should the existence of cerebellar abnormalities be confirmed, they may represent some central pathological abnormality associated with autism. Or they might simply be a marker for more central events occurring during the development of the nervous system when many parts of the brain are forming.

Overall, what can be concluded about the role of atypical hemispheric asymmetry of function in autism? The picture, unfortunately, is far from clear. Delays in language development, rather than deficits as such, characterize much of autistic speech, making the a priori case for left-hemisphere dysfunction weaker. Moreover, autistic children show deficits in the areas of prosody, the social use of language, and the ability to read emotional expression in language. To the extent these functions are lateralized in normal adults, it is the right hemisphere, and not the left, that is involved.

The newest data from neuroimaging studies suggest additional reasons for caution. It is clear that autistic symptoms vary greatly from individual to individual—perhaps there are different forms of autism, with different etiologies or causes. The hypothesis of left-hemisphere dysfunction may be useful if it is pursued on an individual-by-individual basis, rather than by looking at entire groups, but it is very likely that the neurological deficits in autism are more variable and more pervasive than those assumed by the left-hemisphere dysfunction hypothesis. Further research using the tools of modern cognitive neuropsychology should lead to a better understanding of this disorder and to better classifications or discriminations among those grouped together under the label autistic.

Hemispheric Asymmetry and Psychiatric Illness

Schizophrenia is a disorder of complex cognition that is characterized by unusual symptoms such as delusions, hallucinations, disorganization of speech, and loss of normal affect. Depression is characterized by a disturbance of mood in which there are feelings of severe dejection. The symptoms that define schizophrenia and depression mesh loosely with general notions about the functions of the left and right hemispheres that we considered in earlier chapters. The thought disorders and verbal hallucinations that are frequently symptoms of schizophrenia fit with the view of the left hemisphere as the one specialized for analytical and language functions, and the mood disorders that characterize depression are roughly consistent with the conceptualization of the hemispheres as specialized for different aspects of emotion—the left for positive emotion and the right for negative emotion—that was discussed in Chapter 8.

One of the first studies to link psychopathology with a model of hemispheric specialization was conducted by the psychiatrist Pierre Flor-Henry over 25 years ago.[30] Flor-Henry compared 50 cases of temporal lobe epilepsy that also showed psychotic symptoms with 50 cases without psychotic symptoms. When both groups were subdivided on the basis of location of the epileptic focus, he found that a left-hemisphere focus was more common in schizophrenia and a right-hemisphere focus was more common in depression.

Two models of hemispheric involvement in psychosis have been proposed to account for these findings. One is the hemispheric dysfunction hypothesis, in which a given hemisphere is believed to be deficient, possibly in very subtle ways. The psychosis would follow from this deficiency. The second model is the functional hemispheric imbalance hypothesis, in which normal interhemispheric functions mediated by the corpus callosum are thought to be impaired.[31]

Subsequent work on the biological bases of schizophrenia and depression has painted a picture of each disorder in which differential hemispheric involvement, to the extent it exists, is but one piece of a very complex picture of brain dysfunction.

Schizophrenia

Recent studies of patients with schizophrenia have provided evidence of unexpected, generalized abnormalities in brain structure that include enlargement of the ventricles (cavities in the brain that contain cerebrospinal fluid) and diffuse reduction in gray matter, as well as the absence of the expected asymmetry in the planum temporale, at least in some reports.[32] Results from functional neuroimaging show a similar pattern of generalized abnormalities. In general, patients fail to demonstrate normal patterns of task-related, anatomically specific enhancement of metabolic activity. Tasks that require frontal lobe function in normals, for example, show frontal lobe hypometabolism, or underactivation, in schizophrenics. Similar results are found for tasks involving temporal lobe or motor regions. Thus, the abnormalities of brain physiology in schizophrenia appear to be relatively widespread and subtle. Where lateralized deficits have been found, they have tended to involve the left hemisphere. Some studies have identified deficits in the right hemisphere of schizophrenics, however, leading some investigators to postulate models that identify subtypes of schizophrenia and the hemispheric dysfunction associated with each of them.[33]

Increasing evidence has pointed to an important role for the neurotransmitter dopamine in schizophrenia.[34] Some of the strongest evidence pointing to the role of dopamine in schizophrenia comes from studies of the action of antipsychotic drugs that are known to block the action of dopamine. In addition, drugs such as cocaine and amphetamine, which enhance the action of dopamine, induce psychotic symptoms that are virtually indistinguishable from certain forms of schizophrenia. Current theorizing focuses on the possibility that supersensitivity of dopamine receptors in the brains of schizophrenics may underlie the disorder, rather than an excess of dopamine as such. Developments in neuroimaging technologies now permit researchers to measure the function of neurotransmitter receptors in the brain. These techniques should be exceedingly valuable in future investigations of the brain mechanisms underlying schizophrenia and, as we will see next, depression.

Depression

Data from several sources have pointed to a special role for the right hemisphere in depression. Clinical research has shown that unilateral electroconvulsive shock, used occasionally in the treatment of depression, is more effective when applied to the right hemisphere than when it is applied to the left hemisphere. Electroencephalographic studies of depressed patients have generally reported greater activation in the right frontal regions relative to that in the left frontal regions, and PET studies have shown evidence of reduced energy metabolism in the left hemispheres of depressed patients.[35]

Neurotransmitters are also believed to play an important role in depression.[36] The role of neurotransmitters in depression became apparent when it was observed that patients given the drug reserpine for high blood pressure often became severely depressed. The major action of reserpine is to make dopamine and norepinephrine less available for release at the synapse, leading to the idea that dopamine and norepinephrine might be reduced in depression. Although various antidepressant drugs achieve their effects through their action on these neurotransmitters, there is still a great deal to be learned about the relationship of neurochemical dysfunction and depression, and the possibility of differential hemispheric involvement.

Theoretical Considerations

Although a variety of evidence points to some involvement of brain lateralization in psychopathology, each piece alone is not particularly compelling, especially in view of the complexity of the findings. Like reading disability and stuttering, mental disorders most likely have a number of different causes, some of which produce the same overall symptomatology. Abnormalities of brain asymmetry or hemispheric interaction may be involved in certain forms of schizophrenia and depression, but not in all. And in those cases where asymmetry plays a role, that role may vary, depending on the precise form of the disorder under consideration. Careful classification of patients combined with new technologies to measure brain activity should be particularly valuable in addressing the possible role of brain lateralization in psychopathology.

Implications for Treatment

The pathologies considered in this chapter are diverse, ranging from stuttering to schizophrenia. In each case a lateralized abnormality of some sort has been proposed but has not been unequivocally demonstrated. Before attempts are made to apply research findings to the treatment of persons with problems like those just considered, we must be sure that the findings are firmly established. And most important, any treatment must be demonstrated to be effective, independent of any purported neurological rationale. An illustration of these points is the educational program for retarded and brain-damaged children developed over 30 years ago by Glen Doman, a physical therapist, and Carl Delacato, an educational psychologist.[37]

The program, known as "patterning," begins with the assumption that normal cortical dominance develops through a series of stages. The program is individualized for each child and is based on the "level of neurological organization" the child has reached without skipping any developmental stages. For example, children who are not yet walking are required to spend most of their day on the floor, with crawling emphasized. A team of therapists, parents, and volunteers takes turns manipulating the head and limbs of a child who is unable to make the necessary movements alone. Other techniques used in particular children include restricting the use of one arm, occluding one eye, and prohibiting singing and listening to music. The rationale is to develop total cortical dominance extending not only to language but to a dominant eye, hand, and foot.

The Doman and Delacato method is still in use and is promoted through Doman's Institutes for the Achievement of Human Potential in Philadelphia. It has been severely criticized on many grounds, however.[38] First, many of the assumptions Doman and Delacato made are known to be false. For example, hemispheric asymmetry, as noted in Chapter 10, is most likely present at birth and does not develop over time. Moreover, occluding the left eye and restricting musical activities are unlikely to result in development of a dominant left hemisphere. Critics also point out that the method has been promoted in such a way that parents cannot refuse treatment without calling into question their adequacy as parents, and that unsubstantiated claims of success have been made, extending even to claims of making normal children superior. The American Academy of Pediatrics has issued a policy statement concluding that patterning offers "no special merit, that the claims of its advocates are unproven, and that demands on families are so great that in some cases there may be harm in its use."[39] Patterning fails the two criteria we mentioned earlier—a rationale that clearly follows from what is known about the brain, and, most important, evidence that it is truly effective.

We have repeatedly noted the importance of recognizing that many dysfunctions probably have more than one cause. We have also stressed that finding a relationship between a dysfunction and some measure of brain organization does not necessarily imply a causal relationship—both may be caused by an unidentified factor. To assume that similar symptoms always result from the same cause is to grossly oversimplify the intricacies of human brain–behavior relationships. Lateralized dysfunction may be involved in some, but not all, forms of a disorder. It is also important to remember that lateralized dysfunction may not be sufficient by itself to produce a particular problem; other factors may have to operate at the same time before a deficit will occur. A full range of patterns of lateralization are observed in normal persons, an observation strongly suggesting that particular patterns of lateralization per se are not, in themselves, sufficient causes for certain deficits.

PART VII

Hypotheses and Speculation

Beyond the Data

Chapter 12

Attempts at Applying Asymmetry:

"Hemisphericity," Education, and Culture

We have seen evidence that learning and memory can continue separately in the left brain and the right brain after the surgical division of the two hemispheres. Each half of the brain of a split-brain patient is able to sense, perceive, and even conceptualize independently of the other. Furthermore, in virtually every approach to the study of hemispheric processes, especially including those with normal subjects, the data support the existence of hemispheric differences. In earlier chapters we discussed the difficulty investigators have had in characterizing these differences. Some have talked of a verbal–nonverbal distinction. Others argued that the halves of the brain differ in terms of their overall approach to dealing with information.

The rapidly growing body of knowledge dealing with the nature of hemispheric asymmetry has led quite naturally to speculation about the consequences of asymmetry for everyday behavior. Does the specialization seen in the hemispheres of normal individuals correspond to distinct modes of thought? Do some people rely more on the left side of the brain, others more on the right? Do the educational systems of Western civilization emphasize so-called left-brain thinking and perhaps neglect the potential of the right brain? These are some of the popular issues raised by the discoveries discussed in earlier chapters. In this chapter, we will consider several such issues.

Two Brains, Two Cognitive Styles?

Since the first split-brain operations, a progression of labels have been used to describe the processes of the left brain and the right brain. The most widely cited characteristics may be divided into five main groups, which form a kind of hierarchy. Each designation usually includes and goes beyond the characteristics listed above it:

Left hemisphere	Right hemisphere
Verbal	Nonverbal, visuospatial
Sequential, temporal, digital	Simultaneous, spatial, analogical
Logical, analytic	Gestalt, synthetic
Rational	Intuitive
Western thought	Eastern thought

The descriptions near the top of the list seem to be based on experimental evidence; the other designations appear more speculative. The verbal–nonverbal distinction, for example, was the earliest to emerge from split-brain studies and behavioral research with normal subjects. The sequential–simultaneous distinction reflects a current, although not universally accepted, theoretical model holding that the left hemisphere tends to deal with rapid changes in time and to analyze stimuli in terms of details and features, whereas the right hemisphere deals with simultaneous relationships and with the more global properties of patterns.

Many who have speculated on these issues have attempted to go beyond these distinctions. One popular view of the differences between the hemispheres is that the left brain operates in a logical, analytic manner and the right brain works in a Gestalt, synthetic fashion.

Once one starts using such labels to describe the operations of the hemispheres, several questions come to mind. Are they just convenient descriptions of how the hemispheres deal with information? Or do they imply that the hemispheres differ in their styles of thinking? Is it possible to view the specialized functions of the left brain and the right brain as distinct modes of thought?

Historically, philosophers and students of the mind have shown a tendency to divide intellectual faculties into two types. For example, consider the following quotation from a Yogic philosopher who wrote, in 1910:

> The intellect is an organ composed of several groups of functions, divisible into two important classes, the functions and faculties of the right hand, the functions and faculties of the left. The faculties of the right hand are comprehensive, creative, and synthetic; the faculties of the left hand critical and analytic . . . The left limits itself to ascertained truth, the right grasps that which is still elusive or unascertained. Both are essential to the completeness of the human reason. These important functions of the machine have all to be raised to their highest and finest working-power, if the education of the child is not to be imperfect and one sided.[1]

Many Western thinkers have also talked of mental organization as if it were divided into two parts. Rational versus intuitive, explicit versus implicit, analytic versus synthetic, abstract versus concrete, objective versus subjective are some examples of these dichotomies.

Why so many two-part divisions? Do they label truly distinct and separate qualities, or do they just describe the extremes of a set of continuous behaviors? In other words, are we dealing with all-or-none differences, or are there gradations in between? Some have insisted on the former view because, they claim, it conforms best to a neuroanatomical reality—the existence of a left brain and a right brain capable of operating independently. Another view is that the formulation of dichotomies or opposites is just a convenient way of viewing complex situations.

In his influential book, *The Psychology of Consciousness*, psychologist Robert Ornstein has argued that Western men and women have been using only half of their brains and, hence, only half of their mental capacity.[2] He noted that the emphasis on language and logical thinking in Western societies has ensured that the left hemisphere is well exercised. He went on to argue that the functions of the right hemisphere are a neglected part of human abilities and intellect in the West and that such functions are more developed in the cultures, mysticism, and religions of the East. In short, Ornstein identified the left hemisphere with the thought of the technological, rational West and the right hemisphere with the thought of the intuitive, mystical East. Many outlandish claims and misinterpretations have followed in the wake of Ornstein's position. For example, some have equated the left hemisphere with the evils of modern society.[3]

As we have seen, ideas about the nature of hemispheric differences are diverse. They have evolved from verbal–nonverbal distinctions to ever more abstract notions of the relationship between mental function and the hemispheres. In this process, some of the ideas concerning hemispheric differences have moved further and further away from basic research findings. Many scientists have found this disconcerting because the distinction between fact and speculation is often blurred. The term *dichotomania* has been coined to refer to the avalanche of popular literature fostered by the most speculative notions. One investigator has noted:

> It is becoming a familiar sight. Staring directly at the reader frequently from a magazine cover is an artist's rendition of the two halves of the brain. Surprinted athwart the left cerebral hemisphere (probably in stark blacks and grays) are such words as "logical," "analytical," and "Western rationality." More luridly etched across the right hemisphere (in rich orange or royal purple) are "intuitive," "artistic," or "Eastern consciousness." Regrettably, the picture says more about a current popular science vogue than it does about the brain.[4]

Hemisphericity

The concept of hemisphericity—the idea that a given individual relies more on one mode or hemisphere than on the other—is an extension of the idea that the two hemispheres are specialized for different modes of thought. This differential utilization is presumed to be reflected in the individual's "cognitive style," that is, the person's preferences and approach to problem-solving. A tendency to use verbal or analytic approaches to problems is seen as evidence of left-side hemisphericity, whereas those who favor holistic or spatial ways of dealing with information are seen as right-hemisphere people.

Hemisphericity has been claimed by different sources to extend not only to perception but to all kinds of intellectual and personality dimensions. A number of years ago, a cartoon appeared in a well-known magazine showing a fancy country club with a little sign outside that read, "Left Hemisphere People Only." The idea that differences among people may be related to differences in the degree to which they use their two hemispheres is a very appealing one that has captured the imagination of the popular media.

A number of paper-and-pencil tests have been developed with the goal of assessing hemisphericity. Their creators have asserted that by completing one of these tests and having it scored (frequently for a substantial fee) an individual can determine his or her preferred hemisphere. In turn, they have promised, this will be useful information when selecting a career or a spouse, or when making any other choice where hemispheric compatibility seems desirable.

Managers, in particular, are often targeted as potential users of such questionnaires, with claims that the knowledge gleaned from the results can be used for enhancing the productivity of employees as well as for individual and organizational problem-solving. A whole industry has developed around consultants who provide corporate training seminars that promise new marketing and sales directions as well as greater employee performance and satisfaction, all based on the concept of "hemisphericity."[5] Figure 12.1 nicely illustrates this point.

One hemisphericity questionnaire that has undergone the scrutiny of persons other than its developers is "Your Style of Learning and Thinking" (SOLAT).[6] Developed for research purposes by educational psychologist E. P. Torrance and colleagues, the SOLAT questionnaire has 36 items with three alternative responses per item: one indicating left-hemisphere specialization (for example, not good at remembering faces; inhibited in expression of feelings and emotions),

FIGURE 12.1 Dogbert, the management consultant. [DILBERT reprinted by permission of UFS, Inc.]

one indicating right-hemisphere specialization (for example, not good at remembering names; able to express feelings and emotions freely), and one signifying an "integrative" style (for example, equally good at remembering names and faces; controlled in expression of feelings and emotions).[7]

A careful look at the questionnaire shows that the scores correlate highly with tests designed to measure creativity. This correlation is not surprising in view of the logic underlying such tests. As the "nonverbal" hemisphere, the right hemisphere is considered to be responsible for intuition, which, in turn, is seen as a core characteristic underlying creativity. According to this line of reasoning, a test measuring creativity would reflect the degree of right-hemisphere involvement, and hence, hemisphericity. One study that looked at scores on the SOLAT as a function of side of injury in a brain-injured population found no relationship, however, suggesting that the questionnaire is not sensitive to factors related to hemispheric differences.[8]

A similar approach has been taken by Ned Herrmann, developer of the "Herrmann Brain Dominance Instrument (HBDI)."[9] According to his advertising literature, the HBDI is an "extensive, computer-analyzed, scientifically developed questionnaire that is the world standard for identifying brain dominance." In his new book, *The Whole Brain Business Book,* Herrmann asserts that the "the left brain/right brain dichotomy popularized by the press is too simplistic and incomplete to serve as a model on which to base a reliable and valid brain dominance assessment."[10] In its place he offers "whole brain technology" that considers not only the cerebral cortex, but the limbic system, a group of brain structures involved in emotion and motivation, as well. Because both the cortex and limbic system have a left and a right side, this approach led Herrmann to four quadrants or types of mental preference—"analytic/logical," "organized/detailed," "interpersonal/expressive," and "imaginative/conceptual." Understanding and appreciation of whole brain technology, it is claimed, is a powerful key to strategy, productivity, and creativity in business, as well as in personal life.

Yet another recent book claims that an understanding of hemisphericity is the key to successful interpersonal relationships.[11] The author states, "It isn't just a matter of being male or female, but rather, the way in which a person has learned to exercise certain brain functions that over time becomes fixed in particular patterns. Being 'wired' differently from their opposite partner creates problems for couples. This is the root of so many issues . . ." To help readers begin to understand their "brain preference," the author offers 35 pairs of statements in a questionnaire in which readers determine which member of each pair describes them better, for example, A, I am told I am too serious; that I need to lighten up, or B, I am told that I jump to conclusions. "A" items, not surprisingly, count as "left-brain" credit, whereas "B" items count toward "right-brain" dominance. A key provides readers with score ranges that allow them to classify themselves as extremely or moderately left- or right-brained, or balanced left-brained/right-brained. Armed with this knowledge, as well as knowledge about his or her partner's brain preference, the reader can thus, it is claimed, begin to understand the relationship in a new way.

What should we make of these varied and impressive claims for dramatic improvements in life and love that can follow from an understanding of hemisphericity as measured by questionnaires? In evaluating the claims, we need to separate the possible usefulness of the program or therapy being proposed from statements that have been made about what the questionnaires themselves are measuring. Corporate executives may indeed find practical value in thinking about their own cognitive style and in matching work assignments to the talents of employees more closely. The executives are in the best position to determine whether a particular technique results in greater productivity or enhanced employee satisfaction. Similarly, new ways of thinking about a relationship, particularly where there are communication problems, may be quite valuable in dealing with interpersonal difficulties. What we wish to focus on here is the more basic claim that questionnaires being promoted as an entry point to these personal and professional transformations are measuring something called hemisphericity.

A major problem with this assertion is that there is little in the way of scientific evidence linking creativity to the right hemisphere, let alone evidence tying degrees of creativity to the degree of right-hemisphere utilization. Before the idea of hemisphericity can be fairly evaluated, we will need good measures of differential hemispheric activity. There are a number of possible candidates for such a measure, including new neuroimaging techniques, but each currently has problems that limit its usefulness as a measure of hemispheric activity in a particular individual. Such measures may ultimately prove useful in testing the notion that each of us relies more on one hemisphere than on the other. However, should the results prove positive, it would still remain to be seen how effectively the results of paper-and-pencil tests would reflect this differential hemispheric activity. All in all, hemisphericity currently remains an interesting but fundamentally untested hypothesis, and techniques asserting that they are based on the concept of hemisphericity are built on a shaky foundation.

Education and the Hemispheres

The idea that the two hemispheres are specialized for different modes of thought has led naturally to a consideration of their implications for education. Does an elementary school program restricted to reading, writing, and arithmetic educate mainly one hemisphere and leave half of an individual's potential unschooled? Is the entire educational system biased against developing right-hemisphere talents?

Joseph Bogen, one of the pioneers of the commissurotomy procedure, has been an especially avid proponent of developing what he calls "appositional thinking" in school.[12] The word *propositional* was adopted by neurologist John Hughlings Jackson in the nineteenth century to describe the left hemisphere's dominance for speaking, writing, calculation, and related tasks. In contrast, Bogen coined the term *appositional* to refer to the information processing of the right hemisphere in well-lateralized right-handers.

In Bogen's view, society has overemphasized propositionality at the expense of appositionality. Intelligence tests, for example, are aimed at propositional left-hemisphere abilities. Their use is justified by the claim that they predict success in a society that most often measures success monetarily and in terms of productivity. Bogen argued that such measures are very narrow and do not take into account artistic creativity and other right-hemisphere skills that are not easily quantifiable.

The idea that our educational system favors one-half of our mental capability at the expense of the other has been appearing with increasing frequency in educational journals, self-help manuals, and a variety of other publications. Articles usually include a background summary of some of the data on laterality along with the author's personal interpretation of what the data mean. Some end with advice about "boosting right-hemisphere thinking" or "training the right hemisphere."[13]

The major business of the left hemisphere, these articles often claim, is the logical representation of reality and communication with the external world. Thinking, reading, writing, counting, and worrying about time are also usually attributed to the left hemisphere. The business of the right hemisphere, in contrast, is said to be understanding patterns and complex relationships that cannot be precisely defined and may not be logical. The qualities of the right hemisphere, an author will state, are essential for creative insight but tend to be inadequately developed.

An article on mathematics education provides a clear statement of this view:

> The different functions of the right and left hemispheres of the brain require different approaches to education. Due to their emphasis on language and verbal processing, schools have failed to give adequate stimulation to the right side of the brain and thus tend to discriminate against right brain dominant students. Many students show a preferred right brain (intuitive) thinking style and consequently have struggled in school because their thinking style did not conform to typical left brain or logic based.[14]

Classroom teachers at all levels have been exhorted to encourage greater right-brain involvement in their students. Recommendations range from the use of "show and tell" as an activity that stimulates both sides of the brain, to the use of drawings and graphs to augment "left-brain" text, to spending more time listening to music and looking at art, to the greater use of television as a "right-brained input system."[15]

With the possible exception of more television watching, there is little that is controversial about these suggestions. Most primary grade teachers already employ these approaches and find value in them. The problem, as we see it, is the attempt to justify these and other more controversial approaches with claims about what is known about the two hemispheres of the brain.

Our educational systems may be deficient and may limit a broad spectrum of human capabilities. We question, however, the division of styles of thinking along hemispheric lines. It may very well be that in certain stages the formation of new ideas involves intuitive processes independent of analytic reasoning or verbal argument. Preliminary schemes ordering new data or reordering preexisting knowledge could possibly arise from even aimless wanderings of the mind during which a connection is seen between a present and a past event or a remote analogy is established. But are these right-hemisphere functions? We do not think it is as simple as that, and there is certainly no conclusive evidence to that effect. Even television, proposed as we have seen as a way to increase involvement of the right hemisphere, has been shown via an EEG study to activate both sides of the brain in a roughly equivalent manner.[16] Our educational system may miss training or developing half of the brain, but it probably does so by missing out on the talents of both hemispheres.

From Theory to Practice:
Learning to Draw

· · · · · · · · · · ·

The ideas concerning education and the hemispheres considered up to this point have been very general. In this section, we will consider an approach that is much more specific in its recommendations.

Betty Edwards, a California art teacher, has presented her method of teaching people to draw in a popular book entitled *Drawing on the Right Side of the Brain.*[17] Her basic premise is straightforward: Under ordinary conditions, it is the right hemisphere of the brain that has the ability to draw. When left alone, the right hemisphere will produce very respectable drawings, even in untrained adults. The catch is that for most of us, the right brain is not given the opportunity to display its talents. The verbal, analytic, left hemisphere (lacking in artistic ability) becomes involved and interferes. The natural tendency to label and analyze a picture or a scene before drawing it, in Edwards's view, is the source of this interference.

Edwards's method of instruction is designed to reduce the amount of left-hemisphere involvement in the drawing process. One of her first exercises involves having students copy a fairly detailed pencil drawing of a person with the picture held upside down. The reasoning is simple. Held upside down, the picture is no longer easily recognizable. In fact, it is difficult to label any part of it. Thus, Edwards proposed, the upside-down copying task is one in which the right hemisphere may proceed without interference from the left. According to Edwards, most adults will be pleasantly surprised when they finish their drawings and rotate them 180 degrees.

There are several stages in Edwards's method, and we cannot do it justice here. Briefly, however, it claims to create conditions that minimize the likelihood of left-hemisphere involvement. As part of this process, she has suggested that the student verbally reassure the left hemisphere that it is not being abandoned and that a new technique is being tried out only temporarily.

Does Edwards's method work? We know of no research that addresses this question, but her book is filled with before-and-after drawings produced by her adult students. The differences are striking. If they are truly representative, then Edwards's method works, and we do not wish to quarrel with success. We do note, however, that at this point there is no way of knowing whether her methods work for the reasons she claimed. As a general rule, there is no evidence that just one hemisphere is involved in a given cognitive task, including language, which is known to be well lateralized. During language tasks, for example, blood flow is greater to the left hemisphere in most right-handed subjects, but it also increases to a lesser extent in the right hemisphere. There is no reason to believe that this is not also the case for drawing or that the left hemisphere interferes with the right hemisphere as it engages in drawing.

Although split-brain research has shown that the left hemisphere is inferior to the right in ability to draw certain figures, other data show that both hemispheres contribute to drawing, but in different ways. Patients with damage to the parietal lobe show impairments in drawing, regardless of the side of injury; the nature of the impairment, however, varies as a function of side. The left hemisphere appears to be more involved in identification of details and internal elements, whereas the right hemisphere is more involved in orientation, location, and dimensionality.[18]

This analysis of the contribution of the two hemispheres suggests, in fact, an alternative interpretation for Edwards's finding. Rather than producing right-hemisphere involvement in drawing by inverting a picture, inversion may result in greater reliance on left-hemisphere skills by encouraging the individual to break the picture up into smaller parts to be copied feature for feature, line for line. As further support for this interpretation, psychologist Lauren Harris noted that upright faces are more likely to be recognized when presented in the left visual field (and hence to the right hemisphere), whereas inverted faces are better recognized when they are presented to the right visual field (left hemisphere).[19] This finding is consistent with the idea that the left hemisphere is better at the analytic, feature-by-feature approach that is required when a face is no longer recognizable as a face.

It remains for future research to demonstrate why Edwards's method works. For now, the value of the method is independent of its hypothesized mechanism. The value is not increased because of the neuropsychological rationale offered to explain the method, nor does the rationale receive any support because of the method's success.

Science, Culture, and the Corpus Callosum

After accepting the distinction that the left hemisphere is analytic and the right intuitive, the late astronomer–biologist Carl Sagan went on to speculate about how the two modes have interacted to generate the accomplishments of our civilization. In his book *The Dragons of Eden*, Sagan described the right hemisphere as a pattern recognizer that finds patterns, sometimes real and sometimes imagined, in the behavior of people as well as in natural events. The right hemisphere has a suspicious emotional tone, for it sees conspiracies where they do not exist as well as where they do. It needs the left hemisphere to analyze critically the patterns it generates in order to test their reality:

> There is no way to tell whether the patterns extracted by the right hemisphere are real or imagined without subjecting them to left-hemisphere scrutiny. On the other hand, mere critical thinking, without creative and intuitive insights, without the search for new patterns, is sterile and doomed. To solve complex problems in changing circumstances requires the activity of both cerebral hemispheres: the path to the future lies through the corpus callosum.[20]

Sagan went on to suggest that intuitive thinking does well in situations where we have had previous personal or evolutionary experience. "But in new areas—such as the nature of celestial objects close up—intuitive reasoning must be diffident in its claims and willing to accommodate to the insights that rational thinking wrests from Nature."[21] Sagan described science as paranoid thinking applied to nature, a search for natural conspiracies, for connections in data:

> Our objective is to abstract patterns from Nature (right-hemisphere thinking), but many proposed patterns do not in fact correspond to the data. Thus all proposed patterns must be subjected to the sieve of critical analysis (left-hemisphere thinking). The search for patterns without critical analysis, and rigid skepticism without a search for patterns, are the antipodes of incomplete science. The effective pursuit of knowledge requires both functions.[22]

He concluded that the most significant creative activities of a culture—legal and ethical systems, art and music, science and technology—are the result of collaborative work by the left and right hemispheres. We completely agree. Sagan also suggested, "We might say that human culture is the function of the corpus callosum."[23] This may be true, not so much because the corpus callosum interconnects "analytic" with "intuitive" thinking, but because every structure in the brain plays a role in human behavior, and human culture is a function of human behavior.

Chapter 13

The Nature of Hemispheric Specialization

Although much has been said about what each hemisphere can and cannot do, there is still little understanding of the reasons for hemispheric specialization in the first place. There is also little knowledge about the physiological mechanisms that may underlie these fundamental differences. Dealing with these "why" and "how" issues should help answer the "what" of specialization, a question that has preoccupied us throughout much of this book. It is not clear which question is more important or should be answered first. Insight into any one helps reformulate ideas about the other two. An ultimate understanding of hemispheric specialization undoubtedly will arise from the interaction of successively better answers to all three questions.

In earlier chapters, we mentioned different investigators' speculations concerning the evolution and the mechanisms of hemispheric asymmetry. We will now try to bring these speculations together and consider some more recent hypotheses about the nature of hemispheric specialization and callosal function.

Is Dominance Based on Motoric Skills?

Why is the hemisphere that controls speech also the one that usually controls a person's dominant hand? Is it a coincidence, or is there a profound relationship that should tell us something about what is involved in both speech and manipulative skills? Doreen Kimura and her colleagues have obtained evidence that the left hemisphere may be essential for certain types of hand movement.[1] Patients with damage to the left hemisphere but without paralysis of the right side may have difficulty copying a sequence of hand movements and complex finger positions with either the left or the right hand. Kimura suggested that this finding bears a relationship to reports in the clinical literature of persons who are both deaf and mute and had sustained left-hemisphere damage in addition to their earlier speech and hearing disabilities. These individuals used hand-movement communication, but after damage to the left hemisphere, they displayed disturbances of these movements similar to the disruption of speech suffered by normal speakers who sustain such damage.

Doreen Kimura has presented data from a large number of patients with unilateral cerebral pathology that have led her to the conclusion that the left cerebral hemisphere, compared with the right hemisphere, is specialized for motor control of both oral and manual musculature, regardless of whether the movements are communicative in nature or not. She and her colleagues demonstrated, for example, that patients with damage to the left hemisphere, either anterior or posterior, without paralysis of the right side, showed deficits in repeating a variety of hand postures, arm positions, and orientations with respect to the body. This was the case even when those movements were not related to known gestures or movements of the sort normally associated with apraxia. Right-hemisphere patients, in contrast, were comparable to normal subjects.

Repetition of oral movements, both speech-related and nonspeech in nature (blowing, chattering teeth, etc.) showed similar deficits following left-hemisphere damage, although anterior and posterior regions were not equally involved in the repetition of single and multiple oral movements.[2]

Results such as these have led Kimura to conclude that left-hemisphere specialization for speech is a consequence not so much of any asymmetric evolution of symbolic functions as of the evolution of certain motor skills that lend themselves readily to communication. In other words, the left hemisphere evolved language, not because it gradually became more symbolic or analytic per se, but because it became well adapted for some categories of motor activity.

It is possible that the evolutionary advantages offered by the development of a hand skilled at manipulation also happened to be a most useful foundation on which to build a communication system, one that at first was gestural and utilized the right hand but later came to utilize the vocal musculature. As a result, the left hemisphere came to possess a virtual monopoly on control of the motor systems involved in linguistic expression, whether by speech or writing.

Although the differences are considerably less striking than in the case of expression, the left hemisphere also appears to be somewhat superior to the right in its comprehension ability. As noted in Chapter 4, right-handed subjects show a right-ear advantage during dichotic listening for consonant–vowel syllables such as "ba," "da," and "ga." Because these syllables differ only in terms of the rapid frequency changes taking place in the first 50 milliseconds or so of the syllable, the left hemisphere appears to have an advantage in processing this quickly changing information.

But is the left-hemisphere advantage simply one of being able to track rapid frequency changes in speech? There is reason to believe that more is involved. Investigators at the Haskins Laboratories have discovered that the rapid frequency changes that signal *b* in the syllable "ba" are different from those that signal *b* in "be" or "bo." Similarly, the acoustic configuration of other consonants also changes as a function of the vowel in the syllable.[3] Figure 13.1 shows the nature of these changes for *d*.

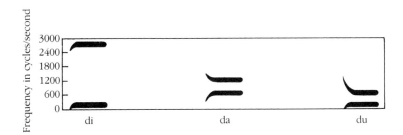

FIGURE 13.1 Idealized spectrogram of sound frequencies produced in voicing "di," "da," and "du." Each sound consists of air vibration concentrated mainly within two frequency ranges, called the first and second formants. Recognizing these sounds involves perceiving the rapid change at the beginning of the formant. Even this early part of the formant changes as the vowel sound changes, despite the fact that all sounds start with *d*.

What do all the different *b*'s or *d*'s have in common that allow our perceptual systems to hear them as identical sounds? Haskins researchers noted that they are similar in terms of the way they are produced. The similarity in production, they argued, is responsible for the similarity in perception.

This idea—the motor theory of speech perception—holds that to perceive speech sounds, the human brain actually figures out what it would have had to do to produce them. Speech researchers have worked hard to explain what allows speech pronounced in so many different ways to be understood so readily. One quality that seems invariant across any particular sound is the way the throat, mouth, lips, and tongue are controlled in its production. The Haskins researchers proposed that in perceiving speech, a listener is in some manner figuring out how he or she would produce the same sounds. Although this theory is not universally accepted, it is of interest to our discussion, for it suggests that finely controlled motor sequences may be an inseparable part of our language communication system, in terms of both production and perception.[4]

Several neuroimaging studies have provided some surprising support for the motor theory of speech perception. A cortical blood-flow study using the xenon-inhalation method reported significant increases in Broca's area during a task in which normal volunteers had to identify words containing a "br" sound in a tape-recorded series of words.[5] A PET study also reported increases in blood flow in Broca's area during a task in which subjects had to decide whether pairs of speech syllables ended in the same consonant or not.[6] The task in both studies involved only perception of speech sounds and not production of speech. The investigators in both studies speculated that their data suggest an active role for the speech production regions of the brain (including Broca's area) in aspects of speech perception.

Manipulospatial Aspects of Right-Hemisphere Skills

What about the right hemisphere? Has it changed during the period in which the left hemisphere acquired its motor and communication skills? Abilities unique to the right hemisphere remain elusive and difficult to define, although spatial ability is strongly implicated. Just as the left hemisphere evolved language, a symbolic system surpassing any single sensory modality, perhaps areas in the right hemisphere evolved ways of representing abstractly the two- and three-dimensional relationships of the external world grasped through vision, touch, and movement. In addition to the spatial tasks considered in earlier chapters, the ability to visualize a complex route or to find a path through a maze seems to depend on the right hemisphere. Although it is usually characterized as more spatial than the left, it is probably more accurately described as more manipulospatial, that is, possessing the ability to manipulate spatial patterns and relationships.

We have just considered how verbal skills may have grown out of the fine-movement skills of the left hemisphere. Perhaps the spatial skills of the right hemisphere are due to another kind of motor skill—the ability to manipulate spatial relationships. Our ability to generate mental maps, rotate images, and conceptualize mechanical contraptions could very well be an abstract, internalized, right-brain counterpart to the motor skills of the left brain.

Are these right-hemisphere skills a result of evolutionary specialization that developed in a fashion complementary to those occurring in the left brain? Or are they more ancient abilities that were at one time bilaterally represented but were essentially displaced in the left by the emergence of language? As noted in Chapter 2, different investigators hold different views on this issue. Jerre Levy, for example, has argued that the cognitive processes used for language and for spatial–perceptual functions are incompatible and, therefore, had to develop in separate areas. By analyzing the tasks and questions most difficult for each hemisphere of split-brain patients, she inferred that the left and right modes of processing would mutually interfere if they existed within the same hemisphere. These kinds of data yield insights into why lateralization took place, but they do not necessarily invalidate the idea that it was mainly the left hemisphere that changed. The issue is not readily decided. Its resolution may depend on much more complete knowledge of what is both common and different about the two hemispheres, as well as the neural mechanisms behind the similarities and differences. Even when we achieve this knowledge, however, it is likely that several equally plausible evolutionary schemes for hemispheric specialization will remain.

Evidence for a Linguistic Basis for Left-Hemisphere Specialization

In contrast to Kimura's view that the left hemisphere is specialized for certain categories of motor activity, another approach holds that the essence of left-hemisphere specialization is the ability of the left hemisphere to deal with the grammar and syntax of language, and that the left hemisphere is uniquely predisposed for the mediation of language. Support for this view may be found in recent work at the Scripps Institute with users of sign language who sustained unilateral brain injury. This work, which was reviewed in Chapter 10 in the context of exposure to spoken language and hemispheric specialization, demonstrated that left-hemisphere damage disrupted the use of sign language to a much greater extent than right-hemisphere injury.[7]

Correlational analyses of the production of sign language versus nonlinguistic hand gestures in these patients, however, did not show the association that Kimura's view would predict. The investigators concluded from these data that at least some aspects of sign language disruption cannot be accounted for solely by a disruption of motor control, and thus that "left hemisphere dominance for language is not driven by physical characteristics of the linguistic signal or motor aspects of its production, but rather stem from higher order properties of the system."[8] The precise nature of those properties, they noted, remains for future research to determine.

Hemispheric Specialization:
The Role of Novelty and Ambiguity

The Routine and the Novel

Learning and new-task performance clearly involve dealing with situations in terms of codes and organizational schemes already present in the brain, that is, dealing with "what is out there" in terms of an already established repertoire of ways of describing and organizing events. This repertoire consists of a whole continuum ranging from biologically fixed visual pattern identification cells to natural language, musical notation, and culturally determined rules of games. Neuropsychologists Elkhonon Goldberg and Louis Costa called these built-in organizational schemes "descriptive systems" and proposed that hemispheric differences in function are rooted in the extent to which an individual's descriptive systems are or are not applicable to ongoing events. They hypothesized that the left hemisphere is highly efficient at processing that takes advantage of well-routinized codes, such as the motoric aspects of language production, and that the right hemisphere is crucial for situations for which no readily apparent descriptive system is available, that is, more novel situations. The model also predicts a shift in the hemisphere involved in a particular task, depending on the extent to which the task becomes efficiently performed and routine.[9]

The Goldberg–Costa model is based partly on observation of the nature of tasks where discrepancies from expected hemisphere involvement seem to appear and partly on some neuroanatomical considerations. As discussed in earlier chapters, not all language-related functions are in the realm of the left hemisphere, nor are all visuospatial functions in the realm of the right hemisphere.

"Classes of materials may differ in the degree of their relevance to existing descriptive systems, thus forming gradients of relative left-right hemispheric involvement in their processing," according to Goldberg.[10] As an example, he noted that the recognition of line drawings of meaningful objects seems to suffer predominantly after posterior left-hemisphere lesions, whereas the recognition of full photographlike pictures may suffer after either left- or right-hemisphere lesions. This difference in the involvement of the two hemispheres in processing these two types of materials cannot be explained in terms of language codability—both are pictures of meaningful objects. It can be explained, however, from a perceptual point of view. Line drawings are the visual models of a whole set or class of real objects, whereas pictures are unique representations (or representations of unique objects). The data just described lead to an example of such a gradient for visual perception, ranging from line drawings of symbols to line drawings of meaningful objects, to detailed pictures of meaningful objects, to nonsense shapes, to human faces, with line-drawing interpretation being most left-hemisphere dependent and face recognition most right-hemisphere dependent[11] (see Figure 13.2).

Goldberg and Costa discussed evidence for differences in neuroanatomical organization of the two hemispheres that may account for two fundamental distinctions in processing. They brought together data suggesting that areas devoted to sensory- and motor-specific functions are greater in the left hemisphere, whereas the right hemisphere is characterized by greater areas of "associative" (higher level, integrative) cortex.[12] Combining other data suggesting that there is more tissue in the right hemisphere with data pointing to an asymmetry in the ratio of gray to white matter in each hemisphere,[13] Goldberg and Costa proposed that there is relatively more white matter in the right hemisphere, a condition indicating greater numbers of connections

Left
Hemisphere ←————————————————————————→ Right
Hemisphere

FIGURE 13.2 An example of visual stimuli that fall into a continuum in terms of left- versus right-hemisphere processing, as suggested by Goldberg et al.

between regions in that hemisphere. Thus, "it appears that there is relatively greater emphasis on interregional integration inherent in the neuronal organization of the right hemisphere, and on intraregional integration in the left hemisphere."[14] In Chapter 1 we mentioned a related conclusion by Josephine Semmes, who proposed that mental processes are distributed over larger regions of brain tissue in the right half of the brain than in the left half.

Goldberg and Costa concluded that, as a result of these anatomical differences, the right hemisphere has a greater capacity for dealing with informational complexity and for processing many modes of representation within a single task, whereas the left hemisphere is superior at tasks requiring detailed fixation on a single, often repetitive, mode of representation or execution.

Ambiguity and the Left and Right Frontal Lobe (or, "What Is the Question?")

Elkhonon Goldberg and colleagues have more recently elaborated on the novel-routine distinctions we have just discussed, dealing, in particular, with evidence for frontal lobe asymmetries in the selection of strategies guided by either internal (memory) or external (environmental) factors. On the one hand, the prefrontal cortex of both hemispheres has long been assumed to be involved when one is challenged by a novel task. On the other hand, the posterior association cortex, also of both hemispheres, is normally thought to provide the storage of cognitive routines and preexisting cognitive representations. Thus, the anterior-to-posterior dimension of the brain appears to be related to processing differences involving novelty versus routinization, in addition to the roles of the right and left hemisphere postulated in earlier work. Goldberg and his colleagues suggest that there is a shift in the cerebral regions controlling a task as a function of learning that involves both axes of the brain: from the right prefrontal (during initial presentation of a novel task) to the left posterior regions (once the task becomes routine).[15]

In addition, they have devised tests to better assess what they consider are frontal lobe contributions to hemispheric asymmetry of function. We interpret most real-life situations and problems based on our own history, needs, and motives, that is, most real-life situations are inherently "projective." This element is, however, totally missing in most laboratory tests of cognitive function, where the problem is stated for the subject explicitly and unambiguously. This precise defining of the problem and its circumstances is exactly why, according to these investigators, laboratory tests fail to see some important differences in hemispheric function. Goldberg and his collaborators have devised a test, called the Cognitive Bias Task, in which response selection is prompted by specific targets but is intended to be ambiguous, allowing responses that range in the extent to which they resemble the target, depending on each subject's preferences.[16] The test in essence establishes the extent to which each subject's responses are guided by the target, that is, are "context-dependent," versus the extent to which responses are not, that is, are "context-independent."

Figure 13.3 presents a sample task and response choices. The use of this test on patients with lesions in either the left or right hemisphere has shown a strong effect with respect to frontal lobe lesions. In right-handed males, left prefrontal lesions produce extreme context independence and right prefrontal lesions produce extreme context dependence. The responses of normal controls fall in the middle. In right-handed females, both left and right prefrontal lesions produce the same effect as right prefrontal lesions in men—extremely context-dependent responses relative to those of controls. Posterior right-hemisphere lesions in females produce context-independent responses similar to those produced by left frontal lesions in men, although the effect is weaker.[17]

These findings as well as the model of frontal asymmetries require further validation and perhaps additional interpretation, but they are consistent with other evidence of greater lateralization of function in men. What is intriguing is the proposition that there may be greater functional heterogeneity within a hemisphere in females, perhaps to make up for the relative hemispheric symmetry.

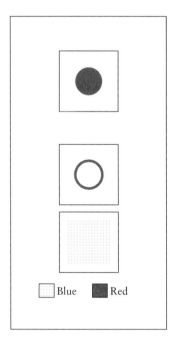

FIGURE 13.3 Example of Cognitive Bias Task trial. The task involves a multiple-choice procedure designed to measure bias (or preference) rather than performance (or accuracy). The stimuli vary along five dimensions: shape, color, number, size, and contour. A "similarity index" is computed between any two stimuli, ranging from 5 (identical) to 0 (differing along all five dimensions). A trial involves the presentation of a target alone followed by two choices below. Subjects look at the target and then select one of the two choices that they like the best. Overall scores reflect the extent to which a subject's choices are guided by the target items, that is, are "context dependent." [After Goldberg et al., 1994.]

A Model of Callosal Function

In our discussions of models of hemispheric asymmetry of function up to this point, only minimal attention has been paid to the functions of the corpus callosum. In Chapter 10 we talked of the corpus callosum as a means of sharing information between the hemispheres or perhaps inhibiting one hemisphere while the other "takes over" some activity.

These hypothesized roles, however, lead to some paradoxical questions. As Jerre Levy has observed, if in fact the corpus callosum provides carbon copy-like information by transferring information from one hemisphere to the other, why have the corpus callosum, "if all you need to do is move your eyes around."[18] After all, most split-brain patients seem to do quite well after they recover from the operation. Conversely, if the corpus callosum only inhibits, allowing each hemisphere to function independently, why is it so complex, so intricate in its connections of so many regions of the brain? We need to develop a model that not only explains the need for its detailed connections, as the carbon copy model does, but also explains how these connections provide unique or truly useful information.

Psychologist Norman Cook considered four possible neurophysiological roles for the corpus callosum: two involving reduction of neural activity (inhibition) and two involving enhancement of neural activity (excitation) in the hemisphere opposite to the site of initial activity.[19] Either inhibition or excitation can operate at the global (diffuse) level, slowing down or activating the entire hemisphere, or at the regional level, doing so only in specific regions in a topographic or "point in one hemisphere" to a "point in the other hemisphere" manner. Cook contended that neither the diffuse nor the topographic excitation model is sufficient—diffuse excitation would amount to using the callosum for purposes of arousing or alerting the other hemisphere, and topographic excitation would provide carbon copy information between hemispheres. In either case, the corpus callosum would tend to accentuate or duplicate what was already happening in the other hemisphere. Cook believed it must do more than that.

Cook similarly rejected the diffuse inhibition possibility, arguing that it is absurd to imagine so large a nerve fiber tract simply serving to shut down one hemisphere while the other is active. Besides, he argued, there is no electrophysiological or metabolic evidence that there is any suppression of overall activity in one hemisphere as the other becomes more active. This elimination process left Cook with the topographic inhibitory model, which he discussed in terms of how it can serve to accentuate functional asymmetries.

To understand his model, we must first accept two assumptions, both of which have considerable support from experimental data. The first is that arousal and attentional mechanisms located deep in the brain tend to activate regions of both hemispheres symmetrically. The brain's main arousal system, the reticular activating formation, does in fact consist of subcortical groups of cell bodies and pathways that are not separated by cutting the callosum. As mentioned in Chapter 3, cerebral blood-flow data have also shown that when there are increases in metabolism, they tend to occur in regions of both hemispheres, even during speech production. The other assumption is that related aspects of some item in memory are represented in the brain anatomically near each other, or at least that access to these related aspects is provided by neighboring neurons.

Cook contended that topographic inhibition across the corpus callosum suppresses in one hemisphere exactly the same neuronal pattern of activity that originated in the other, but at the same time allows activity to develop in surrounding neurons representing complementary (e.g., contextual) aspects of the original information. Figure 13.4 illustrates how this might occur.

In most language-related activity it would be excitation in the left that inhibits equivalent neurons in the right and promotes surrounding context-associated processing. As an example, excitation of the cortical neurons that represent "cat" in the left hemisphere would inhibit "cat" in the right hemisphere while allowing excitation of peripheral cat-related neural assemblies ("kitten, lion, dog," etc.) in that hemisphere. If the ongoing language is, "The cat pounced on the

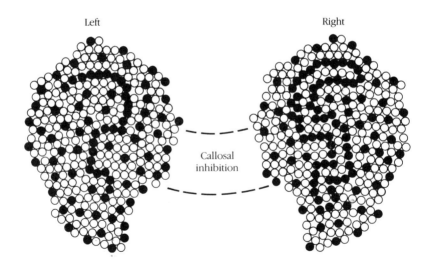

Left   Right

Callosal
inhibition

FIGURE 13.4 An example of topographic inhibition, mediated by the corpus callosum, creating a suppression of activity in the same grouping of cells of the right hemisphere that are active in the left. This is accompanied by increased activity in the immediately surrounding neurons in the right hemisphere that are thought to encode related or contextual information. Dark circles represent neurons or columns of neurons that are firing. [From Cook, "Callosal Inhibition: The Key to the Brain Code," Fig. 1, p. 102, in *Behavioral Science*, 1984.]

mouse," then not only would individual words produce related contextual items in the right but also the meaning of the left hemisphere's sentence, as a whole, would generate right-hemispheric contextual meaning.

These complementary aspects of whatever item is being processed are the result of a "mirror-image negative relationship" between equivalent areas of the two hemispheres, created or at least accentuated by continuous topographic inhibition across the cerebral commissures. In the case of language, this model implies that whatever the left hemisphere asserts explicitly, the right hemisphere connotes in a more generalized pattern, with the explicit message omitted. Thus, by producing two distinctly different patterns of neural excitation within bilaterally identical regions (each of which was aroused by the general attentional system), "callosal homotopic (i.e., equivalent) inhibition allows the 'two brains' momentarily to hold different perspectives on the same information."[20]

Language-related examples are just one type of example of how this system works, according to Cook. The idea of complementary functions of equivalent areas extends to other functions, including perception where, for example, perception of a visual figure versus its contextual background also operates in a similar manner. Cook's assumption that equivalent (homotopic) areas of the two hemispheres end up active for complementary aspects is supported by what is known about subtle language and cognitive deficits after right-hemisphere injury, such as the deficits in context, metaphor, and humor discussed in Chapter 7.

Global Versus Local Processing and the Hemispheres

There is some reason to believe that the cerebral hemispheres tend to encode objects and the perceptual world at different levels of scale. The perceptual world can be organized hierarchically: The forest consists of trees, which in turn consist of leaves and other parts. There is the perennial joke about the person who cannot see the forest (or the "whole" picture) for the trees. Neuropsychological evidence and some neuroimaging experiments have recently suggested that attending to "the forest" depends on activating the right hemisphere.

In one study, brain-injured patients were asked to identify which of two possible target letters (by pressing one of two keys) was present on each trial. Stimuli were large letters (the "global" level), which were formed by arranging sets of smaller letters (the "local" level). Subjects did not know whether the target letter would appear at the global or local level. Patients with right-hemisphere superior temporal gyrus lesions had selective difficulty identifying letters at the global level, whereas patients with left-hemisphere damage in this area had selective difficulty identifying letters at the local level.[21] Other neuropsychological studies have also indicated that unilateral lesions to the temporal and parietal cortex lead to different attentional and perceptual impairments, a result indicating a left-hemisphere bias for local and a right-hemisphere bias for global processing.[22]

A recent PET study has provided direct evidence for this hemispheric asymmetry in normal subjects.[23] The investigators used what they termed "hierarchically" organized stimuli similar to the ones used with brain-injured patients in two separate experiments. In the first, a directed attention task, subjects were asked to attend to and name either the global or local aspects of the figures in separate blocks of trials. The figures are illustrated in Color plate 16. Both large and small figures were used to check for a possible confounding of differences in stimulus size on the local–global issue (i.e., to control for size effects). The results of this experiment showed asymmetric activation of visual areas in the occipital lobes: Attention to the global aspect of the figures activated the right lingual gyrus, whereas locally directed attention activated the left inferior occipital cortex. The investigators were surprised by the fact that this asymmetry was not in the temporal–parietal areas, as predicted by the clinical studies, but was evident in prestriate visual cortex, an area known to be involved in the early stages of visual processing. They had expected that the prestriate visual cortex would be symmetrically activated by the invariant or identical stimuli across trials. They speculated that this result demonstrated a high-level asymmetric effect by selective attention on the processing of identical input in primary (i.e., early sensory stage) visual areas (see Color plate 17).

In the second experiment, a divided attention task, a preselected target letter appeared at either the global or the local level (i.e., as the letter made up of smaller letters or as one of the small letters), and the subjects were required to say at which of the two levels the target had appeared. The analysis determined the blood-flow changes that correlated with the number of attentional target switches between the two perceptual levels. Results showed that the number of target switches from local to global (and vice versa) covaried with temporal–parietal activation in the left and right hemisphere. The most significant positive correlation was observed between cerebral blood-flow in the right temporal–parietal area and the amount of time that attention was sustained to either the global or local level (see Color plate 17). It was concluded that the temporal–parietal cortices, especially the right, mediate the distribution or maintenance of selective attention in situations where the subject does not know in advance the level at which the relevant stimulus will occur.

Some investigators have claimed that hemispheric specialization for global versus local levels of analysis is really a result of the hemispheric differences in spatial frequency encoding that were discussed in Chapter 4. Low spatial frequencies carry information about global attributes of visual stimuli, whereas high spatial frequencies carry information about local attributes, a difference possibly leading to some of the right- and left-hemispheric advantages observed for global versus local processing.

Emerging Principles
of Visuospatial Lateralization

Psychologists Halle Brown and Stephen Kosslyn have argued that hemispheric differences can be best explained in terms of explicit principles that apply to specific psychological functions, as opposed to broad generalizations involving simple dichotomies, such as analytic versus holistic. They have pointed out that contemporary research suggests that most hemispheric differences are ones of degree, that is, both hemispheres are capable of most computations but differ in the relative efficacy of individual processes rather than overall capabilities.

Brown and Kosslyn contended that principles are emerging that explain patterns of cerebral lateralization as long as one deals with specific types of processing, that is, principles that appear to apply to the visuospatial domain should not be assumed to apply to auditory, linguistic, or other domains.[24] "Global" versus "local" processing (or whole versus part) is an example of a specific dichotomy that appears to apply to hemispheric differences in visual and spatial domains. Different principles of hemispheric organization may apply to the auditory domain. For example, one study using trained musicians found a left-ear advantage for recognizing components of melodies and a right-ear advantage for overall melody patterns, the reverse of what would have been expected had the global–local dichotomy been applicable to the auditory domain.[25]

Brown and Kosslyn noted that there are several other principles emerging regarding hemispheric asymmetries in visuospatial function. They suggested that another set of findings provides evidence that the right hemisphere represents specific visual forms in memory better than the left, whereas the left hemisphere represents abstract, visual categories better than the right, similar to the Goldberg–Costa model discussed earlier.

Furthermore, Brown and Kosslyn suggested that there is a hemispheric asymmetry for representing specific forms or shapes versus the spatial relationships among shapes. This view is partly based on experiments showing that the right hemisphere is much better at "metric coordinate" spatial relationships, such as whether a dot is less or more than three millimeters from a line. The left hemisphere processes "categorical" spatial relationships, for example, whether a dot is above or below a line, more efficiently than the right hemisphere does.

These asymmetries may not, at first glance, seem consistent. Why is the right better at "global" level analysis of part–whole relationships (and low spatial frequencies) and the left superior in dealing with more global visual categories? Both appear to be "holistic" processes. This question illustrates exactly why the term *holistic* may be too general to apply to hemispheric asymmetries. At first glance, it also seems paradoxical that component parts (as in the evidence for left superiority in local or part analysis) and specific forms (as in the evidence for right superiority for specific visual forms in memory) are represented more effectively in different hemispheres.

Kosslyn contended that computer simulation models offer a hypothesis that ties together such apparently contradictory findings. Before we consider this topic, we will briefly turn to the idea of computer simulation and the parallel distributed processing (PDP) model of neural function.

Computer Simulation
and PDP Models of Neural Networks

PDP Model of Neural Networks

The PDP model of neural networks has been a very influential framework for modeling ways in which the brain may store information and for computer simulation of other brain functions. It was developed by computing theorists interested in examining ways of coding information that may resemble or mimic ways in which the brain deals with information.[26] Although not, strictly speaking, an alternative to modular models, PDP makes some assumptions that are at odds with some of the assumptions of modularity.

The main principles of PDP relevant to neural coding are

> *Distributed representation of knowledge* In PDP systems, representations consist of patterns of activation distributed over a population of units. Different entities can therefore be represented by the same set of units, because the pattern of activation across the units will be distinctive. Long-term memory knowledge is encoded in the pattern of connection strengths distributed among a population of units.[27]

> *Graded nature of information processing* In PDP systems, processing is not all or none: Representations can be partially active, for example, through partial or subthreshold activation of some of those units that would normally be active. Partial knowledge can be embodied in connection strengths, either before learning has been completed or after partial damage.[28]

> *Interactivity* The units in PDP models are highly interconnected; thus, mutual influence among different parts of the system is the rule rather than the exception. This influence can be excitatory, as when one part of a distributed representation activates the remaining parts (pattern completion), or it can be inhibitory, as when different representations compete with one another to become active or to maintain their activation.[29]*

---

*The interactivity assumption is the part most incompatible with the assumptions of strict modularity, for if normal operation of some part of the system depends on the influence of some other part, it may not operate normally after that other part has been damaged.

Although we will not delve into it here, computer simulation has been used to test the sufficiency of the PDP hypotheses to account for neuropsychological findings, that is, to account for a set of dissociations in mental capabilities found to occur in certain kinds of brain damage. Psychologist Martha Farah, for example, showed that the PDP model accounted for the set of deficits and spared abilities in three neuropsychological syndromes better than did a traditional model invoking strict modularity of function.[30]

Two additional concepts arising from PDP models are "coarse encoding" and "conjunctive encoding."[31] Conjunctive encoding uses a separate definite unit of memory or memory trace (for example, a connection between cells) to stand for every aspect and every important relationship (conjunction) between items. Such an encoding scheme is highly specific but quickly runs out of units. In coarse encoding, each elementary unit of memory is broadly tuned, so properties or features specified by a unit overlap to various degrees with those specified by others. Any part or feature of, say, a visually presented item, is then represented by activity in a group of units within whose overlapping representational boundaries it falls. Although efficient and quite flexible, the coarse encoding system breaks down when it has to encode large numbers of highly similar, simultaneous events.

Do the Hemispheres Make Use of Different Neural Circuits?

The psychological plausibility of PDP is controversial, especially concerning its adequacy for language and reasoning. However, it may be useful as a model for many neural functions. Several investigators have suggested that the PDP concepts of "conjunctive encoding" and "coarse encoding" appear to apply to many of the differences observed in hemispheric processing.

Psychologist S. H. Woodward has proposed a relationship between two different patterns of neuronal connectivity and the specialized functions of the two cerebral hemispheres. Bringing together some PDP concepts of memory storage and some basic neurophysiological data, Woodward proposed that left-hemisphere processing relies primarily on tight connections between vertical columns of neurons, whereas right-hemisphere processing depends on weaker and longer horizontal connections.[32] Figure 13.5 illustrates the prominent horizontal and vertical dimensions evident in the major layers of cor-

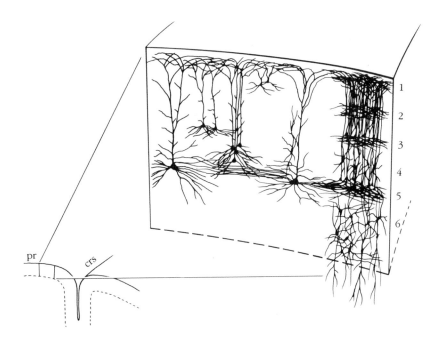

FIGURE 13.5 A cross section through a cortical gyrus, illustrating the prominent horizontal and vertical dimensions of assemblies of cortical neurons and their interconnections. The interconnections are formed by both axons and dendrites, mostly from pyramidal cells. The numbers identify the main cortical laminae, or layers. [Adapted from Scheibel, Davies, Lindsay, and Scheibel, "Basilar dendritic bundles of giant pyramidal cells," Fig. 1, p. 309, in *Experimental Neurology* 42, 307–319, 1974.]

tical neurons and their interconnections. Both vertical and horizontal circuitry have been well studied by neurophysiologists, and there is no conclusive evidence that the connections actually differ in some way in the two hemispheres. What could differ, however, is which kind of circuitry is more utilized in each hemisphere. Woodward noted a striking parallel between coarse and conjunctive encoding models of PDP theory and the kinds of processing horizontal and vertical neuronal connections can offer.

In conceptualizing hemispheric differences along these lines, the left is presumed to be dominated by highly coupled, nonoverlapping connections between vertically arranged cell neighbors, as schematized

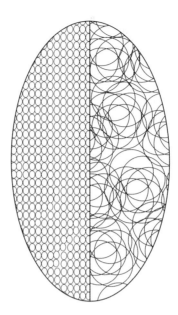

FIGURE 13.6 This diagram represents an idealization of hypothesized differences in the way neural circuitry is utilized by right- and left-hemisphere functioning. In the left, it is mostly highly coupled, nonoverlapping connections between vertically arranged cell neighbors that are important. In the right, horizontal axonal connections dominate, and cell groups over large distances overlap in their connections, which are "weaker" than the vertical connections that the left tends to depend on. [Adapted from Woodward, 1988.]

on the left side of Figure 13.6. Precision coding of small differences, like those needed for articulation or fine motor movements, would depend on this "columnar" organization. The right-hemisphere anatomy is presumed to be dominated by overlapping horizontal axonal connections, thought to involve greater distances and more cell groups, and to be weaker or less precise than the tight vertical columns of neurons in the left, as schematized on the right side of Figure 13.6. The encoding potential of this kind of anatomy resembles that of coarse encoding and seems to be more applicable to encoding more diffuse, less repetitive information. The efficiency of coarse encoding increases as features of a stimulus become more dispersed and variable. "These characteristics appear to correspond closely to classical notions of the right hemisphere as excelling in the integration of spatially and temporally disparate features and the representation of stimulus 'wholes and continuities.'"[33]

Steven Kosslyn has invoked PDP models and similar anatomical analogies in arguing that hemispheric differences in visuospatial processing are a result of processing the output of neurons with different sized receptive fields.[34] He used PDP-based computer modeling to show that the left hemisphere's superiority can be explained if it tends to process outputs from neurons with relatively small receptive fields (as schematized on the left side in Figure 13.6), whereas the right hemisphere's superiority is more consistent with processing of outputs from neurons with relatively large overlapping receptive fields (right side of Figure 13.6). For example, Kosslyn demonstrated that categorical spatial relations, such as those we discussed earlier in terms of left-hemisphere superiority, can be computed more effectively if the input is filtered through a set of small, relatively nonoverlapping receptive fields that allow "pockets" of space to be delineated, such as those above or below a reference point. In contrast, metric spatial relations, such as those discussed earlier with respect to right-hemisphere superiority, can be computed more effectively if the input is filtered through large, highly overlapping receptive fields, which promote the use of "coarse encoding." These models are also consistent with the spatial frequency findings—larger receptive fields will encode lower spatial frequencies more efficiently (at which the right hemisphere is superior), whereas smaller receptive fields will encode higher spatial frequencies more efficiently (at which the left hemisphere is superior).

It is unlikely that these hemispheric differences in encoding are caused by "hard-wired" anatomical variations. Because the vertical and horizontal anatomies do not appear to be lateralized, hemispheric differences must arise in physiological use rather than in anatomy itself.

Neurophysiologists have shown that activities within a hemisphere tend to suppress or inhibit horizontal connections and that vertical circuitry tends to dominate local cortical patterns. It has been suggested that transcallosal input to the right hemisphere permits increasing utilization of horizontal, coarse coding-type storage and processing,[35] but the biological reality of such hypotheses remains to be established.

A Little About Models, Reductionism, and Explanation

Levels of Description

We have mentioned "bottom-up" and "top-down" processing in the context of sensory–perceptual function. In that context, bottom-up refers to how basic operations at the input level lead to higher level functions and top-down refers to how higher level mental operations may constrain or modify the basic operations on the basis of factors such as prior experience, expectations, and context. There is a more general issue suggested by such distinctions—namely, what level of brain and/or mental function does one study to achieve an "understanding of the brain."

Most investigators in neuroscience and cognitive science acknowledge that there are multiple levels of description of the operations of the nervous system, from "molecules to thoughts" or "neurons to psyche," and that one of the goals of science is a complete description of the nervous system at all these levels. There are differences of opinion, however, as to how to arrive at this complete description and sometimes as to which levels are more important.[36]

One approach is to begin with the most elementary levels of description, such as the biophysics of neurons, believing that it will be impossible to understand higher levels of organization if one does not know precisely what is being organized. This approach is often referred to as "bottom-up," alluding to the idea one is analyzing a complex process in terms of its constituent processes. It is also often called the reductionist approach, based on the assumption that any complex, high-level function can be explained by "reducing" it to its components. The success of reductionist approaches in many areas of science, especially in physics and chemistry, has made many scientists believe it is the only way to explain and to learn to manipulate natural phenomenon. Others, however, feel that the reductionist approach is insufficient to account for brain function and, especially, the relationship between brain activity and mental processes.

An alternative approach, often called "top-down," is to begin with higher level nervous system function and see how it constrains what lower level processes need to do in order to account for the higher

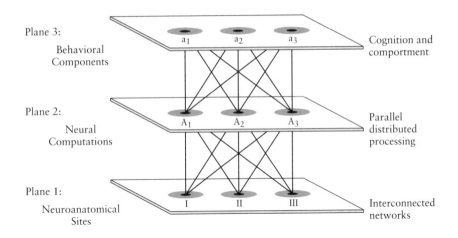

Plane 3:
Behavioral
Components

a_1 a_2 a_3

Cognition and
comportment

Plane 2:
Neural
Computations

A_1 A_2 A_3

Parallel
distributed
processing

Plane 1:
Neuroanatomical
Sites

I   II   III

Interconnected
networks

FIGURE 13.7 Schematic illustration of interrelationships among anatomical, computational, and behavioral planes. [After M. Mesulam, 1990.]

processes. It is argued that our understanding of lower levels will be facilitated if we know what higher function they serve. Thus, cognitive neuroscientists forge ahead with studying perception, memory, etc., while acknowledging that our understanding of the more elementary level of description is far from complete.

Figure 13.7 illustrates an example of three "planes" or levels of description proposed by neurologist Marcel Mesulam and shows some of the "interrelationships" among anatomical, computational, and behavioral planes.[37] This schematic is only a rough approximation, but nevertheless, it conveys the spirit of the approach to brain research taken by many cognitive neuroscientists. It should also suggest the care that should be taken in applying data and explanations from one level of description to another.

A Critique of Functionalist Cognitive Science

Nobel laureate Gerald Edelman has criticized the pervasive functionalist approach of cognitive science, insisting that mental functions cannot be properly studied by theoretical constructs based on cognitive psychology and computer modeling—rather they have to be rooted in the real biology of brain and brain evolution. In the terms discussed in the preceding section, Edelman is thus espousing the importance of the "bottom-up" approach to brain–behavior research. "Emboldened by an apparent convergence of interests, some scientists have relied on the concept of mental representations and on a set of assumptions collectively called the functionalist position. From this viewpoint, people behave according to knowledge made up of symbolic mental representations. Cognition consists of the manipulation of these symbols. Psychological phenomena are described in terms of functional processes."[38]

These functions or computations involve operating on representations or manipulating symbols and are assumed to be largely independent of variations in the structure of the nervous system, especially of individual variations arising in development. Part of this functionalist approach, according to Edelman, is the use of computer analogies in which the brain (or more correctly, the mind) is like a computer and the world is like a computer tape. In effect, the functionalist approach to the brain assumes that the world is so ordered that signals received can be "read" in terms of logical thought.

Edelman maintained that a description of the mind cannot proceed "liberally"—that is, in the absence of a detailed biological description of the brain. In addition, many cognitive scientists are ignoring evidence that the way in which the categorization of objects and events occurs in animals and in humans does not at all resemble logic or computation. Human memory, for example, "involves a rich texture of previous knowledge that cannot be adequately represented by the impoverished language of computer science—'storage,' 'retrieval,' 'input,' 'output.'"[39]

Edelman's own work offers an alternative based on a theory of neuronal group selection, in which object recognition, for example, results from selective matching of sensory events to a preexisting and diverse repertoire of neuronal patterns, established in the course of an organism's development. (This view avoids, according to Edelman, any notions of "instructive" type explicit information transfer to the organism.) Although his theory is controversial, the points Edelman made about cognitive science should not be taken lightly.

Left and Right in Biology and Physics

French biologist Louis Pasteur discovered in the nineteenth century that molecules of tartaric acid could assume either of two mirror-image forms and that a certain plant mold could act on one, but not on the other, form of the acid. This specificity meant that the plant mold, in effect, could tell left from right! Pasteur assumed that his discovery implied that a fundamental asymmetry exists in the molecular structure of the plant mold itself and wrote, "This important criterion (of molecular asymmetry) constitutes perhaps the only sharply defined difference which can be drawn at the present time between the chemistry of dead or living matter." He went on to speculate that "life is dominated by asymmetrical actions. I can even imagine that all living species are primordially, in their structure, in their external forms, functions of cosmic asymmetry."[40]

Are the origins of asymmetry in humans and in certain other life forms to be found in more fundamental aspects of nature—in the fundamental forces operating in biology and physics? The forces of nature have long been assumed to preserve parity, a concept derived from physics that means, in its most general sense, that phenomena remain unchanged if reflected through a plane or viewed in a mirror. In other words, natural interactions in the world look just as normal viewed in a mirror as they do viewed directly. It is only the presence of human artifacts (such as writing) or the knowledge of the exact arrangements of an original scene that can give away whether a picture is mirror-reversed or not. The laws governing a mirrored scene, including how objects interact, appear to be exactly the same as those governing the original. Pasteur's idea of a cosmic asymmetry, however, although perhaps not justified by the limited data on which it was based, was nevertheless prophetic of some recent developments in biology and physics.

Molecular Biology

The discovery of deoxyribonucleic acid (DNA) as the genetic material in cells and the discovery of DNA's helical structure was heralded as a major contribution to biology and genetics. The double strands of each DNA molecule encode genetic information in terms of the sequencing of component amino acids. The two long strands are wound around each other in a clockwise spiral; thus, the DNA molecule cannot be superimposed on its mirror reflection. Some investigators have speculated that this and other asymmetries at the molecular level underlie the gross asymmetry in some organisms, including the leftward displacement of the heart and, perhaps, handedness and cerebral lateralization in humans. They argue that these gross asymmetries must lie in the molecular mechanisms that control the development of the organism's structure.[41] Although each cell contains identical DNA molecules containing all of the information necessary to form the complete organism, the cells differentiate to form different kinds of tissue. It is thought that the genetic information in each cell interacts with some other source of "positional" information in the growing embryo that determines the cell type and ultimately the actual shape and structure of the organism.[42]

The mechanisms regulating the growth of structure and form are not known, and the existence of a positional code is only hypothesized. Psychologists Corballis and Beale suggested that any systematic differences in the formation of left and right would be part of this code and that genes themselves do not encode the direction of asymmetry. They argued that the positional code must consist of a structural asymmetry at the molecular level. Whether or not the asymmetries are expressed depends on interaction of the positional code with the genetic code. As noted in Chapter 10, Corballis and Beale proposed that, in most people, handedness and cerebral lateralization are under the influence of a left–right gradient contained in the positional code that results in right-handedness and the left cerebral control of speech. In a small minority, however, this positional code gradient "is denied expression, and the directions of handedness and cerebral lateralization are assigned randomly and independently."[43]

Parity in Nuclear Physics

As previously mentioned, the forces of nature have long been assumed to preserve parity; that is, normal interactions in the world do not in any way define left and right in the sense that such concepts could be derived from asymmetries in the way things work (or forces operate). Even the deflection of a compass needle to the left or the right by a wire carrying parallel current could not be used to define these directions, because the designations of the needle's "north" and "south" poles are essentially arbitrary. A mirror image of an experiment set up to deflect a compass needle with an electric current would look perfectly normal, because the observer would assume the needle's poles were reversed.

In 1957, however, physicists discovered that some instances of the so-called weak nuclear force (or weak interaction) involving radioactive emissions from atoms did not conserve parity. The nucleus of the cobalt-60 atom was shown to emit electrons more frequently from one end than from the other. Thus, the north and south poles of a magnetic field could be defined in an absolute way by stating that if cobalt-60 nuclei are lined up in the field, then the south pole is that toward which the greater number of electrons are emitted.[44] This asymmetry would also allow one to distinguish between a compass needle's deflection (in the presence of a current-carrying wire) in the real world and in a mirror.

The issue of whether a fundamental distinction exists between left and right in the physical laws of the universe remains a debated one. Some physicists have appealed to "deeper" principles to argue that parity is still preserved, such as the essentially arbitrary nature in which "positive" and "negative" electric charge is defined, along with the consequent labeling of the direction of current flow. Even the direction of time flow is brought in as a factor to help preserve the sense of absolute symmetry in natural interactions. Nevertheless, there is a sense now that, at least at relatively fundamental levels of analysis of physical interactions, natural asymmetries do occur.

Are these more or less fundamental physical asymmetries the basis for the asymmetries evident at the level of molecular biology? At first glance it seems unlikely, because it is not evident how asymmetries at the level of weak nuclear interactions have any influence at the biochemical level; chemical interactions, after all, depend on the electromagnetic force, a much stronger force than that associated with nuclear decay. It is thought that the influence of these asymmetries at the level of chemical interactions is negligible, yet some theorists have speculated that, given the time scale of biochemical evolution on Earth, the influence would be substantial.[45] In addition, there is some evidence that parity is not conserved at the level of electromagnetic and, therefore, chemical interactions.[46]

In reviewing these and other data for asymmetries in nature, Corballis and Beale concluded that "they do strengthen our conviction that the systematic asymmetries of morphology, molecular biology, and subatomic interactions are ultimately linked, and that there is, after all, an absolute, universal distinction between left and right."[47]

Chapter 14

Mind–Body, Consciousness, and the Hemispheres

Speculation concerning the implications of hemispheric asymmetry has followed closely behind discoveries with split-brain patients and other investigations into the functioning of the halves of the brain. This is not surprising, for great indeed is the temptation to account for observations about our own minds and the varieties of human experience in light of discoveries about the brain. Much speculation has touched on the nature of consciousness. What does laterality research have to offer the age-old question about the relationship between mind and body (or between mind and brain)? Does it provide any experimental evidence for Freud's concept of the "unconscious"? Does each hemisphere in a split-brain patient possess a consciousness of its own?

The effort to understand human consciousness is an inquiry older than science itself. It is at the heart of the riddle of self-identity that has preoccupied philosophers, theologians, mystics, and any individual who has asked: "Who—or what—am I? How is it that I am here now?" Some contemporary brain scientists, emboldened by technical abilities that appear to capture such intangibles as a subject imagining events that have not occurred, believe they are getting closer to understanding human consciousness or, at the least, how the brain gives rise to subjective experience. They hope that by studying the activity of the brain during perception, language, and memory, they will discover the organizing principles underlying all subjective experience.

The questions do not stop there, for the general issue of the relationship between mind and brain strikes deep into other profound dilemmas, such as the extent to which we have "free will" versus the extent to which our lives, decisions, and actions are "predetermined," and to issues of personal responsibility—"Am I at fault, or is it my damaged brain?"

We cannot do justice to such issues in a single book, much less a single chapter. Instead, we will present brief glimpses of some of the fascinating, thought-provoking attempts that psychologists, neuroscientists, and philosophers have made into understanding consciousness, or perhaps more accurately, the issues surrounding what it would mean to understand it. We will naturally concentrate more on issues involving consciousness where the study of hemispheric asymmetries may have a bearing, but we will do so within the broader perspective of mind–brain relationships in general.

The issues are diverse, and discourse about even one topic may operate at several levels. Discussions about consciousness can be especially confusing because the term is used somewhat differently by different investigators. There are a number of areas of brain research where the investigators involved believe their data have implications for consciousness. These include the effects of split-brain surgery, evidence for unconscious processes in patients with unusual syndromes, the denial of illness or even of paralyzed or missing limbs in certain brain injuries, confabulation and hallucination in certain patients with damaged sensory input, and the relationship of sleep to conscious wakefulness. We will survey some of this evidence as well as some of the controversial ideas that have emerged as investigators have attempted to extend the implications of left brain and right brain beyond the data.

Two Brains, Two Minds?

More than four centuries ago, the great French philosopher René Descartes concluded that the pineal gland, at the base of the brain, is the seat of consciousness, or more precisely, where the mental and physical realms interact. He based his conclusion on his belief in the unity of consciousness and on the fact that the pineal gland was the only brain part he could find that was not double in structure.

Assigning the interaction of the mental and physical to part of the body seems an inconsistent twist in Descartes's thinking if one examines his writings on the relationship between body and mind. Although Descartes enjoyed mechanically analyzing some of the functions of living things and had great interest in human anatomy, he felt there was something about human beings that could not be explained in these terms. He saw the human body as similar to the bodies of animals, but he questioned whether the human mind could be part of the same physical world. An analysis of one's own thought, he felt, cannot prove the existence of anything outside personal experience. Descartes concluded that an absolute distinction must be made between the mental and the physical.

The assertion that the mind is independent of the body came to be known as Cartesian dualism. Some modern skeptics have referred to it as the "ghost in the machine" idea. The philosophical issues revolving around the relationship between body and mind in general are referred to as the mind–body problem.

Although a simplification, the views and theories of most philosophers and scientists on the relationship of mind and body can be classified into three major categories: mentalist (or idealist), dualist, and materialist (or physicalist). The mentalist view is that mind, spirit, or consciousness is in some way the primary substance of the universe, or that these, in effect, create the universe and our impression of all physical things. Even though this idea is not adhered to by many in recent times, it keeps reappearing in interesting forms.[1] The dualist view was originally elaborated by Descartes but has continued into modern times in different versions, including variations on how mental and physical processes are related. Some dualist theories view them as co-occurring in a strictly parallel fashion ("parallelism") and some postulate interaction between them ("interactionism"). The materialist view is probably the most well known and is reflected in the "neurophilosophy" of many brain investigators and contemporary thinkers who contend that mind, consciousness, and all mental events are reducible to, and explainable in terms of, the activity of the nervous system—although some also add the body as well.

Even those who may not see the need to examine the formal philosophy of developing a cognitive neuroscience have to inevitably ask "more scientific" questions about the relationships of the external world and internal mental events. "How much of the world as we apprehend it, or of the structure of our experience and thought of it, is due to reality, how much to the mechanisms of perception and thought, how much to mutable theory or assumption, and how much to contingent human purposes, social structures or conventions?"[2] The scientific study of cognition demands that serious respect be paid to all of these questions.

Implications of Split-Brain Research

Within the past two and a half decades, work with split-brain patients has raised questions about the implications of split-brain surgery for the mind–body problem. If the surgeon's knife accomplishes a separation of consciousness, then splitting the brain is splitting the mind. One is then forced, the argument goes, to accept the fact that mind is brain, or at least that mind arises from the workings of the brain.

Although one can argue with the premise that split consciousness implies mind is brain, most of the controversy in this areas focuses on whether such patients can actually be shown to possess two realms of consciousness, at least some of the time. In Chapter 2 we saw how this question was discussed on a theoretical level by Gustav Fechner and William McDougall. Fechner claimed that the split-brain operation would result in a doubling of consciousness, whereas McDougall contended that consciousness would remain unaffected by such a procedure.

One hundred years later, Roger Sperry argued that the results of split-brain research support Fechner's prediction of a doubling of consciousness in these patients:

> Everything we have seen so far indicates that the surgery has left
> these people with two separate minds, that is, two separate spheres
> of consciousness. What is experienced in the right hemisphere seems
> to lie entirely outside the realm of experience of the left hemisphere.
> This mental dimension has been demonstrated in regard to perception,
> cognition, volition, learning, and memory.[3]

For Sperry, the impression of mental unity in split-brain patients is an illusion, a consequence of the sharing by the two sides of the brain of the same position in space, the same sensory organs, and the same experiences in everyday situations outside the lab.

In contrast, Sir John Eccles (also a Nobel laureate, for his work in physiology) denied that there are two separate minds in a split-brain patient or that consciousness is in any way split by commissurotomy.[4] He claimed that the right hemisphere cannot truly think. He made a distinction between "mere consciousness," which humans share with animals, and the world of language, thought, and culture, which is uniquely human and essential to any idea of a mind.

In Eccles's opinion, everything that is truly human derives from the left hemisphere, where the speech center typically resides and where interactions between brain and mind occur. The split-brain patient who blushes or smiles when a pinup is flashed to her right hemisphere not only cannot report why she did so but truly does not know why she blushed. The right hemisphere cannot know because only the left hemisphere can have thoughts or knowledge.

Although such controversies are highly confounded by subjective definitions of consciousness, some attempts have been made to be more precise in using this term. One approach is to form an operational definition, which is a definition in terms of the procedures that may be used to measure a concept. Along these lines, Donald McKay, whose primary field is artificial intelligence, has noted that the split brain cannot be viewed as a split mind until it can be shown that each separated half has its own independent system for assigning values to events, setting goals, and establishing response priorities.

An experiment to address this point was conducted by Joseph LeDoux and Michael Gazzaniga with their unique commissurotomy patient, P.S. The study took advantage of the considerably greater than usual linguistic capabilities in P.S.'s right hemisphere, which was able to express itself by arranging Scrabble letters with the left hand in response to questions. LeDoux and Gazzaniga's intention was to ask subjective questions of each hemisphere separately and to compare the results.

On each trial, P.S. was asked a question orally. The key word or words were replaced by the word "blank." The missing word or words were then visually presented in either the left visual field (to the right hemisphere) or in the right visual field (to the left hemisphere). The questions included, "Who (are you)?" "Would you spell the name of your favorite (hobby)?" "What is (tomorrow)?" The italicized items were the key words actually flashed in the respective visual field. When they were presented to the right hemisphere, P.S. was asked to use the Scrabble letters to spell out his answers.

P.S. was also asked to rate how he felt about a particular word by pointing to a number from one (like very much) to 5 (dislike very much). Some of the words were chosen because of their personal significance to the patient. They included "Paul" (his name) and "Liz" (his girlfriend's name). A sample question is, "How much do you like?" A word would then appear in either the left or the right visual field.

The results showed both that P.S.'s right hemisphere could answer the questions asked and that its answers and evaluations sometimes differed from those of the left hemisphere. For example, ratings by the right hemisphere were consistently closer to the "dislike" end of the scale in the word-rating test than were those by the left hemisphere. When asked the job he would pick, the right hemisphere spelled out "automobile race," in contrast to P.S.'s normal left-hemisphere verbal assertion that he wanted to be a draftsman.

Regarding the issue of double consciousness, the investigators stated:

> Each hemisphere in P.S. has a sense of self and each possesses its own system for subjectively evaluating current events, planning for further events, setting response priorities, and generating personal responses. Consequently, it becomes useful now to consider the practical and theoretical implications of the fact that double consciousness mechanisms can exist.[5]

Although P.S. is a special case because of the extent of verbal capabilities in both his hemispheres, the theoretical implications of demonstrating an apparent double consciousness in the same person extend beyond this one case. In addition to illustrating the older claim that splitting the brain can split the mind, LeDoux and Gazzaniga felt that their observations suggest "the nature and origin of those mental qualities unique to man." These, they felt, are dependent on an active language system:

> When this system is absent, as in the right hemisphere of most split-brain patients, . . . the organism functions mainly at the perceptual motor level. Though certain cognitive skills can be demonstrated in such instances, the richness and characteristic flexibility of human behavior seems to be lacking in the absence of linguistic sophistication . . . Add a rich linguistic system to an isolated mass of non-verbal tissue as in the right hemisphere of P.S., and a human being with the capacity to value, aspire, and reflect on life experience emerges.[6]

The idea that consciousness is dependent on language or linguistic processes is not entirely new. Several philosophers and linguists have subscribed to so-called verbal access theories of consciousness. These theories have in common the concept that the brain events experienced as conscious are the events processed by the language system of the brain.

Language, Consciousness, and the Left Hemisphere

. . . .

Anosognosia and the Left Hemisphere's Story Line

We discussed in earlier chapters how right-hemisphere lesions often lead to left hemispatial neglect. A rarer syndrome that can also occur with right-hemisphere stroke is called anosognosia and involves a vehement denial on the part of the patient of their disabilities. The denial usually comes in the form of statements that there is nothing wrong with the paralyzed left side of their body. Sometimes the patient may even insist that the paralyzed left arm or leg belongs to someone else.

Neurologist Vilayanur Ramachandran has provided fascinating case reports of such patients, whose denial of disability can range from rationalizations to explain why one arm does not move, such as "I have severe arthritis in my shoulder, doctor. You know that hurts," to outright confabulations about what the paralyzed arm is doing, as in the following case:

Doctor: Can you use your right hand?
Patient: Yes.
Doctor: Can you use your left hand?
Patient: Yes.
Doctor: Are both hands equally strong?
Patient: Yes.
Doctor: Can you point to my nose with your right hand?
(The patient proceeds to do so)
Doctor: Can you point to my nose with your left hand?
(The patient's hand lies paralyzed in front of her.)
Doctor: Mrs. D, are you pointing to my nose?
Patient: Yes.
Doctor: Can you see it pointing?
Patient: Yes, it is about two inches from your nose.
(The patient's hand continues to lie paralyzed in front of her.)

Ramachandran speculated that this kind of self-deception is a very exaggerated form of normal psychological defense mechanisms that arise from certain specialized functions of the left hemisphere. One of these, he claims, is imposing consistency on the staggering amount of data flooding our brains. "At any given moment in our waking lives our brains are flooded by a bewildering variety of sensory inputs, all of which must be incorporated into a coherent perspective that's based on what stored memories already tell us is true about ourselves and the world. To act, the brain must have some way of selecting from this superabundance of detail and ordering it into a consistent belief system, a story that makes sense of the available evidence."[7]

Normally, according to Ramachandran, this is an adaptive mechanism that keeps the brain from being hounded into directionless indecision by the combinatorial explosion of possible scenarios that might come from the material available to the senses. The left hemisphere's role is to create a model and maintain it at all costs. The right hemisphere's role is to detect anomalies. "When anomalous information reaches a certain threshold, its job is to force the left hemisphere to revise the entire model and start from scratch. The left tries to cling. The right tries to force paradigm shifts."[8] In certain cases of right-hemisphere injury, the right hemisphere's anomaly detection role is damaged, leaving the left free to confabulate and deny without any constraints.

Verbal Mechanisms in Mental Unity: Evidence from the "Split Brain"

Ramachandran's hypothesized role for left-hemisphere mechanisms in anosognosia bears a striking resemblance to the explanation given by Gazzaniga and LeDoux over 20 years ago for some unusual verbal rationalizations provided by their commissurotomy patient P.S. P.S. was presented with pairs of visual scenes flashed simultaneously to each side of a fixation point and asked to use his hands to point to pictures, from among several placed in front of him, that were related to what he had seen flashed on the screen. He did this quite well. For example, when a snow scene was presented to the right hemisphere and a chicken claw was presented to the left, P.S. quickly responded correctly by choosing a picture of a chicken from a series of four cards with his right hand and a picture of a shovel from a series of four cards with his left hand. Of particular interest was his verbal interpretation when asked to "explain" his choices. "I saw a claw and I picked the chicken, and you have to clean out the chicken shed with a shovel," he replied.[9]

This kind of response occurred trial after trial. The verbal left hemisphere accurately identified why it had picked the answer and then, without hesitation, would incorporate the right hemisphere's response into the framework. While the investigators knew exactly why the right hemisphere had made its choice, P.S.'s left hemisphere presented as fact what was merely a guess.

Gazzaniga and LeDoux saw in these results the suggestion that the major task of the "verbal self" is to construct a reality based on actual behavior. They felt that verbal mechanisms are not always privy to the origin of our actions and can attribute cause to actions not actually accessible to them: "It is as if the verbal self looks out and sees what the person is doing, and from that knowledge it interprets a reality."[10]

Another View of Unawareness of Deficit (Verbal Access Revised)

Neuropsychologist Elkhonon Goldberg and colleagues have argued that the higher incidence of anosognosia or unawareness of deficit with right-hemisphere lesions reflects a general hemispheric asymmetry in self-awareness evident in normal subjects.[11] They suggested that left hemisphere-controlled cognitive processes are more readily available to self-awareness than those controlled by the right hemisphere for reasons that transcend natural language and that are more fundamental than the ones implied by "verbal access" models of conscious processes.

They proposed that in normal cognition the operational content of the processes controlled by the right hemisphere is less available to introspection and awareness than those of the left hemisphere, because (as discussed in Chapter 13) the left hemisphere mediates various well worked out, routinized representational systems or codes whereas the right does not rely on such codes (and excels in dealing with novelty). Goldberg and colleagues argued that natural language is but one example of routinized representational systems operative in human cognition (and primarily within the left hemisphere). Other representational systems that are outside language but still exist at a cultural level include mathematical formalisms, musical and dance notations, and games with special notations such as chess. Still other routinized codes arise as the result of an individual's continuous exposure to a new class of stimuli or cognitive demands. These develop idiosyncratically rather than by way of cultural learning.

Goldberg and colleagues proposed that people are more aware of the content of mental operations that rely on such routinized, left-hemisphere, codes and thus are more aware of their disintegration following brain damage. The cognitive operations in a task involving right-hemisphere mechanisms are more obscure or "fuzzy" to the subject under normal conditions, and their disintegration in pathology is also less apparent.

The Origins of Consciousness and the "Bicameral Mind"

Until as recently as 3,000 years ago, members of the group *Homo sapiens* were virtually automatons, lacking both a concept of self-fulfillment and a sense of the brevity of life. They heard voices inside their heads and called them gods. These gods told them what to do and how to act. Their minds were divided into two parts: an executive part called "god" and a follower part called "man." When writing and more complex human activity started weakening the authority of the auditory hallucinations, this "bicameral mind" slowly broke down. The voices of the gods fell silent, and what we call consciousness was born.

This is the radical theory of Princeton psychologist Julian Jaynes, who has proposed that the speech of the gods occurred in the right hemisphere and was heard by the auditory and speech centers of the left hemisphere by means of the cerebral commissures. Perhaps, he suggested, the pattern-recognition and spatial-processing mechanisms of the right hemisphere were communicating with the left hemisphere through primitive language.

Jaynes supported many of his contentions by reference to ancient literature and to history. He felt that the *Iliad,* for example, describes a people who are not conscious. They do not decide to fight, and they do not plan strategy or do anything else without the intervention of a god or some hallucination.

> These auditory and visual hallucinations, occurring whenever a novel situation arose, show us the structure of the bicameral mind. Achilles, like all bicameral people, had a split mind. One part, the executive god part, stored up all admonitory experience and fitted things into a pattern and told the follower or person part what to do through an auditory hallucination.[12]

To Jaynes, consciousness depends on linguistic processes and the creation of an internal, metaphorical "I." Consciousness is a smaller part of our mental life than previously assumed. A great deal of our mental activity is not conscious but automatic: We do not think about it. This is one reason why it should not be so difficult to imagine ancient humans going through life without the "self-consciousness" we have developed. They may not have been able to view themselves at a distance or to imagine themselves doing something in the future.

> Consciousness is learned on the basis of language and taught to others. It is a cultural invention rather than a biological necessity . . . We know now that the brain is more plastic, more capable of being organized by the environment than we previously supposed . . . We can assume that the neurology of consciousness is plastic enough to allow the change from the bicameral mind to consciousness to be made largely on the basis of learning and culture.[13]

Although there is considerable controversy concerning Jaynes's theory, the idea of connecting the voices of gods in ancient times to a stage in the cultural development of language is fascinating. But there may be a simpler connection than that proposed by Jaynes. Instead of equating the voices of the gods with the right hemisphere's attempt to speak to the left, ancient men and women can be viewed as having misinterpreted internalized speech developing in the left hemisphere. It is possible that in the early phases of the evolution of language, humans were caught off guard by the fact that they could speak to themselves.

Alternative Opinions About the Role of Language in Conscious Thought

Jaynes's theory is a bold example of theories dealing with the topic of consciousness in terms of linguistic mechanisms. We have mentioned several prominent investigators who felt that the left hemisphere was responsible for consciousness because it possessed the verbal skills "necessary" for consciousness. Not all researchers and theorists believe that language is a prerequisite for consciousness, or for thought, however.

Consider the following self-reflection by the eminent geneticist Francis Galton:

It is a serious drawback to me in writing, and still more in explaining myself, that I do not think as easily in words as otherwise. It often happens that after being hard at work, and having arrived at results that are perfectly clear and satisfactory to myself, when I try to express them in language I feel that I must begin by putting myself upon quite another intellectual plane. I have to translate my thoughts into a language that does not run very evenly with them. I therefore waste a vast deal of time in seeking appropriate words and phrases, and am conscious, when required to speak on a sudden, of being often very obscure through mere verbal maladroitness, and not through want of clearness of perception. That is one of the small annoyances of my life.[14]

Others have also contended that words and verbal mechanisms cannot be equated with thought or consciousness. The mathematician Hadamard claimed that words were totally absent from his mind when he was concentrating and that every word he read or heard disappeared the moment he began to think it over.[15] The philosopher Schopenhauer probably expressed this general viewpoint most adamantly when he wrote, "thoughts die the moment they are embodied by words."[16]

The Right Hemisphere and the Unconscious

Arthur Koestler, a well-known writer, argued that the "creative act" usually occurs through other than conscious analytic intention. In his book *The Act of Creation*, Koestler mentioned the idea of incubation periods: putting a problem aside for a time in the hope of coming up with an insight later. He also suggested that the unconscious does a great deal of matchmaking or forming of analogies.

Several famous scientists have recounted how they found a solution to a problem during a dream. Otto Loewi, who won the 1936 Nobel prize in physiology or medicine for showing that nerve impulses are transmitted by means of chemical agents, described how the critical experiment came to him in a near-sleep state. He had come up with the idea of chemical transmission 17 years earlier but had put it "aside" for lack of a way to test it. Fifteen years later, he performed experiments (unrelated to his old idea) for which he had designed a technique to detect fluids secreted by a frog's heart. One night, two years later:

> I awoke, turned on the light, jotted down a few notes on a tiny slip of thin paper. Then I fell asleep again. It occurred to me at six o'clock in the morning that during the night I had written down something most important, but I was unable to decipher the scrawl. The next night, at three o'clock, the idea returned. It was the design of an experiment to determine whether or not the hypothesis of chemical transmission that I had uttered seventeen years ago was correct. I got up immediately, went to the laboratory, and performed a simple experiment on a frog heart according to the nocturnal design.[17]

In an experiment in which he removed the salt solution surrounding a stimulated frog heart and then applied it to a second heart, Loewi unequivocally proved that nerves influence the heart (and most other tissue) by releasing specific chemical substances from their terminals. A careful review of the chain of events leading to Loewi's experiment dispels any notion that it was an accidental or purely intuitive discovery. The background for it had been set by years of rigorous work. However, the act of connecting two critical ideas apparently came while he was in an unconscious or semiconscious state.

Koestler attributed a role to the unconscious in discovery, calling it the "type of thinking prevalent in childhood and in primitive societies, which has been superseded in the normal adult by techniques of thought which are more rational and realistic." As for the incubation period (such as the 17-year period in Loewi's case), Koestler called it "thinking aside" or a rebellion against constraints that is "a temporary liberation from the tyranny of overprecise verbal concepts, of the axioms and prejudices ingrained in the very texture of specialized ways of thought."[18]

The temptation to reinterpret insights such as these in terms of the laterality data is obviously great. As noted in Chapter 2, some investigators have suggested that dreaming is part of the realm of the right hemisphere. A few have proposed that the right hemisphere does all the dreaming; others proposed that the dream state allows the right hemisphere to express itself more freely than usual because the left hemisphere does not dominate or interfere. Sigmund Freud, the father of psychoanalysis, believed that the qualities of the unconscious mind are revealed through the logic of dreams.

The Freudian Unconscious

Do the discoveries with split-brain patients have any consequences for Freud's theories? David Galin has suggested they do. According to Galin, they provide a neurological validation for Freud's notion of an unconscious mind. Galin pointed out that the right hemisphere's mode of thought is similar to Freud's description of the "unconscious," and he noted a parallel between the functioning of the isolated right hemisphere and mental processes that are repressed, unconscious, and unable to control behavior directly. Examples of the latter include the extensive use of images, lesser involvement in the perception of time and sequence, and a limited language of the sort that appears in dreams and slips of the tongue.

Galin believed that the two hemispheres usually operate in an integrated fashion, but at certain times may be blocked from communicating with each other. Galin described several ways in which the two hemispheres of an ordinary person could function as if they had been surgically disconnected. In one interesting example, he talked of the inhibition of information transfer because of conflict: "Imagine the effect on a child when his mother presents one message verbally, but quite another with her facial expression and body language; 'I am doing it because I love you, dear' say the words, but 'I hate you and will destroy you,' says the face."[19]

Galin believed that although each hemisphere is exposed to the same sensory input, it effectively receives a different input because each emphasizes only one of the messages. The left will attend to the verbal cues, and the right will attend to the nonverbal cues. When they are in conflict, Galin argued, the left hemisphere may disconnect the transfer of conflicting information from the other side. During such moments of disconnection, the left hemisphere alone governs consciousness. Mental events in the right hemisphere, however, continue a life of their own and act as a "Freudian" unconscious, as an "independent reservoir of inaccessible cognition," which may create uneasy emotional states in a person.

Can Hemispheres Be Independent Selves?

When the word *teacup* is projected tachistoscopically on a screen, with *tea* presented to the left and *cup* to the right of a fixation point, a split-brain patient cannot read the whole word. Instead, the patient will say the word was *cup*, because the verbal left hemisphere saw what was to the right of fixation (the right visual field). The patient's left hand, under control of the mute right hemisphere, will point to the word *tea* in an array of words that includes *cup* and *teacup*. Some theorists feel this situation is a convincing argument for the duality of mind in the split-brain patient. Roland Puccetti argued that the patient's responses indicate a true perceptual experience in each hemisphere. "So here it appears that what is going on in each hemisphere is not just an initial registration of the visual material but a reading out—verbally in one case, manually in the other—of what was actually seen."[20]

But Puccetti went beyond the issue of whether there are two minds in a split-brain patient to propose that, in fact, double consciousness is the normal situation in humans without the operation. In the intact human brain, under the same experimental conditions, the word *teacup* is seen at the same time in both hemispheres, one-half of the word coming directly to each hemisphere and the other half coming indirectly via the corpus callosum (see description of the visual system in Chapter 2). Why then, Puccetti asked, does the subject not see *teacup teacup* instead of just *teacup*, if consciousness spans both hemispheres?

Some would answer that the duplication is only in the initial sensory registration of the stimulus that is not at a conscious level—the double sensory representations are fused in the processing that leads to our "seeing" the stimulus. Puccetti contended, however, that each hemisphere normally does "see" the whole visual field; that is, each hemisphere is conscious of *teacup*, just as each hemisphere is conscious of half that word when the corpus callosum is split. Thus, cutting the corpus callosum does not in itself produce a divided mind but, rather, only deprives two existing minds of half their normal visual input (the ipsilateral half-field), subsequent to which the separate consciousnesses become evident. In the intact brain, neither half-brain has introspective access to the conscious contents of the other. The callosal connections do not provide this; rather, they provide transfer of more basic sensory information.

But why this duplication of conscious experience? Puccetti claimed, as others have, that duplication has to occur at the sensory level, that each half-brain must supply information about what it is seeing to the other half. But at the same time, he contended, conscious unity must be confined to each hemisphere; otherwise, there would be a doubling of the sensory field at a conscious level, and this would be counterproductive when dealing with any visual target. Thus, there is no overall mind spanning the two half-brains.

Why is it that we are not aware of two separate conscious entities within our heads? Why do the two half-brains seem to work so well together? Puccetti felt that the cross-cuing phenomenon provides part of the answer. Experiments with split-brain patients have shown that the disconnected left (verbal) hemisphere will actually claim possession of material presented to only the right hemisphere. What is significant in these cases is that "the verbal half-brain insists it has this knowledge, under the surface somewhere, and implies that there is no other conscious center that has it."[21]

Puccetti also argued that the right hemisphere's continuing to faithfully cue the speaking hemisphere, as in a game of charades, under such experimental conditions attests to its lifetime role in a secondary position to the left hemisphere in most matters of communication with the outside world. Little is changed for the mute right hemisphere after commissurotomy.

Puccetti's hypothesis of duality of consciousness in the normal brain, as one might expect, has a large number of critics. Nevertheless, it is an interesting approach to questions brought to mind by split-brain research.

What Kind of "Selves" Are Hemispheres?

Philosopher Daniel Dennett has mocked the personalization attributed to brain parts:

> So *what is it like* to be the right hemisphere self in a split-brain patient? This is the most natural question in the world, and it conjures up a mind-boggling—and chilling—image: there you are, trapped in the right hemisphere of a body whose left side you know intimately (and still control) and whose right side is now as remote as the body of a passing stranger. You would like to tell the world what it is like to be you, but you can't! You're cut off from all verbal communication by the loss of your indirect phone lines to the radio station in the left hemisphere. You do your best to signal your existence to the outside world, tugging your half of the face into lopsided frowns and smiles, and occasionally (if you are a virtuoso right hemisphere self) scrawling a word or two with your left hand.[22]

Dennett goes on to say that this exercise in imagination simply is not the case because commissurotomy does not leave in its wake organizations both distinct and robust enough to support such a separate self. The conditions for accumulating the sort of narrative richness and independence that constitutes a "fully fledged" self are not present:

> For brief periods during carefully devised experimental procedures, a few of these patients bifurcate in their response to a predicament, temporarily creating a second center of narrative gravity . . . the life of the second rudimentary self lasts a few minutes at most, not much time to accrue the sort of autobiography of which fully fledged selves are made.[23]

Philosopher–psychologist Daniel N. Robinson of Georgetown University has also argued that issues pertaining to the unity of consciousness are largely unaffected by split-brain data. Robinson acknowledged the scientific merit of new findings and theories regarding the lateralization of psychological processes. However, he saw only one consistent finding in research with split-brain patients that can be claimed to have relevance to issues of "split selves" or "double consciousness." This, he said, is the personal state of "epistemic contradiction," the contradictory knowledge-claims sometimes encountered in the testing of commissurotomized patients. The same patient, often at nearly the same time, will assert and deny a specific claim or fact of memory: "The left hand, as the expression goes, may not know what the right one is doing, or as today's commentator would say, the left brain doesn't know what the right one is saying, because the right one cannot speak." These contradictions "are used in defense of the notion of the disunity or multiplicity of self or," Robinson went on, "the duality of self, apparently because there happen to be two hemispheres."[24]

The plain fact, Robinson argued, is that any number of experimental operations produce just this state in perfectly normal observers. For example, observers under certain cuing conditions will "recall" a number or a letter that, after it was initially presented briefly in an array, they could not recognize at all.[25] In certain psychophysical experiments observers will respond just as quickly to a flash they claim they do not "see" as to the same flash when it is presented alone.[26] Robinson mentioned other examples such as "hysterical" patients who adopt entirely distinct identities, sleepwalkers who complete elaborate actions and do not recall anything about it afterward, and hypnotic subjects who deny what they know.

> For those who would use such findings as proof of a multiplicity of selves, there is an embarrassment of riches to which commissurotomies add very little, but for those committed to the duality thesis, the findings are actually too good for the thesis to be true. States of

epistemic contradiction are, as it happens, not limited to two per person. Recall Eve's three faces, and Binet turned up cases involving many more. Needless to say, however, none of these cases included any evidence of more than two hemispheres.[27]

The real problem, Robinson contended, has to do with meanings and interchangeable use of such words as "self," "self-identity," "personal identity," and "person." A person is a human being, often of unknown identity, possessing certain attributes not present to the same degree in the rest of the animal kingdom—a collection of attributes shared by many entities of a certain kind. One can answer "it is a person" to a what question.

To know who that person is, we must go beyond the attributes that established personhood and establish the personal identity. If we inquire as to name, occupation, address, and details of a person's life, we may assert that we know the actual identity of the person—the personal identity. This is different from self-identity, however, because, for example, that specific person may be amnesic and therefore ignorant of the very identity we established. Nevertheless, the amnesic person is not doubtful of existing and "surely must be granted a self, and will claim as much whether we grant it or not."[28]

Robinson contended that some of the effects observed in split-brain patients and the other examples of contradictory knowledge-claims may be taken as evidence of multiple personal identities and even multiple self-identities, but in no case are they evidence of multiple selves. And, we add, it may be most reasonable to view them simply as laboratory manifestations of the many unconscious processes going on within a person's head that psychology and physiology have been attempting to document over the last hundred years.

Conscious Versus Unconscious Processes in the Clinic

Scientists have become more interested in experimental dissociations between conscious and unconscious processes, evident in certain neuropsychological case studies, and the implications these may have for understanding the physiological basis of consciousness itself. The ability to experimentally study some neurophysiological aspect underlying different states of consciousness arose in the late 1950s when the discovery of rapid eye movements during different stages of sleep led to a great deal of excitement. Work with split-brain patients in the 1960s and 1970s, as discussed earlier in this chapter, also seemed to offer possible insight into the nature of consciousness, especially through experiments that investigated the possibility of two independent streams of consciousness. More recently, there has been considerable interest in the extent to which brain damaged patients exhibit preserved access to nonconscious, or implicit, knowledge despite a profound impairment of conscious, or explicit, knowledge. We have already discussed, in earlier chapters, several instances of this: in cases of severe memory loss where patients can be shown to possess evidence of having learned tasks that they have no conscious recollection of doing. We have also seen neglect patients who will correctly "guess" at stimuli they claim they did not see in explicit visual-field testing.

There are other clinical examples of such dissociations in conscious and unconscious processes. "Blindsight" is one of the most famous and involves considerable evidence for some aspects of visual information unconsciously affecting or "getting through" to patients who have damage to the visual areas of the cortex and appear blind on formal visual testing.[29] Some of this evidence is similar to that obtained with the "forced choice" paradigm we mentioned in the study of visual extinction in neglect patients, where, if forced to guess, the patient does much better than chance despite claiming not to have seen anything. Other evidence indicates that such patients have information about location and movement of object stimuli despite not being able to identify the actual objects. Many other examples exist of unconscious learning effects in patients and even in normal subjects in whom analogous phenomena can be demonstrated under laboratory conditions.

What is it that such cases, and the obvious existence of many cerebral operations of which we are not conscious, can tell us about consciousness in general? There are differences of opinion on this, but a number of investigators feel that such phenomena offer the opportunity to study aspects of consciousness in an empirical manner under laboratory-controlled conditions. Furthermore, the neuroanatomical stuctures involved in the syndromes may serve as a basis for a truly physiological model of consciousness.

Stefan Kohler and Morris Moscovitch, in reviewing the literature involving unconscious visual processing, arrived at three models that have different implications for the neural substrate of consciousness.[30]

According to the *degraded representation* model, both conscious and unconscious processes are mediated by the same neural mechanisms. The other two models, however, posit that consciousness is dependent on specific neural substrates that are different from those implicated in unconscious processes. In the *disconnection* model, neural mechanisms involved in unconscious processes connect, in a serial manner, to those involved in consciousness. Moreover, this model assumes that the neural mechanism mediating conscious awareness is a dedicated system that serves all domains, that is, all unconscious processing systems connect to one conscious awareness system. In contrast, the *distinct knowledge* model proposes parallel processing with respect to consciousness across multiple domains. This means that each sensory-perceptual modality or domain has its own neural substrates for unconscious and conscious stages of processing.

The latter two models, according to Kohler and Moscovitch, would direct the search for the neural basis of consciousness in different ways. The distinct knowledge model will direct the search along the many brain regions that are involved in perceptual processes that lead to explicit knowledge in specific domains. In contrast, the disconnection model will direct the search toward a dedicated structure or network without which consciousness cannot exist in any domain.

Although neither model has yet been systematically pursued, Kohler and Moscovitch suggest tentative hypotheses based on the role of the hippocampus in conscious recollection (see discussion in Chapter 8) and other data indicating that the human visual system has two subsystems, one for object identification (the ventral or "what" path), and another for location and guidance of visual action (the dorsal or "where" path). Although connections between these two visual systems and the hippocampus are not well documented in humans, in the monkey the ventral path has strong projections to the hippocampal formations, whereas projections from the dorsal path to the hippocampus are sparse.

Assuming this is also the situation in humans, Kohler and Moscovitch suggested it offers the opportunity to more carefully examine several predictions concerning conscious recollection: that only visual knowledge that is consciously (explicitly) apprehended can be recollected at a later time and that the regions necessary for consciousness are those that project to the hippocampal formation. They cautioned that they do not claim the hippocampal formation to be the repository or gateway of consciousness. Instead, they see it as a structure that needs "conscious input" for its operation and may, therefore, serve as a guide or pointer to those regions that are involved in consciousness.

The Binding Problem

One of the often discussed mysteries of human brain function concerns how multiple cerebral processes result in unified perceptual experience. How does the brain "bind" the fragmented pieces of information coming from different objects and parts of the scene, as well as from different senses, into a single coherent image? Several philosophers, including Emanuel Kant and David Hume, have considered some form of this problem. In more recent times, brain researchers have looked for more neurobiological explanations. One hypothesis is that there must be one place in the brain where information from all other parts is fed. Another is that binding occurs via temporal synchrony or timing; the synchrony of neural activation across multiple regions is what produces binding.

Electrical Synchrony Model

Electrophysiologist Rodolfo Llinas has asserted that timing is the answer, and he has proposed a controversial and provocative theory explaining it on the basis of 40 cycle-per-second (Hz) brain wave activity.[31] Using magnetoencephalography (MEG, described in Chapter 3), Llinas has shown that a 40 cycle-per-second (Hz) wave continuously sweeps the brain from front to back every 0.0125 second. Because a section of the thalamus has cells that fire in a natural pattern of 40 cycles per second, Llinas believes it is their firing rhythm that is the source of the rhythmicity detected at the surface of the cortex.

The thalamus is known to serve as a major relay station for the body's sensory systems, before their signals go on to the primary sensory regions of the cortex. Llinas suggested that the thalamus can ensure that the sensory cells in the cortex, including cortical regions subserving different sensory modalities, are coordinated into a rhythm of electrical activity that is at or near 40 cycles a second. This continuous electrophysiological sweep or scanning wave could be the binding signal that links information from the parts of the cortex that handle auditory, visual, motor, and other sensory signals.

The brain creates images, in his view, as follows: The wave of impulses from around the thalamus's intralaminar nucleus "polls" all the sensory regions mapped out across the cortex once every 0.0125 second. The regions that have active cells, representing some sensory input, are locked into the same rhythm as the scanning wave, and send back a train of nervous impulses to the thalamus, all precisely timed in a coherent pattern. According to Llinas, all the coherent impulses that are received in a given cycle are perceived as a single image. "The sensory messages of sight, sound, smell and touch, are thus bound together, not in a single place but in a single instant of time."[32]

Similarities of REM Sleep and Conscious Wakefulness ("A Person's Waking Life Is a Dream Guided by the Senses.")

Llinas has also suggested that changes in the oscillatory states indicate an intriguing relationship between waking consciousness and sleep, in which consciousness is essentially a dreamlike state guided by the senses. In studying the differences between deep ("delta") sleep, rapid eye movement (REM, or dream) sleep, and the awake state, Llinas found that the awake and REM sleep states are identical with respect to the presence of 40-Hz oscillations, but they differ in their electrical response to external sensory stimuli. While awake and REM states both show evoked potential responses to an external stimulus, the rhythmic 40-Hz activity during REM is not abruptly "reset" by an external stimulus in the same way that 40-Hz activity is reset by a novel or startling stimulus when the subject is awake.

These findings indicate that the 40-Hz thalamus–cortex resonance is active and has very similar properties during wakefulness and REM sleep. Both states generate cognitive experiences but, Llinas suggested, the dream state is characterized by an increased attentiveness to an internal state in the sense that external stimuli do not perturb it.

Llinas also has a hypothesis for why we dream, partially based on the fact one usually either dreams about recent events or about ongoing problems. Dreaming, he believed, may be the necessary consequence of the parallel nature of neuronal organization. Llinas suggested that at the end of the day we may have many partial solutions to a particular question being considered prior to our falling asleep and that in dreaming we "download" them and thus prevent the overloading of circuits with the accumulation of an ever-increasing set of ongoing partial solutions. He has found support for this point of view in the excellent solutions to problems that can arise in dreams, much in the same way that Otto Loewi described his nocturnal insight about the role of chemical agents in neuronal transmission.

The Relevance of Questions Regarding the Unity of Perceptual Experience

As intriguing as are some of the issues (and proposed solutions) regarding the unity of perceptual and conscious experience, it is entirely possible that the questions surrounding these issues are themselves misleading and inappropriate. Is it really necessary to worry about "where" information is brought together in the brain, for example, where "binding" of different sensory events takes place? After all, we *are* our whole brain (and body); do we need to worry about how sensory events within the brain are unified? Do we need to account for the apparent unity of conscious experience by searching for a brain region where different streams of information processing are integrated into a coherent whole? For that matter, do we need to be concerned with how or why the existence of two hemispheres does not appear to result in conflicting streams of consciousness for the person whose brain they constitute?

There is an emerging sentiment on the part of a small group of scientists and philosophers that many such questions result from an erroneous perspective on how different categories of mental functions can be related to physiological events.[33] This error in perspective is probably most evident in the way many models of information processing in the brain appear to lead to the "homunculus problem." Many models inevitably lead to the question of who or what it is that "looks" at the results of the proposed processing steps—a little man in the head, or "homunculus," a figure resembling the distorted figure often drawn to show the disproportionate representation of different body parts in the sensory–motor cortex of the brain? Clearly, this problem is a result of asking the wrong question or approaching the operations of the brain in a wrong way. "Where" something takes place has served a useful purpose in identifying many functional localization principles of the brain. It is probably not, however, an appropriate question or approach to many of the human faculties we ascribe to the brain.

Is the Mind-Body Problem a Dead Issue?

In the exciting rush of new discoveries and observations of brain–behavior relationships, the idea is sometimes fostered that "understanding" the mind (or at least some mental functions) is just around the corner. In addition, because it is often easy to refute naive or simplistic assignments of consciousness to either specific structures (as in earlier days) or to steps in information processing (as sometimes done in more recent times), some writers have fostered the general impression that philosophical and even psychological questions having to do with problems of relating mental events to physical events are nonsense, to be replaced by a new "neurophilosophy" that assumes mental events are completely relatable to neurophysiological events.

In fact, there are still important conceptual and philosophical issues to be addressed in attempting to discover and explain the physiology underlying "cognitive operations." These are not dismissed by mocking Descartes's use of the pineal gland or by refuting John Eccles's pronouncement about where in physiology "consciousness" enters the scene. Unfortunately, the relative ease with which some attempts at dealing with consciousness have been attacked seems to have also trivialized serious questioning of the mind–brain "identity." As noted in Chapter 3, a physiological correlate of some mental event is not identical to the event. Mental life may never be relatable to externally measured physiology—not because it does not arise from brain activity, but because what we experience inwardly is not explainable in terms of discretely measurable processes. Perhaps certain specific sensory aspects of the experience can be related in some causal manner to specific physiology, but the conscious experience as a whole probably has temporal and mechanistic background characteristics completely different from the time, structure, and process we are attempting to measure.

But will we measure "it" in the future? As physician and writer Jonathan Miller said:

> Indeed, the method by which we are acquainted with consciousness
> is so fundamentally different from the method by which we aquaint
> ourselves with brains that I suspect, as philosopher Colin McGinn does,
> that although we don't have to invoke anything other than brain—
> no magic that contravenes the laws of nature—we will never fully
> understand the connection.[34]

Miller concluded:

There is obviously much more to be learned about the relationship between brains and minds, and it will be years, perhaps centuries, before we come up against the "cognitive closure" so courageously identified by Professor McGinn. The fact that such research is destined to describe an asymptotic curve, which approaches but never reaches the limit, does not preclude the necessity of our following it.[35]

Postscript

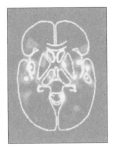

At the time the first edition of *Left Brain, Right Brain* was written, popularization of the implications of cerebral laterality research had almost become a cultural (and perhaps, countercultural) phenomenon. New findings from brain science were extended well beyond what could be justified by the data. The evidence was seen by some as demonstrating the existence of untapped resources of the mind as well as offering an explanation of cultural differences, individual differences in cognitive style, altered states of consciousness, and creativity, among others. The line between science and speculation was too often blurred, and there was no ready way for most readers to make the necessary distinctions between them. *Left Brain, Right Brain* set out to correct this problem: to separate fact from speculation, to show that the exuberance of popular accounts did not diminish the reality of profound asymmetries in cerebral organization, and to help convey some of the real issues, drama, and spirit associated with brain research. In the course of our writing, we became even more impressed with the reality of hemispheric differences and their potential for helping us understand the brain mechanisms underlying higher mental functions.

We have used the study of hemispheric asymmetries as an organizational and instructive approach in leading the reader on a journey from historical to contemporary research on brain-behavior and mind-brain connections. Much of that research, however, no longer has an explicit focus on hemispheric differences. Over time, the emphasis on "laterality" of function in brain research has subsided as new and increasingly sophisticated questions about cerebral organization are being asked and, to some extent, answered. Asymmetry of function often remains tacitly in the background, something to be taken for granted, so much so that a neuroimaging scientist presenting data at a meeting may even forget to mention the fact that most of the language effects being reported occurred in the left hemisphere!

Although the emphasis of most such research and of this book has certainly gone beyond simply searching for hemispheric differences, functional asymmetries remain a fundamental principle of cerebral organization that plays a central, if not always explicit, role in cognitive neuroscience. It is also a principle that is yet to be fully understood and explained. The late Justine Sergent, a neuropsychologist and neuroimaging researcher, had discussed the relevance of research into hemispheric asymmetries:

"The problem of the functional asymmetry of the brain lies at the core of human neuropsychology. . . . This constitutes a paradoxical phenomenon that has no equivalent in nature. Indeed both logic and experience lead us to believe that two symmetrical structures, made of the same tissue and having the same anatomical organization, should possess the same properties and functions, as in the case of the eyes, lungs, kidneys or ears. This is not so for the brain, and the structural similarity of its two main components is not accompanied by functional equivalence. . . . The understanding and specification of the respective roles of the cerebral hemispheres in the control of cognition and behavior are inescapable considerations in any account of the functional organization of the brain."[1]

It is possible that some of the most profound human mental abilities are a result of nature's forfeiting, to an extent, a very old, stable, and successful method of changing the brain: bilaterally symmetric evolution. Why so much of nature involves mirror-symmetrical structure, and why the brain has for the most part evolved in a mirror-symmetrical fashion, is a theoretical issue that largely remains a subject of conjecture.

One suggestion is that a doubled structure is less subject to damage. Mechanisms on one side can easily take over functions lost on the other because they are basically doing the same thing. Once asymmetries developed, this advantage was lost. Substituting for this loss of redundancy, however, was the added survival value of language, sophisticated mental mapping capabilities, and whatever other talents the integrated action of the asymmetric components of the two hemispheres could generate.

In studying these asymmetries, researchers are going beyond what is different about the halves of the brain. They are uncovering principles that help us ask better questions about how mental function can be related to brain function and what it means to "explain" our behavior in terms of physiological processes.

The discovery of some orderly relationships between the locus of brain activity and covert mental function encourages the idea that localization is at least a step toward uncovering the cerebral mechanisms behind mental abilities. Investigators have touched on issues of consciousness, emotion, and the unity of experience. Some of these may be premature attempts using insufficient data and inappropriate definitions, but they are steps—first steps—in the long endeavor to understand the brain and, perhaps, ourselves.

Notes

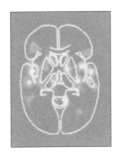

Chapter 1

[1] A. Harrington, *Medicine, Mind, and the Double Brain* (Princeton, NJ: Princeton University Press, 1987).

[2] W. Gibson, "Pioneers in Localization of Brain Function," *Journal of the American Medical Association* 180 (1962): 944–951.

[3] P. Broca (1863), cited in R. J. Joynt, "Paul Pierre Broca: His Contribution to the Knowledge of Aphasia," *Cortex* 1 (1964): 206–213.

[4] P. Broca (1864), cited in M. Critchley, *Aphasiology and Other Aspects of Language* (London: Edward Arnold, 1970).

[5] P. Broca (1865), cited in S. Dimond, *The Double Brain* (London: Churchill-Livingstone, 1972).

[6] B. Bramwell, "On Crossed Aphasia," *Lancet* 8 (1899): 1473–1479.

[7] J. H. Jackson, *Selected Writings of John Hughlings Jackson*, ed. J. Taylor (New York: Basic Books, 1958).

[8] Ibid.

[9] Ibid.

[10] Ibid.

[11] T. Weisenberg and K. E. McBride, *Aphasia: A Clinical and Psychological Study* (New York: Commonwealth Fund, 1935).

[12] J. D. Bradshaw, *Clinical Neuropsychology: Behavioral and Brain Science* (San Diego: Academic Press, 1995).

[13] O. Dalin (1745), cited in A. L. Benton and R. J. Joynt, "Early Descriptions of Aphasia," *Archives of Neurology* 3 (1960): 205–222.

[14] Bradshaw, *Clinical Neuropsychology*.

[15] J. Semmes, "Hemispheric Specialization, a Possible Clue to Mechanism," *Neuropsychologia* 6 (1968): 11–26.

[16] W. Penfield and L. Roberts, *Speech and Brain Mechanisms* (Princeton, NJ: Princeton University Press, 1959).

[17]C. A. Mateer, R. L. Rapport, and D. D. Polly, "Electrical Stimulation of the Cerebral Cortex in Humans," in *Neuromethods,* ed. A. Boulton, G. Baker, and M. Hiscock (Clifton, NJ: Humana Press, 1990).

[18]G. A. Ojemann, "Cortical Stimulation and Recording in Language," in *Localization and Neuroimaging in Neuropsychology: Foundations of Neuropsychology,* ed. A. Kertesz (San Diego: Academic Press, 1994); G. A. Ojemann, "Investigating Language During Awake Neurosurgery," in *Neuroscience, Memory, and Language. Decade of the Brain,* ed. R. D. Broadwell (Washington, DC: US Government Printing Office, 1995).

[19]M. Jones-Gotman, I. Rouleau, and P. Snyder, eds., "Special Issue: Clinical and Research Contributions of the Intracarotid Amobarbitol Procedure to Neuropsychology," *Brain and Cognition* 33 (1997): 1–132.

[20]T. Rasmussen and B. Milner, "The Role of Early Left-Brain Injury in Determining Lateralization of Cerebral Speech Functions," in *Evolution and Lateralization of the Brain,* ed. S. Dimond and D. Blizzard (New York: New York Academy of Sciences, 1977).

[21]D. W. Loring, K. Meador, G. Lee, A. Murro, J. Smith, H. Flanigin, B. Gallagher, and D. King, "Cerebral Language Lateralization: Evidence from Intracarotid Amobarbitol Testing," *Neuropsychologia* 28 (1990): 831–838.

[22]P. J. Snyder, R. A. Novelly, and L. J. Harris, "Mixed Speech Dominance in the Intracarotid Sodium Amytal Procedure: Validity and Criteria Issues," *Journal of Clinical and Experimental Neuropsychology* 12 (1990): 629–643.

[23]Bradshaw, *Clinical Neuropsychology.*

[24]T. Shallice, *From Neuropsychology to Mental Structure* (Cambridge: Cambridge University Press, 1988).

[25]N. Geschwind, "Disconnection Syndromes in Animals and Man," *Brain* 88 (1965): 585–644.

[26]A. W. Ellis and A. W. Young, *Human Cognitive Neuropsychology* (London: Erlbaum, 1988).

[27]D. Marr, "Early Processing of Visual Information," *Philosophical Transactions of the Royal Society of London* B 275 (1976): 483–524.

Chapter 2

[1]T. C. Erikson, "Spread of Epileptic Discharge," *Archives of Neurology and Psychiatry* 43 (1940): 429–452.

[2]J. E. Bogen, "Some Historical Aspects of Callosotomy for Epilepsy," in *Epilepsy and the Corpus Callosum 2* (New York: Plenum, 1995).

[3]A. Harrington, *Medicine, Mind, and the Double Brain* (Princeton, NJ: Princeton University Press, 1987).

[4]Bogen, "Some Historical Aspects of Callosotomy."

[5]R. E. Myers, "Function of Corpus Callosum in Interocular Transfer," *Brain* 79 (1956): 358–363; R. E. Myers and R. W. Sperry, "Interhemispheric Communication Through the Corpus Callosum. Mnemonic Carry-Over

Between the Hemispheres," *Archives of Neurology and Psychiatry* 80 (1958): 298–303.

[6]R. W. Sperry, "Hemisphere Deconnection and Unity in Conscious Awareness," *American Psychologist* 23 (1968): 723–733.

[7]M. S. Gazzaniga, *The Bisected Brain* (New York: Appleton-Century-Crofts, 1970).

[8]S. M. Ferguson, M. Rayport, and W. S. Corrie, "Neuropsychiatric Observations on Behavioral Consequences of Corpus Callosum Section for Seizure Control," in *Epilepsy and the Corpus Callosum*, ed. A. G. Reeves (New York: Plenum, 1985).

[9]J. Levy, C. Trevarthen, and R. W. Sperry, "Perception of Bilateral Chimeric Figures Following Hemispheric Disconnection," *Brain* 95 (1972): 61–78.

[10]L. Franco and R. W. Sperry, "Hemisphere Lateralization for Cognitive Processing of Geometry," *Neuropsychologia* 15 (1977): 107–114.

[11]T. A. Nielsen, J. Montplaisir, R. Carcotte, and M. Lassonde, "Sleep, Dreaming, and EEG Coherence Patterns in Agenesis of the Corpus Callsoum: Comparisons with Callosotomy Patients," in *Callosal Agenesis*, ed. M. Lassonde and M. A. Jeeves (New York: Plenum, 1994).

[12]C. R. Clark and G. M. Geffen, "Corpus Callosum Surgery and Recent Memory," *Brain* 112 (1989): 165–175.

[13]E. Phelps, W. Hirst, and M. S. Gazzaniga, "Deficits in Recall Following Partial and Complete Commissurotomy," *Cerebral Cortex* 1 (1991): 492–498.

[14]E. Zaidel, "Language in the Right Hemisphere Following Callosal Disconnection," in *Handbook of Neurolinguistics*, ed. H. Whitaker and B. Stemmer (San Diego: Academic Press, 1998).

[15]Ibid.

[16]K. Baynes and J. C. Eliassen, "The Visual Lexicon: Its Access and Organization in Commissurotomy Patients," in *Right Hemisphere Language Comprehension: Perspectives from Cognitive Neuroscience*, ed. M. Beeman and C. Chiarello (New York: Erlbaum, 1997).

[17]E. Zaidel and A. M. Peters, "Phonological Encoding and Ideographic Reading by the Disconnected Right Hemisphere: Two Case Studies," *Brain and Language* 14 (1981): 205–234; Baynes and Eliassen, "The Visual Lexicon."

[18]K. Baynes, J. C. Eliassen, and M. S. Gazzaniga, "Agraphia Without Alexia: Isolation of Graphemic Output in a Split Brain Patient," 26th Annual Meeting of the Society for Neuroscience, November 1996.

[19]Zaidel, "Language in the Right Hemisphere."

[20]A. Kertesz, "Recovery of Aphasia," in *Behavioral Neurology and Neuropsychology*, ed. T. E. Feinberg and M. J. Farah (New York: McGraw-Hill, 1997).

[21]M. Beeman and C. Chiarello, eds., *Right Hemisphere Language Comprehension: Perspectives from Cognitive Neuroscience* (New York: Erlbaum, 1997).

[22]R. D. Nebes, "Direct Examination of Cognitive Function in the Right and Left Hemispheres," in

Asymmetrical Function of the Brain, ed. M. Kinsbourne (Cambridge: Cambridge University Press, 1978).

23. Franco and Sperry, "Hemisphere Lateralization for Cognitive Processing of Geometry."

24. J. Levy-Agresti and R. W. Sperry, "Differential Perceptual Capacities in Major and Minor Hemispheres," *Proceedings of the National Academy of Sciences USA* 61 (1968): 115.

25. J. Levy, "Psychobiological Implications of Bilateral Asymmetry," in *Hemispheric Function in the Human Brain,* ed. S. Dimond and S. Beaumont (New York: Halstead Press, 1974).

26. C. Trevarthen and M. Kinsbourne, cited in J. Levy, "Cerebral Asymmetries as Manifested in Split Brain Man," in *Hemispheric Disconnection and Cerebral Function,* ed. M. Kinsbourne and W. L. Smith (Springfield, IL: Charles C. Thomas, 1974).

27. J. Levy and C. Trevarthen, "Metacontrol of Hemispheric Function in Human Split Brain Patients," *Journal of Experimental Psychology: Human Perception and Performance* 2 (1976): 299–312.

28. J. Levy, "The Regulation and Generation of Perception in the Asymmetric Brain," in *Brain Circuits and Functions of the Mind, Essays in Honor of Roger Sperry,* ed. C. Trevarthen (Cambridge: Cambridge University Press, 1990).

29. R. W. Sperry, "Lateral Specialization in the Surgically Separated Hemispheres," in *The Neurosciences Third Study Program,* ed. F. O. Schmitt and F. C. Worden (Cambridge, MA: MIT Press, 1974).

30. M. S. Gazzaniga and S. A. Hillyard, "Language and Speech Capacity of the Right Hemisphere," *Neuropsychologia* 9 (1971): 273–280.

31. J. D. Holtzman, J. J. Sidtis, B. T. Volpe, D. H. Wilson, and M. S. Gazzaniga, "Dissociation of Spatial Information for Stimulus Localization and the Control of Attention," *Brain* 104 (1981): 861–872.

32. M. C. Corballis, "Visual Integration in the Split Brain," *Neuropsychologia* 31 (1995): 937–959.

33. N. Geschwind, "The Frequency of Callosal Syndromes in Neurological Practice," in *Epilepsy and the Corpus Callosum,* ed. A. G. Reeves (New York: Plenum, 1985).

Chapter 3

1. N. A. Lassen, D. H. Ingvar, and E. Skinhoj, "Brain Function and Blood Flow," *Scientific American* 239 (1978): 62–71.

2. J. Risberg, J. H. Halsey, E. L. Wills, and E. M. Wilson, "Hemispheric Specialization in Normal Man Studied by Bilateral Measurements of the Regional Cerebral Blood Flow: A Study with the ^{133}Xe Inhalation Technique," *Brain* 98 (1975): 511–524.

3. R. Kuzniecky, J. M. Mountz, G. Wheatley, and R. Morawetz, "Ictal Single Photon Emission Computed Tomography Demonstrates Localized Epileptogenesis in Cortical Dysplasia," *Annals of Neurology* 34 (1993): 627–631.

[4]G. Deutsch, J. Mountz, H. Liu, and L. Harrell, "Physiological and Cognitive Activation Measured by Tc-99m HMPAO Brain SPECT Compared with Quantitative Xe-133 rCBF," *Journal of Nuclear Medicine* 36 (1995): 63.

[5]G. Deutsch, W. T. Bourbon, A. C. Papanicolaou, and H. M. Eisenberg, "Visuospatial Tasks Compared via Activation of Regional Cerebral Blood Flow," *Neuropsychologia* 26 (1988): 445–452.

[6]P. T. Fox, S. E. Peterson, M. I. Posner, and M. E. Raichle, "Language-Related Brain Activation Measured with PET: Comparison of Auditory and Visual Word Presentations," *Journal of Cerebral Blood Flow and Metabolism* 7, Supplement 1 (1987): S294.

[7]J. V. Haxby, C. L. Grady, B. Horwitz, L. G. Ungerleider, M. Mishkin, R. E. Carson, P. Herscovitch, M. B. Schapiro, and S. I. Rapoport, "Dissociation of Object and Spatial Visual Processing Pathways in Human Extrastriate Cortex," *Proceedings of the National Academy of Sciences USA* 88 (1991): 1621–1625; B. Horwitz, C. L. Grady, J. V. Haxby, L. G. Ungerleider, M. B. Schapiro, M. Mishkin, and S. I. Rapoport, "Functional Associations Among Human Posterior Extrastriate Brain Regions During Object and Spatial Vision," *Journal of Cognitive Neuroscience* 4 (1992): 311–322.

[8]B. Shaywitz, S. E. Shaywitz, K. Pugh, R. T. Constable, P. Skudlarski, R. K. Fulbright, R. A. Bronen, J. M. Fletcher, D. P. Shankweiler, L. Katz, and J. C. Gore, "Sex Differences in the Functional Organization of the Brain for Language," *Nature* 373 (1995): 607–609.

[9]G. F. Eden, J. W. VanMeter, J. M. Rumsey, J. Maisog, R. P. Woods, and T. A. Zeffiro, "Abnormal Processing of Visual Motion in Dyslexia Revealed by Functional Brain Imaging," *Nature* 382 (1996): 66–69.

[10]D. Kotz, "Mapping the Human Mind," *Journal of Nuclear Medicine* 36 (1995): 11–32; R. Shulman, "Interview with Robert G. Shulman," *Journal of Cognitive Neuroscience* 8 (1996): 474–480.

[11]A. Gevins, "Electrophysiological Imaging of Brain Function," in *Brain Mapping: The Methods,* ed. A. Toga and J. Mazziotta (San Diego: Academic Press, 1996).

[12]D. Galin and R. Ornstein, "Lateral Specialization of Cognitive Mode: An EEG Study," *Psychophysiology* 9 (1972): 412–418.

[13]D. L. Molfese, R. B. Freeman, Jr., and D. S. Palermo, "The Ontogeny of the Brain Lateralization for Speech and Nonspeech Stimuli," *Brain and Language* 2 (1975): 356–368.

[14]C. C. Wood, W. R. Goff, and R. S. Day, "Auditory Evoked Potentials During Speech Perception," *Science* 173 (1971): 1248–1251.

[15]A. C. Papanicolaou, A. L. Schmidt, B. D. Moore, and H. M. Eisenberg, "Cerebral Activation Patterns in an Arithmetic and a Visuospatial Processing Task," *International Journal of Neuroscience* 20 (1983): 283–288.

[16]A. S. Gevins, J. Leong, M. E. Smith, J. Le, and R. Du, "Mapping Cognitive Brain Function

with Modern High-Resolution Electroencephalography," *Trends in the Neurosciences* 18 (1995): 429–436; A. S. Gevins and J. Illes, "Neurocognitive Networks of the Human Brain," in *Windows on the Brain*, ed. R. A. Zappulla, F. F. LeFever, J. Jaeger, and R. Bilder, *Annals of the New York Academy of Sciences* 620 (1991): 22–44.

[17]D. S. Barth, W. Sutherling, J. Engel, Jr., and J. Beatty, "Neuromagnetic Localization of Epileptiform Spike Activity in the Human Brain," *Science* 218 (1982): 891–894.

[18]G. L. Romani, S. J. Williamson, and L. Kaufman, "Characterization of the Human Auditory Cortex by the Neuromagnetic Method," *Experimental Brain Research* 47 (1982): 381–393.

[19]A. C. Papanicolaou, "An Introduction to Magnetoencephalography with Some Applications," *Brain and Cognition* 27 (1995): 331–352; A. C. Papanicolaou, S. Baumann, R. L. Rogers, C. Saydjari, E. G. Amparo, and H. M. Eisenberg, "Localization of Auditory Response Sources Using Magnetoencephalography and Magnetic Resonance Imaging," *Archives of Neurology* 47 (1990): 33–37.

[20]G. Deutsch, "A Critical Overview of the Contributions of Functional Neuroimaging to Neuropsychology," *Journal of Experimental and Clinical Neuropsychology* 14 (1992): 86–87.

[21]N. Geschwind and W. Levitsky, "Human Brain: Left–Right Asymmetries in Temporal Speech Region," *Science* 161 (1968): 186–187.

[22]J. A. Wada, R. Clark, and A. Hamm, "Cerebral Hemispheric Asymmetry in Humans," *Archives of Neurology* 32 (1975): 239–246; S. F. Witelson and W. Pallie, "Left Hemisphere Specialization for Language in the Newborn: Anatomical Evidence of Asymmetry," *Brain* 96 (1973): 641–646.

[23]J. Chi, E. Dooling, and F. Gilles, "Left–Right Asymmetries of the Temporal Speech Areas of the Human Fetus," *Archives of Neurology* 34 (1977): 346–348.

[24]A. Scheibel, I. Fried, L. Paul, A. Forsythe, U. Tomiyasu, A. Wechsler, A. Kao, and J. Slornick, "Differentiating Characteristics of the Human Speech Cortex: A Quantitative Golgi Study," in *The Dual Brain*, ed. D. Benson and E. Zaidel (New York: Guilford, 1985).

[25]A. M. Galaburda, J. Corsiglia, G. D. Rosen, and G. F. Sherman, "Planum Temporale Asymmetry, Reappraisal Since Geschwind and Levitsky," *Neuropsychologia* 25 (1987): 853–868.

[26]W. M. Cowan, J. Fawcett, D. O'Leary, and B. Stanfield, "Regressive Events in Neurogenesis," *Science* 225 (1984): 1258–1265.

[27]G. Edelman, *Neural Darwinism* (New York: Basic Books, 1987).

[28]G. Rosen, G. Sherman, and A. Galaburda, "Interhemispheric Connections Differ Between Symmetrical and Asymmetrical Brain Regions," *Neuroscience* 33 (1989): 525–533.

[29]M. LeMay and A. Culebras, "Human Brain-Morphologic Differences in the Hemispheres Demonstrable by Carotid Anteri-

ography," *New England Journal of Medicine* 287 (1972): 168–170.

[30] M. LeMay and N. Geschwind, "Asymmetries of the Human Cerebral Hemispheres," in *Language Acquisition and Language Breakdown*, ed. A. Caramazza and E. Zurif (Baltimore: Johns Hopkins University Press, 1978).

[31] W. H. Oldendorf, "Principles of Imaging Structure by Nuclear Magnetic Resonance," *Archives of Neurology* 32 (1983): 239–246.

[32] H. Steinmetz, J. Volkmann, L. Jancke, and H. Freund, "Anatomical Left–Right Asymmetry of Language-Related Temporal Cortex Is Different in Left- and Right-Handers," *Annals of Neurology* 29 (1991): 315–319.

[33] H. Steinmetz, L. Jancke, A. Kleinschmidt, G. Schlaug, J. Volkmann, and Y. Huang, "Sex But No Hand Difference in the Isthmus of the Corpus Callosum," *Neurology* 42 (1992): 749–752.

Chapter 4

[1] J. Hellige, "Divided Visual Field Techniques," in *The Blackwell Dictionary of Neuropsychology*, ed. J. G. Beaumont, P. M. Knealy, and M. J. C. Rogers (Cambridge, MA: Blackwell, 1996).

[2] M. P. Bryden, "Dichotic Listening," in *The Blackwell Dictionary of Neuropsychology*, ed. J. G. Beaumont, P. M. Knealy, and M. J. C. Rogers (Cambridge, MA: Blackwell, 1996).

[3] D. Kimura, "Functional Asymmetry of the Brain in Dichotic Listening," *Cortex* 3 (1967): 163–168.

[4] J. J. Sidtis, "Dichotic Listening After Commissurotomy," in *Handbook of Dichotic Listening: Theory, Methods, and Research*, ed. K. Hugdahl (Chichester: John Wiley, 1988).

[5] E. L. Schwartz, R. Desimone, T. D. Albright, and C. G. Gross, "Shape Recognition and Inferior Temporal Neurons," *Proceedings of the National Academy of Sciences USA* 80 (1984): 5776–5778.

[6] M. Corballis, "Neuropsychology of Perceptual Functions," in *Neuropsychology*, ed. D. Zaidel (San Diego: Academic Press, 1994).

[7] Ibid.

[8] R. Klatzky and R. Atkinson, "Specialization of the Cerebral Hemispheres in Scanning for Information in Short-Term Memory," *Perception and Psychophysics* 10 (1971): 335–338.

[9] S. Sasanuma, M. Itoh, K. Mori, and Y. Kobayashi, "Tachistoscopic Recognition of Kana and Kanji Words," *Neuropsychologia* 15 (1977): 547–553.

[10] M. H. VanKleeck, "Hemispheric Differences in Global Versus Local Processing of Hierarchical Visual Stimuli by Normal Subjects: New Data and a Meta-Analysis of Previous Studies," *Neuropsychologia* 27 (1989): 1165–1178.

[11] J. Sergent and J. B. Hellige, "Role of Input Factors in Visual-Field Asymmetries," *Brain and Cognition* 5 (1986): 174–199.

[12] A. Grabowska and A. Nowicka, "Visual-Spatial-Frequency Model of Cerebral Asymmetry: A Critical Survey of Behavioral and Electrophysiological Studies,"

Psychological Bulletin 120 (1996): 434–449.

[13]M. P. Bryden, "An Overview of the Dichotic Listening Procedure and Its Relation to Cerebral Organization," in *Handbook of Dichotic Listening: Theory, Methods, and Research,* ed. K. Hugdahl (Chichester: John Wiley, 1988).

[14]R. Zatorre, "Perceptual Asymmetry in the Dichotic Fused Words Test and Cerebral Speech Lateralization Determined by the Carotid Amytal Test," *Neuropsychologia* 27 (1989): 1207–1219.

[15]T. A. Mondor and M. P. Bryden, "The Influence of Attention Upon the Dichotic REA," *Neuropsychologia* 29 (1991): 1179–1190.

[16]M. P. Bryden and T. A. Montor, "Attentional Factors in Visual Field Asymmetries," *Canadian Journal of Psychology* 45 (1991): 427–447.

[17]M. Kinsbourne, "The Mechanisms of Hemisphere Asymmetry in Man," in *Hemispheric Disconnection and Cerebral Function,* ed. M. Kinsbourne and W. L. Smith (Springfield, IL: Charles C. Thomas, 1974).

[18]P. A. Reuter-Lorenz, M. Kinsbourne, and M. Moscovitch, "Hemispheric Control of Spatial Attention," *Brain and Cognition* 12 (1990): 240–266.

[19]K. Hugdahl, "Dichotic Listening: Probing Temporal Lobe Functional Integrity," in *Brain Asymmetry,* ed. R. Davidson and K. Hugdahl (Cambridge, MA: MIT Press, 1995).

[20]E. Zaidel, J. M. Clarke, and B. Suyenobo, "Hemispheric Independence: A Paradigm Case for Cognitive Neuroscience," in *Neurobiology of Higher Cognitive Function,* ed. A. B. Scheibel and A. F. Wechsler (New York: Guilford, 1990).

[21]M. Banich, "Interhemispheric Processing: Theoretical Considerations and Empirical Approaches," in *Brain Asymmetry,* ed. R. Davidson and K. Hugdahl (Cambridge: MIT Press, 1995).

[22]J. B. Hellige, "Cerebral Laterality and Metacontrol," in *Recent Advances in Laterality,* ed. F. Kitterle (Hillsdale, NJ: Erlbaum, 1991).

[23]Ibid.

[24]Banich, "Interhemispheric Processing."

[25]R. A. Harshman and M. E. Lundy, "Can Dichotic Listening Measure Degree of Lateralization?" in *Handbook of Dichotic Listening: Theory, Methods, and Research,* ed. K. Hugdahl (Chichester: John Wiley, 1988).

[26]J. Hellige, *Hemispheric Asymmetry; What's Right and What's Left* (Cambridge, MA: Harvard University Press, 1993).

Chapter 5

[1]W. Dennis, "Early Graphic Evidence of Dextrality in Man," *Perceptual and Motor Skills* 8 (1958): 147–149; R. A. Dart, "The Predatory Implement Technique of Australopithecus," *American Journal of Physical Anthropology* 7 (1949): 1–38; R. S. Uhrbrock, "Laterality in Art," *Journal of Aesthetics and Art Criticism* 32 (1973): 27–35; S. Coren and C. Porac, "Fifty Centuries of Right Handedness: The Historical Record," *Science* 198 (1977): 631–632.

[2]M. C. Corballis, "The Origins and Evolution of Human Laterality," in *Neuropsychology and Cognition*, vol. 1, ed. R. N. Malateska and L. C. Hartlage (The Hague: Martinus Nijhoff Publishers, 1982).

[3]F. Fabbro, "Left and Right in the Bible from a Neuropsychological Perspective," *Neuropsychologia* 24 (1994): 161–183.

[4]M. Barsley, *Left Handed People* (North Hollywood, CA: Wilshire Book Co., 1979).

[5]C. Sagan, *The Dragons of Eden* (New York: Random House, 1977).

[6]J. A. Froude, *Thomas Carlyle in London, 1834–1881* (London: Longmans, Green, 1884).

[7]D. J. Cunningham, "Right Handedness and Left Handedness," *Journal of the Royal Anthropological Institute of Great Britain and Ireland* 32 (1902): 273–296.

[8]R. C. Oldfield, "The Assessment and Analysis of Handedness: The Edinburgh Inventory," *Neuropsychologia* 9 (1971): 97–114.

[9]M. P. Bryden and X. Steenhuis, "Issues in the Assessment of Handedness," in *Cerebral Laterality: Theory and Research* (Hillsdale, NJ: Erlbaum, 1991); I. C. McManus, "Handedness," in *The Blackwell Dictionary of Neuropsychology*, ed. J. G. Beaumont, P. M. Knealy, and M. J. C. Rogers (Cambridge: Blackwell, 1996).

[10]I. C. McManus and M. P. Bryden, "The Genetics of Handedness, Cerebral Dominance, and Lateralization," in *Handbook of Neuropsychology*, ed. I. Rapin and S. Segalowitz (New York: Elsevier, 1992).

[11]R. Collins, "On the Inheritance of Direction and Degree of Asymmetry," in *Cerebral Lateralization in Nonhuman Species*, ed. S. Glick (Orlando, FL: Academic Press, 1985).

[12]M. Annett and M. P. Alexander, "Atypical Cerebral Dominance: Predictions and Tests of the Right Shift Theory," *Neuropsychologia* 34 (1996): 1215–1227.

[13]N. Geschwind and N. Galaburda, *Cerebral Lateralization: Biological Mechanisms, Associations and Pathology* (Cambridge, MA: MIT Press, 1987).

[14]M. W. O'Boyle and C. P. Benbow, "Handedness and Its Relationship to Mathematical Talent," in *Left Handedness: Behavioral Implications*, ed. S. Coren (Amsterdam: North-Holland Elsevier, 1990).

[15]M. P. Bryden, I. C. McManus, and B. Bulman-Fleming, "Evaluating the Empirical Support for the Geschwind-Behan-Galaburda Model of Cerebral Lateralization," *Brain and Cognition* 26 (1994): 103–167.

[16]S. Coren, "Twinning is Associated with an Increased Risk of Left-Handedness and Inverted Writing Posture," *Early Human Development* 40 (1994): 23–27; C. Derom, E. Thiery, R. Vlietinck, R. Loos, and R. Derom, "Handedness in Twins According to Zygosity and Chorion Type: A Preliminary Report," *Behavior Genetics* 26 (1996): 407–408.

[17]A. Akerman and S. Fischbein, "Twins—Are They at Risk? A Longitudinal Study of Twins and Nontwins from Birth to 18 Years of Age," *Acta Geneticae Medicae*

et Gemellologiae 40 (1991): 29–40.

[18]P. Bakan, "Nonright-handedness and the Continuum of Reproductive Casualty," in *Left Handedness: Behavioral Implications and Anomalies* [*Advances in Psychology*, vol. 67], ed. S. Coren (Amsterdam: North-Holland Elsevier, 1990).

[19]M. Schwartz, "Left Handedness and Prenatal Complications," in *Left Handedness: Behavioral Implications and Anomalies,* ed. S. Coren (Amsterdam: North-Holland Elsevier, 1990).

[20]P. Satz, D. L. Orsini, E. Saslow, and R. Henry, "The Pathological Left-Handedness Syndrome," *Brain and Cognition* 4 (1985): 27–46; P. Satz, D. L. Orsini, E. Saslow, and R. Henry, "Early Brain Injury and Pathological Left-Handedness: Clues to a Syndrome," in *The Dual Brain,* ed. E. Zaidel (New York: Guilford, 1985).

[21]D. W. Loring, K. Meador, G. Lee, A. Murro, J. Smith, H. Flanigin, B. Gallagher, and D. King, "Cerebral Language Lateralization: Evidence from Intracarotid Amobarbitol Testing," *Neuropsychologia* 28 (1990): 831–838.

[22]A. R. Luria, *Traumatic Aphasia* (The Hague: Mouton, 1970); A. Subirana, "The Prognosis in Aphasia in Relation to Cerebral Dominance and Handedness," *Brain* 81 (1958): 415–425.

[23]M. Peters, "Handedness and Its Relation to Other Indices of Cerebral Lateralization," in *Brain Asymmetry,* ed. R. Davidson and K. Hugdahl (Cambridge, MA: MIT Press, 1995).

[24]A. Kertesz, "Recovery of Aphasia," in *Behavioral Neurology and Neuropsychology,* ed. T. E. Feinberg and M. J. Farah (New York: McGraw-Hill, 1997).

[25]J. W. VanStrien and A. Bouma, "Sex and Familial Sinistrality Differences in Cognitive Abilities," *Brain and Cognition* 27 (1995): 137–146.

[26]J. Levy and M. Reid. "Variations in Writing Posture and Cerebral Organization," *Science* 194 (1976): 337.

[27]A. M. Weber and J. L. Bradshaw, "Levy and Reid's Neurological Model in Relation to Writing Hand/Posture: An Evaluation," *Psychological Bulletin* 90 (1981): 74–78; J. Levy, "Handwriting Posture and Cerebral Organization: How Are They Related?" *Psychological Bulletin* 91 (1982): 589–608.

[28]D. C. Bourassa, I. C. McManus, and M. P. Bryden, "Handedness and Eye-Dominance: A Meta-analysis of Their Relationship," *Laterality* 1 (1996): 5–34.

[29]L. J. Elias and M. P. Bryden, "Footedness Is a Better Predictor of Language Lateralization than Handedness," *Laterality,* in press.

[30]L. B. Day and P. F. MacNeilage, "Postural Asymmetries and Language Lateralization in Humans (*Homo sapiens*)," *Journal of Comparative Psychology* 110 (1996): 88–96.

[31]M. W. O'Boyle and J. B. Hellige, "Cerebral Hemisphere Asymmetry and Individual Differences in Cognition," *Learning and Individual Differences* 1 (1989): 7–35.

[32]D. V. M. Bishop, *Handedness and Developmental Disorder* (Oxford:

Blackwell Scientific Publishers, 1990).

[33] J. Levy, "Possible Basis for the Evolution of Lateral Specialization of the Human Brain," *Nature* 224 (1969): 614–615.

[34] M. W. O'Boyle and C. P. Benbow, "Handedness and Its Relationship to Ability and Talent," in *Left Handedness: Behavioral Implications and Anomalies,* ed. S. Coren (Amsterdam: North-Holland Elsevier, 1990).

[35] C. Mebert and G. Michel, "Handedness in Artists," in *Neuropsychology of Left Handedness,* ed. J. Herron (New York: Academic Press, 1980).

[36] S. Coren and D. F. Halpern, "Left Handedness—A Marker for Decreased Survival Fitness," *Psychological Bulletin* 109 (1991): 90–106.

[37] D. F. Halpern, R. Gilbert, and S. Coren, "PC or Not PC? Contemporary Challenges to Unpopular Research Findings," *Journal of Social Distress and the Homeless* 5 (1996): 251–271; M. E. Salive, J. M. Guralnik, and R. J. Glynn, "Left-Handedness and Mortality," *American Journal of Public Health* 83 (1993): 265–267.

[38] K. Hugdahl, P. Satz, M. Mitrushina, and E. N. Miller, "Left-Handedness and Old Age: Do Left-Handers Die Earlier?" *Neuropsychologia* 31 (1993): 325–333.

[39] L. Harris, "Do Left Handers Die Sooner than Right Handers," *Psychological Bulletin* 113 (1993): 203–234; D. Halpern and S. Coren, "Left Handedness and Life Span: A Reply to Harris," *Psychological Bulletin* 114 (1993): 235–241.

[40] S. Coren and F. H. Previc, "Handedness as a Predictor of Increased Risk of Knee, Elbow, or Shoulder Injury, Fractures, and Broken Bones," *Laterality* 1 (1996): 139–152.

Chapter 6

[1] M. Coltheart, E. Hull, and D. Slater, "Sex Differences in Imagery and Reading," *Nature* 253 (1975): 438–440.

[2] D. F. Halpern, *Sex Differences in Cognitive Abilities* (New York: Erlbaum, 1992); A. Feingold, "Cognitive Gender Differences: Where Are They and Why Are They There?" *Learning and Individual Differences* 8 (1996): 25–32.

[3] H. Lansdell, "A Sex Difference in Effect of Temporal Lobe Neurosurgery on Design Preference," *Nature* 194 (1962): 852–854.

[4] J. McGlone, "Sex Differences in Functional Brain Asymmetry," *Cortex* 14 (1978): 122–128.

[5] J. Inglis and J. S. Lawson, "Sex Differences in the Effects of Unilateral Brain Damage on Intelligence," *Science* 212 (1981): 693–695.

[6] J. A. Wada, R. Clark, and A. Hamm, "Cerebral Hemisphere Asymmetry in Humans," *Archives of Neurology* 32 (1975): 239–246.

[7] J. J. Kulynych, K. Vladar, D. W. Jones, and D. R. Weinberger, "Gender Differences in the Normal Lateralization of the Supratemporal Cortex: MRI Surface-Rendering Morphometry of

Heschl's Gyrus and the Planum Temporale," *Brain* 115 (1992): 1521–1541.

8 S. F. Witelson and D. L. Kigar, "Sylvian Fissure Morphology and Asymmetry in Men and Women: Bilateral Differences in Relation to Handedness in Men," *Journal of Comparative Neurology* 323 (1992): 326–340.

9 F. Aboitiz, A. B. Scheibel, and E. Zaidel, "Morphometry of the Sylvian Fissure and the Corpus Callosum, with Emphasis on Sex Differences," *Brain* 115 (1992): 1521–1541.

10 L. Allen, M. Richey, Y. Chai, and R. Gorski, "Sex Differences in the Corpus Callosum of the Living Human Being," *Journal of Neuroscience* 11 (1991): 933–942.

11 S. F. Witelson, "Neuroanatomical Bases of Hemispheric Functional Specialization in the Human Brain: Possible Developmental Factors," in *Hemispheric Communications: Mechanisms and Models,* ed. F. L. Kitterle (Hillsdale, NJ: Erlbaum, 1995).

12 S. F. Witelson, I. I. Glezer, and K. L. Kigar, "Women Have Greater Density of Neurons in Posterior Temporal Cortex," *Journal of Neuroscience* 15 (1995): 3418–3428.

13 B. A. Shaywitz, S. E. Shaywitz, K. R. Pugh, R. T. Constable, P. Skudlarski, R. K. Fulbright, R. A. Bronen, J. M. Fletcher, D. P. Shankweiler, L. Katz, and J. C. Gore, "Sex Differences in the Functional Organization of the Brain for Language," *Nature* 373 (1995): 607–609.

14 D. Voyer, "On the Magnitude of Laterality Effects and Sex Differ-

ences in Functional Lateralities," *Laterality* 1 (1996): 51–83; M. Hiscock, R. Inch, C. Jacek, C. Hiscock-Kalil, and K. M. Kalil, "Is There a Sex Difference in Human Laterality? I. An Exhaustive Survey of Auditory Laterality Studies from Six Neuropsychology Journals," *Journal of Clinical and Experimental Neuropsychology* 16 (1994): 423–435; M. Hiscock, M. Israelian, R. Inch, C. Jacek, and C. Hiscock-Kalil, "Is There a Sex Difference in Human Laterality? II. An Exhaustive Survey of Visual Laterality Studies from Six Neuropsychology Journals," *Journal of Clinical and Experimental Neuropsychology* 17 (1995) 590–610.

15 Voyer, "On the Magnitude of Laterality Effects and Sex Differences."

16 I. Silverman and M. Eals, "Sex Differences in Spatial Abilities: Evolutionary Theory and Data," in *The Adapted Mind,* ed. J. H. Barlow, L. Cosmides, and J. Tooby (New York: Oxford University Press, 1992).

17 J. Levy, "Lateral Differences in the Human Brain in Cognition and Behavioral Control," in *Cerebral Correlates of Conscious Experience,* ed. P. Buser and A. Rougeul-Buser (New York: North-Holland Publishing Co., 1978).

18 N. Geschwind and A. M. Galaburda, *Cerebral Lateralization: Biological Mechanisms, Associations, and Pathology* (Cambridge, MA: MIT Press, 1987).

19 R. J. Nelson, *An Introduction to Behavioral Endocrinology* (Sunderland, MA: Sinauer Associates, 1995).

[20]M. L. Collaer and M. Hines, "Human Behavioral Sex Differences: A Role for Gonadal Hormones During Early Development?" *Psychological Bulletin* 118 (1995): 55–107.

[21]E. Hampson, "Spatial Cognition in Humans: Possible Modulation by Androgens and Estrogens," *Journal of Psychology and Neuroscience* 20 (1995): 397–404.

[22]J. M. Reinisch and S. A. Sanders, "Effects of Prenatal Exposure to Diethylstilbestrol (DES) on Hemispheric Laterality and Spatial Ability in Human Males," *Hormones and Behavior* 26 (1992): 62–75.

[23]D. Kimura, "Sex, Sexual Orientation, and Sex Hormones Influence Human Cognitive Function," *Current Opinion in Neurobiology* 6 (1996): 259–263.

[24]S. D. Moffat and E. Hampson, "A Curvilinear Relationship Between Testosterone and Spatial Cognition in Humans: Possible Influence of Hand Preference," *Psychoneuroendocrinology,* 21 (1996): 323–337.

[25]D. Kimura and E. Hampson, "Cognitive Pattern in Men and Women Is Influenced by Fluctuations in Sex Hormones," *Current Directions in Psychological Science* 3 (1994): 57–61.

[26]Moffat and Hampson, "A Curvilinear Relationship Between Testosterone and Spatial Cognition in Humans: Possible Influence of Hand Preference."

[27]Ibid.

[28]L. S. Allen and R. A. Gorski, "Sexual Orientation and the Size of the Anterior Commissure in the Human Brain," *Proceedings of the National Academy of Sciences USA* 89 (1992): 7199–7202.

[29]C. M. McCormick and S. F. Witelson, "Functional Cerebral Asymmetry and Sexual Orientation in Men and Women," *Behavioral Neuroscience* 108 (1994): 525–531.

[30]B. A. Gladue and J. M. Bailey, "Spatial Ability, Handedness, and Human Sexual Orientation," *Psychoneuroendocrinology* 20 (1995): 487–497.

[31]J. Hall, and D. Kimura, "Sexual Orientation and Performance on Sexually Dimorphic Motor Tasks," *Archives of Sexual Behavior* 24 (1995): 395–407.

[32]C. P. Benbow and D. Lubinski, "Psychological Profile of the Mathematically Talented: Some Sex Differences and Evidence Supporting Their Biological Basis," in *Women, Men, and Gender,* ed. M. Walsh (New Haven: Yale University Press, 1997).

[33]M. W. Boyle, C. P. Benbow, and J. E. Alexander, "Sex Differences, Hemispheric Laterality, and Associated Brain Activity in the Intellectually Gifted," *Developmental Neuropsychology* 11 (1995): 415–443.

[34]D. F. Halpern and T. M. Wright, "A Process-Oriented Model of Cognitive Sex Differences," *Learning and Individual Differences* 8 (1996): 3–24.

[35]D. F. Halpern, "Changing Data, Changing Minds: What the Data on Cognitive Sex Differences Tell Us and What We Hear," *Learning and Individual Differences* 8 (1996): 73–82.

Chapter 7

[1] A. W. Ellis and A. W. Young, *Human Cognitive Neuropsychology* (London: Erlbaum, 1988).

[2] Ibid.

[3] E. Goldberg, "Rise and Fall of Modular Orthodoxy," *Journal of Clinical and Experimental Neuropsychology* 17 (1995): 193–208.

[4] M. Farah, "Neuropsychological Inference with an Interactive Brain: A Critique of the 'Locality' Assumption," *Brain and Behavioral Sciences* 17 (1994): 43–104.

[5] K. W. Walsh, *Neuropsychology: A Clinical Approach* (London: Churchill-Livingstone, 1995); K. M. Heilman and E. Valenstein, *Clinical Neuropsychology* (New York: Oxford University Press, 1993); J. Bradshaw and J. Mattingly, *Clinical Neuropsychology: Behavioral and Brain Science* (San Diego: Academic Press, 1995).

[6] A. Kreindler, C. Calavrezo, and L. Mihailescu, "Linguistic Analysis of One Case of Jargon Aphasia," *Revue Roumaine de Neurologic* 8 (1971): 209–228.

[7] J. W. Brown, *Aphasia, Apraxia and Agnosia* (Springfield, IL: Charles C. Thomas, 1972).

[8] A. K. Coughlan and E. K. Warrington, "Word-Comprehension and Word-Retrieval in Patients with Localized Cerebral Lesions," *Brain* 101 (1978): 163–185; S. J. Dimond, *Neuropsychology: A Textbook of Systems and Psychological Functions of the Human Brain* (London: Butterworths, 1980).

[9] N. Geschwind, "Disconnexion Syndromes in Animals and Man," *Brain* 88 (1965): 237–294; N. Geschwind, "The Organization of Language and the Brain," *Science* 170 (1970): 940–944.

[10] Dimond, *Neuropsychology*.

[11] Geschwind, "Disconnexion Syndromes in Animals and Man."

[12] J. C. Marshall, "On the Biology of Language Acquisition," in *Biological Studies of Mental Processes*, ed. D. Caplan (Cambridge, MA: MIT Press, 1980).

[13] T. Shallice, *From Neuropsychology to Mental Structure* (Cambridge: Cambridge University Press, 1988); Ellis and Young, *Human Cognitive Neuropsychology*.

[14] S. Petersen, P. Fox, M. Posner, M. Mintun, and M. Raichle, "Positron Emission Tomographic Studies of the Processing of Single Words," *Journal of Cognitive Neuroscience* 1 (1989): 153–170.

[15] J. Binder and S. Rao, "Human Brain Mapping With Functional Magnetic Resonance Imaging," in *Localization and Neuroimaging in Neuropsychology*, ed. A. Kertesz (San Diego: Academic Press, 1994); J. R. Binder, J. A. Frost, T. A. Hammeke, R. W. Cox, S. M. Rao, and T. Prieto, "Human Brain Language Areas Identified by Functional Magnetic Resonance Imaging," *Journal of Neuroscience* 17 (1997): 353–362.

[16] Binder and Rao, "Human Brain Mapping with Functional Magnetic Resonance Imaging."

[17] G. Deutsch and J. Halsey, "Cortical Blood Flow Indicates Frontal Asymmetries Dominate in Males But Not in Females During Task Performance," *Journal of Cere-*

bral Blood Flow and Metabolism 11 (1991): 787; R. Zatorre, A. Evans, E. Meyer, and A. Gjedde, "Lateralization of Phonetic and Pitch Discrimination in Speech Processing," Science 256 (1992): 846–849.

[18] J. F. Demonet, F. Chollet, S. Ramsay, D. Cardebat, J. L. Nespoulous, R. Wise, and R. Frackowiak, "The Anatomy of Phonological and Semantic Processing in Normal Subjects," Brain 115 (1992): 1753–1768.

[19] B. M. Mazoyer, N. Tzourio, V. Frak, A. Syrota, N. Murayama, O. Levrier, G. Salamon, D. Dehaene, L. Cohen, and J. Mehler, "The Cortical Representation of Speech," Journal of Cognitive Neuroscience 5 (1993): 467–479.

[20] R. S. Frackowiak, "Frontal Mapping of Verbal Memory and Language," Trends in Neuroscience 17 (1994): 109–115.

[21] Mazoyer et al., "Cortical Representation of Speech."

[22] K. Stromswold, D. Caplan, N. Alpert, and S. Rauch, "Localization of Syntactic Comprehension by Positron Emission Tomography," Brain and Language 52 (1996): 452–473.

[23] H. Damasio, T. Grabowski, D. Tranel, R. Hichwa, and A. Damasio, "A Neural Basis for Lexical Retrieval," Nature 380 (1996): 499–505.

[24] Ibid.

[25] D. Tranel, H. Damasio, A. Damasio, and J. Brandt, "Separate Concepts are Retrieved from Separate Neural Systems: Neuroanatomical and Neuropsychological Double Dissociations," Society for Neuroscience Abstracts 21 (1995): 1497; D. Perani et al., "Different Neural Systems for the Recognitions of Animal and Man-Made Tools," Society for Neuroscience Abstracts 21 (1995): 1498.

[26] J. W. Brown, Mind, Brain, and Consciousness (New York: Academic Press, 1977).

[27] Dimond, Neuropsychology.

[28] G. A. Ojemann, "Subcortical Language Mechanisms," in Studies in Neurolinguistics, vol. 1, ed. H. Whitaker and H. A. Whitaker (New York: Academic Press, 1976); G. A. Ojemann, "Asymmetric Function of the Thalamus in Man," Annals of the New York Academy of Science 299 (1977): 380–396.

[29] A. Smith, "Speech and Other Functions After Left (Dominant) Hemispherectomy," Journal of Neurology, Neurosurgery and Psychiatry 29 (1966): 467–471; C. W. Burkland and A. Smith, "Language and the Cerebral Hemispheres," Neurology 27 (1977): 627–633.

[30] A. Smith, "Nondominant Hemispherectomy," Neurology 19 (1969): 442–445.

[31] Geschwind, "Disconnexion Syndromes in Animals and Man."

[32] M. Coltheart, "Deep Dyslexia: A Right-Hemisphere Hypothesis," in Deep Dyslexia, ed. M. Coltheart, K. Patterson, and J. C. Marshall (London: Routledge and Kegan Paul, 1980).

[33] D. Hines, "Differences in Tachistoscopic Recognition Between Abstract and Concrete Words as a Function of Visual Half-Field and Frequency," Cortex 13 (1977): 66–73.

[34]Petersen et al., "Positron Emission Tomographic Studies."

[35]G. McCarthy, A. Blamire, D. Rothman, R. Gruetter, and R. Shulman, "Echoplanar Magnetic Resonance Imaging Studies of Frontal Cortex Activation During Word Generation in Humans," *Proceedings of the National Academy of Sciences USA* 90 (1993): 4952–4956.

[36]A. Nakagawa, "Role of Anterior and Posterior Attention Networks in Hemispheric Asymmetries During Lexical Decisions," *Journal of Cognitive Neuroscience* 3 (1991): 313–321.

[37]M. Posner and M. Raichle, *Images of Mind* (New York: Scientific American Library, 1994).

[38]M. Danly and B. Shapiro, "Speech Prosody in Broca's Aphasia," *Brain and Language* 16 (1982): 171–190.

[39]K. M. Heilman, R. Scholes, and R. T. Watson, "Auditory Affective Agnosia: Disturbed Comprehension of Affective Speech," *Journal of Neurology, Neurosurgery and Psychiatry* 38 (1975): 69–72.

[40]E. D. Ross and M. M. Mesulam, "Dominant Language Functions of the Right Hemisphere?" *Archives of Neurology* 36 (1979): 144–148.

[41]E. D. Ross, "The Aprosodias: Functional-Anatomic Organization of the Affective Components of Language in the Right Hemisphere," *Annals of Neurology* 38 (1981): 561–589.

[42]D. F. Benson, B. Dobkin, L. J. Gonzalez-Roth, N. Helman-Estabrook, and A. Kertesz, "Assessment: Melodic Intonation Therapy," *Neurology* 44 (1994): 566–568.

[43]E. Winner and H. Gardner, "The Comprehension of Metaphor in Brain-Damaged Patients," *Brain* 100 (1977): 717–729; N. S. Foldi, M. Cicone, and H. Gardner, "Pragmatic Aspects of Communication in Brain-Damaged Patients," in *Language Functions and Brain Organization,* ed. S. J. Segalowitz (New York: Academic Press, 1983).

[44]W. R. Gowers, *A Manual of Diseases of the Nervous System* (London: J. & A. Churchill, 1893).

[45]M. Kinsbourne, "The Minor Cerebral Hemisphere as a Source of Aphasic Speech," *Archives of Neurology* 25 (1971): 302–306.

[46]A. C. Papanicolaou, B. D. Moore, H. S. Levin, and H. M. Eisenberg, "Evoked Potential Correlates of Right Hemisphere Involvement in Language Recovery Following Stroke," *Archives of Neurology* 44 (1987): 521–524.

[47]G. Deutsch, A. C. Papanicolaou, and H. M. Eisenberg, "CBF During Tasks Intended to Differentially Activate the Cerebral Hemispheres: New Normative Data and Preliminary Applications in Recovering Stroke Patients," *Journal of Cerebral Blood Flow and Metabolism* 7 Supplement (1987): S306.

[48]M. Fiorelli, J. Blin, S. Bakchine, D. Laplane, and J. C. Baron, "PET Studies of Cortical Diaschisis in Patients with Motor Hemi-Neglect," *Journal of Neurological Sciences* 104 (1991): 135–142.

[49]E. K. Warrington, "Constructional Apraxia," in *Handbook of Clinical Neurology,* vol. 4, ed. P. J. Vinken and G. W. Bruyn

(Amsterdam: Elsevier/North-Holland Biomedical Press, 1969).

[50] M. Krams, M. P. Deiber, R. Frackowiak, and R. Passingham, "Broca's Area and Mental Preparation," *NeuroImage* 3 Supplement (1996): S392.

[51] A. L. Benton, "Visuoperceptive, Visuospatial, and Visuoconstructive Disorders," in *Clinical Neuropsychology,* ed. K. M. Heilman and E. Valenstein (Oxford: Oxford University Press, 1979).

[52] P. F. Roland, E. Meyer, T. Shibaski, Y. Yamamoto, and C. Thompson, "Regional Cerebral Blood Flow Changes in Cortex and Basal Ganglia During Voluntary Movements in Normal Human Volunteers," *Journal of Neurophysiology* 48 (1982): 467–478.

[53] R. Watson, W. Fleet, L. Rothi, and K. Heilman, "Apraxia and the Supplementary Motor Area," *Archives of Neurology* 43 (1986): 787–792.

[54] Binder and Rao, "Human Brain Mapping."

[55] K. M. Stephan, G. R. Fink, R. E. Passingham, D. Silbersweig, A. Ceballos-Baumann, C. D. Firth, and R. S. Frackowiak, "Functional Anatomy of the Mental Representation of Upper Extremity Movements in Healthy Subjects," *Journal of Neurophysiology* 73 (1995): 373–386.

[56] R. Massarelli, J. Decety, M. Raybaudi, M. Roth, C. Delon-Martin, C. Segebarth, and M. Jeannerod, "Recruitment of Primary Motor Cortical Area M1 During Motor Task Simulation Revealed by Functional Magnetic Resonance Imaging (fMRI) and Angiography (fMRA)," *NeuroImage* 3 Supplement (1996): S397.

[57] J. Decety, H. Sjöholm, E. Ryding, and D. H. Ingvar, "Motor Imagery Activates the Cerebellum: A Single-Photon Emission Computed Tomography Study with the Intravenous ^{133}Xe Injection Method," *Journal of Cerebral Blood Flow and Metabolism* 9 Supplement (1989): S742.

[58] J. H. Halsey, U. Blauenstein, E. Wilson, and E. Wills, "Regional Cerebral Blood Flow Comparison of Right and Left Hand Movement," *Neurology* 29 (1979): 21–28.

[59] S. G. Kim, J. Ashe, K. Hendrich, J. M. Ellermann, H. Merkle, K. Ugurbil, and A. P. George, "Functional Magnetic Resonance Imaging of Motor Cortex: Hemispheric Asymmetry and Handedness," *Science* 93 (1993): 615–617.

[60] V. Mattay, A. Santha, J. Van Horn, R. Sexton, J. Frank, and D. Weinberger, "Motor Function and Hemispheric Asymmetry: A Whole Brain Echo Planar fMRI Study," *NeuroImage* 3 Supplement (1996): S398.

[61] F. Binkofski, J. Classen, and R. Seitz, "Disturbance of Visualspatial Movement Control by Unilateral Posterior Thalamic Lesions," *NeuroImage* 3 Supplement (1996): S375.

[62] D. A. Rottenberg, J. Sidtis, S. Strothers, K. Rehm, J. Anderson, R. Savoy, N. Lange, and J. Arnold, "Temporal Changes in a Multidimensional Covariance Pattern During Figure Tracing: Evidence of Motor Learning?" *NeuroImage* 3 Supplement (1996):

S408; J. Moeller, C. Ghez, F. Ghilardi, and D. Eidelberg, "Patterns of Brain Activation in Motor Sequence Learning: O-H$_2$O/PET Studies," *NeuroImage* 3 Supplement (1996): S401.

[63] A. L. Benton, "The Neuropsychology of Facial Recognition," *American Psychologist* 35 (1980): 176–186; Benton, "Visuoperceptive, Visuospatial, and Visuoconstructive Disorders."

[64] J. Sergent, S. Ohta, and B. MacDonald, "Functional Neuroanatomy of Face and Object Recognition," *Brain* 115 (1992): 15–36.

[65] Ibid.

[66] J. Sergent and J. L. Signoret, "Outstanding Issues in the Study of Prosopagnosia," *Journal of Clinical and Experimental Neuropsychology* 13 (1991): 34.

[67] E. Goldberg, "Associative Agnosias and the Functions of the Left Hemisphere," *Journal of Clinical and Experimental Neuropsychology* 12 (1990): 467–484.

[68] Ibid.

[69] Ellis and Young, *Human Cognitive Neuropsychology.*

[70] D. Marr, *Vision* (San Francisco: W. H. Freeman, 1982).

[71] Ellis and Young, *Human Cognitive Neuropsychology.*

[72] M. J. Farah, M. J. Soso, and R. M. Dasheiff, "Visual Angle of the Mind's Eye Before and After Unilateral Occipital Lobectomy," *Journal of Experimental Psychology: Human Perception and Performance* 18 (1992): 241–246.

[73] S. M. Kosslyn and K. N. Ochsner, "In Search of Occipital Activation During Visual Mental Imagery," *Trends in Neuroscience* 17 (1994): 290–292; S. M. Kosslyn, N. M. Alpert, W. L. Thompson, V. Maljkovic, S. Weise, C. F. Chabris, S. E. Hamilton, S. L. Rauch, and F. S. Buonano, "Visual Mental Imagery Activates Topographically Organized Visual Cortex," *Journal of Cognitive Neuroscience* 5 (1993): 263–287.

[74] G. Goldenberg, I. Podreka, M. Steiner, K. Willmes, E. Suess, and L. Deecke, "Regional Cerebral Blood Flow Patterns in Visual Imagery," *Neuropsychologia* 27 (1989): 641–664.

[75] P. E. Roland and B. Gulyas, "Visual Imagery and Visual Representation," *Trends in Neuroscience* 17 (1994): 281–287.

[76] L. Trojano and D. Grossi, "A Critical Review of Mental Imagery Defects," *Brain and Cognition* 24 (1994): 213–243.

[77] M. J. Farah, M. S. Gazzaniga, J. D. Holtzman, and S. M. Kosslyn, "A Left Hemisphere Basis for Visual Imagery?" *Neuropsychologia* 23 (1985): 115–118; M. J. Farah, "Current Issues in the Neuropsychology of Image Generation," *Neuropsychologia* 33 (1995): 1455–1471.

[78] C. Stangalino, C. Semenza, and S. Mondini, "Generating Visual Mental Images: Deficit After Brain Damage," *Neuropsychologia* 33 (1995): 1473–1483.

[79] J. Decety, D. Perani, M. Jeannerod, V. Bettinardi, B. Tadary, R. Woods, J. C. Mazziota, and F. Fazio, "Mapping Motor Representations with Positron Emission Tomography," *Nature* 371 (1994): 601–602; G. Golden-

berg, I. Podreka, M. Steiner, P. Reanzen, and L. Deecke, "Contributions of Occipital and Temporal Brain Regions to Visual and Acoustic Imagery—A SPECT Study," *Neuropsychologia* 29 (1991): 695–702.

[80]S. M. Kosslyn, M. Behrmann, and M. Jeannerod, "The Cognitive Neuroscience of Mental Imagery," *Neuropsychologia* 33 (1995): 1335–1344.

[81]S. M. Kosslyn, V. Maljkovic, S. E. Hamilton, G. Horwitz, and W. L. Thompson, "Two Types of Image Generation: Evidence for Left and Right Hemisphere Processes," *Neuropsychologia* 33 (1995): 1485–1510.

[82]Ibid.

[83]G. Deutsch, J. M. Mountz, and E. San Pedro, "Mental Rotation and Phonological Tasks Investigated with a New Xenon rCBF SPECT Method," *NeuroImage* 5 (1997): S128.

Chapter 8

[1]K. Keilman, R. Watson, and E. Valenstein, "Neglect: Clinical and Anatomic Aspects," in *Behavioral Neurology and Neuropsychology,* ed. T. Feinberg and M. Farah (New York: McGraw-Hill, 1997).

[2]R. Rafal, "Hemispheric Neglect: Cognitive Neuropsychological Aspects," in *Behavioral Neurology and Neuropsychology,* ed. T. Feinberg and M. Farah (New York: McGraw-Hill, 1997).

[3]G. Deutsch, J. Tweedy, and B. Lorinstein, "Some Temporal and Spatial Factors Affecting Visual Neglect," *International Journal of Neuroscience* 12 (1981): 271.

[4]M. Kinsbourne, "Orientational Bias Model of Unilateral Neglect: Evidence from Attentional Gradients Within Hemispace," in *Unilateral Neglect: Clinical and Experimental Studies,* ed. I. H. Robertson and J. C. Marshall (Hillsdale, NJ: Erlbaum, 1993).

[5]K. Heilman, R. Watson, and E. Valenstein, "Neglect and Related Disorders," in *Clinical Neuropsychology,* ed. K. Heilman and E. Valenstein (New York: Oxford University Press, 1993).

[6]M. Corbetta, F. Miesen, G. Shulman, and S. Petersen, "A PET Study of Visuospatial Attention," *Journal of Neuroscience* 13 (1993): 1202–1226.

[7]M. Posner and M. Raichle, *Images of Mind* (New York: Scientific American Library, 1994).

[8]S. Weintraub and M.-M. Mesulam, "Right Cerebral Dominance in Spatial Attention: Further Evidence Based on Ipsilateral Neglect," *Archives of Neurology* 44 (1987): 621–625.

[9]E. Bisiach, "Understanding Consciousness: Clues from Unilateral Neglect and Related Disorders," in *The Neuropsychology of Consciousness,* ed. A. Milner and M. Rugg (London: Academic Press, 1992).

[10]K. S. Lashley, "In Search of the Engram," in *Symposium of the Society for Experimental Biology,* No. 4 (London: Cambridge University Press, 1950).

[11]W. Penfield and P. Perot, "The Brain's Record of Auditory and Visual Experience. A Final Summary and Discussion," *Brain* 86

(1963): 595–696; W. Penfield and L. Roberts, *Speech and Brain Mechanisms* (Princeton, NJ: Princeton University Press, 1959).

[12] G. Deutsch and J. R. Tweedy, "Cerebral Blood Flow in Severity Matched Alzheimer and Multi-infarct Patients," *Neurology* 37 (1987): 431–438.

[13] G. A. Miller, "The Magical Number Seven, Plus or Minus Two: Some Limits on Our Capacity for Processing Information," *Psychological Review* 63 (1956): 81–97.

[14] S. M. Kosslyn and O. Koenig, *Wet Mind: The New Cognitive Neuroscience* (New York: Free Press-Macmillan, 1995).

[15] R. Frackowiak, "Functional Mapping of Verbal Memory and Language," *Trends in Neurosciences* 17 (1994): 109–115.

[16] R. P. Kesner, "Mnemonic Functions of the Hippocampus: Correspondence Between Animals and Humans," in *Conditioning Representation of Neural Function*, ed. C. D. Woody (New York: Plenum, 1983); B. Milner, "Hemispheric Specialization: Scope and Limits," in *The Neurosciences: Third Research Program*, ed. F. O. Schmitt and F. G. Warden (Cambridge, MA: MIT Press, 1974).

[17] M. Moscovitch and C. Umilta, "Conscious and Nonconscious Aspects of Memory: A Neuropsychological Framework of Modules and Central Systems," in *Perspectives on Cognitive Neuroscience*, ed. R. G. Lister and H. J. Weingartner (Oxford: Oxford University Press, 1991); M. Moscovitch, "Memory and Working-with-Memory: A Component Process Model Based on Modules and Central Systems," *Journal of Cognitive Neuroscience* 4 (1992): 257–267.

[18] M. Moscovitch, "Confabulation and the Frontal System: Strategic vs Associative Retrieval in Neuropsychological Theories of Memory," in *Varieties of Memory and Consciousness: Essays in Honor of Endel Tulving*, ed. H. L. Roediger and F. I. M. Craik (Hillsdale, NJ: Erlbaum, 1989).

[19] Kosslyn and Koenig, *Wet Mind: The New Cognitive Neuroscience*.

[20] C. B. Blakemore and M. A. Falconer, "Long-Term Effects of Anterior Temporal Lobectomy on Certain Cognitive Functions," *Journal of Neurology, Neurosurgery and Psychiatry* 30 (1967): 364–367; B. Milner and H. L. Teuber, "Alteration of Perception and Memory in Man: Reflections on Methods," in *Analysis of Behavioral Change*, ed. L. Wieskrantz (New York: Harper & Row, 1968).

[21] G. Deutsch, A. C. Papanicolaou, H. M. Eisenberg, D. W. Loring, and H. S. Levin, "CBF Gradient Changes Elicited by Visual Stimulation and Visual Memory Tasks," *Neuropsychologia* 24 (1986): 283–287.

[22] T. Shallice and G. Vallar, "The Impairment of Auditory-Verbal Short-Term Storage," in *Neuropsychological Impairments of Short-Term Memory*, ed. G. Vallar and T. Shallice (Cambridge: Cambridge University Press, 1990).

[23] E. DeRenzi and P. Nichelli, "Verbal and Non-Verbal Short-Term Memory Impairment Following

Hemispheric Damage," *Cortex* 11 (1975): 341–354.

24. C. J. Marsolek, S. M. Kosslyn, and L. R. Squire, "Form-Specific Visual Priming in the Right Cerebral Hemisphere," *Journal of Experimental Psychology: Learning, Memory, and Cognition* 18 (1992): 492–508; L. R. Squire, "Declarative and Nondeclarative Memory: Multiple Brain Systems Supporting Learning and Memory," *Journal of Cognitive Neuroscience* 4 (1992): 232–243.

25. R. L. Buckner, S. E. Petersen, J. G. Ojemann, F. M. Miezin, L. Squire, and M. E. Raichle, "Functional Anatomical Studies of Explicit and Implicit Memory Retrieval Tasks," *Journal of Neuroscience* 15 (1995): 12–29; D. L. Schacter, N. Alpert, C. Savage, S. Rauch, and M. Alpert, "Conscious Recollection and the Human Hippocampal Formation: Evidence From Positron Emission Tomography," *Proceedings of the National Academy of Sciences USA* 93 (1996): 321–325.

26. K. A. Paller, "Recall and Stem Completion Priming Have Different Electrophysiological Correlates and Are Modified Differentially by Directed Forgetting," *Journal of Experimental Psychology: Learning, Memory, and Cognition* 16 (1990): 1021–1032; K. A. Paller and M. Kutas, "Brain Potentials During Memory Retrieval: Neurophysiological Support for the Distinction Between Conscious Recollection and Priming," *Journal of Cognitive Neuroscience* 4 (1992): 375–391.

27. R. Badgaiyan and M. Posner, "Priming Reduces Input in Right Posterior Cortex During Stem Completion," *Neuroreport,* 7 (1996): 2975–2978.

28. Schacter et al., "Conscious Recollection and the Human Hippocampal Formation."

29. S. Kapur, F. I. M. Craik, E. Tulving, A. Wilson, S. Houle, and G. M. Brown, "Neuroanatomical Correlates of Encoding in Episodic Memory: Levels of Processing Effect," *Proceedings of the National Academy of Sciences USA* 91 (1994): 2008–2011.

30. E. Tulving, S. Kapur, F. I. M. Craik, M. Moscovitch, and S. Houle, "Hemispheric Encoding/Retrieval in Episodic Memory: Positron Emission Tomography Findings," *Proceedings of the National Academy of Sciences USA* 17 (1994): 2016–2020.

31. A. Owen, B. Milner, M. Petrides, and A. Evans, "A Specific Role for the Right Parahippocampal Gyrus in the Retrieval of Object-Location: A Positron Emission Study," *Journal of Cognitive Neuroscience* 8 (1996): 588–602.

32. Tulving et al., "Hemispheric Encoding/Retrieval in Episodic Memory"; T. Shallice, P. Fletcher, C. Frith, P. Grasby, R. Frackowiak, and R. Dolan, "Brain Regions Associated with Acquisition and Retrieval of Verbal Episodic Memory," *Nature* 368 (1994): 633–635.

33. J. Kinoshita, "Mapping the Mind," *New York Times Magazine,* October 18 (1992): 44–54.

34. M. Mishkin, "A Memory System in the Monkey," *Philosophical Transactions Review Society of*

London, Series B: Biological Sciences 298 (1982): 85–92; L. R. Squire, *Memory and Brain* (New York: Oxford University Press, 1987).

[35] R. Desimone, "The Physiology of Memory: Recordings of Things Past," *Science* 258 (1992): 245–246.

[36] Mishkin, "Memory System in the Monkey."

[37] M. Colombo, M. R. D'Amato, H. R. Rodman, and C. G. Gross, "Auditory Association Cortex Lesions Impair Auditory Short-Term Memory in Monkeys," *Science* 247 (1990): 336.

[38] G. Goldenberg, I. Podreka, M. Steiner, and K. Wilmes, "Regional Cerebral Blood Flow Patterns in Imagery Tasks—Results of Single Photon Emission Computed Tomography," in *Cognitive and Neuropsychological Approaches to Mental Imagery,* ed. D. M. Engelkamp and J. T. E. Richardson (Dordrecht: Martinus Nijhoff, 1988).

[39] A. R. Damasio, "Category-Related Recognition Defects as a Clue to the Neural Substrates of Knowledge," *Trends in Neuroscience* 13 (1990): 95–98.

[40] F. C. Bartlett, *Remembering* (Cambridge: Cambridge University Press, 1931).

[41] D. Schacter, E. Reiman, T. Curran, L. S. Yun, D. Bandy, K. McDermott, and H. Roediger, "Neuroanatomical Correlates of Veridical and Illusory Recognition Memory: Evidence from PET," *Neuron* 17 (1996): 267–274.

[42] R. S. Frackowiak, "Functional Mapping of Verbal Memory and Language," *Trends in Neuroscience* 17 (1994): 109–115.

[43] D. Schacter, T. Curran, L. Galluccio, W. Milberg, and J. Bates, "False Recognition and the Right Frontal Lobe," *Neuropsychologia* 14 (1996): 793–808.

[44] B. Milner, "Laterality Effects in Audition," in *Interhemispheric Relations and Cerebral Dominance,* ed. V. Mountcastle (Baltimore: Johns Hopkins University Press, 1962); J. E. Bogen and H. W. Gordon, "Musical Tests of Functional Lateralization with Intracarotid Amobarbital," *Nature* 230 (1971): 524–525.

[45] H. W. Gordon and J. E. Bogen, "Hemispheric Lateralization of Singing After Intracarotid Sodium Amobarbital," *Journal of Neurology, Neurosurgery and Psychiatry* 37 (1974): 727–738.

[46] R. J. Zatorre, "Musical Perception and Cerebral Function: A Critical Review," *Music Perception* 2 (1984): 196–221.

[47] J. L. Bradshaw and J. B. Mattingly, *Clinical Neuropsychology: Behavioral and Brain Science* (San Diego: Academic Press, 1995).

[48] I. Peretz, "Processing of Local and Global Musical Information by Unilateral Brain-Damaged Patients," *Brain* 113 (1990): 1185–1205.

[49] M. Mazzoni, P. Moretti, L. Pardossi, M. Vista, A. Muratorio, and M. Puglioli, "A Case of Music Imperception," *Journal of Neurology, Neurosurgery and Psychiatry* 56 (1993): 322–324.

[50] J. Sergent, E. Zuck, S. Terriah, and B. MacDonald, "Distributed

Neural Network Underlying Musical Sight-Reading and Keyboard Performance," *Science* 257 (1992): 106–109.

[51] T. Elbert, C. Pantev, C. Wienbruch, B. Rockstroh, and E. Taub. "Increased Cortical Representation of the Fingers of the Left Hand in String Players." *Science* 270 (1995): 305–307.

[52] G. Schlaug, L. Jancke, Y. Huang, J. Staiger, and H. Steinmetz. "Increased Corpus Callosum Size in Musicians," *Neuropsychologia* 33 (1995): 1047–1055.

[53] K. S. LaBar and J. LeDoux, "Emotion and the Brain," in *Behavioral Neurology and Neuropsychology,* ed. T. Feinberg and M. Farah (New York: McGraw-Hill, 1997); W. James, *The Principles of Psychology* (New York: Holt, 1890).

[54] P. Eckman, R. W. Levenson, and W. V. Friesen, "Autonomic Nervous System Activity Distinguishes Emotions," *Science* 221 (1983): 1208–1210.

[55] K. M. Heilman and R. T. Watson, "Arousal and Emotions," in *Handbook of Neuropsychology,* vol. 3, ed. F. Boller and J. Grafman (Amsterdam: Elsevier, 1989).

[56] G. Hohmann, "Some Effects of Spinal Cord Lesions on Experimental Emotional Feelings," *Psychophysiology* 3 (1966): 143–156.

[57] A. Damasio, *Descartes' Error: Emotion, Reason, and the Human Brain* (New York: Putnam, 1994).

[58] S. Schachter, "The Interaction of Cognitive and Physiological Determinants of Emotional State," in *Advances in Experimental Social Psychology,* vol. 1, ed. L. Berkowitz (New York: Academic Press, 1970).

[59] A. C. Papanicolaou, *Emotion: A Reconsideration of the Somatic Theory* (New York: Gordon and Breach, 1989).

[60] G. Gainotti, "Reactions 'catastrophiques' et manifestations d'indifférence au cours des atteintes cerebrales," *Neuropsychologia* 7 (1969): 195–204.

[61] G. F. Rossi and G. Rosadini, "Experimental Analysis of Cerebral Dominance in Man," in *Brain Mechanisms Underlying Speech and Language,* ed. C. H. Millikan and F. L. Danley (New York: Grune & Stratton, 1967); H. Terzian, "Behavioral and EEG Effects of Intracarotid Sodium Amytal Injection," *Acta Neurochirurgia (Wein)* 12 (1964): 230–239.

[62] Terzian, "Behavioral and EEG Effects."

[63] H. A. Sackheim, M. S. Greenberg, A. L. Weiman, R. C. Gur, J. P. Hungerbuhler, and N. Geschwind, "Hemispheric Asymmetry in the Expression of Positive and Negative Emotions: Neurological Evidence," *Archives of Neurology* 39 (1982): 210–218.

[64] K. M. Heilman, R. Scholes, and R. T. Watson, "Auditory Affective Agnosia: Disturbed Comprehension of Affective Speech," *Journal of Neurology, Neurosurgery and Psychiatry* 38 (1975): 69–72.

[65] D. M. Tucker, R. T. Watson, and K. M. Heilman, "Affective Discrimination and Evocation in Patients with Right Parietal Disease," *Neurology* 27 (1977): 947–950.

[66] J. C. Borod, F. Andelman, L. K. Obler, J. R. Tweedy, and

J. Welkowitz, "Right Hemisphere Specialization for the Appreciation of Emotional Words and Sentences: Evidence from Stroke Patients," *Neuropsychologia* 30 (1992): 827–844.

[67] D. Van Lancker and J. J. Sidtis, "Identification of Affective-Prosodic Stimuli by Left- and Right-Hemisphere-Damaged Subjects: All Errors Are Not Created Equal," *Journal of Speech and Hearing Research* 35 (1992): 963–970.

[68] J. C. Borod, "Interhemispheric and Intrahemispheric Control of Emotion: A Focus on Unilateral Brain Damage," *Journal of Consulting and Clinical Psychology* 60 (1992): 339–348.

[69] H. A. Sackheim, R. C. Gur, and M. Saucy, "Emotions Are Expressed More Intensely on the Left Side of the Face," *Science* 202 (1978): 434–436.

[70] J. C. Borod and H. S. Caron, "Facedness and Emotion Related to Lateral Dominance, Sex, and Expression Type," *Neuropsychologia* 18 (1980): 237–242.

[71] J. Borod, E. Koff, and B. White, "Facial Asymmetry in Posed and Spontaneous Expressions of Emotion," *Brain and Cognition* 2 (1983): 165–175.

[72] B. B. Schiff and B. MacDonald, "Facial Asymmetries in the Spontaneous Response to Positive and Negative Emotional Arousal," *Neuropsychologia* 28 (1990): 777–785.

[73] R. J. Davidson, "Cerebral Asymmetry and Emotion: Conceptual and Methodological Conundrums," *Cognition and Emotion* 7 (1993): 115–138.

[74] R. J. Davidson and S. K. Sutton, "Affective Neuroscience: The Emergence of a Discipline," *Current Opinion in Neurobiology* 5 (1995): 217–224.

[75] R. E. Wheeler, R. J. Davidson, and A. J. Tomarken, "Frontal Brain Asymmetry and Emotional Reactivity: A Biological Substrate and Affective Style," *Psychophysiology* 30 (1993): 82–89.

[76] A. J. Tomarken, R. J. Davidson, R. E. Wheeler, R. C. Doss, "Individual Differences in Anterior Brain Asymmetry and Fundamental Dimensions of Emotion," *Journal of Personality and Social Psychology* 62 (1992): 676–687.

[77] A. J. Tomarken and R. J. Davidson, "Frontal Brain Activation in Repressors and Non-Repressors," *Journal of Abnormal Psychology* 103 (1994): 339–349.

[78] W. C. Drevets, T. O. Videen, J. L. Price, S. H. Preskorn, S. T. Carmichael, and M. E. Raichle, "A Functional Anatomical Study of Unipolar Depression," *Journal of Neuroscience* 12 (1992): 3628–3641.

[79] Davidson and Sutton, "Affective Neuroscience: The Emergence of a Discipline."

[80] Borod, "Interhemispheric and Intrahemispheric Control of Emotion."

[81] H. Gardner, H. H. Brownell, W. Wapner, and D. Michelow, "Missing the Point: The Role of the Right Hemisphere in the Processing of Complex Linguistic Materials," in *Cognitive Processing in the Right Hemisphere*, ed. E. Perecman (New York: Academic Press, 1983).

[82]K. M. Heilman and R. T. Watson, "Arousal and Emotions," in *Handbook of Neuropsychology*, vol. 3, ed. F. Boller and J. Grafman (Amsterdam: Elsevier, 1989).

[83]K. M. Heilman, H. D. Schwartz, and R. T. Watson, "Hypoarousal in Patients with the Neglect Syndrome and Emotional Indifference," *Neurology* 28 (1978): 229–232.

Chapter 9

[1]F. Nottebohm, "The Song Circuits of the Avian Brain as a Model System in Which to Study Vocal Learning, Communication, and Manipulation," *Discussions in Neuroscience* 10 (1994): 72–80.

[2]Ibid.

[3]J. Cynx, H. Williams, and F. Nottebohm, "Hemispheric Differences in Avian Song Discrimination," *Proceedings of the National Academy of Sciences USA* 89 (1992): 1372–1375.

[4]J. S. McCasland, "Neuronal Control of Bird Song Production," *Journal of Neuroscience* 7 (1987): 23–39.

[5]L. J. Rogers, *The Development of Brain and Behavior in the Chicken* (Wallingford: CAB International, 1995).

[6]J. Bradshaw and L. Rogers, *The Evolution of Lateral Asymmetries, Language, Tool Use, and Intellect* (San Diego: Academic Press, 1993).

[7]P. F. MacNeilage, M. G. Studdert-Kennedy, and B. Lindblom, "Primate Handedness Reconsidered," *Behavioral and Brain Sciences* 10 (1987): 247–303.

[8]Ibid.

[9]J. Fagot and J. Vauclair, "Manual Laterality in Non-Human Primates: A Distinction Between Handedness and Manual Specialization," *Psychological Bulletin* 109 (1991): 76–89.

[10]J. Vauclair and J. Fagot, "Manual Specialization in Gorillas and Baboons," in *Primate Laterality: Current Behavioral Evidence of Primate Asymmetries*, ed. J. P. Ward and W. D. Hopkins (New York: Springer-Verlag, 1993).

[11]R. A. W. Lehman, "Manual Preference in Prosimians, Monkeys and Apes," in *Primate Laterality: Current Behavioral Evidence of Primate Asymmetries*, ed. J. P. Ward and W. D. Hopkins (New York: Springer-Verlag, 1993).

[12]C. R. Hamilton, "Hemispheric Specialization in Monkeys," in *Brain Circuits and Functions of the Mind*, ed. C. B. Trevarthen (Cambridge: Cambridge University Press, 1990); C. R. Hamilton, "Functional Lateralization in Monkeys," in *Recent Advances in Laterality*, ed. F. Kitterle (Hillsdale, NJ: Erlbaum, 1991).

[13]R. Vogels, R. C. Saunders, and G. Borban, "Hemispheric Lateralization in Rhesus Monkeys Can Be Task Dependent," *Neuropsychologia* 32 (1994): 425–438.

[14]G. H. Yeni-Komshian and D. Benson, "Anatomical Study of Cerebral Asymmetry in the Temporal Lobe of Humans, Chimpanzees, and Rhesus Monkeys," *Science* 192 (1976): 387–389.

[15]M. Lemay and N. Geschwind, "Hemispheric Differences in the Brains of Great Apes," *Brain, Behavior, and Evolution* 11 (1975): 48–52.

[16]C. P. Groves and N. K. Humphrey, "Asymmetry in Gorilla Skulls: Evidence of Lateralized Brain Function?" *Nature* 244 (1973): 53–54.

[17]S. D. Glick, J. N. Carlson, K. L. Drew, and R. M. Shapiro, "Functional and Neurochemical Asymmetry in the Corpus Striatum," in *Duality and Unity of the Brain,* ed. D. Ottoson (New York: Plenum, 1987).

[18]S. Cabib, F. R. D'Amato, P. J. Neveu, B. Deleplanque, M. LeMoal, and S. Puglisi-Allegra, "Paw Preference and Brain Dopamine Asymmetries," *Neuroscience* 64 (1995): 427–432.

[19]E. Mach (1885), cited in S. D. Glick and D. Ross, "Lateralization of Function in the Rat Brain. Basic Mechanism May Be Operative in Humans," *Trends in the Neurosciences* 12 (1981): 196–199.

[20]M. R. Petersen, M. D. Beecher, S. R. Zoloth, D. B. Moody, and W. C. Stebbins, "Neural Lateralization of Species-Specific Vocalizations by Japanese Macaques," *Science* 202 (1978): 324–326.

[21]W. D. Hopkins, K. D. Morris, S. Savage-Rumbaugh, and D. Rumbaugh, "Hemispheric Priming by Meaningful and Non-meaningful Symbols in Language Trained Chimpanzees: Further Evidence of a Left Hemisphere Advantage," *Behavioral Neuroscience* 106 (1992): 575–582.

[22]Ibid.

[23]R. J. Davidson, N. H. Kalin, and S. E. Shelton, "Lateralized Response to Diazepam Predicts Temperamental Style in Rhesus Monkeys," *Behavioral Neuroscience* 107 (1993): 1106–1110.

[24]N. Geschwind, "Implications for Evolution, Genetics, and Clinical Syndromes," in *Cerebral Lateralization in Nonhuman Species,* ed. S. Glick (Orlando, FL: Academic Press, 1985).

[25]Ibid.

[26]A. Bisazza, C. Cantalupo, A. Robins, L. J. Rogerts, and G. Vallortigara, "Right Pawedness in Toads," *Nature* 379 (1996): 408.

Chapter 10

[1]E. H. Lenneberg, *Biological Foundations of Language* (New York: Wiley, 1967).

[2]L. S. Basser, "Hemiplegia of Early Onset and the Faculty of Speech with Special Reference to the Effects of Hemispherectomy," *Brain* 85 (1962): 427–460.

[3]M. Kinsbourne, "The Ontogeny of Cerebral Dominance," in *Developmental Psycholinguistics and Communication Disorders,* ed. D. Aaronson and R. W. Reiber (New York: New York Academy of Sciences, 1975).

[4]B. T. Woods and H. L. Teuber, "Changing Patterns of Childhood Aphasia," *Annals of Neurology* 3 (1978): 273–280.

[5]D. Bishop, "Language Development After Focal Brain Damage," in *Language Development in Exceptional Circumstances,* ed. D. Bishop and K. Mogford (Hove, UK: Erlbaum, 1993).

[6]M. Dennis and H. Whitaker, "Language Acquisition Following Hemidecortication: Linguistic Superiority of the Left Over the Right Hemisphere," *Brain and Language* 3 (1976): 404–433.

[7] D. V. M. Bishop, "Linguistic Impairment After Left Hemidecortication for Infantile Hemiplegia? A Reappraisal," *Quarterly Journal of Experimental Psychology* 35 (1983): 199–207.

[8] R. E. Stark, K. Bleile, J. Brandt, J. Freeman, and E. P. G. Vining, "Speech-Language Outcomes of Hemispherectomy in Children and Young Adults," *Brain and Language* 51 (1995): 406–421.

[9] A. M. Galaburda, "Anatomic Basis of Cerebral Dominance" in *Brain Asymmetry*, ed. R. Davidson and K. Hugdahl (Cambridge, MA: MIT Press, 1995).

[10] D. Molfese and J. C. Betz, "Electrophysiological Indices of the Early Development of Lateralization for Language and Cognition and Their Implications for Predicting Later Development," in *Brain Lateralization in Children: Developmental Implications*, ed. D. L. Molfese and S. J. Segalowitz (New York: Guilford, 1988).

[11] D. L. Molfese and V. J. Molfese, "Discrimination of Language Skills at Five Years of Age Using Event Related Potentials Recorded at Birth," *Developmental Neuropsychology*, in press.

[12] M. Hiscock and M. Kinsbourne, "Phylogeny and Ontogeny of Cerebral Lateralization," in *Brain Asymmetry*, ed. R. Davidson and K. Hugdahl (Cambridge, MA: MIT Press, 1995).

[13] R. Bijeljac-Babic, S. McAdam, I. Peretz, and J. Mehler, "Dichotic Perception and Laterality in Neonates," *Brain and Language* 37 (1989): 591–605.

[14] J. Pujol, P. Vendrell, C. Junque, J. L. Marti-Vilalta, and A. Capdevila, "When Does Human Brain Development End? Evidence of Corpus Callosum Growth Up to Adulthood," *Annals of Neurology* 34 (1993): 71–75.

[15] S. Witelson, "Neuroanatomic Bases of Hemispheric Functional Specialization in the Human Brain: Developmental Factors," in *Neurodevelopment, Aging, and Cognition*, ed. I. Kostovic, S. Knezevic, H. M. Wisniewski, and G. J. Spilch (Boston: Birkhauser, 1992).

[16] M. Y. Yazan, B. E. Wexler, M. Kinsbourne, B. Peterson, and J. F. Lichman, "Significance of Individual Variations in Callosal Area," *Neuropsychologia* 33 (1995): 769–779.

[17] J. M. Clarke, C. M. McCann, and E. Zaidel, "The Corpus Callosum and Language: Anatomical–Behavioral Relationships," in *Right Hemisphere Language Comprehension: Perspectives from Cognitive Neuroscience*, ed. M. Beeman and C. Chiarello (Hillsdale, NJ: Erlbaum, 1997).

[18] M. Lassonde and M. A. Jeeves, Eds., *Callosal Agenesis: A Natural Split Brain?* (New York: Plenum, 1994).

[19] Ibid.

[20] M. Lassonde, H. C. Sauerwein, and F. Lepore, "Extent and Limits of Callosal Plasticity: Presence of Disconnection Symptoms in Callosal Agenesis," *Neuropsychologia* 33 (1995): 989–1007.

[21] C. Temple and J. Isley, "Sounds and Shapes: Language and Spatial Cognition in Callosal Agenesis," in *Callosal Agenesis*, ed. M. Lassonde and M. A. Jeeves (New York: Plenum, 1994).

[22]Ibid.

[23]M. Morgan, "Embryology and Inheritance of Asymmetry," in *Lateralization in the Nervous System,* ed. S. Harnad, R. Doty, L. Goldstein, J. Jaynes, and G. Krauthamer (New York: Academic Press, 1977).

[24]M. Corballis and M. J. Morgan, "On the Biological Basis of Human Laterality: I. Evidence for a Maturational Left-Right Gradient," *Behavioral and Brain Sciences* 2 (1978): 261–336.

[25]R. Rymer, *Genie: An Abused Child's Flight from Silence* (New York: HarperCollins, 1993).

[26]S. Krashen, "Lateralization, Language Learning, and the Critical Period: Some New Evidence," *Language Learning* 23 (1973): 63–74.

[27]G. Hickok, U. Bellugi, and E. S. Klima, "The Neurobiology of Sign Language and Its Implications for the Neural Basis of Language," *Nature* 381 (1996): 699–702.

[28]M. Paradis, "Language Lateralization in Bilinguals: Enough Already," *Brain and Language* 39 (1990): 576–586; A. Berquier and R. Ashton, "Language Lateralization in Bilinguals: More Not Less Is Needed: A Reply to Paradis," *Brain and Language* 43 (1992): 528–533.

[29]D. Klein, B. Milner, R. J. Zatorre, E. Meyer, and A. C. Evans, "The Neural Substrates Underlying Word Generation: A Bilingual Functional-Imaging Study," *Proceedings of the National Academy of Sciences USA* 92 (1995): 2899–2903; D. Klein, R. J. Zatorre, B. Milner, E. Meyer, and A. C. Evans, "The Neural Substrates of Bilingual Language Processing: Evidence from Positron Emission Tomography," in *Aspects of Bilingual Aphasia,* ed. M. Paradis (London: Pergamon, 1995).

[30]K. Kim, N. R. Relkin, K. Lee, and J. Hirsch, "Distinct Cortical Areas Associated with Native and Second Languages," *Nature* 388 (1997): 171–174.

Chapter 11

[1]J. M. Rumsey, "Biology of Developmental Dyslexia," *Journal of the American Medical Association* 268 (1992): 912–915; D. D. Duane and D. B. Gray, Eds., *The Reading Brain: The Biological Basis of Dyslexia* (Parkland, MD: York Press, 1991).

[2]Rumsey, "Biology of Developmental Dyslexia."

[3]S. T. Orton, *Reading, Writing, and Speech Problems in Children* (New York: Norton, 1937).

[4]M. P. Bryden, "Does Laterality Make Any Difference? Thoughts on the Relation Between Cerebral Asymmetry and Reading," in *Brain Lateralization in Children,* ed. D. Molfese and S. Segalowitz (New York: Guilford, 1988).

[5]Ibid.

[6]A. M. Galaburda, G. P. Sherman, G. D. Rosen, F. Aboitiz, and N. Geschwind, "Developmental Dyslexia: Four Consecutive Patients with Cortical Anomalies," *Annals of Neurology* 18 (1985): 222–233.

[7]P. Humphreys, W. E. Kaufmann, and A. Galaburda, "Developmental Dyslexia in Women: Neuropathological Findings in Three

Cases," *Annals of Neurology* 28 (1990): 727–738.

[8] J. P. Larsen, T. Hoien, I. Lundberg, and H. Odegaard, "MRI Evaluation of the Size and Symmetry of the Planum Temporale in Adolescents with Developmental Dyslexia," *Brain and Language* 39 (1990): 289–301.

[9] R. A. Duara, A. Kushch, K. Gross-Glenn, W. W. Barker, B. Jallad, S. Pascal, D. A. Lowenstein, J. Sheldon, M. Rabin, and B. Levin, "Neuroanatomic Differences Between Dyslexic and Normal Readers on Magnetic Resonance Imaging Scans," *Archives of Neurology* 48 (1991): 410–416.

[10] R. T. Schultz, N. K. Cho, L. H. Staib, L. E. Kier, J. M Fletcher, S. E. Shaywitz, D. P. Shankweiler, L. Katz, J. C. Gore, J. S. Duncan, and B. A. Shaywitz, "Brain Morphology in Normal and Dyslexic Children: The Influence of Sex and Age," *Annals of Neurology* 35 (1994): 732–742.

[11] C. M. Leonard, L. J. Lombardino, L. R. Mercado, S. R. Browd, J. I. Breier, and O. F. Agee, "Cerebral Asymmetry and Cognitive Development in Children: A Magnetic Resonance Imaging Study," *Psychological Science* 7 (1996): 89–95.

[12] Ibid.

[13] N. T. Kraus, J. McGee, T. D. Carrell, S. G. Zecker, T. G. Nicol, and D. B. Koch, "Auditory Neurophysiologic Responses and Discrimination Deficits in Children with Learning Problems," *Science* 173 (1996): 971–973.

[14] P. Tallal, S. L. Miller, G. Bedi, G. Byma, Z. Wang, S. S. Nagarajan, C. Schreiner, W. M. Jenkins, and M. M. Merzenich, "Language Comprehension in Language-Learning Impaired Children Improved with Acoustically Modified Speech," *Science* 271 (1996): 81–84; M. M. Merzenich, W. M. Jenkins, P. Johnston, C. Schreiner, S. L. Miller, and P. Tallal, "Temporal Processing Deficits of Language-Learning Impaired Children Ameliorated by Training," *Science* 271 (1996): 77–81.

[15] Tallal et al., "Language Comprehension in Language-Learning Impaired Children."

[16] G. F. Eden, J. W. VanMeter, J. M. Rumsey, J. Maisog, R. P. Woods, and T. A. Zeffiro, "Abnormal Processing of Visual Motion in Dyslexia Revealed by Functional Brain Imaging," *Nature* 382 (1996): 66–69.

[17] D. V. M. Bishop, *Handedness and Developmental Disorder* (Oxford: Blackwell, 1990).

[18] Ibid.

[19] P. T. Fox, R. J. Ingham, J. C. Ingham, T. B. Hirsch, J. H. Downs, C. Martin, P. Jerabek, T. Glass, and J. L. Lancaster, "A PET Study of the Neural Systems of Stuttering," *Nature* 382 (1996): 158–162.

[20] I. Rapin, "Autistic Children: Diagnosis and Clinical Features," *Pediatrics* 87 Supplement (1991): 751–761.

[21] L. Selfe, *Nadia: A Case of Extraordinary Drawing Ability in an Autistic Child* (New York: Academic Press, 1977).

[22] D. Fein, M. Humes, E. Kaplan, D. Lucci, and L. Waterhouse, "The Question of Left Hemisphere Dysfunction in Infantile

Autism," *Psychological Bulletin* 95 (1984): 258–281.

[23] G. Dawson, "Cerebral Lateralization in Autism: Clues to the Role in Language and Affective Development," in *Brain Lateralization in Children,* Molfese and Segalowitz.

[24] G. Dawson, S. Warrenburg, and P. Fuller, "Cerebral Lateralization in Individuals Diagnosed as Autistic in Early Childhood," *Brain and Language* 15 (1982): 353–368.

[25] G. Dawson, C. Phillips, and L. Galpert, "Hemispheric Specialization and the Language Abilities of Autistic Children," *Child Development* 57 (1986): 1440–1453.

[26] K. Aiken, "Examining the Evidence for a Common Structural Basis to Autism," *Developmental Medicine and Child Neurology* 33 (1991): 930–938.

[27] T. Schifter, J. M. Hoffman, H. Hatter, M. W. Hanson, R. E. Coleman, and G. R. DeLong, "Neuroimaging in Infantile Autism," *Journal of Child Neurology* 9 (1994): 155–161.

[28] J. M. Mountz, L. C. Tolbert, D. W. Lill, C. R. Katholi, and H. G. Lie, "Functional Deficits in Autistic Disorder: Characterization by ^{99m}Tc-HMPAO and SPECT," *Journal of Nuclear Medicine* 36 (1995): 1156–1162.

[29] D. S. Peterson, "Neuroimaging in Child and Adolescent Neuropsychiatric Disorders," *Journal of the American Academy of Child and Adolescent Psychiatry* 34 (1995): 1560–1576.

[30] P. Flor-Henry, "Schizophrenic-like Reactions and Affective Psychoses Associated with Temporal Lobe Epilepsy: Etiological Factors," *American Journal of Psychiatry* 26 (1969): 400–403.

[31] J. H. Gruzelier, "Hemispheric Imbalance: Syndromes of Schizophrenia, Premorbid Personality, and Neurodevelopmental Influences," *Handbook of Schizophrenia,* vol. 5, ed. S. Steinhauer, J. H. Gruzelier, and J. Zubin (Amsterdam: Elsevier, 1991).

[32] J. M. Gold and D. R. Weinberger, "Cognitive Deficits and the Neurobiology of Schizophrenia," *Current Opinion in Neurobiology* 5 (1995): 225–230.

[33] J. Cutting, *The Right Cerebral Hemisphere and Psychiatric Disorders* (Oxford: Oxford University Press, 1990).

[34] R. Kahn, M. Davidson, and K. Davis, "Dopamine and Schizophrenia Revisited," in *Biology of Schizophrenia and Affective Disease,* ed. S. Watson (Washington, DC: American Psychiatric Press, 1996).

[35] M. S. George, T. T. Ketter, and R. M. Post, "Prefrontal Cortex Dysfunction in Clinical Depression," *Depression* 2 (1994): 59–72.

[36] R. Berman, J. Krystal, and D. Charney, "Mechanisms of Action of Antidepressants: Monoamine Hypotheses and Beyond," in *Biology of Schizophrenia and Affective Disease,* ed. S. Watson (Washington, DC: American Psychiatric Press, 1996).

[37] G. Doman, *What to Do About Your Brain-Injured Child* (Garden City Park: Avery Publishing, 1994).

[38]R. A. Cummins, *The Neurologically-Impaired Child: Doman-Delacato Technique Reappraised* (London: Croom Helm, 1988).

[39]Position Statement on Doman-Delacato Treatment of Neurologically Handicapped Children, American Academy of Pediatrics.

Chapter 12

[1]S. Aurobindo, quoted in J. E. Bogen, "The Other Side of the Brain. VII: Some Educational Aspects of Hemispheric Specialization," *UCLA Educator* 17 (1975): 24–32.

[2]R. Ornstein, *The Psychology of Consciousness* (New York: Harcourt Brace Jovanovich, 1977).

[3]A. Harrington and O. Godehard, "Whole Brain Politics and Brain Laterality Research," *European Archives of Psychiatry and Neurological Sciences* 239 (1989): 141–143.

[4]H. Gardner, "What We Know (and Don't Know) about the Two Halves of the Brain," *Harvard Magazine* 80 (1978): 24–27.

[5]A. McGee-Cooper, *You Don't Have to Go Home from Work Exhausted* (New York: Bantam, 1992).

[6]E. P. Torrance and C. Reynolds, *Norms-Technical Manual for "Your Style of Learning and Thinking"* (Athens, GA: Department of Educational Psychology, University of Georgia, 1980).

[7]E. P. Torrance, C. P. Reynolds, T. Riegel, and O. Ball, "Your Style of Learning and Thinking" Forms A and B: Preliminary Norms, Abbreviated Notes, Scoring Keys, and Selected References," *Gifted Child Quarterly* 21 (1977): 563–573.

[8]L. J. Zalewski, C. A. Sink, and D. J. Yachimowicz, "Using Cerebral Dominance for Education Programs," *Journal of General Psychology* 119 (1992): 45–57.

[9]N. Herrmann, *The Creative Brain* (Lake Lure, NC: Brain Books, 1991).

[10]N. Herrmann, *The Whole Brain Business Book* (New York: McGraw-Hill, 1996).

[11]R. Cutter, *When Opposites Attract* (New York: Dutton, 1994).

[12]J. E. Bogen, "The Other Side of the Brain. VII: Some Educational Aspects of Hemispheric Specialization," *UCLA Educator* 17 (1975): 24–32.

[13]P. R. Johnson and C. R. Daumer, "Intuitive Development: Communication in the Nineties," *Public Personnel Management* 22 (1993): 257–268.

[14]A. Kitchens, "Left Brain/Right Brain Theory: Implications for Developmental Math Instruction," *Review of Research in Developmental Education* 8 (1991): 20–23.

[15]I. Sonnier, Ed., *Methods and Techniques of Holistic Education* (Springfield, IL: Charles C. Thomas, 1985); I. Sonnier, Ed., *Hemisphericity as a Key to Understanding Individual Differences* (Springfield, IL: Charles C. Thomas, 1992); L. J. Harris, "Right Brain Training: Some Reflections on the Application of Research on Cerebral Hemispheric Specialization to Education," in *Brain Lateralization in Children,* ed. D. L. Molfese and

S. J. Segalowitz (New York: Guilford, 1988).

[16]K. V. Fite, *Television and the Brain: A Review* (New York: Children's Television Workshop, 1994).

[17]B. Edwards, *Drawing on the Right Side of the Brain* (Los Angeles: J. P. Tarcher, 1989).

[18]E. K. Warrington, "Constructional Apraxia," in *Handbook of Clinical Neurology*, vol. 4, ed. P. J. Vinken and G. W. Bruyn (Amsterdam: North-Holland, 1986).

[19]Harris, "Right Brain Training."

[20]C. Sagan, *The Dragons of Eden* (New York: Random House, 1977).

[21]Ibid.

[22]Ibid.

[23]Ibid.

Chapter 13

[1]D. Kimura, *Neuromotor Mechanisms in Human Communication* (New York: Oxford University Press, 1993).

[2]Ibid.

[3]I. Mattingly and M. Studdert-Kennedy, *Modularity and the Motor Theory of Speech Perception* (Hillsdale, NJ: Erlbaum, 1991).

[4]Ibid.

[5]G. Deutsch and J. H. Halsey, Jr., "Cortical Blood Flow Indicates Active Motor Component During Speech Sound Discrimination Task," *Journal of Clinical and Experimental Neuropsychology* 12 (1990): 416.

[6]R. J. Zatorre, A. C. Evans, E. Meyer, and A. Gjedde, "Lateralization of Phonetic and Pitch Discrimination in Speech Processing," *Science* 256 (1992): 846–849.

[7]G. Hickok, U. Bellugi, and E. S. Klima, "The Neurobiology of Sign Language and Its Implications for the Neural Basis of Language," *Nature* 381 (1996): 699–702.

[8]Ibid.

[9]E. Goldberg and L. D. Costa, "Hemispheric Differences in the Acquisition and Use of Descriptive Systems," *Brain and Language* 14 (1981): 144–173.

[10]E. Goldberg, H. G. Vaughan, Jr., and L. J. Gerstman, "Nonverbal Descriptive Systems and Hemispheric Asymmetry: Shape versus Texture Discrimination," *Brain and Language* 5 (1978): 249–257.

[11]Ibid.

[12]A. Galaburda, "Anatomic Basis of Cerebral Dominance," in *Brain Asymmetry*, ed. R. Davidson and K. Hugdahl (Cambridge, MA: MIT Press, 1995).

[13]H. A. Whitaker and G. A. Ojemann, "Lateralization of the Higher Cortical Functions: A Critique," in *Evolution and Lateralization of the Brain*, ed. S. J. Dimond and D. A. Blizard, *Annals of the New York Academy of Sciences* 299 (1977): 459–473; R. C. Gur, I. K. Packer, J. P. Hungerbuhler, M. Reivich, W. D. Obrist, W. S. Amarnek, and H. A. Sackheim, "Differences in the Distribution of Gray and White Matter in Human Cerebral Hemispheres," *Science* 207 (1980): 1226–1228.

[14]Goldberg and Costa, "Hemispheric Differences in the Acquisition and Use of Descriptive Systems."

[15]E. Goldberg, K. Posell, and M. Lovell, "Lateralization of Frontal Lobe Functions and Cognitive Novelty," *Journal of Neuropsychiatry* 6 (1994): 371–378.

[16]E. Goldberg, K. Podell, R. Harner, M. Lovell, and S. Riggio, "Cognitive Bias, Functional Cortical Geometry, and the Frontal Lobes: Laterality, Sex, and Handedness," *Journal of Cognitive Neuroscience* 6 (1994): 276–296.

[17]Goldberg et al., ibid.; Goldberg et al., "Lateralization of Frontal Lobe Functions and Cognitive Novelty"; E. Goldberg and K. Podell, "Lateralization in the Frontal Lobes: Searching the Right (and Left) Way," *Biological Psychiatry* 38 (1995): 569–571.

[18]J. Levy, "Interhemispheric Collaboration: Single Mindedness in the Asymmetrical Brain," in *Hemispheric Function and Collaboration in the Child*, ed. C. T. Best (New York: Academic Press, 1985).

[19]N. D. Cook, "The Transmission of Information in Natural Systems," *Journal of Theoretical Biology* 108 (1984): 349–367; N. D. Cook, "Callosal Inhibition: The Key to the Brain Code," *Behavioral Science* 29 (1984): 98–110.

[20]Ibid.

[21]M. Lamb, I. Robertson, and R. Knight, "Component Mechanisms Underlying the Processing of Hierarchially Organized Patterns: Inferences from Patients with Unilateral Cortical Lesions," *Journal of Experimental Psychology: Learning, Memory, and Cognition* 16 (1990): 471–483.

[22]J. C. Marshall and P. W. Halligan, "Seeing the Forest but Only Half the Trees," *Nature* 373 (1995): 521–523.

[23]G. R. Fink, P. W. Halligan, J. D. Marshall, C. D. Frith, R. Frackowiak, and R. Dolan, "Where in the Brain Does Visual Attention Select the Forest and the Trees?" *Nature* 382 (1996): 626–628.

[24]H. Brown and S. Kosslyn, "Cerebral Lateralization," *Current Opinion in Neurobiology* 3 (1993): 183–186.

[25]I. Peretz and M. Babai, "The Role of Contour and Intervals in the Recognition of Melody Parts: Evidence from Cerebral Asymmetries in Musicians," *Neuropsychologia* 30 (1992): 277–292.

[26]G. Hinton, J. L. McClelland, and D. E. Rumelhart, "Distributed Representations," in *Parallel Distributed Processing. Explorations in the Microstructure of Cognition*, ed. D. E. Rumelhart, J. L. McClelland, and the PDP Research Group (Cambridge, MA: MIT Press, 1986).

[27]M. Farah, "Neuropsychological Inference with an Interactive Brain: A Critique of the 'Locality' Assumption," *Behavioral and Brain Sciences* 17 (1994): 43–104.

[28]Ibid.

[29]Ibid.

[30]Ibid.

[31]G. Hinton et al., "Distributed Representations."

[32]S. H. Woodward, "An Anatomical Model of Hemispheric Asymmetry," *Journal of Clinical and Experimental Neuropsychology* 10 (1988): 68.

[33]Ibid.

[34] S. Kosslyn, C. Chabris, C. Marsolek, and O. Koenig, "Categorical Versus Coordinate Spatial Representations: Computational Analyses and Computer Simulations," *Journal of Experimental Psychology: Human Perception and Performance* 18 (1992): 562–577; H. Brown and S. Kosslyn, "Cerebral Lateralization," *Current Opinion in Neurobiology* 3 (1993): 183–186.

[35] Woodward, "Anatomical Model of Hemispheric Asymmetry."

[36] Farah, "Neuropsychological Inference with an Interactive Brain."

[37] M. M. Mesulam, "Distributed Locality and Large-Scale Neurocognitive Networks," *Behavioral and Brain Sciences* 17 (1994): 74–76; M. M. Mesulam, "Large-scale Neurocognitive Networks and Distributed Processing for Attention, Language and Memory," *Annals of Neurology* 28 (1990): 597–613.

[38] G. Edelman, *Bright Air, Brilliant Fire* (New York: Basic Books, 1992).

[39] Ibid.

[40] R. Dubos, *Pasteur and Modern Science* (London: Heinemann, 1960).

[41] M. C. Corballis and I. L. Beale, *The Ambivalent Mind* (Chicago: Nelson-Hall, 1983).

[42] L. Wolpert, "Pattern Formation in Biological Development," *Scientific American* 239 (1978): 124–137.

[43] Corballis and Beale, *The Ambivalent Mind*.

[44] Ibid.

[45] B. Norden, "The Asymmetry of Life," *Journal of Molecular Evolution* 11 (1978): 313–332.

[46] E. M. Henley, "Parity and Time-Reversal Invariance in Nuclear Physics," *Annual Review of Nuclear Science* 19 (1969): 367–427.

[47] Corballis and Beale, *The Ambivalent Mind*.

Chapter 14

[1] A. Goswami, *The Self-Aware Universe: How Consciousness Creates the Material World* (New York: Putnam, 1993).

[2] M. Ayers, "Philosophy, Knowledge, and Reality," in *The Neurological Boundaries of Reality,* ed. E. M. R. Critchley (London: Farand Press, 1994).

[3] R. W. Sperry, "Brain Bisection and Consciousness," in *Brain and Conscious Experience,* ed. J. Eccles (New York: Springer-Verlag, 1966).

[4] J. Eccles, *The Brain and Unity of Conscious Experience: The 19th Arthur Stanley Eddington Memorial Lecture* (Cambridge: Cambridge University Press, 1965).

[5] J. E. LeDoux, D. H. Wilson, and M. S. Gazzaniga, "A Divided Mind: Observation on the Conscious Properties of the Separated Hemispheres," *Annals of Neurology* 2 (1977): 417–421.

[6] Ibid.

[7] V. S. Ramachandran and D. Rogers-Ramachandran, "Denial of Disabilities in Anosognosia," *Nature* 382 (1996): 501; S. Blakeslee, "Figuring Out the Brain from Its Acts of Denial; One Hemisphere Models the World, the Other Faults It,"

New York Times, vol. 145, January 23, 1996.

[8] Blakeslee, "Figuring Out the Brain from Its Acts of Denial; One Hemisphere Models the World, the Other Faults It."

[9] M. S. Gazzaniga and J. E. LeDoux, The Integrated Mind (New York: Plenum, 1978).

[10] Ibid.

[11] E. Goldberg and W. Barr, "Three Possible Mechanisms of Unawareness of Deficit," in Awareness of Deficit After Brain Injury: Clinical and Theoretical Issues, ed. G. Prigatano and D. Schacter (New York: Oxford University Press, 1991).

[12] J. Jaynes, cited in S. Keen, "Reflections on the Dawn of Consciousness," Psychology Today 11 (1977): 58.

[13] Ibid.

[14] R. Penrose, The Emperor's New Mind (New York: Oxford University Press, 1989).

[15] J. Hadamard, The Psychology of Invention in the Mathematical Field (Princeton, NJ: Princeton University Press, 1945).

[16] Ibid.

[17] O. Loewi, Perspectives in Biology and Medicine 4 (Chicago: University of Chicago Press, 1960).

[18] A. Koestler, The Act of Creation (New York: Dell, 1964).

[19] D. Galin, "Implications for Psychiatry of Left and Right Cerebral Specialization," Archives of General Psychiatry 31 (1974): 572–583.

[20] R. Puccetti, "The Case for Mental Duality: Evidence from Split-Brain Data and Other Considerations," The Behavioral and Brain Sciences 4 (1981): 93–123.

[21] R. W. Sperry, E. Zaidel, and D. Zaidel, "Self-Recognition and Social Awareness in the Disconnected Minor Hemisphere," Neuropsychologia 17 (1979): 153–166.

[22] D. C. Dennett, Consciousness Explained (Boston: Little Brown, 1991).

[23] Ibid.

[24] D. N. Robinson, "Cerebral Plurality and the Unity of Self," American Psychologist 37 (1982): 904–910.

[25] G. Sperling, "The Information Available in Brief Visual Presentations," Psychological Monographs 74 (1960): (11, Whole No. 498).

[26] D. H. Raab, "Backward Masking," Psychological Bulletin 60 (1963): 118–129.

[27] Robinson, "Cerebral Plurality and the Unity of Self."

[28] Ibid.

[29] M. S. Gazzaniga, R. Fendrich, and C. Mark Wessinger, "Blindsight Reconsidered," Current Directions in Psychological Science 3 (1994): 93–95.

[30] S. Kohler and M. Moscovitch, "Unconscious Visual Processing in Neuropsychological Syndromes: A Survey of the Literature and Evaluation of Models of Consciousness," in Cognitive Neuroscience, ed. M. D. Rugg (Cambridge, MA: MIT Press).

[31] R. R. Llinas, "Perception as an Oneiric-like State Modulated by the Senses," in Large-scale Neuronal Theories of the Brain, ed. C. Koch and J. Davis (Cambridge, MA: MIT Press, 1994); S. Blakeslee, "How the Brain Might Work: A New Theory of Consciousness," New York

Times, vol. 144, March 21, 1995.

[32] Blakeslee, "How the Brain Might Work: A New Theory of Consciousness."

[33] G. Edelman, *Bright Air, Brilliant Fire* (New York: Basic Books, 1992); M. Kinsbourne, "Septo-hippocampal Comparator: Consciousness Generator or Attention Feedback Loop?" *Behavioral and Brain Sciences* 18 (1995): 687–688.

[34] J. Miller, "Trouble in Mind," *Scientific American* 267 (1992): 180.

[35] Ibid.

Postscript

[1] J. Sergent, "Visualizing the Working Cerebral Hemispheres," in *Hemispheric Communication: Mechanisms and Models,* ed. F. Kitterle (Hillsdale, N.J.: Erlbaum, 1995).

Index

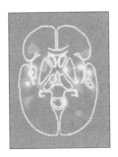

Agenesis. *See* Corpus callosum, agenesis of
Agnosia, 17, 188–190. *See also* Facial agnosia; Neglect
Alexia. *See* Reading disability and asymmetry; Aphasia, disorders of reading and writing
Allen, L., 144
Alpha rhythm. *See* Electrophysiological techniques, alpha rhythm
Alzheimer's disease, 205
American Sign Language. *See* Sign language
Amnesia. *See* Memory
Amusia. *See* Music
Analytic-holistic dichotomy, 49, 105
Anatomical asymmetries, 86–93. *See also* Neuroimaging, structural
  in animals, 244–245
  cerebral angiography, 89–90
  computerized tomography (CT), 90
  development of, 88–89
  and handedness, 91
  Heschyl's gyrus, 88
  in infants and fetuses, 256–257
  interpretation of data, 92–93
  magnetic resonance imaging (MRI), 91–92
  planum temporale, 86–88
  reading disability and, 274–275
  sex differences, 143–145

Animal asymmetries, 237–249
  anatomical studies, 244–245
  avian asymmetries, 238–240
  behavioral tests, 246–247
  bird song, 238–239
  paw preference, 125, 240–242
  pharmacological asymmetries, 245–246
  split-brain studies, 240–244
  theoretical implications, 247–248
Annett, M., 126, 127
Anomia, 25. *See also* Aphasia, anomia
Anosognosia, 337
Aphasia, 162–167
  anomia, 166
  arrest, 20
  Broca's aphasia, 163–164
  conduction aphasia, 165
  in children, 252–253
  crossed aphasia, 13
  disorders of reading and writing, 176–177
  factors in recovery, 45, 131, 175–176, 181–182
  global aphasia, 167
  hemispherectomy and, 175–176
  history of, 11–14
  classification, 162–167
  subcortical, 174–175
  theoretical issues in, 167

Wernicke's aphasia, 164–165, 176
Word deafness, 166
Aphasic arrest. *See* Electrical stimulation of brain
Aphemia, 12. *See also* Aphasia
Apraxia, 15, 182–188
    hemispheres, role of, 184–185
    types of, 182–184
Associations/dissociations, 26
Asymmetry
    cytoplasmic model, 263–264
    in nature, 326–328
    role of environment, 264–267
Asymmetry of function. *See* Hemispheric asymmetry
Attention, 202–203
    attentional bias, 101–102, 109–110
Auburtin, E., 11
Auditory studies. *See* Dichotic listening
Autism, 128, 280–284
Awareness. *See* Consciousness

Bakan, P., 129
Banish, M., 112, 114
Barsley, M., 121
Basser, L. S., 252
Beale, I., 328, 329
Behavioral studies of asymmetry. *See also* Visual-field studies; Dichotic listening
    degree of asymmetry, 115
    and handedness, 131
    hemispheric interaction, 112–115
    interpretation, 111–113
    models of, 101–102, 111–112
    reliability, 110
    and Wada test, 108–109
Bellugi, U., 265
Benbow, C., 153
Benton, A., 185, 190
Bilingualism, 266–267
Binder, J., 168, 170, Color Plate 12
Binding problem. *See* Consciousness, binding problem

Bird song. *See* Animal asymmetries, bird song
Blindsight, 349
Blood flow, cerebral. *See* Neuroimaging, functional—metabolic techniques

Bogen, J., 34, 34, 298
Borod, J., 230, 232
Bouillaud, J.B., 10
Bradshaw, J., 79
Brain/behavior relationships, 93–95. *See also* Chapters 7 and 8
Brain imaging, *See* Neuroimaging
Broca, P., 11–13, 23
    Broca's aphasia. *See* Aphasia, Broca's aphasia
    Broca's area, 12, 88, 170–171, 223, 306
    cerebral localization, 11–12, 23
Broca's rule, 13, 22
Brown, H., 317, 318
Brown, J., 174
Bryden, M. P., 109, 128, 133, 273
Buckner, R., 214
Bulman-Fleming, B., 128
Burger, H., 74

Callosal agenesis. *See* Corpus callosum, agenesis of
Carlyle, T., 122
Cerebral angiography. *See* Anatomical asymmetries
Cerebral blood flow. *See* Neuroimaging, functional—metabolic techniques
Cerebral commissures. *See* Commissures, cerebral; Corpus callosum
Cerebral dominance, 14–15. *See also* Hemispheric asymmetry
Cerebral localization, 10–12, 23, 94
Chiasm. *See* Optic chiasm
Chimeric figure studies, 50–51, 154
Clinical data, problems of interpretation, 27–28, 159–162. *See also* specific topics
Cognitive Bias Task, 311, 312
Cognitive neuropsychology, 25–28, 160–161
    agnosia, perspectives on, 193–195
    approaches to memory, 211
    assumptions of, 25–29
    history, 23–25
Cognitive neuroscience, 2–3, 29
Cognitive style and asymmetry, 292–294. *See also* Information-processing asymmetries
    Hemisphericity

Collins, R., 125
Commissures, cerebral. See also Corpus callosum
    role of, 56–57
Commissurotomy. See Split-brain surgery
Completion, visual, 49–50, 54, 202
Computerized tomography (CT), 63. See also Neuroimaging, structural
Conduction aphasia. See Aphasia, conduction aphasia
Consciousness, 32, 331–355. See also Mind-body relationships
    bicameral mind, 340–341
    binding problem 351–353
    neural substrate models, 349–350
    and REM sleep, 352–353
    role of language, 337–342
    in split-brain patients, 52–53, 334–336, 345–346
    and unconscious, 342–348, 348–350
    unity of, 32, 52–53, 346–348
Cook, N., 313, 314, 315
Corballis, M., 264, 328, 329
Coren, S., 136, 137
Corpus callosum, 31. See also Commissures
    agenesis of, 261–263
    development of, 243 245
    handedness, 91–92
    in musicians, 224
    role of, 31–32, 259–260, 302, 312–315
    sex differences, 91–92, 144
    sexual orientation, 152
Costa, L., 308, 309, 310
Covariance Analysis, 70–72, 79
Creativity, 342–343
Cross cuing, 53–54
Crossed aphasia. See Aphasia, crossed aphasia
Crowding hypothesis, 135, 149
CT scan. See Computerized tomography
Cunningham, D., 122

Damasio, A., 173, 174, 218
Damasio, H., 173, 174
da Vinci, L., 135
Davidson, R., 232, 233, 234, 247

Dax, M., 13
Day, L., 133
Deep dyslexia. See Aphasia, disorders of reading and writing
Delacato, C., 287, 288
Dennett, D., 346
Dennis, M., 254
Depression, 286
Descartes, R., 332, 333, 354
Development of asymmetry, 251–268. See also Plasticity
    anatomical asymmetry, 88–89, 256–257
    in bilinguals, 266–267
    changes with age, 258–259
    developmental gradient, 263–264
    exposure to language, role of, 265–266
    and hemispherectomy, 253–255
Diaschisis, 160, 181–182
Diazepam, 247
Dichotic listening, 98–100, 103. See also specific subject areas
    across lifespan, 258–259
    problems in interpreting data, 107–110
    and Wada test, 108–109
Dichotomania, 294
Dimond, S., 166
Direct electrical stimulation of brain. See Electrical stimulation of brain
Disconnection syndrome. See Split brain surgery, disconnection syndrome
Disorders of purposeful movement. See Apraxia
Dissociations. See Associations/ dissociations
Doman, D., 287, 288
Dominance, cerebral. See Cerebral dominance
Drawing and asymmetry, 300–301
Dreaming
    and creativity, 343
    right-hemisphere role in, 343
    in split-brain patients, 41
Dualism, 333
Dyslexia, 127. See also Learning disabilities; Aphasia, reading and writing disorders
    visual abnormalities, 227

Ear asymmetry. *See* Dichotic listening
Eccles, J., 334, 335, 354
Edelman, G., 325, 326
Eden, G., 277
Education and asymmetry, 298–301
Edwards, B., 300
EEG. *See* Electrophysiological techniques, electroencephalogram (EEG)
Electrical stimulation of brain, 20–21
  aphasic arrest, 20
  and localization of memory, 204
Electrophysiological techniques, 74–83
  alpha rhythm, 75
  electroencephalogram (EEG), 74–76
  event-related potentials (ERP), 76–77
  evoked fields, 80–83
  magnetoencephalogram (MEG), 79–80
  new approaches, 79
  probe-evoked potentials, 77–78
  problems in interpretation, 83–86
Ellis, A., 25
Emission tomography. *See* Positron emission tomography (PET) and Single photon emission, tomography (SPECT)
Emotion, 225–234. *See also* Intonation
  models of, 225–227
  perception of, 229–233
  reactions to Wada test, 227
  responses to hemispheric injury, 227–229
  role of hemispheres, 233–234
Epilepsy, 19–20
  split-brain surgery as treatment, 33–36
Evoked fields. *See* Electrophysiological techniques, evoked fields
Event-related potentials (ERP). *See* Electrophysiological techniques, event-related potentials
Eye preference, 132–133. *See also* Visual-field studies

Face recognition, 191–192. *See also* Facial agnosia
  in split brain patients, 40–41
Facial agnosia (prosopagnosia), 17, 190–191, 218
Fagot, J., 241, 242

Farah, M., 197, 320
Fechner, G., 32, 334
Fink, G., 316, 317, Color Plates 16, 17
Flor-Henry, P., 285
Footedness, 132–133
Fox, P., 279, 280
Frackowiak, R., 171
Franco, L., 48
Freud, S., 343
  Freudian theories, 344
Functional asymmetries. *See* Hemispheric asymmetry; Handedness
Functionalism, 325, 326
Functional neuroimaging. *See* Neuroimaging, functional

Galaburda, A., 88, 89, 127, 128, 129, 134, 149, 256, 265, 274
Galin, D., 75, 344
Gall, F., 10
Galton, F., 341
Gardner, H., 234
Gazzaniga, M., 44, 46, 335, 336, 338–339
Gender differences in asymmetry. *See* Sex differences in asymmetry
Genetic factors in handedness. *See* Handedness, genetic models
Genie, 265
Geschwind, N., 57–58, 86, 87, 88, 127, 128, 129, 134, 149, 166, 248, 265, 273
Gesture, asymmetry in, 265–266, 304–305
Gevins, A., 79
Glick, S., 245
Global aphasia. *See* Aphasia, global
Global vs. local processing, 315–317, 318
Goldberg, E., 192, 193, 194, 308, 309, 310, 311, 339, 340
Gorski, R., 144

Hadamard, J., 342
Hall, J., 152
Halpern, D., 136, 137, 155, 156
Hamilton, C., 243
Handedness, 119–137. *See also* Left-handedness
  and aphasia, 131
  in autism, 281–282

Broca's rule, 13, 22
and cognitive function, 134–136
current theories, 131 137
environmental theories, 125
and footedness, 132–133
and functional asymmetry, 22,
130–131
genetic models, 125–127
and immune system, 127–129
measurement of, 123–124
nineteenth-century theories of,
122–123
paw preference in animals, 125,
240–242
"right shift" theory, 126–127
in twins, 129
visuospatial functions, 134–135
writing posture, 132
Haxby, J., 71
Heilman, K., 202, 229, 234
Hellige, J., 113, 116
Hemispherectomy, 175–176
in children, 253–255
Hemispheric asymmetry. See also
Anatomical asymmetries
in animals. See Animal
asymmetries
and apraxic disorders, 184–185
in bilinguals, 266–267
corpus callosum, role of,
312–315
development of. See Development of
asymmetry
evolution of, 305–308
information processing. See
Information-processing
asymmetries
and psychiatric illness. See Psychiatric
illness and asymmetry
memory, 210–213
models of, 111–116, 303–329
sex differences. See Sex differences
in asymmetry
Hemisphericity, 294–297
questionnaires, 295–296
training seminars, 295–296
Herrmann, N., 296
Hickok, G., 265
Hippocampus, 41, 208, 350
Hopkins, W., 246

Hormones
and cognitive function (including
mathematical ability), 149–155
and handedness, 127–129
sexual orientation, 151–152
Horwitz, B., 71, 72
Hubel, D., 217
Hugdahl, K., 137
Hume, D., 351
Humor, role of right hemisphere in,
180–181

Imagery. See Visual imagery
Immune system. See Left-handedness,
immune system
Implicit processes, 55, 208–209
Information-processing asymmetries,
48–52, 103–105. See also Cognitive
style
Inglis, J., 143
Ingram, R., 279, 280
Ingvar, D., 187
Inhibition, 40, 229, 259–261, 312–315
Interhemispheric transfer of informa-
tion, 54–55, 56, 259–261. See also
Commissures, cross cuing, Inhibition
Intonation. See Right hemisphere,
intonation
Isley, J., 262

Jackson, J.H., 14, 15–16, 160, 298
Jaynes, J., 340, 341

Kana/Kanji, 104–105
Kant, E., 351
Kapur, S., 215
Kimura, D., 98, 99, 100, 152, 304, 307,
308
Kinsbourne, M., 109, 110, 151, 181,
202
Klima, E., 265
Kohler, S., 349, 350
Koestler, A., 342, 343
Kosslyn, S., 196, 197, 317, 318, 323
Kraus, N., 275

Language, 162. See also Speech
disorders of, 162–182
after hemispherectomy, 175–176
and intonation, 179–180

neuroimaging studies, 168–174
role in mental units, 338–342
role of right hemisphere, 178–182
in split brain patients, 42–45
Lansdell, H., 140
Larsen, J., 274
Lashley, K., 204
Lassen, N., 64
Lassonde, M., 262
Lateral preferences. *See* Handedness;
Left-handedness
Lateralization. *See* Hemispheric asymmetry; Development of asymmetry
Lateralized stimuli. *See* Visual-field
studies; Dichotic listening;
Lawson, J., 143
Learning disabilities, 272–278
LeDoux, J., 335, 336, 338, 339
Left hemisphere
and apraxia, 182–185
and autism, 281–283
gestures, 304–305
role in music, 220–221
role in psychopathology, 285–286
in speech and language, 168–172,
173–174, 304–305
Left-handedness, 119–137. *See also*
Handedness
in artists, 135
and asymmetry, 91
and autism, 281–283
birth stress, 129
cognitive abilities, 134–136
and creativity, 135–136
crowding hypothesis, 135
current theories, 124–130
effects of brain damage, 129–130,
252
familial sinistrality, role of, 91,
131–132
historical bias against, 120–121
immune system, 127–129
and mortality, 136–137
nineteenth-century theories of,
122–123
pathological, 130, 134
and stuttering, 278–279
in twins, 129
visuospatial functions, 134–135
writing posture, 132

LeMay, M., 89–90
Lenneberg, E., 252
Leonard, C., 275
Lepore, F., 262
Levitsky, W., 86, 87
Levy, J., 49, 50, 51, 113, 132, 134, 135,
149, 307, 312
Lichtheim, L., 23
Liepmann, H., 15
Lindblom, B., 241
Llinas, R., 351, 352
Localization, cerebral. *See* Cerebral
localization
Loewi, O., 342, 343, 353

Mach, E., 245
MacNeilage, P., 133, 241
Magnetic resonance imaging (MRI), 63,
64, 72–74. *See also* Neuroimaging,
functional,
Neuroimaging, structural; and studies
under specific topics
Magnetoencephalogram (MEG). *See*
Electrophysiological techniques, mag-
netoencephalogram,
(MEG)
Marr, D., 26
Materialism, 333
Mathematical ability, 128, 152–154
handedness, 153
hemispheric asymmetry, 153
hormones, 153
Mazoyer, R., 171
McDougall, W., 32, 334
McGlone, J., 140
McKay, D., 334
MEG. *See* Electrophysiological
techniques, magnetoencephalogram
(MEG)
Melodic intonation therapy. *See* Right
hemisphere, intonation
Memory, 204–220
amnesia, 204–206
convergence zones, 174, 218
false memory, 218–219
hemispheric differences, 210–213
hippocampus, 208–210
in split-brain patients, 41–42, 211
models, 206–210
neuroimaging studies, 211–220

Mentalism, 333
Merzenich, M., 276,278
Mesulam, M., 203, 325
Metabolic scanning, 63–74. *See also*
  Neuroimaging, functional—metabolic
  techniques
    limitations, 64–65, 83–86
Metacontrol
  in neurologically normal brains,
    113–114
  in split-brain patients, 51–52
Miller, J., 356
Mind-body relationships, 94,
  331–336, 354–355. *See also*
  Consciousness
Modules. *See* modularity
Modularity, 26–27, 161, 209
  and memory, 209–210
  in musicians, 222–223
Molfese, D., 257
Molfese, V., 257
Morgan, M., 264
Moscovitch, M., 209, 210, 214, 215,
  349, 350
Motor theory. *See* Speech, motor
  theory
Mountz, J., 68, 283, Color Plates 1, 2,
  15
Movement. *See also* Apraxia
  imagined, 185–187
  imaging studies, 187–188
MRI (Magnetic resonance imaging). *See*
  Neuroimaging, functional; Neuroimag-
  ing, structural
Music and the hemispheres,
  220–224
    amusia, 18
    brain injury and, 221
    brain organization, 223–224
    corpus callosum, 224
    melodic intonation therapy, 180
    role of right hemisphere, 18,
      220–222
Myers, R., 33

Nadia, 281
Nakagawa, A., 179
Neglect, 17, 199–204, 337
  brain injury associated with, 199
  models of, 202–204

Neuroimaging, functional, 63–86
  electrophysiological techniques,
    74–83
  limitations, 64–65, 83–86
  metabolic techniques, 63–74
  subtraction method, 70, 85
Neuroimaging, structural, 63, 89–93.
  See also Anatomical asymmetries
Neuronal loss, 88, 89
Neuropsychological disorders. *See* spe-
  cific disorders
Neuropsychology, 3, 23–25, 159–160.
  See also Cognitive neuropsychology
Nottebohm, F., 238
Nuclear magnetic resonance (NMR).
  See Neuroimaging, functional—
  metabolic techniques; Neuroimaging,
  structural

Ojemann, G., 20, 175
Optic chiasm, 33, 37
Ornstein, R., 75, 293
Orton, S., 272, 273, 277

Parallel distributed processing (PDP),
  161, 318–323
Parity, 328, 329
Pasteur, L., 326–327
Pathological left-handedness. *See* Left-
  handedness, pathological
Pathologies. *See also* specific
  pathologies
    implications for treatment, 287–288
Patterning, 287–288
Paw preference, 240–242. *See also* Ani-
  mal asymmetries
    in primates, 241–242
    in toads, 249
Penfield, W., 20–21, 204
Perceptual disorders, 188–198. *See also*
  Agnosia; Neglect
PET. *See* Positron emission tomography;
  Neuroimaging, functional—metabolic
  techniques
Petersen, S., 168, Color Plate 11
Phrenology, 74
Plasticity, 252, 254, 255, 264. *See also*
  Development of asymmetry
Positron emission tomography (PET),
  63, 64, 69–72. *See also* Neuroimaging,

functional—metabolic techniques, and studies under specific topics
Posner, M., 168, 178, 179
Probe-evoked potentials. See Electrophysiological techniques, probe-evoked potentials
Prosopagnosia. See Facial agnosia
Psychiatric illness and asymmetry, 284–287. See also Depression; Schizophrenia
    role of neurotransmitters, 286
    theoretical issues, 287
Psychologist's fallacy, 85
Puccetti, R., 345, 346

Raichle, M., 168, 178
Ramachandran, B., 337, 338
Ravel, M., 221
Rayport, M., 40
Reading disability and asymmetry. See also Dyslexia
    anatomical asymmetries, 274–275
    deep dyslexia, 177
    disorders resulting from injury, 176–177
    interpretation of data, 277–278
    mirror-image reversals, 273
    "patterning," 287–288
Reductionism, 324, 325
Reid, M., 132
Resolution, temporal and spatial, 64, 65
Right hemisphere, 15–19
    depression, 286
    discovery of functions, 15–16
    dreaming, role in, 343
    emotion, 227–233, 233–234
    humor, 180–181
    intonation, 179–180
    language, 42–45, 178–182
    manipulative basis for superiorities, 306–307
    music, 18, 220–222
    perceptual disorders, 188–193
    reading abilities, 176–177
    recovery from aphasia, role in, 131, 175–176, 181–182
    Sagan model, 302
    the unconscious, 342–348
    visuospatial functions, 16–17, 45–48, 185

Right-ear advantage. See Dichotic listening
Risberg, J., 66
Robinson, D. 347–348
Roland, P., 185, 196
Ross, E., 179, 180

Saccadic eye movements, 36
Sackheim, H., 228
Sagan, C., 121, 301–302
Satz, P., 130
Sauwerwein, H., 262
Schachter, D., 214, 215, 220
Schachter, S., 226
Schizophrenia, 284, 285–286. See also Psychiatric illness and asymmetry
Schlaug, G., 224
Schopenhauer, 342
Schwartz, M., 129
Semantic priming. See Interhemispheric transfer of information
Semmes, J., 310
Sergent, J., 105, 106, 107, 191, 222, Color Plate 14
Sex differences in asymmetry, 139–156
    anatomical studies, 143–145
    behavioral studies, 147
    and cognition, 139–140, 145–146
    difficulty in studying, 142–143, 147–148
    effects of brain damage, 140–142
    hormones, 149–154
    possible origins, 148–149
    significance, 155–156
Sexual orientation, 151–152
Shaywitz, B., 145, 146
Shaywitz, S., 145, 146
Sign language, 265–266
Singing. See Music
Single photon emission tomography (SPECT), 64, 67–69. See also Neuroimaging, functional, and specific topics
Sinistrality. See Left-handedness
Smith, A., 175
Sodium amobarbital. See Wada test
SPECT. See Single photon emission tomography; Neuroimaging, functional, and studies under specific topics

Speech
  speech-evoked potentials in infants,
    257–258
  and hemispheres in split-brain
    patients, 44–45
  motor theory of perception,
    305–306
  parallels with bird song, 239
  Wada test, 22
Speech disorders. *See* Aphasia
Sperry, R., 33, 36, 46, 48, 334
Splenium. *See* Corpus callosum
Split-brain patients, 29. *See also* Split
  brain surgery; Animal asymmetries,
  split brain research
  cautions about interpreting data, 42,
    57–58
  consciousness in, 52–53, 334–336,
    345–346
  cross cuing, 53–54
  dreaming in, 41
  facial recognition, 40–41
  information-processing styles,
    48–52
  memory in, 41–42, 211
  mental unity, 338–339
  right-hemisphere language,
    42–45
  visuospatial functions, 45–48
Split-brain surgery, 31–35
  in animals, 33–34, 242–244
  disconnection syndrome, 39–40
  effects on consciousness, 52–53,
    334–336, 345–346
  effects on interhemispheric transfer of
    information, 36–39
  everyday behavior after, 39–42,
    52
  first human operations, 33–36
  as treatment for epilepsy, 31,
    33–36
Squire, L., 212
Steinmetz, H., 91
Strategies. *See* Information-processing
  asymmetries
Stroke, 9, 160
Studdert-Kennedy, M., 241
Stuttering and asymmetries,
  278–280
Superior colliculus, 54

Tallal, P., 276, 278
Temple, C., 262
Testosterone
  role in handedness, 128
  role in sex differences in cognition,
    149–151, 153–154
Teuber, H.L., 253
Thalamus, 174–175
Torrance, E. P., 295
Trevarthen, C., 50, 113
Twins, handedness, 129

Unconscious, 342–348
  Freudian theories, 344
  memory, 209–210

Van Wagenen, W., 33, 36
Verbal access theories. *See*
  Consciousness
Verbal/nonverbal dichotomy, 49,
  102–103, 292
Visual completion. *See* Completion,
  visual
Visual-field studies, 98. *See also* specific
  topics
  mechanisms underlying asymmetries,
    100–102
  methodology, 36–39
  problems in interpreting data,
    107–110
Visual imagery, 41, 195–198
Visual pathways, 71
Visuospatial functions
  and handedness, 134–135
  principles of, 317–318
  in right hemisphere, 16–17, 185
  in split-brain patients. 45–48
Vogel, P., 34, 35
Voyer, D., 147

Wada, J., 21
Wada test, 21–22
  dichotic listening, 108–109
  emotional reactions to, 227
  and handedness, 22,
    108–109
  in stutterers, 279
Weintraub, S., 203
Wernicke, K., 14, 87
Wernicke's area, 87

Wernicke's aphasia. *See* Aphasia,
  Wernicke's aphasia
Whitaker, H., 254
Weisel, T., 217
Wilson, D., 43
Witelson, S., 144–145
Woods, B., 253
Woodward, S., 320

Word deafness. *See* Aphasia, word
  deafness
Writing posture. *See* Handedness,
  writing posture

Zaidel, E., 43, 44, 45, 111,
  112
Zatorre, R., 221